# Windows 2000 Reducing TCO

## Little Black Book

Robert E. Simanski

**President, CEO**
*Keith*
*Weiskamp*

**Publisher**
*Steve Sayre*

**Acquisitions**
**Editor**
*Stephanie Wall*

**Marketing**
**Specialist**
*Tracy*
*Schofield*

**Project Editor**
*Toni Zuccarini*
*Ackley*

**Technical**
**Reviewer**
*John Green*

**Production**
**Coordinator**
*Wendy Littley*
*Meg E. Turecek*

**Cover Designer**
*Jody Winkler*

**Layout Designer**
*April Nielsen*

## Windows 2000 Reducing TCO Little Black Book

### Limits Of Liability And Disclaimer Of Warranty

### Trademarks

The Coriolis Group, LLC
14455 North Hayden Road, Suite 220
Scottsdale, Arizona 85260

480/483-0192
FAX 480/483-0193
http://www.coriolis.com

Library of Congress Cataloging-in-Publication Data
Simanski, Robert E.
   Windows 2000 reducing TCO little black book / by Robert E. Simanski.
      p.   cm.
   ISBN 1-57610-315-3
      1. Microsoft Windows (Computer file).   2. Microcomputer workstations.
3. Computer networks--Management.   I. Title.
QA76.76.O63S55854   2000
005.4'4769--dc21                                99-42713
                                                   CIP

Printed in the United States of America
10  9  8  7  6  5  4  3  2  1

14455 North Hayden Road • Suite 220 • Scottsdale, Arizona 85260

Dear Reader:

Coriolis Technology Press was founded to create a very elite group of books: the ones you keep closest to your machine. Sure, everyone would like to have the Library of Congress at arm's reach, but in the real world, you have to choose the books you rely on every day *very* carefully.

To win a place for our books on that coveted shelf beside your PC, we guarantee several important qualities in every book we publish. These qualities are:

- *Technical accuracy*—It's no good if it doesn't work. Every Coriolis Technology Press book is reviewed by technical experts in the topic field, and is sent through several editing and proofreading passes in order to create the piece of work you now hold in your hands.

- *Innovative editorial design*—We've put years of research and refinement into the ways we present information in our books. Our books' editorial approach is uniquely designed to reflect the way people learn new technologies and search for solutions to technology problems.

- *Practical focus*—We put only pertinent information into our books and avoid any fluff. Every fact included between these two covers must serve the mission of the book as a whole.

- *Accessibility*—The information in a book is worthless unless you can find it quickly when you need it. We put a lot of effort into our indexes, and heavily cross-reference our chapters, to make it easy for you to move right to the information you need.

Here at The Coriolis Group we have been publishing and packaging books, technical journals, and training materials since 1989. We're programmers and authors ourselves, and we take an ongoing active role in defining what we publish and how we publish it. We have put a lot of thought into our books; please write to us at **ctp@coriolis.com** and let us know what you think. We hope that you're happy with the book in your hands, and that in the future, when you reach for software development and networking information, you'll turn to one of our books first.

Keith Weiskamp
President and CEO

Jeff Duntemann
VP and Editorial Director

*To my beloved sons, Joseph and John, who came through for me with help, understanding, and moral support, time and time again during the period when I was writing this book. You will never know how much this has meant to me.*

*To my darling cats, Tubbu and Stripes, who kept me company during my long hours at the keyboard and made sure that I took breaks to play with them. You get me up in the morning, look out for me during the day, and put me to bed at night. My home would be a very lonely place without you.*

*To all of the developers at Microsoft who worked on Windows 2000. You have given us a significant new product that will make the lives of network administrators much easier.*

*Finally, to you, the reader of this book. The goal of meeting your needs and expectations has been foremost in my mind throughout the entire writing process. I only hope that I have lived up to the task.*

≥▲

# About The Author

I have been in the publishing industry for more than 30 years—and I have loved every minute of it. Well, almost every minute.

I started out in 1965 as a newspaper reporter and photographer for *The Catholic Review*, a weekly newspaper in Baltimore, Maryland. After working for several other papers, I became an editor in the public relations office of The Catholic University of America, Washington, DC, where I wrote and edited their alumni magapaper. The publication won scads of awards but unfortunately they didn't do much to help my salary.

By 1978 I had a growing family, so I took a better-paying job with a trade association. From that time on, I have specialized in editing and managing publications for trade associations. Over the years, I have edited three magazines, produced marketing materials and many other types of publications, and founded a desktop publishing department. Eventually I began to develop Web sites as well.

As personal computers became popular in the early 1980s, I saw that if I wanted to continue to be marketable in my field, I needed to become computer-literate. In 1986, I bought my first personal computer, a Kaypro PC. Much to my surprise, I found that I was good with computers.

Soon I joined the Capital PC User Group, one of the largest and strongest user groups in the country. In 1990, shortly after the release of Microsoft Windows 3, I became a volunteer for the group's Member Help Line. Today I am listed as a resource in at least half a dozen areas. This experience has given me insights into the kinds of problems that many users have with today's computer hardware and software.

I started my own freelance business, Your Publications Pro!, in 1993, but continued to hold full-time jobs as well. In two of those positions I served as network administrator. In 1997, I decided to work for myself full-time. At present, I specialize in general writing, editing, and publication production; technical writing and editing; Web site development and maintenance; and computer consulting and troubleshooting.

I am divorced and have two fine sons, Joe and John. I live in a town house with Tubbu and Stripes, my two male tabby cats. When not at the computer or holding a conversation with a cat, I enjoy listening to classic jazz, watching tapes of historic sports events, and watching good movies of any vintage. I guess that makes me a classic couch potato.

**Robert E. Simanski**
rsimanski@mindspring.com

# Acknowledgments

Although I have been a writer, editor, and publisher for more than 30 years, this is my first full-length book for the computer market. The credit for helping me to penetrate this market belongs to my agent, Martha Kaufman Amitay of Adler & Robin Books Literary Agency. I will be forever grateful to Martha for her professionalism, faith, and dedication through years of false starts and dashed hopes. I would also like to thank my friend, Gabriel Goldberg, who referred me to Martha's agency.

Next, I would like to thank Stephanie Wall, my Acquisitions Editor at The Coriolis Group. She gave me both the opportunity to do this book and the flexibility to change its direction when it became apparent that this was necessary. In addition, the delays in the release of the shipping version of Windows 2000 also meant delays in the releases of the beta versions needed to write this book. Stephanie and I worked together every step of the way, sharing information and ideas. Together, we changed the production schedule of this book several times to match the projected release dates of both the betas and the shipping version.

In today's publishing environment, a book of this type is the work of many people. Computer books, particularly those that deal with software, must be published in a timely fashion. As the author is writing the next chapter, others are editing and designing earlier chapters, while still others are developing a marketing campaign for the new book.

Windows 2000 was still very much a work in progress while this book was being produced. Writing about new technologies that often changed from one beta release to another was much more challenging than I had anticipated. If there was one thing that made my life easier, it was the professionalism, patience, and understanding of the production staff at Coriolis. In more than 34 years in the publishing industry, I have never worked with a better crew. They deserve the credit for everything that is good about this book. The flaws and errors are mine alone.

First, I would like to thank Toni Zuccarini Ackley, who served as Project Editor. Toni kept things on track even when I was letting her down. She patiently tolerated all of my delays, problems, and excuses, never once acting less than professional. Frankly, I don't know how she managed to put up with me.

John Green, the technical editor, kept me honest. He not only called my attention to flaws and inaccuracies but also, whenever possible, showed me how to correct them. In addition, he was kind enough to say so when he thought that I had made a good point. Nancy Sixsmith, the copy editor, helped to ensure that the text made sense and saved me from some embarrassing errors.

Poor editors—and there are far too many of them—impose their own ideas and writing style on an author's manuscript. Toni and John are rare gems—everything that good editors should be. They made the text as accurate and consistent as possible while still allowing my own ideas and style to come through.

A book is more than just a manuscript set in type. Good format, design, and production can enhance its value and usefulness, while poor format, design, and production can sabotage the best of manuscripts. The credit for the excellent appearance of this book belongs to Wendy Littley, Production Coordinator; Jesse Dunn, Cover Designer; and April Nielsen, Layout Designer.

To each of these people—and to those who also deserve credit but whom I have unintentionally neglected to mention—I am deeply grateful.

# Contents At A Glance

# Table Of Contents

*Immediate Solutions*

## Chapter 6
## Using The Group Policy Editor ............................................... 187

## Chapter 9
## Using Security Templates ....................................................... 263

# Introduction

The purpose of this book is to show you, the network administrator, how to use the new features in Windows 2000 to reduce the Total Cost of Ownership (TCO) of your network and the systems connected to it. Whether you are running a small, local area network with one location and a dozen users, or a large enterprise network with many users on several continents, this book will help you to manage your network efficiently and effectively.

Although reducing TCO may be of primary concern to business owners and their financial directors, it means much more than dollars and cents on a balance sheet. For you, the network administrator, reducing TCO can help you to get home at a decent hour and to receive fewer emergency calls during your scarce free time. By helping you to prevent user-created problems and by automatically repairing damaged software installations, it can also reduce work-related stress for yourself and everyone else on your network. Finally, it can help you to improve your stature with the top executives in your organization. In other words, you might actually be able to have that life that your friends and family have been begging you to get.

This book has been written primarily for experienced administrators who are in the process of migrating their networks from Windows NT or NetWare to Windows 2000, or who are evaluating the new release for future deployment. It will also be helpful to new administrators who have been given the task of building a small network from scratch or migrating from a Windows 95 or Windows 98 peer-to-peer network.

## About This Book

Despite its compact size, you will find that this book offers detailed coverage of many of the important new features in Windows 2000, including the Active Directory, Group Policy, IntelliMirror, and Microsoft Management Console. In fact, these four subjects are threads that run throughout the entire book.

These features have been broken out into a baker's dozen of main chapters plus three appendixes. Each main chapter begins with an In Brief section that gives you the basic information that you need to understand the features covered in the chapter and how they can help you.

The bulk of each chapter is an Immediate Solutions section with practical examples of how to use the features covered in the chapter. In every chapter except the first, these solutions are broken down into precise, step-by-step procedures. Many of the solutions are illustrated with large, clear screenshots of the dialog boxes that you will be seeing.

You can use these procedures as if they were recipes. I have made every effort to assume nothing and to leave nothing to chance. This book was written with my server and my workstation side by side. In almost every case, I performed each procedure on the server one step at a time, describing each step in my word processor before I went on to the next one.

Throughout the writing of this book, my goal has been to do more than just tell you how to use a feature. Wherever possible, I have tried to put it into perspective for you as well. There were times when the value of a feature was not always immediately apparent to me. I often found myself asking, "What am I missing here?" In most cases, after some thought I was able to come up with scenarios that made sense and present them to you. On one or two occasions, however, I could not, and when this happened, I let you know. This does not mean that *you* will not find the feature valuable. Most likely, it means that I do not know everything that I ought to know.

Interspersed throughout every chapter, you will find candid and informative notes, tips, and warnings. Most of them were drawn from my own experience working with the software. You will find that I have not pulled any punches, either. If something did not work for me, you will know about it.

# What You Will Learn From This Book

The first two chapters of this book will give you the background orientation that you will need to use it successfully. Chapter 1 will tell you about the components in Microsoft's Zero Administration Initiative, the starting point for many of the innovations in Windows 2000. Chapter 2 will introduce you to the Microsoft Management Console, the new, standardized interface used by all of the administrative tools in Windows 2000.

Beginning with Chapter 3, this book will teach you how to use dozens of features in Windows 2000 that are geared to reducing TCO. You will find that most of them are related to one or more of three new fundamental technologies in Windows 2000: the Active Directory, Group Policy, and IntelliMirror:

- *Active Directory (Chapters 3 through 5)*—The Active Directory is the tool that you will use to organize your network and the objects within it. All of the objects in your network are contained in the Active Directory, where you can find them easily and quickly. You will learn how to use the Active Directory to organize your domains, sites, organizational units, groups, users, computers, and printers.

- *Group Policy (Chapters 6, 9, 10, 11, 13, and Appendix A)*— Group Policy is the tool that you will use to manage users and computers on your network. The Group Policy Editor replaces the System Policy Editor of Windows NT 4 and takes the concept of policy-based management much further. You will learn how to use group policy to manage the security of your network and control the Windows desktop environments of your users.

- *IntelliMirror (Chapters 7, 11, 12, and 13)*—IntelliMirror makes it possible for your users' Windows environments, software, and data files to follow them wherever they are on your network. In addition, it can ensure that their network-based data files are available to them even when they are working offline. You will learn how to create roaming user profiles so that your users see the same Windows environment regardless of the workstation that they are using. You will also learn how to use software management to make the applications that they need available to them at any time—applications that can be automatically installed, updated, repaired, and uninstalled from a remote network location. You will also learn how Remote Installation Services (Appendix B) can help you to extend software management to the unattended installation of the Windows 2000 Professional operating system on compatible workstations.

The primary purpose of the Active Directory and Group Policy is to *help you*. How you use them may also help your users indirectly, but for the most part, this will be transparent to them. IntelliMirror, on the other hand, *helps you to help your users*. The benefit of having all of the applications and files that they need available to them, in their familiar Windows environment, no matter where they are on your network, will be immediately apparent to them. This will require migrating their workstations to Windows 2000 Professional, but the benefits should more than offset the inconvenience to them.

As you can see, some chapters make extensive use of more than one of these three core technologies. In fact, you will find yourself using the Active Directory in almost every chapter and Group Policy almost as frequently.

# TCO And The Zero Administration Initiative

There is a reason why many publishers advise their authors to write their introduction last, rather than first. The process of researching and writing a book is a dynamic one. You soon find that the book takes on a life of its own, compelling you to follow paths that you had not planned to take. In some cases, the paths did not even exist when you started. In the end, you wind up with a book that hopefully is better, but most definitely is different from the one that you had expected to write.

Such has been the case with this book, which grew out of Microsoft's Zero Administration Initiative for Windows (ZAW), announced in 1997. Microsoft stated that its primary goal was to reduce Total Cost of Ownership (TCO), a subject that, then as now, was of great concern to both business executives and network administrator. The original outline for this book dealt exclusively with the announced components of that initiative.

As I began to work with Windows 2000, however, I realized that anything that helped network administrators to manage their networks better automatically helped to reduce TCO. Almost every new feature in Windows 2000, as well as every improvement to an existing feature, fell into this category. The focus of the book changed from a narrow focus on the components of the ZAW to a much broader emphasis on showing readers how to use the new features in Windows 2000 to reduce TCO.

In a book of this size, it would have been impractical to try to cover every feature in Windows 2000 that could help to reduce TCO in some way. In deciding on the features to cover in the main chapters, I asked myself these questions:

- Was it a core component of Windows 2000, included in the default installation for a domain controller?

- Was it a feature that a large number of readers would be likely to use once they understood its value?

- Could the reader be taught how to use it with easy-to-follow, step-by-step procedures?

Most of the important new features for reducing TCO met those criteria. Two other relevant features, Remote Installation Services and the Windows Scripting Host, did not. Remote Installation Services is an optional component of Windows 2000 Server. It requires that you also install two other optional components, the Dynamic Host Configuration Protocol (DHCP) and Domain Name Services (DNS). The Windows Scripting Host requires that you know a scripting language such as VBScript. Because of this, these features are covered in appendixes rather than in the main chapters.

# A Final Note

I hope that this book will become your trusted companion in helping you to use the powerful new features in Windows 2000 to reduce your organization's Total Cost of Ownership. My primary goal in writing it was to do what was right by you, the reader, regardless of the time and effort that it took.

Ever since buying my first PC in 1986 and joining the Capital PC User Group soon afterward, I have been a firm believer in the concept of users helping users. I welcome your questions, criticisms, suggestions, war stories, or whatever else you care to share with me. Please feel free to contact me at **rsimanski@mindspring.com** or visit my Web site at **www.yourpubpro.com**.

# Microsoft's Zero Administration Initiative

# *In Brief*

Microsoft's Zero Administration Initiative for Windows is designed to reduce total cost of ownership (TCO) by helping network administrators gain control of client workstations. Understanding each of the components of the initiative will help you see how they fit together and help you to use them effectively.

When Microsoft Corporation released the Zero Administration Kit for Windows NT 4 in June 1997, it launched the first wave of a new, integrated series of products and technologies designed to reduce the TCO of networked personal computers. One of its primary goals was to make the job of managing large networks easier for network administrators in several important areas, such as:

- Unifying and sharing resources over far-flung, enterprise-wide networks.
- Managing large numbers of users and workstations.
- Automating time-consuming tasks, such as software installation.

Taken together, these new tools and enabling technologies constitute Microsoft's Zero Administration Initiative for Windows. Some of the components of the initiative were introduced in 1997 for use with Windows NT 4. However, most debuted as an integral part of the initial release of Windows 2000 Server, and a few others are still being developed.

The first part of this chapter reviews the events that led to the concern over TCO and the network-management problems faced by information technology (IT) professionals today. The second part looks at each of the components of the Zero Administration Initiative. By understanding these components, you will see how they fit together and have the knowledge to select the ones that best meet your needs.

## The Need For The Initiative

The Zero Administration Initiative is a response to the growing concern of business owners and executives about the total cost of personal computers in a business setting. That cost—which has been estimated to be as high as $16,000 per workstation—includes not only the initial dollars spent on hardware and software, but also the expense of employee training, hardware and software upgrades, and system maintenance. Many business leaders have become frustrated because, although they believe that personal computers (PCs) have the potential to significantly increase the productivity of their employees, that potential is not being fully realized. Total cost of ownership is of even greater concern in the mainframe arena. Because of this, IT administrators are seeking to integrate personal computers into their systems to run applications that either don't exist for their mainframes or cannot be run cost-effectively on them.

The challenge faced by IT professionals today is a byproduct of one of the advantages of the personal computer—namely, that it is a *personal* computer. Before personal computers became popular in the early 1980s, most computer networks consisted of either large centrally located mainframes or smaller workgroup-oriented minicomputers. Users sat at terminals that were linked to a central computer. These terminals consisted solely of video displays and keyboards, and had no processing power of their own. All of the processing power, as well as the software that harnessed it, resided in the central computer, which was controlled and managed by professionals in what was then often called the Data Processing Department.

The PC radically changed that scenario. For the first time, business executives—many of whom had never bothered to use the slow terminals connected to the mainframe—had an affordable workstation with its own processing power, running reasonably priced software that could help them perform important tasks such as financial management. This new type of workstation was independent of the main system and the data processing professionals who ran it.

At first, only senior managers could justify having a personal computer. As competition among manufacturers increased, however, prices began to drop, and personal computers soon found their way onto the desktops of professionals at all levels.

Those early adopters relished the independence that the new systems offered. Many of them became power users; as personal computers became both more powerful and more prevalent, these employees became unofficial "computer gurus" in their offices. In influence, if not authority, they often equaled the data processing managers.

With a computer on every desk (or at least in every department), there was a need to share resources such as files and printers, and the computer industry developed technologies for networking them. Before long, it was possible to network large numbers of personal computers in widely separated locations.

Someone had to manage these networks, and the task could not be left to the office guru. As the mainframe-oriented data processing managers of the 1960s and 1970s gave way to IT professionals with experience in personal computers, responsibility for the networks returned to the same departments that used to run the mainframes and minicomputers.

The name of the department might have changed from Data Processing to Information Technology, but its role had not. What had changed, however, was the relationship between the IT professionals and their end users.

Although today's typical network administrators may have the same level of responsibility as their predecessors, they almost certainly do not have the same level of influence and control. To make things even more difficult, they are faced with several problems that were unheard of in the mainframe days:

- As PCs have become more powerful, they have taken over more and more of the roles that were previously associated with mainframes and minicomputers. The local area network (LAN), confined to a handful of servers in a small, manageable area, has grown into an enterprise-wide network that uses many servers and spans large geographical areas. Application servers, Web servers, and database servers have been added to the file and print servers of the LAN.

- PC users have become used to their independence and are reluctant to relinquish it. Power users often install their own software without regard to its impact on their system. Almost everyone uses screen savers and desktop wallpaper, despite the fact that they can drain system resources and cause systems to lock up.

- Computer viruses are a major problem. I know of cases in which employees have lost months—or even years—of work because someone used a diskette from an outside source without scanning it for viruses first.

- Improvements in computer hardware accelerated dramatically in the 1990s. New generations of central processors were introduced about every 18 months, and enhancements to existing lines reached the market several times a year. Computer manufacturers are now forced to change their product lines every three or four months to remain competitive, which makes it impossible for you to standardize on proven products for any length of time.

Even though you may buy all your hardware from one supplier, the $1,500 system that you order today won't be the same as the one you got three months ago. Sometimes, you might not know what components are in it until you open the case.

- Software developers release new versions of programs every 12 to 24 months. These new versions take advantage of the latest generation of hardware, which makes last year's computers obsolete long before the end of their useful service lives.

The Zero Administration features of Windows 2000 Server, together with those in Systems Management Server 2 and other new tools, offer you, as a network administrator, some much-needed relief. They give you the tools to regain control of client workstations. They enable you to run automated tasks, such as software installation, from your server, instead of having to install software manually at each workstation. Who knows? You may even regain control of your evenings and weekends!

**1. Microsoft's Zero Administration Initiative**

# *Immediate Solutions*

To a large extent, the Zero Administration Initiative makes use of capabilities that are already present in Windows 2000 Server, Windows 98, and, to a lesser extent, in Windows NT 4 and Windows 95. The components of the initiative help you to make full use of those capabilities.

There are several different types of components in the initiative. They include optional management tools such as Systems Management Server and the Zero Administration Kit, new techniques for dealing with the underlying infrastructures of the operating systems that you use, and new enabling technologies that have been built into Windows 2000 Server and Windows 98. Some of the tools can also be used with Windows NT 4 and Windows 95.

The initiative includes six software components, one technique that you can use in combination with features built into Windows 2000 Server, and one enabling technology. The components include the Active Directory, the Microsoft Management Console (MMC), Systems Management Server (SMS), the Zero Administration Kit, the Web Administration Utility for Windows NT Server, and the Windows Scripting Host. The technique is called policy-based management. With the exception of the Active Directory, which is one of the most important new features of Windows 2000 Server, these components were first introduced in 1997 as enhancements to Windows NT 4 Server.

The enabling technology—Windows Management Instrumentation (WMI)—is present in Windows 2000 Server. Its impact and value to you, however, will depend on how well it is supported by third-party vendors. It will take several years before the potential is fully realized.

Let's take a close look at each one, in order of their importance to the subject of this book.

## Microsoft Management Console

The Microsoft Management Console, or MMC, is not a tool in itself; it is a customizable framework for the network-management tools that you choose to install in it. The MMC is based on snap-ins, which are similar to the plug-ins used by Web browsers and other applications.

Microsoft has included about two dozen preconfigured consoles for Windows 2000 Server, each with one or more snap-ins, and is urging third-party developers of management tools for Windows 2000 Server to use the console interface as well. Some snap-ins are standalone, some are extensions that enhance the capabilities of other snap-ins, and still others can be used either way.

The MMC enables you to assemble the tool sets that you need for specific tasks. By putting together several custom tool sets, you can create task-oriented views that are as simple or as complex as you need them to be. For example, you might have separate views for network-, system-, and user-oriented tasks. You can also create custom consoles for users to whom you have delegated some administrative responsibilities—for example, department managers. Users can download the custom sets to their local systems. If the users don't already have the necessary snap-ins, they are downloaded to their systems automatically the first time they attempt to use them. See Figure 1.1 for an example of a console.

The MMC uses a Windows Explorer-like interface that shows you the components on your network that can be managed by the snap-ins installed in the console. It uses the Explorer folder metaphor. The main window has the usual menu bar. Within the main window is a

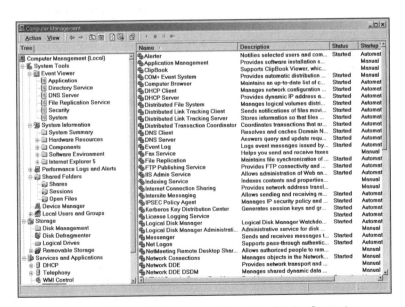

*Figure 1.1    The Microsoft Management Console with the Computer Management snap-in.*

split child window. The top pane, called a command bar, includes the toolbars and drop-down lists used by the installed snap-ins. Below the command bar, the bottom-left pane, called the console tree, displays folders containing objects that can be managed by the snap-ins. The bottom-right pane, called the details pane, shows the objects in the selected folder.

As in Windows Explorer, you can expand and contract folders in the tree display. For example, in the left pane you might have a parent folder for event logs. Expanding the folder, you might see child folders for application, security, and system logs. If you select the system log in the left pane, the right pane displays a list of events recorded in the log.

| *Related solution:* | *Found on page:* |
|---|---|
| Using Predefined Consoles In Windows 2000 Server | 45 |

# Active Directory

The Active Directory, introduced in Windows 2000 Server, is Microsoft's version of a network directory service. A directory service offers a way for users to find and identify other users and resources on a network. It has been likened to a phone book for a network. Enter the name of a user or resource, and the network directory service gives you the information you need to access the person or resource.

One of the problems with large networks is that they often have many network-based directories. Network file systems, email systems, and groupware programs each have their own directory structure. Users often have to log on to each service separately. Complex structures are difficult to administer and costly to support.

In response, Microsoft introduced the Active Directory, a vehicle for integrating these multiple directory structures. Active Directory, a feature of Windows 2000 Server, provides a unified interface for directory services from different providers. Through a single point of administration, you can manage your network resources regardless of the network environment in which they exist. These resources can include files, peripherals, host connections, databases, Web access, users, services, and network resources.

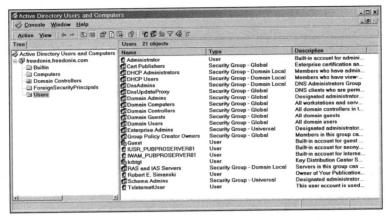

*Figure 1.2    The Active Directory Users and Computers console.*

Microsoft has provided several preconfigured consoles for managing various aspects of the Active Directory. See Figure 1.2 for an example of one.

Although all aspects of the Active Directory are covered in subsequent chapters, the component of greatest importance to Zero Administration is the Active Directory Users and Computers console. This console provides a consistent mechanism for you to add users, manage printers, and control servers and workstations.

# Policy-Based Management

It is important to understand how the Microsoft Management Console and the Active Directory work because they provide the framework and environment for almost everything you do in Windows 2000 Server. Policy-based management, however, is the most important subject covered in this book. A solid understanding of policy-based management is essential if you are to get the full benefit of the Zero Administration features in Windows 2000 Server.

Policy-based management enables you to tap into the existing capabilities of the underlying architectures of 32-bit Windows operating systems, and use these capabilities to manage your network more effectively. Through policy-based management, you can deal with such issues as user access and system security by creating system and group policies and user profiles on your server, and then synchronizing them

**9**

with the operating systems on client workstations. You can even perform backups or scan workstations for viruses directly from the server. Finally, you can create policies to automate tasks such as updating operating systems, installing new applications, managing users, and locking down desktop systems.

The primary tool for policy-based management in Windows 2000 Server is the Group Policy Editor, which replaces the System Policy Editor of Windows NT 4. The Security Configuration Editor, which enables you to create custom security policies and assign security settings to a policy object, is also of significant interest. Other policy-based management features in Windows 2000 Server enable you to manage user profiles, set disk quotas, and manage software.

| Related solutions: | Found on page: |
|---|---|
| Managing Group Policies Assigned To Active Directory Objects | 196 |
| Enabling User Profiles In Windows 98 And Windows 95 | 223 |
| Accessing And Viewing Disk Quota Settings | 244 |
| Using The Security Configuration And Analysis Snap-in | 297 |
| Preparing To Implement Software Management | 334 |

# Windows Scripting Host

The Windows Scripting Host enables you to create simple scripts that can be executed directly from either the Windows desktop or the command shell. The scripts are similar to DOS batch files and are appropriate for simple situations in which interaction with the user is not required. A login script is a good candidate for using the capabilities of the Windows Scripting Host.

The tool is compatible with all 32-bit Windows operating systems (including Windows NT 4 or greater and Windows 95 or greater) and comes with Windows 98, as well as with Windows 2000 Server and Windows 2000 Professional. It includes scripting engines for both Visual Basic and JavaScript. Both command-shell and Windows-based versions are included.

Other tools and technologies in the Zero Administration Initiative allow you to manage groups of users through policy scripts. The Windows Scripting Host gives you the opportunity to manage subgroups, or even individual users, by creating scripts that run automatically in specific circumstances, such as when a user logs onto the network. Network administrators have used login scripts for many years, of course. Windows Scripting Host scripts, however, like DOS batch files, are not limited to login situations.

---

**TIP:**   *Windows 98 comes with the Windows Scripting Host and several sample scripts. To make sure that it is installed on your Windows 98 system, open Control Panel/Add/Remove Programs. From the Windows Setup page, select Accessories, and then choose Details. If the box next to Windows Scripting Host is not checked, check the box and follow the prompts to install it. You'll find the sample scripts under your Windows folder, in the \samples\wsh folder.*

*As of this writing, if you are a member of the Microsoft Developer Network, you can download the Windows Scripting Host for Windows 95 or Windows NT 4, as well as sample scripts, from Microsoft's Web site at **msdn.microsoft.com/scripting/default.htm?/scripting/ windowshost/**. In the event that this URL has changed, you can log onto Microsoft's main Web site and search on both "Windows Script Host" and "Windows Scripting Host." (I have seen it referred to both ways by Microsoft.)*

---

# Zero Administration Kit

The Zero Administration Kit was the first component of the Zero Administration Initiative to be released by Microsoft. It is a set of tools, techniques, and guidelines that help you use the existing features in Windows NT Server 4 and Systems Management Server to set and maintain policies on client workstations. At this writing, Microsoft has not announced a version for Windows 2000 Server. This is probably because many of the voids that the kit attempted to fill in Windows NT have been addressed by the management features in Windows 2000.

The purpose of the kit, which relies heavily on the System Policy Editor in Windows NT 4 Server, is to show network administrators how to manage and control the Windows desktops on their client workstations. It includes sample policies to start you on your way.

For example, you can tightly control the operating system interface that is presented to members of different groups on your network. You can give those employees who require a high level of flexibility at their workstations the tools and options that they need to do their work. In contrast, for those who use only one application, you can remove the distractions presented by their desktop operating system, so that the application loads automatically when they log on to the network—just like the old mainframe/dumb terminal days.

The Zero Administration Kit comes with two predefined profiles for workstation clients: TaskStation and AppStation. The TaskStation profile is designed for situations in which the user needs only one application, such as a proprietary line-of-business program. In TaskStation mode, the user never sees the Windows desktop shell interface. The Start menu and the Taskbar do not exist for them. When they log onto the network, their application opens immediately. No other software is installed on their system, and they cannot access any of the features of the operating system. Their files are stored on the network and simply cached on their local drive.

The AppStation profile is designed for the end user who runs several applications and needs a certain amount of flexibility at their work-station. Some, but not all, of the features of the operating system are available to them. You, as network administrator, determine what those features are in your policy for the AppStation group. For ex-ample, you can disable some or all of the applets in Control Panel, preventing the user from tinkering with configuration settings or changing the appearance of their desktop. You can also control what they see on the Start menu and can disable the Shut Down command, where appropriate.

These profiles attach to the user, not to the workstation, which per-mits users to "roam" from one workstation to another. If a TaskStation user logs onto another system—for instance, one normally used by a member of the AppStation group—they will see only the TaskStation interface that you have designated for them. The situation also works in reverse; an AppStation member can log onto a workstation that is normally used by a TaskStation employee and still have their AppStation interface available to them.

The Zero Administration Kit can also be used in conjunction with Systems Management Server to automate the installation of operat-ing system software and business applications on client systems. There are separate versions of the kit for Windows 95 and Windows NT Workstation clients. The Windows 95 version lacks the security fea-tures of the Windows NT version because of differences in the oper-ating systems.

Because the Zero Administration Kit is limited to Windows NT 4 Server, it is not covered in detail in this book. Instead, you will learn how to use the Group Policy Editor and other features of Windows 2000 Server to create equivalents of the AppStation and TaskStation interfaces.

**TIP:** *At this writing, you can download the Windows 95, Windows 98, and Windows NT 4 Workstation versions of the Zero Administration Kit from Microsoft's Web site at* ***www.microsoft. com/windows/zak/getzak.htm****. In the event that this URL has changed, you can log onto Microsoft's main Web site and search on "Zero Administration Kit."*

| Related solution: | Found on page: |
|---|---|
| Working With Offline Files | 414 |

# IntelliMirror

Although not listed as a component of the Zero Administration Initiative, IntelliMirror (a sophisticated caching technology introduced in Windows 2000 Server) is seen by many as an important tool that makes life easier for administrators. Microsoft describes it as "persistent caching of data and configuration information," which is a complex way of describing a relatively simple concept.

Application software, user profiles, and user-created data files are stored on your server and downloaded to the client workstation, as needed. Instead of being used to hold installed applications and permanent copies of working files, the hard drive on the workstation is used as a very large disk cache. Software components are downloaded as they are used, not all at once. Data files are transferred the first time the user accesses them. The user works with the copy on their local drive, reducing traffic on the network except when they are saving a file.

Every time they save the file, it is saved to the network as well as to their local drive, where it is stored with a cryptic file name different from the name used for the network copy. The next time the user opens the file, the local copy is checked against the network version. If the network version is newer, it is downloaded to the user's workstation. If not, the local copy of the file is used.

One advantage of IntelliMirror is that it reduces network traffic. Another is that its ability to synchronize files enables the user to continue to work on the file offline without having to remember to copy it to the local drive and back to the network later on. The next time the user logs on, the file is copied back to the network if it is newer than the network version. If someone else has modified the network version in the meantime, the user receives an overwrite warning.

Because users' software, data files, and configuration information are stored on the network, users can change workstations and still use their familiar configurations. If a user's normal workstation fails, it becomes much easier than before to get that person up-and-running quickly on another system. On the other hand, if the network should go down, the user can continue to work on their local copy of the file.

There is at least one serious drawback to IntelliMirror. When users access a software program on the network, only the necessary components are downloaded to their workstations, not the entire installation. If users are working offline—as is often the case with notebook users—and they attempt to use a software feature that they didn't need before, it will not be available to them. Be prepared for some angry long-distance phone calls from your marketing department's road warriors.

# Web Administration Utility

The Web Administration Utility makes it possible for you to administer your server remotely by using any compatible Web browser—including those running on Windows, Macintosh, and Unix platforms. Although it is not a replacement for your industrial-strength, on-site administrative tools, you will find it useful when you need to perform a simple management task away from the office. Through it, you can administer accounts, shares, sessions, servers, and printers.

The utility, which is designed to work with Windows NT 4 as well as Windows 2000 Server, works in conjunction with Internet Information Server (IIS). When you install IIS on your system, it generates Web pages with forms that you can use to administer your network. To access a form from your remote system, just enter its Uniform Resource Locator (URL) in your Web browser.

**TIP:**   At this writing, you can download the Web Administration Utility from Microsoft's Web site at **www.microsoft.com/ntserver/nts/downloads/management/NTSWebAdmin/ default.asp**. In the event that this URL has changed, you can access Microsoft's main Web site at **www.microsoft.com** and search on "Web Administration Utility."

# An Enabling Technology And Other New Features

The Zero Administration Initiative features discussed previously are covered in depth in subsequent chapters. In addition, Windows 2000 includes an enabling technology that could become important to you in the next few years, as well as several other relevant new features.

The enabling technology—Windows Management Instrumentation—is also implemented in Windows 98. Whether or not you will see much benefit from it will depend on the extent to which both Microsoft and third-party developers adopt it.

## Windows Management Instrumentation

Windows Management Instrumentation (WMI) enables you to monitor and control the hardware on your local workstations. In discussing WMI, Microsoft refers to "well-instrumented computer software and hardware components." What it means is this: Hardware designed for Windows Management Instrumentation is able to engage in bidirectional communication with Windows NT Server through intermediary software, so that when there is a problem, the hardware can send your server an alert message.

WMI, which is an extension of the Windows Driver Model (WDM), provides an interface through which hardware components can provide information and notification to Windows 2000 Server. When a hardware device needs to send information to a server, it sends the information to the hardware-specific WDM Mini Driver supplied by its manufacturer. This driver, in turn, passes the information to the standard WDM driver supplied by Microsoft. The WDM driver then transmits the information to the WMI interface.

Suppose that a hard drive has a worn spindle that is causing it to vibrate. During one of these mini-earthquakes, the disk head hits the platter, which damages a sector on the drive and causes the data in the sector to become corrupted. If you formatted the drive for the NTFS file system native to Windows 2000, the file system might be able to recover the data automatically. Unfortunately, it only masks (instead of corrects) the underlying problem, which is that you have a hard drive that is about to buy the farm.

Through the bidirectional communications channel made available by WMI, an alert is sent to your server. You respond to the alert, replace the drive before it crashes, download the necessary files to the new drive, and get the workstation back on line with a minimum of disruption. When you install the new drive, this information is transmitted to WMI, which records the fact that the drive was replaced.

WMI pulls together information from hardware, drivers, and applications and stores the consolidated information in a central management information pool. This storage component conforms to the requirements of Web-based Enterprise Management, and it uses the Common Information Model as a way to allow you to access and react to the information.

The uses of WMI are not limited to disaster prevention. The technology can also help you to perform the following tasks:

- Monitor and respond to other types of faults and alerts reported by hardware and software
- Perform preemptive maintenance
- Exercise control over upgrades and versions
- Plan for capacity and manage performance
- Manage security and assets
- Manage operations
- Automate management tasks

WMI uses Internet technology to allow you to remotely manage systems, networks, and users.

Until now, you had to use specific protocols (such as the Simple Network Management Protocol) to accomplish remote management for the task at hand. WMI, however, does not depend on any specific vendor, protocol, or management standard. It uses a task-oriented approach rather than a protocol-oriented one.

Each component in the environment that you are managing is seen as an object; its properties are stored in classes. These classes are organized into hierarchies, which in turn are grouped by areas of interest—for example, network, applications, and systems. These areas of interests are called schemas, and each schema is a subset of the entire managed environment. These schemas and protocols are open and easily extended. Developers can create extensions to schemas to add new classes and properties.

## Other Relevant New Features

Other features introduced in Windows 2000 Server that will be of interest to you include the following:

- *More control over services*—When a service fails in Windows 2000 Server, you now have three choices: restart the service, run a program, or reboot the machine.

- *Improved power management*—In Windows 2000 Server, you can establish power-management policies for various workstations. For example, you might want to force desktop workstations to go into sleep mode when they are idle; or, on the other hand, have them remain on all night for periodic maintenance, backup, or software installation.

- *Easy setup of remote access*—Until now, users who attempted to set up remote access to your network on their home computers have had to configure the connection on their own—this was no mean task, even with the Dial-Up Networking feature of recent versions of Windows. A new feature in Windows 2000 Server allows you to create a ready-made configuration package for the user, which you can send by email or post on a Web page. All the user has to do is download the package to his or her system, and then click on it to make a connection to your network.

# Systems Management Server

Systems Management Server (SMS) is an optional, extra-cost management tool. It is designed to help you distribute software to your workstation clients and manage the software once it is installed.

Version 1.2 for Windows NT Server 4, which was released in 1997, was closely tied to both policy-based management and the Zero Administration Kit. Some of its software-management features found their way into Windows 2000 Server. Therefore, when Microsoft released version 2 of SMS in the fall of 1998, it took a new direction with the product.

SMS is now geared primarily to large installations that require a flexible, easily expanded means of managing software installed on workstations. Because of its size and complexity, it would be impossible to cover it adequately in this book. However, because of its importance to the Zero Administration Initiative, a brief overview of SMS may be useful to you.

SMS provides you with tools for automating software and hardware inventory, software distribution, and remote diagnostics. It can be used together with leading enterprise-oriented network management platforms as well as with smaller-scale, third-party network management applications.

Until now, installing new software and updating existing installations have been very labor-intensive. You probably had to do them at each workstation, one at a time, after hours and on weekends. If you're as busy as most administrators, you had to do them on a catch-as-catch-can basis, fixing the "problem" workstations first and neglecting others. As a result, you wound up with different versions of the same operating systems and applications software on your workstations, which made troubleshooting even more difficult than normal.

SMS enhances the software-management capabilities that are already present in Windows 2000 Server. By integrating SMS with these capabilities, you can automate software management on a large scale. Here's how it works:

The latest versions of your operating system and primary applications software are stored on your server. When a user logs on, the operating system on the client workstation checks itself against the copy on the server. If there have been any updates or bug fixes, they are downloaded to the workstation. A similar process occurs when the user launches an application. All of this happens "silently," without requiring the user to intervene. If you have a large number of workstations to upgrade, you can schedule unattended batch updates.

Using the same technology, application software on the client workstation diagnoses itself when it is started. If a key file is deleted or becomes corrupted, the software repairs itself by downloading a replacement file from the server.

Other important features of SMS include remote inventory, software metering, remote diagnostics, and remote automatic software distribution.

## Remote Inventory And Software Metering

The need for accurate software inventories has become increasingly important in recent years because organizations have become sensitive to the need to comply with software licensing requirements. Until now, however, in most cases the only way you could monitor what software was on what workstation was to visit each workstation yourself.

SMS allows you to retrieve hardware and software information on any workstation within your network, including one halfway around the world. Version 2 also gives you the ability to monitor software usage. This can be useful if your licensing arrangements are tied to the number of people using the software at the same time, rather than to the number of systems on which the software may be used. Lotus Development Corporation offers this type of economical licensing arrangement, and—no doubt—other developers do as well.

## Remote Diagnostics

Systems Management Server can also save you trips to the workstation to diagnose problems by providing you with remote control, event forwarding, and network analysis tools.

## Software Distribution

New features in Windows 2000 Server can be used to distribute software to individual workstations. SMS enhances these features in several ways:

- *Cross-platform distribution*—With SMS, you can distribute software to workstations that are running under a variety of operating systems, not just 32-bit Windows platforms. In addition to Windows 2000 Professional, Windows NT 4 Workstation, Windows 95, and Windows 98, the list includes DOS, Windows 3.1, Macintosh, and OS/2. You can distribute software even if these workstations are connected to servers that run a different network operating system, such as Novell NetWare or IBM LanServer.

- *Off-hours distribution*—You can schedule software distribution to synchronize upgrades on multiple clients. Because the upgrades are "silent" and do not require that the user be logged on, you can do this after hours.

- *Patching*—SMS has the capability to patch a binary file, so you don't have to transmit the entire file to the workstation. With the large executable files that are common today, this helps to reduce traffic on your network.

- *Reporting and rollback*—SMS monitors and reports on the success of an installation. For large installations, you can test the likelihood of success before you launch the complete process. As each software component is installed, the information is entered into a database. Shared Dynamic Link Libraries (DLLs) are flagged, preventing you from inadvertently deleting them later on.

If an installation fails or you later need to uninstall an application, you can do a controlled rollback. The historical record of the installation also makes it easier to re-create an installation when a laptop is lost or the hard drive on a desktop system stops working.

**Chapter 2**

# Using The Microsoft Management Console

# In Brief

As noted in Chapter 1, Windows 2000 Server includes three key components of Microsoft's Zero Administration Initiative for Windows—the Microsoft Management Console (MMC), the Active Directory, and the Group Policy Editor—as well as other useful Zero Administration tools. Because you will use the MMC for most of your administrative tasks, including managing the Active Directory and working with group policies, I cover the MMC in detail in this chapter.

## Overview Of The Microsoft Management Console

It is important to understand that the MMC is not a program that you run. Rather, it is a standardized interface for the administrative tools in Windows 2000 Server. Microsoft's goal was to develop a common user interface for all of the administrative tools in each of its operating systems. Over time, the company plans to convert all such tools for use with the MMC interface. It is also encouraging third-party developers to do the same.

Most of the administrative tools in Windows 2000 Server use the MMC interface. These tools are also called *consoles*. In effect, a tool set, or console, runs within the Microsoft Management Console environment. The terminology can be confusing. When I refer to a console (lowercase), I am referring to a set of tools that uses the MMC, rather than to the MMC itself. You got a preview of some of the consoles if you used the Configure Server Wizard when you installed Windows 2000 Server.

### Snap-Ins

The individual consoles contain one or more components called *snap-ins*. Many snap-ins come with Windows 2000 Server itself and most are installed in one or more of the preconfigured consoles that come with Windows 2000 Server. You can also create your own custom consoles and install the snap-ins of your choice.

There are two types of snap-ins, standalone and extension. A *standalone snap-in* does not require any other snap-in to perform its function. An *extension snap-in* is attached to another snap-in and is controlled by the parent snap-in. As a matter of fact, snap-ins can serve in both capacities, and most of the snap-ins provided with Windows 2000 Server work in both ways. The standalone version may have a full set of capabilities that can be applied to many different objects. On the other hand, the extension version acts only on the object controlled by the parent snap-in and may offer only those capabilities needed by the parent. You'll see examples of these later in this chapter.

Note that I use the term "parent snap-in" and not "standalone snap-in." The reason is that some extension snap-ins can in turn use other extension snap-ins. In addition to snap-ins, consoles may contain ActiveX controls, Web pages, Taskpads similar to those in Windows NT 4 Server, and other components.

Your favorite third-party administrative tools are likely to be converted to snap-ins in the near future, if they have not already been converted. This does not mean that the third-party tools you have been using with Windows NT Server 4 will not work with Windows 2000 Server. Whether any given tool will work depends on the tool itself, not on its user interface.

# Learning A New Set Of Tools

Virtually all of the most frequently used administrative tools in Windows NT Server 4 have been replaced by snap-ins. These include User Manager for Domains, System Policy Editor, and Server Manager, as well as numerous Control Panel applets. Some of the remaining applets, such as the Device Manager component of the System applet, also appear as snap-ins.

For a quick look at the consoles installed on your system, click the Start menu button at the lower-left corner of your screen and then select Programs|Administrative Tools. You will see a list of about two dozen tools, depending on the features installed with your copy of Windows 2000 Server. Most, if not all, of these tools will be consoles.

In my opinion, the MMC interface is definitely more efficient than the collection of administrative tools in Windows NT Server 4. Nevertheless, you need to devote some time to becoming familiar with the new interface and learning how to find and use the new tools for accomplishing the tasks that you need to perform. There are several new features that you are almost certain to find useful:

- *Ease of Customization*—You can customize any console, adding and deleting snap-ins as needed. More importantly, you can create your own custom consoles. The snap-ins are not limited to any specific console, and you can use the same snap-in in several different consoles. If you find that Microsoft's choice of snap-ins for any given console does not work well for you, you can create your own custom console from scratch. You will learn how to do this later in this chapter, as we build some custom consoles that relate to Zero Administration. Consoles are saved as a file with an .MSC extension. Most of the consoles installed with Windows 2000 Server appear in the C:\winnt\system32 folder, assuming that the operating system is installed in the default drive and folder. Consoles that you create will be saved in a folder called My Administrative Tools, accessible through the list of programs on the Start menu.

**NOTE:** *Even though the name of the operating system had been changed to Windows 2000 in Beta 3 and all of the splash screens had been updated, the default installation folder is still \winnt.*

- *Ease of Distribution*—You can create custom consoles for use by other administrators on your network, making it easier for you to delegate some of your responsibilities and distribute the consoles as easily as you can any other file, even as email attachments. If the recipient does not have all of the required snap-ins, the first time he or she uses the console the required snap-ins will be automatically and transparently downloaded from the server to the user's workstation and installed on that system, provided that the user is logged onto the network. In addition, by customizing the view within a console and then selecting the appropriate user mode on the Console page of the console's Options menu, you can create a read-only subset of a console that allows users to access only those features that you want them to use. For further information, see "Locking Down A Console" in the Immediate Solutions section.

**TIP:** *Preconfigured consoles that you modify and save with a different name are saved to the \system32 folder by default and do not show up in the Administrative Tools menu. If you want them to show up when you select My Administrative Tools from the Programs menu or the Administrative Tools window in Control Panel, save them to the folder C:\Documents and Settings\Administrator\Start Menu\Programs\My Administrative Tools.*

The MMC will change the way you work with Windows 2000 Server, so now we will take a close look at what it is and how it works. In the Immediate Solutions section later in this chapter, you will see how to use the preconfigured consoles shipped with Windows 2000 Server; then, you will learn how to create your own custom consoles.

# How The Microsoft Management Console Works

To see the Microsoft Management Console (MMC) in practice, let's look at both the bare-bones MMC interface and a console with many features.

## The MMC Console Interface

To see an example of the basic MMC interface, click the Start menu and then select Run. In the command-line window, enter the following:

```
mmc /a
```

This will open an empty console window, as shown in Figure 2.1. The MMC uses Microsoft's Multiple Document Interface (MDI). Any given console consists of at least two windows, one parent window and one child window.

The parent window, as in all consoles, consists of the basic MMC interface. At the top, under the title bar, is a command bar common to

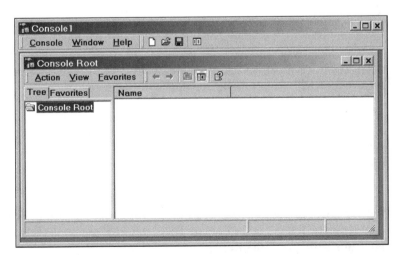

*Figure 2.1    The basic Microsoft Management Console interface prior to the installation of snap-ins.*

all consoles. At the left of the command bar are three drop-down menus: Console, Window, and Help. The Console menu contains the options necessary to configure and customize the console itself. The Window and Help menus contain the standard options that are common to the Microsoft Windows interface. At the right of the menu bar is a toolbar with icons for creating, opening, and saving consoles, as well as for opening a new window.

Contained within the parent window is a child window. The appearance of this window depends on the design and configuration of the selected snap-in. In most cases, it has its own command bar with drop-down menus at the left and a toolbar just to the right of the menus. The content of both the command bar and the toolbar depends on the snap-in you are using and the nature of the selected object on which you will act.

In the middle of the console is a split window resembling the one used by Windows Explorer with a console tree at the left and a details pane at the right. The panes are empty because no snap-ins have been installed. In most cases, the console tree shows a series of folders containing the functions of the installed snap-in or set of snap-ins. The contents of the selected folder are displayed in the details pane.

Later, you will learn how to create your own custom consoles using the basic MMC interface. For now, exit the console without saving it.

# A Working Console

To see an example of a preconfigured working console, click on Start|Programs|Administrative Tools. You will see a list of all of the predefined consoles installed on your system. The contents of the list will vary slightly according to the features that are installed with Windows 2000 Server, so let's look at a common—and powerful—console. Select the Computer Management console, shown in Figure 2.2.

In this console, the panes in the split window are occupied, and the command bar for the console appears above them. Note that the functions displayed in the console tree in the left pane are contained in group folders. As with Windows Explorer, you expand a folder by single-clicking on the plus sign to the left of its name. In this case, there are nested folders containing other folders or objects, and you must drill down several levels to find what you need. When you select a folder in the left pane, the contents of that folder appear in the right pane, just as in Windows Explorer.

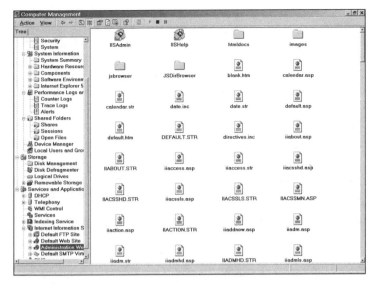

*Figure 2.2    The full Computer Management console with the console tree expanded.*

What you see in a console window depends on where the window is rooted in relation to the entire tree. Initial windows open at the console root so that you can view the entire tree. The same is true of windows that you create using the New Window command on the Window menu of the console's toolbar.

By using other options, you can also open new windows at any point along the console tree, effectively hiding the parts of the tree that are above it. Then, you can close the earlier windows. You might want to use this method when you are creating custom consoles for other administrators. In so doing, you can help them to focus only on those tasks that are relevant to their responsibilities and prevent them from seeing the entire console tree. Note that the entire tree is still present in the console; it's just that portions are hidden from the user's view. See Figure 2.3 for an example.

Most of the objects you see in the console tree are containers. A container is any item on the tree to which an object can be added. Although most containers are folders, there is another type of container called a *viewable item*. When you select a viewable item, it displays a list, text, or graphics in the details pane.

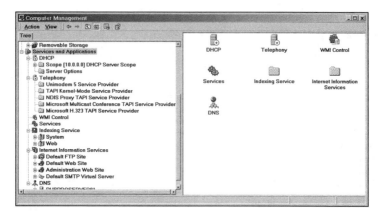

*Figure 2.3    A collapsed view of a portion of the Computer Management console.*

One type of item that you will see in the console tree, but that does not contain any objects, is called a *leaf*. When you select a leaf in the console tree, it displays a group of many items in the details pane. Although these items could also be part of the console tree, their large number makes this impractical.

When you first open the Computer Management console, you see three main folders in the console tree: System Tools, Storage, and Services and Applications. Click the plus sign to the left of each folder to expand it one level.

The contents of each folder depend on the features that you chose when you installed Windows 2000 Server. Under System Tools, for example, you may see as many as seven folders, including System Information, Services, Shared Folders, Event Viewer, and Device Manager. Under Storage, you will most likely find four folders: Logical Drives, Disk Management, Disk Defragmenter, and Remote Storage. Under Services and Applications, you may find such folders as Indexing Service, DNS, and Internet Information Services.

---

**NOTE:**    *If you install Windows 2000 Server to a blank drive, as opposed to upgrading an existing installation, and you are not logged onto your network at the time, the installation routine will configure your computer as a standalone system even though you may be physically connected to a network. The Computer Management console will be configured to manage only your local computer. The snap-ins that are installed will be those appropriate for a standalone system. If you later promote your system to a domain controller, the Local Users and Groups snap-in extension will be removed. The reason is that because the system is now a domain controller, users and groups should be handled through the Active Directory Users and Computers console.*

---

# Drilling Down Through The Console Tree

To give you an idea of the fine granularity that is possible within a console, expand the System Information folder by clicking the plus sign next to its name. Now expand each of its child folders fully. See Figure 2.4 for an example of what the console tree for your system may look like at this point. Once you have fully expanded a folder, you can take action on the objects in the last folder.

Return to the snap-in command bar above the split window. All snap-in command bars have at least two drop-down menus, Action and View, and some have other menus as well. The Action menu is context-sensitive. Its options will depend on the object that you have selected in the details pane, and its function is similar to that of the right-click context menu.

The View menu will be familiar to you from the similar menu on virtually all folders in recent versions of Windows. Here, you can also customize the display, toggling items on and off as needed. The toolbar next to the menus is context-sensitive, displaying icons for some—but not always all—of the options on the right-click context menu.

The description bar is normally deselected by default. When selected, it appears just below the command bar, above the console tree and details pane. In some cases, when you select a folder in the console tree, the task that you can perform on the objects in the details pane is shown here.

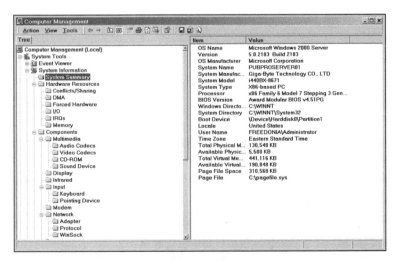

*Figure 2.4    Drilling down the console tree in the Computer Management console.*

# Understanding User And Author Modes

You can use the MMC in two different modes: User and Author. In User mode, you can use the features already built into the console, but you cannot modify it. It's like working with a read-only file. In Author mode, you can not only use these features but also modify the console itself. Three levels of User mode offer varying degrees of flexibility—they are Full Access; Limited Access, Multiple Windows; and Limited Access, Single Window.

Although you will normally want to work in Author mode, at least until you have the consoles configured the way you want them, you might also need to create and distribute custom consoles to people to whom you have delegated some administrative responsibilities. In those cases, you might want to lock a custom console in one of the User modes to prevent people from modifying your consoles. Table 2.1 describes the four modes available in the Console property sheet of the Options dialog box. See Figure 2.5 for an example of a Console property sheet. Later in this chapter, I cover how to implement these modes.

*Table 2.1    Microsoft Management Console operating modes.*

| Operating Mode | What It Allows |
| --- | --- |
| Author Mode | Allows you to access all of the console's functionality, including the ability to add or remove snap-ins, create new windows, and navigate all portions of the console tree. |
| User Mode—Full Access | Allows you to manage the windows in the console and provides you with full access to the console tree in the left pane. However, it does not allow you to add or remove snap-ins or change the options for the console itself. Although the Save command is removed from the File menu, changes that do not directly affect the snap-ins installed in the console, such as changes to the View menu settings, are saved automatically when you exit the console. |
| User Mode—Limited Access, Multiple Windows | Includes all of the restrictions of the Full Access mode. In addition, it limits your ability to open new windows or to access areas of the console tree that were not shown when the console was saved. Although multiple child windows may be open because the author of the console set them up that way, you do not have the ability to close them. |
| User Mode—Limited Access, Single Window | Inherits all of the preceding restrictions and also limits the view to a single window. Essentially, it freezes the view that existed when the console was saved. |

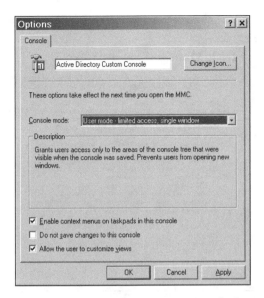

*Figure 2.5   The Console property sheet in the console Options dialog box.*

# The MMC Help System

The MMC help system, shown in Figure 2.6, uses Microsoft's new HTML-based help engine. The system displays a combined table of contents, offering both general help for the MMC interface and specific help for each snap-in installed in the console. The availability and quality of help for each snap-in depend entirely on its developer.

---

*TIP:*   *While you are becoming familiar with all of the new features of Windows 2000 Server, you might find it preferable to use the Help option on the Start menu instead of the Help feature in a specific console. This online help file includes detailed information about every major function of the operating system, including help for each of the preconfigured consoles. You can keep it open as you switch from console to console. On the other hand, if you use the Help function in a specific console, the Help window will close when you close the console.*

---

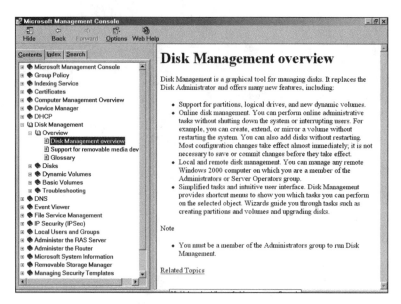

*Figure 2.6    The Microsoft Management Console help system.*

# Immediate Solutions

## User Mode Procedures

This section is devoted to basic procedures that all users need to know, such as opening a console, using its windows, and navigating the help system. It serves as a foundation to "Author Mode Procedures," where you will learn how to create your own consoles.

### Opening A Preconfigured System Administration Console

Most of the preconfigured system administration consoles provided by Microsoft are contained in shortcuts in the Administrative Tools folder. You must have administrative privileges on the system that you are using in order to access them.

There are two ways to access this folder: through the Start menu or through Control Panel. The first is probably the easiest for most people.

To access the consoles through the Start menu, follow these steps:

1. Click the Start menu button at the left of the Taskbar and then choose Programs|Administrative Tools.

2. Select the desired tool from the context-sensitive menu.

To access the consoles through Control Panel, follow these steps:

1. Double-click the My Computer icon on your Windows desktop.

2. Double-click the Control Panel icon to open its window.

3. Double-click the Administrative Tools icon in Control Panel.

Alternately, you can follow these steps:

1. Click the Start menu button.

2. Select Settings|Control Panel|Administrative Tools.

---

**TIP:** *You can save yourself some time by creating shortcuts to the Administrative Tools folder on your desktop and on the Start menu. Open Control Panel, right-click on the Administrative Tools icon to select it, drag it to an empty area of your Windows desktop, and release the mouse button. You'll see a menu with several options. Select Create Shortcut(s) Here. While you're still in Control Panel, right-click and drag the same icon to the Start menu button.*

---

## Opening A Custom Administrative Tool

Custom consoles that you create from scratch will, by default, be saved in the My Administrative Tools folder on your system, assuming that you have logged on as administrator. If you want to be able to access your custom consoles easily, make sure that they are saved to that folder.

To open a custom console, follow these steps:

1. Click the Start menu button.
2. Select Programs|My Administrative Tools.
3. Select the desired tool.

If you have saved your console to another folder, then you need to navigate to it on your own, either through the standard Windows File Open dialog box in the console (in this case, it is Console|Open) or by using Windows Explorer. If for some reason you have chosen to save your console in a folder other than the default, I recommend that you create a shortcut to the console in the My Administrative Tools folder so that you will be able to access it easily.

If you choose to use Windows Explorer to open your console, navigate to the folder in which the file is stored. All consoles have an .MSC extension. Double-click on the file to open the console.

## Finding A "Lost" Console

At some point, it's bound to happen. You've modified a preconfigured console and saved it under a new name, but when you want to use it again, it doesn't show up under either Administrative Tools or My Administrative Tools.

Many, but not all, of the preconfigured console files provided by Microsoft are in the \winnt\system32 folder. If you don't see your file there, the simplest way to find it is to use the Search feature on the Start menu:

1. Click the Start menu button.
2. Select Search|For Files And Folders.
3. When the Search Results window opens, enter the following in the Search For Files Named edit window:

   ```
   *.msc
   ```

4. In the Look In edit window, select Local Hard Drives.

5. Check the Advanced checkbox and make sure that the Search Subfolders box is checked.

6. Click the Search Now button.

The search engine will scan your hard drives for all files with the specified extension. You can double-click on a file to open the console. With the search results still on your screen, right-click and drag the files from the search results screen to your folder and create shortcuts there. See Figure 2.7 for an example of a search.

## Opening A Console With The Run Command

When you want to create your own custom console, the simplest way to open a blank console is to use the Run command on the Start menu. You can also use this to open an existing console, assuming that you know the full path name to the file.

One advantage of this method is that you can use the **/a** command-line switch to open the console in Author Mode regardless of its default mode setting. This is useful when you need to modify a console that has been saved with a restrictive User Mode setting.

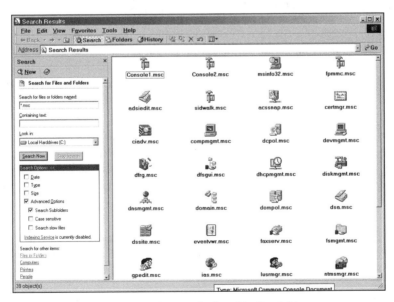

*Figure 2.7    The search results are displayed in the right pane.*

> **NOTE:**   The **/s** command-line switch used with earlier releases of the Microsoft Management
> Console is no longer needed. This switch suppressed the opening splash screen, which is not
> found in the current version. Also, the preconfigured consoles that come with Windows 2000
> Server are now saved in User Mode—Full Access by default. In most of the beta releases,
> including the Corporate Preview Program beta, they defaulted to Author Mode.

To open a new, empty console for editing, follow these steps:

1. Click the Start menu button.

2. Select Run, and then enter this command:

   ```
   MMC /a
   ```

   This will open a new console in Author Mode.

3. To open an existing console for editing, include the full path to
   the file as well:

   ```
   MMC pathname /a
   ```

For example, your command might be something such as this, but
with the command on one continuous line:

```
MMC "C:\Documents and Settings\Administrator\Start Menu\
   Programs\MyConsole.msc" /a
```

If you simply want to use the console and not edit it, you don't need
the **/a** switch.

> **TIP:**   If the name of the file includes spaces, don't forget to put quote marks around it, as
> shown in the preceding example. Otherwise, the command interpreter will treat everything up to
> the first space as the name of the file and everything after the space as command-line switches.
> To help avoid this error, use the underscore instead of a space whenever you are naming your
> own files and folders.

If you prefer to open a command-prompt window rather than use the
Run command, the syntax shown previously will work there as well.
Using the Run command is quicker, for me at least.

## Working With Console Windows

Windows and panes within a console can be resized according to the
standard Microsoft Windows conventions. Main and child windows
can be maximized, minimized, or displayed at normal size, and the
console tree and details panes can be widened or narrowed as needed.

In addition, several other window controls are available. For example, in the Microsoft Management Console itself, you can hide or display the console tree, the Action and View menus, the standard toolbar, the status bar, the description bar, and the Taskpad navigation tabs. See Figure 2.8 for an example. For snap-ins, you can hide or display their menus and toolbars. To customize these settings, select View|Customize. In the Customize View dialog box, you can toggle the listed items on and off by selecting or unselecting their respective checkboxes.

## Using The MMC Help System

Microsoft has provided a very good online help system for Windows 2000 Server, with both practical examples and explanations of concepts, and the help available for the MMC is fairly thorough. As noted in the "In Brief" section, the quality and quantity of help for any given console or snap-in depends on the developer. Microsoft has provided consistently good help for the preconfigured consoles that it provides with Windows 2000 Server.

Within a given console, you can access the help system in one of four ways:

- Click the Help menu on the main toolbar.
- Click the Help button on the main or console toolbars.

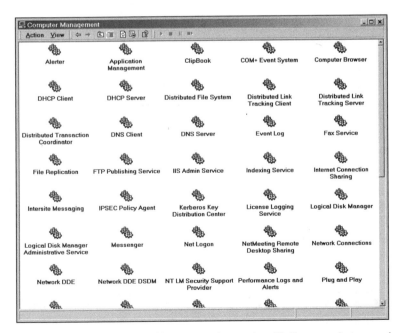

*Figure 2.8    The Computer Management console with the console tree and description bar hidden.*

- Click the system icon at the top-left corner of the main title bar.
- Press the F1 key.

Any of these actions will open a browser-like, frame-based Help window with a table of contents in the left frame and the selected help page displayed in the right window. Carrying through the same interface used in the console (or Windows Explorer, for that matter), you double-click on an item in the left frame to expand the list of topics and subtopics available. In some cases, you might need to drill down several levels to find the object for which you are looking.

You will find two main headings, one for help with the MMC interface itself and another for help with the specific console that you are using. If you don't immediately find the topic in which you are interested, use the Index or Find features, which are enhanced versions of similar features in previous versions of Windows.

The help engine in Windows 2000 Server has been greatly improved over its predecessors. The Find feature will display a list of "hits." When you select a topic for display in the right window, you'll find all of the hits highlighted. To refine your search and limit it to a specific phrase, enclose the search phrase in quotation marks.

# Author Mode Procedures

Now, let's get to the good stuff, where you'll learn how to customize the predefined consoles, create your own consoles, and distribute them to other users to whom you have delegated authority. You'll start with modifying a preconfigured console and then move on to creating and distributing your own custom consoles.

## Customizing A Console

The Active Directory Sites And Services console offers a good place to start because it leaves room for being fleshed out with additional snap-ins relating to the Active Directory. To open it in Author Mode, enter this command:

```
mmc /a c:\winnt\system32\dssite.msc
```

**NOTE:**  *If your server is not a domain controller, the Active Directory may not have been installed. If the tool is not on the list, open any of the other consoles. You won't do any harm to it because you'll save the console under another name.*

As soon as the console has opened, save it under another name for safety:

1. Click the Console menu at the top-left corner of the window.

2. Select Save As.

3. By default, the file will be saved in the same folder as the source file, usually the \winnt\system32 folder. You want to save it in your personal tools folder, so use the dialog box tools to navigate to the folder C:\Documents and Settings\Administrator\ Start Menu\Programs\My Administrative Tools.

4. Change the file name to My_Active_Directory_Console.msc and save the file.

## Adding A Snap-In

Expand the folders in the console tree to become familiar with their content. As you will see, this console covers only a few of the features of the Active Directory. You'll want a more powerful tool, so let's add several other snap-ins that relate to the Active Directory:

1. Click the Console menu.

2. Select Add/Remove Snap-ins. This will open the Standalone page of the Add/Remove Snap-in dialog box.

3. In the main window, you'll see a list of currently installed snap-ins. Make sure that Active Directory Sites And Services is showing in the Snap-ins Added To drop-down list box near the top of the dialog box, and then select the Add button at the bottom-left of the page.

4. You will see an Add/Remove Standalone Snap-In dialog box with a list of all the available standalone snap-ins that have been installed on your system. Among them should be Active Directory Domains And Trusts and Active Directory Users And Computers. Select each one in turn and click the Add button at the bottom of the new dialog box. Figure 2.9 shows an example of the dialog box.

5. As you add each one, its name will appear in the first dialog box. When you are finished, click the Close button in the new dialog box.

6. Now click on the Extensions tab at the top of the dialog box. At the top of the page is a Snap-ins That Can Be Extended drop-down list box. You will see that only two of the snap-ins, Active Directory Sites And Services and Active Directory Users And

*Figure 2.9    The Add Standalone Snap-In dialog box showing all of the snap-ins installed on the user's system.*

Computers, can be extended with snap-ins. As you select each one, the list of available extensions will be shown.

7. Make sure that the Add All Extensions checkbox above the list of available extensions is checked. By checking this box, you are selecting all of the appropriate extensions that have been installed on your system. If you copy the console to a system that has different installed snap-ins, the console will use what's available on that system. On the other hand, if you select snap-ins manually, the selected snap-in must be available wherever the console is used. If it has not been installed, the snap-in will be downloaded automatically from the server to the system.

   When you select Add All Extensions, the checkbox to the left of each extension will be grayed out, indicating that it has been automatically selected. In the current example, there may be only one available extension, Group Policy, and its checkbox may be marked but grayed out. When you select the Add All Extensions option, the checkboxes of all the extensions on the list will appear this way. See Figure 2.10 for an example of an Extensions page.

8. Click OK to return to the console window. Your new snap-ins should appear in the console tree. Save the file by clicking Console|Save.

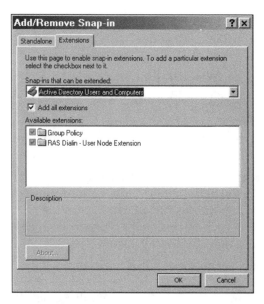

*Figure 2.10    The Extensions page of the Add/Remove Snap-in dialog box.*

## Removing A Snap-In

It was probably overkill to add all three snap-ins. Unless your network consists of multiple domains with trust relationships, you probably don't need the Active Directory Domains And Trusts snap-in, so let's remove it:

1. Click Console|Add/Remove Snap-Ins. This will reopen the Standalone page of the Add/Remove Snap-In dialog box. Again, make sure that the Active Directory Sites And Services Snap-In is selected in the drop-down list box at the top of the page. You will see a list of all snap-ins attached to the selected one.

2. Highlight the Active Directory Domains And Trusts snap-in.

3. Click the Remove button at the bottom of the dialog box.

4. Click OK to return to the console.

5. Save the file.

## Modifying The Window Display

Let's suppose that you administer a large network with several domains, and you have delegated some administrative responsibilities to domain administrators. You want to provide them with a modified version of your new customized console. Perhaps they only need the

Active Directory Users And Computers snap-in. What you want to do is show them only a part of the console tree:

1. Save the file under a new name, such as Domain_Administrator_Directory_Tools.msc.

2. In the console tree, select Active Directory Users And Computers.

3. From the Action menu above the console tree (or from the right-click menu, if you prefer), select New Window From Here. This will hide everything in the tree above the selected folder.

4. The original window is still present, as you'll see by clicking the Window menu at the top of the console. You want to eliminate it in the version that you will send to others, so click the Window menu, open a window that you don't want, and close it. Do this until you have only the desired window.

5. Perhaps your domain administrators don't need to see the console tree. Select View|Customize, and then uncheck the Console Tree option to eliminate it. Now, they will see only the details pane.

6. If you're like me, you may prefer the Details view in Windows Explorer and most other windows, so the details panes in my consoles tend to default to this view. However, your domain administrators might be more familiar with the Large Icon view. Click the View menu and select it. The details pane will now look like the default My Computer window with which many Windows users are familiar. Refer to Figure 2.8 for an example.

7. Save the file.

## Locking Down A Console

You have the console pretty much the way you want it, but now you need to make sure that it stays that way when the domain administrators use it. Try the different User Mode options:

1. Select Console|Options.

2. In the drop-down list box, select the desired User Mode. (Refer to Table 2.1.)

3. Check the Do Not Save Changes To This Console checkbox. This does not mean that you, as author, cannot change the console; it simply prevents others from doing so. Even if they add a snap-in, it will only remain for the current session. See Figure 2.11 for an example of the dialog box.

4. Click the Apply button, and then click OK to return to the console window.

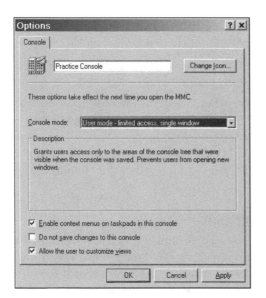

*Figure 2.11   Locking down a console in the Console page of the Options dialog box.*

5. Save the file.

6. When you return to the console, it will appear as if nothing has changed. Here's the kicker: You have to exit the console and then reopen it to see the effects of your changes. Exit the console now.

7. Click Start|Programs|My Administrative Tools and reopen the console. Chances are that you'll need to make additional changes. To do so, you must open the file in Author Mode. You will need to use the command prompt or Run command and the command line switches covered earlier in this chapter.

## Creating A Console From Scratch

It's sometimes easier to create a console from scratch than to modify an existing one:

1. Click the Start menu button and then select the Run command.

2. Enter the following command:

```
mmc /a
```

You will see a blank, empty console in Author Mode. By default, it will be called Console1.

3. Click Console|Save. Make sure that the Save dialog box is open to the My Administrative Tools folder.

4. Give the file a meaningful name and save it. Windows 2000 Server will automatically add the .MSC extension.

5. Follow the steps outlined earlier in the chapter in the sections "Adding A Snap-In," "Modifying The Window Display," and "Locking Down A Console," with one exception: When you add snap-ins, you must add them to the console root because you are creating a console from scratch rather than modifying an existing one.

## Distributing Your Console

A console is a file, and you can distribute your customized console in the same way that you do any other file. You can even send it as an email attachment. You might want to make sure that the recipient puts it in his or her My Administrative Tools folder. If the console requires a snap-in that the recipient does not have, the necessary snap-in will be downloaded from your server and installed on his or her system the first time the recipient uses the console.

## Creating A Custom Console For Zero Administration

In upcoming chapters, you'll make heavy use of some of the preconfigured consoles, especially in your work with the Active Directory and with group and security policies. To make things easier, let's put together a custom console focusing on Zero Administration.

First, open a new, blank console as described earlier in this chapter in the section "Creating A Console From Scratch." Save it under the name Zero_Administration_Toolkit.msc.

Add the following standalone snap-ins:

- Active Directory Sites And Services
- Active Directory Users And Computers
- Computer Management
- Disk Management
- Distributed File System
- Security Configuration and Analysis
- Security Templates

In the Extensions page of the Add/Remove Snap-Ins dialog box, cycle through each of the snap-ins and make sure that all of the available extensions have been added.

# Using Predefined Consoles In Windows 2000 Server

Here is a list of predefined consoles that are installed with Windows 2000 Server and examples of tasks that you can perform with them. Your list of available consoles may differ slightly depending on the Windows 2000 Server features installed on your system:

- *Active Directory Sites and Services*—Manage the Active Directory at the domain level. Use this console to:
  - Configure a default first-site domain controller.
  - Delegate control.
  - Set up replication within a site.
  - Set up replication between two sites.
  - Create a link between two sites.
  - Create a bridge to another site.
  - Define a site.
  - Add a new server to a site.
  - Add a subnet to a site.
  - Add a domain controller to a site.
  - Move a domain controller.
  - Repair a domain controller.
  - Configure site settings.
- *Active Directory Domains and Trusts*—Use this console to change the domain mode, create an explicit domain trust, or add User Principal Name (UPN) suffixes.
- *Active Directory Users and Computers*—Use this to administer Active Directory objects and information. Types of objects include domains, organizational units, groups, computers, and users.
- *Component Services*—Use this console to configure and administer Common Object Model (COM) components.
- *Computer Management*—Manage hardware and services on a local computer. Use this console to:
  - Monitor system events.
  - Create and manage shared resources.
  - View a list of users connected to a specific computer.

- Start and stop system services.
- Configure storage devices.
- View Device Manager and add or update device drivers.
- Manage server applications and services affecting a specific computer.

- *Configure Your Server*—This is the console that appears whenever you load Windows 2000, unless you have disabled it. Use this console to add and configure important new features.

- *Data Sources (ODBC)*—Use this console to add, remove, and configure Open Database Connectivity (ODBC) data sources and drivers.

- *Distributed File System*—Manage the Distributed File System (DFS). Use this console to:
  - Create a new DFS root.
  - Add a share to the DFS root.
  - Replicate a DFS root or share.

- *DHCP*—Manage the Dynamic Host Configuration Protocol (DHCP). Use this console to:
  - Connect to and start DHCP servers.
  - Monitor and configure DHCP servers.
  - Manage scopes and superscopes.
  - Manage options.
  - Manage clients and leases.
  - Manage Bootstrap Protocol (BOOTP) clients.

- *Directory Services Migration Tool*—Use this console to help your Windows 2000 network co-exist with Novell Directory Services.

- *DNS*—Manage the zones in your Domain Naming System (DNS) server setup. Use this console to create a new zone and update server data files.

- *Domain Controller Security Policy*—Use this console to edit the default group policy for a domain controller. This is the local computer policy for the controller.

- *Domain Security Policy*—Use this console to edit the default group policy for your domain.

- *Event Viewer*—View logs of application, system, and security events. Use this console to monitor hardware and software activities.

- *Internet Services Manager*—Manage Internet Information Services. Use this console to set properties relating to your network's Web, FTP, and Gopher services.

- *Licensing*—Manage software licenses. Use this console to:
  - View the Per Seat and Per Server licenses across your organization.
  - Manage the purchasing or deleting of licenses for software on your network servers.
  - View usage statistics.
  - Balance your network's licensing replication load.
  - Change the licensing mode of Microsoft BackOffice software from Per Server to Per Seat.
  - Create license groups.

- *Local Security Policy*—Use this console to edit the default group policy security settings for the local computer.

- *Performance*—Use this console to display graphs of system performance and configure data logs and alerts.

- *Remote Storage*—Maintain adequate space on your local drives. Use this console to:
  - Manage local volumes.
  - Copy files to remote storage.
  - Establish the desired free space.
  - Specify selection criteria and rules for moving files to remote storage.
  - Set the runaway limit for users.
  - Change the file-copying schedule.
  - Validate volume files.
  - Modify remote files.
  - Discontinue volume management.

- *Routing and Remote Access*—Manage the Routing and Remote Access Service. Use this console to:
  - Start and stop the service.

- Add a server.

- Rebuild the server list.

- *Server Extensions Administrator*—Use this console to manage the FrontPage Server Extensions.

- *Services*—Use this console to start and stop services on the local system.

- *Telnet Server Administration*—Use this console to view and modify Telnet server settings and connections.

All of these tools, as well as others, appear in the Administrative Tools folder. Click the Start button, and select Programs|Administrative Tools. You can also access the folder in Control Panel. See Figure 2.12 for an example of the Administrative Tools window.

| Related solutions: | Found on page: |
| --- | --- |
| Managing Domains, Trees, And Forests | 76 |
| Managing Sites | 79 |
| Managing The Schema | 94 |
| Administering Computer Accounts | 117 |
| Administering Groups | 164 |
| Administering Organizational Units | 172 |

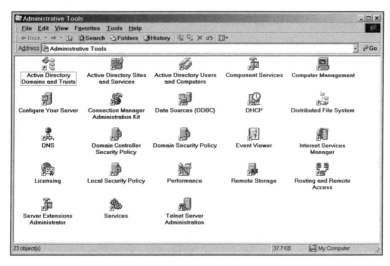

*Figure 2.12   The Administrative Tools Window in Control Panel with a typical configuration of consoles and other tools.*

# Finding Reference And Troubleshooting Information

This final section of the chapter includes information that will help you find the Windows 2000 Server equivalents of the Windows NT 4 administrative tools, show you how to navigate the MMC interface using the keyboard, and help you troubleshoot problems with consoles.

## Finding Equivalents Of Windows NT 4 Tools

I hope the preceding list of predefined consoles will give you a good idea of the purpose of each one. If you have been working with Windows NT Server 4, however, you may be wondering where your old tools have gone. Table 2.2 shows you how to accomplish many administrative tasks previously done with Windows NT 4 tools.

*Table 2.2   Administrative tool realignment in Windows 2000 Server.*

| Task | Windows NT 4 Tool | Windows 2000 Equivalent |
| --- | --- | --- |
| Manage trust relationships. | User Manager for Domains | Active Directory Domains and Trusts |
| Manage user accounts and groups. | User Manager for Domains | Active Directory Users and Computers |
| Assign logon scripts. | User Manager for Domains | Group Policy Editor snap-in |
| Manage shares. | My Computer or Windows NT Explorer | Distributed File System |
| Manage domain security policy. | User Manager for Domains | Group Policy Editor snap-in |
| Configure computer security policy. | System Policy Editor | Group Policy Editor snap-in |
| Manage the computers in a domain. | Server Manager | Active Directory Users and Computers |
| Manage a server's shared resources. | Server Manager | Distributed File System |
| Manage disk storage. | Disk Administrator | Disk Management Snap-in |
| Manage server connections. | Server Manager | Computer Management |
| Add hardware to a computer. | Several Control Panel applets | Hardware Wizard in Control Panel |
| Configure devices. | Device option in Control Panel | Computer Management |
| Configure network interface cards. | Network applet in Control Panel | Hardware Wizard in Control Panel |

## Controlling The Microsoft Management Console With The Keyboard

Selection and navigation in the MMC user interface follows standard Microsoft Windows conventions. For example, single-clicking an item selects it in either the console tree or the details pane. Double-clicking an item in the tree expands or contracts the portion of the tree below it, as does single-clicking the plus (+) or minus (-) sign to the left of most objects in the tree. Right-clicking on an item displays the context-sensitive shortcut menu for the selected item.

For those who prefer navigating with keyboard commands, Table 2.3 lists the navigation controls in the MMC. Where alternate commands exist, they are shown in parentheses.

Keyboard shortcuts can take the place of many mouse actions in the MMC. In most cases, they follow standard Microsoft Windows conventions. Table 2.4 lists the standard keyboard commands that apply to both the main console window and the child windows belonging to the snap-ins.

*Table 2.3   Keyboard navigation in consoles.*

| Keystroke Or Combination | What It Does |
|---|---|
| Tab (F6) | Moves to the next pane in the active console window. |
| Shift+Tab (Shift+F6) | Moves to the previous pane in the active console window. |
| Ctrl+Tab (Ctrl+F6) | Moves to the next console window. |
| Ctrl+Shift+Tab (Ctrl+Shift+F6) | Moves to the previous console window. |
| Right arrow (+ on the numeric keypad) | Expands the selected item in the console tree. |
| Left arrow (- on the numeric keypad) | Contracts the selected item in the console tree. |
| * on the numeric keypad | Expands the entire console tree from the root downward. |
| Up arrow | Selects the previous item in a pane. |
| Down arrow | Selects the next item in a pane. |
| Page Up | Selects the first visible item in a pane. |
| Page Down | Selects the last visible item in a pane. |
| Home | Selects the very first item in a pane. |
| End | Selects the very last item in a pane. |
| Alt+right arrow | Select the next item in a pane. |
| Alt+left arrow | Select the previous item in a pane. |

*Table 2.4   Keyboard shortcuts in consoles.*

| Keystroke Or Combination | What It Does |
|---|---|
| Alt+Spacebar | Activates the main Window menu. |
| Alt+- (hyphen) | Opens the Window menu for the active console window. |
| Alt+A | Opens the Action menu for the active window. |
| Alt+V | Opens the View menu for the active window. |
| Alt+F4 | Closes the current console. |
| Ctrl+M | Opens the Add/Remove Snap-ins dialog box. |
| Ctrl+N | Opens a new, empty console. |
| Ctrl+O | Opens an existing console. |
| Ctrl+P | Prints the current page or active pane. |
| Ctrl+S | Saves the current console. |
| Ctrl+W | Opens a new window. |
| Ctrl+F4 | Closes the active window. |
| Ctrl+F5 | Restores the active window. |
| Ctrl+F10 | Maximizes the active window. |
| Shift+F10 | Opens the Action shortcut menu for the selected item. |
| Enter | Opens the Properties dialog box for the selected item, or in some cases, the item itself. |
| F1 | Opens context-sensitive Help for the selected item. |
| F2 | Opens an edit box for renaming the selected item. |
| F5 | Refreshes the display in all console windows. |

**2. Using The Microsoft Management Console**

## Troubleshooting The Microsoft Management Console

Because the MMC is an interface rather than a program in and of itself, you are not likely to have much trouble with it. Rather, whatever problems you may encounter are more likely to be due to the snap-ins written for use with the MMC.

Nevertheless, there are two areas where you might run into some problems:

- *Lack of help for a specific snap-in*—If you can't find help for a particular snap-in, particularly one from a third-party developer, it may be because the developer either has not provided online help or has not written it so that it can be merged into the MMC Help table of contents. Instead, the developer may have written a separate help file, accessible from the Help menu or the Help button on the toolbar of the snap-in.

- *Cannot find an expected snap-in in the list of installed snap-ins—* If an expected snap-in is not listed among the available snap-ins installed on your system, it may be because the feature that it controls has not been installed. For example, if Internet Information Services has not been installed on your system, you will not see the Internet Services snap-in listed. To add a feature to Windows 2000 Server, follow these steps:

    1. Open Control Panel, click Add/Remove Programs, and then select the Add/Remove Windows Components option to run the Windows Components Wizard.

    2. The wizard will scan your system to determine which features have been installed, then present you with a list of all available features. Select the feature that you want to add and follow the prompts.

# Chapter 3

# Managing Domains, Sites, And Schemas

*(continued)*

# *In Brief*

I have devoted three chapters of this book, beginning with this one, to the Active Directory, one of the most important new features of Windows 2000 Server. Many of the Zero Administration tools that you will use are tied closely to the Active Directory. Therefore, it is important that you have a full understanding of the Active Directory, so that you will know how to use its features and tools to accomplish your network-management tasks.

Although virtually every management tool in Windows 2000 Server uses the Active Directory to one degree or another, there are four Microsoft Management Consoles that are specifically devoted to it. In this chapter, you will learn how to use three consoles that enable you to manage the enterprise-wide aspects of your network: Active Directory Sites and Services, Active Directory Domains and Trusts, and Active Directory Schema. In Chapters 4 and 5, you will learn how to use the Active Directory Users and Computers console to perform everyday tasks. These include creating and managing computer and user accounts, groups, and organizational units.

# What Is The Active Directory?

The purpose of any directory is to help you find something of interest and importance to you. A telephone directory, for example, enables you to find the telephone number of someone you need to contact. If you know the person's name and have a general idea of where she is located, a telephone directory will help you find her telephone number.

In a network environment, a directory serves much the same purpose. It helps users to find and access resources on your network—including hardware, software, data files, and people. This is the primary purpose of the Active Directory. Equally important, the Active Directory, in combination with the Microsoft Management Console, provides a structure that makes it easier than before for you to manage these resources and other objects on your network. It does this by grouping all of the objects on your network in one central location, where you can manage them with a series of Microsoft Management

Consoles that have a common interface. All of the directory-based applications that ship with Windows 2000 Server have been integrated into the Active Directory.

The Active Directory's scope encompasses your entire enterprise, regardless of its size. It organizes the objects on your network into a hierarchical pyramid, starting at the top. This arrangement makes it possible for you to view and manage virtually everything on your network, regardless of its location (assuming that you have the necessary rights and permissions).

# Active Directory Domains And Trusts

The main purpose of the Active Directory Domains and Trusts console is to enable you to make the resources on your network easily available to everyone on your network. With the Active Directory, you can do this without placing an undue burden on network resources, even if your users are in different domains. Information about resources in other domains is contained in a global catalog that is available to each person in each domain. Figure 3.1 shows the console.

The Active Directory does not discard the domain-based architecture of Windows NT 4; rather, it builds on and enhances the domain concept. Although certain global groups, such as administrators, can operate in more than one domain, you will normally assign most of the objects in your network, such as computers and users, to a specific domain. Because so much happens at the domain level, the data for the Active Directory is maintained on the domain controller.

Although Windows 2000 Server preserves the domains in a Windows NT 4 network,there are important enhancements in Windows 2000 Server. In Windows NT 4 Server, each domain has a primary domain controller and many domains have one or more backup controllers. In

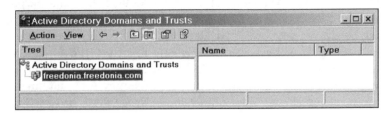

*Figure 3.1   The Active Directory Domains and Trusts console.*

3. Managing Domains, Sites, And Schemas

Windows 2000 Server, all controllers within a domain that are running Windows 2000 Server are on an equal footing with each other. This arrangement is possible because the Active Directory automatically replicates data among all of the controllers in a domain. In a mixed environment, domain controllers that are still running Windows NT will see the Windows 2000 controllers as primary domain controllers.

---

**NOTE:**   *If you upgrade from Windows NT 4 Server, and the system you upgrade is either a primary or a backup domain controller, the installation routine configures your system as a domain controller. When it does, it installs the necessary components, including the Active Directory. If you install Windows 2000 Server on a new system or upgrade a system that is not a domain controller, you will see a Configure Server Wizard when you reboot the system after installation completes. This wizard leads you through the process of promoting the system to a domain controller.*

---

Active Directory Domains and Trusts offers two ways for organizing multiple domains on your network: trees and forests. When you create or promote the first domain controller on your network, the Configure Server Wizard essentially forces you to create both a new domain tree and a new domain forest. As you create or promote a new domain controller, you are given an opportunity to either create a new tree and forest, or join the controller to an existing tree.

---

**NOTE:**   *You cannot create new domains, trees, or forests by using the Active Directory Domains and Trusts administrative tool. You can only create them at the time when you promote a server to a domain controller, using the Configure Server Wizard. The tool is used to manage only ones that you have already created.*

---

Most large organizations require more than one domain, and some organizations have many domains. The Active Directory improves upon the Windows NT 4 domain model in the ease with which you can add multiple domains to the Active Directory.

The most common reason to create multiple domains is to reduce the volume and nature of the replication traffic on your network. By creating logical spin-offs of your principal domain, and by delegating at least some level of control of the new domains to others, you can reduce the traffic on your network significantly and make it easier to administer as well.

**3. Managing Domains, Sites, And Schemas**

Here are some other examples of situations where multiple domains can be useful:

- Large geographically spread-out organizations, in which certain sites are connected by very slow links. For example, all of your North American sites (and all of your European sites) might be connected by high-speed lines. However, the connections between your North American sites and your European ones might be over a slow transatlantic line. In that case, you might want to create separate domains for North America and Europe.

- Highly decentralized organizations, in which each division is managed by a separate autonomous administrator. These administrators can establish their own domains and implement their own security policies.

- International organizations, in which it is important to preserve and support the local language and culture.

## Joining Domains In Trees And Forests

You can create trust relationships between domains by creating a domain tree. Each new domain that you create becomes a child of the parent domain. Once you establish a trust relationship between your current domain and each of the other domains in your tree, similar relationships between each domain and every other linked domain are established automatically at the same time.

By default, Windows 2000 Server establishes two-way transitive-trust relationships between domains. When users from any of the domains in the tree log onto your network, they automatically have access to the resources in all of the trees. This makes it much easier to establish trust relationships than in Windows NT 4 Server.

Figure 3.2 shows an example of a domain tree. The relationship of each subordinate domain to the primary domain is automatically applied to each of the other subordinate domains as well.

Domain forests are groups of two or more domain trees. Each domain tree in a forest has its own separate naming structure, which is the primary difference between a domain tree and a domain forest. All domains in all forests share the same schema and global catalog.

Although the domain tree is often the preferred way to link multiple domains, because it is easy for your users to access information and resources on them, sometimes this arrangement is

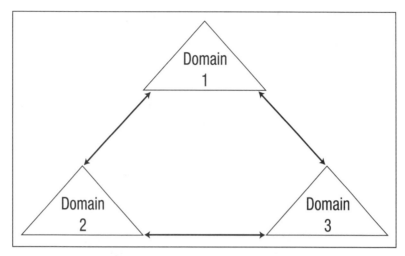

*Figure 3.2   An example of a domain tree with two-way transitive-trust
relationships.*

impractical or simply not an option. In that case, creating a forest
becomes a good alternative.

Here's an example of when a forest is appropriate: Two companies
have merged, but each has kept its own identity and DNS name. You
can make each one a separate domain or tree on your network, and
then join them to a forest with other domains. This enables each company to keep its identity while still making it possible for its employees to share resources on other domains.

Figure 3.3 illustrates an example of a domain forest. Note that, unlike domains within a tree, you must establish each relationship
individually.

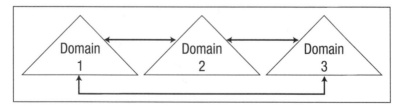

*Figure 3.3   An example of a domain forest with two-way transitive-trust
relationships established between each domain.*

# Establishing Trust Relationships Between Domains

When joining two domains in a tree, you can create one of two types of trust relationships between the domains:

- *Two-Way Transitive Trust*—This is the default trust relationship. It is designed to simplify the administration of relationships between domains.

- *One-Way Trust*—This type of relationship, which is more restrictive than a two-way trust, must be explicitly added or removed by selectively creating or modifying a relationship between two domains.

### Two-Way Transitive Trusts

With a two-way transitive trust, the relationships among linked domains are bidirectional and transitive from one domain to another. Users in any domain can access resources in any other domain. This type of relationship is created automatically when you either add a child domain to an existing tree or join two domain trees to create a forest. When you do this, and you allow the default relationship between the parent and child to stand, two things happen:

- The child domain automatically trusts all other domains that are trusted by the parent.

- All domains that trust the parent also trust the child.

When you join two domain trees in a forest, a two-way transitive trust is established between the root domains of each tree in the forest. This is what makes it possible for users to access resources on any domain in the forest.

### Explicit One-Way Trusts

There may be times when you do not want to establish a two-way trust relationship, but you need to have some way for users from one domain to access specified resources on another domain. For example, you might need to share certain resources with a business partner.

Explicit one-way trusts allow you to selectively enable access to your resources from users in the other domain. This type of relationship affects only the two domains in question and can be revoked when the need for it no longer exists. It is equivalent to the domain trust relationship used in Windows NT 4 Server.

In a one-way trust, access flows in one direction only. The host domain is called the *trusting domain*, whereas the domain that has been granted access to the host is called the *trusted domain*.

# The Active Directory Sites And Services Manager

A site consists of a group of computers that are in a well-defined location and share good, fast network connections with each other. It is not part of the domain's namespace. A domain can have any number of sites, and different areas within the site can be in different domains.

In addition, the Active Directory Sites and Services console contains information about some of the services that are available on the current domain controller. By default, they are not displayed. To view them, select ViewlShow Services Node. In the default configuration, the services include public key services, including certificate templates and enrollment services, Routing And Remote Access Service, and Windows NT Directory Service. Figure 3.4 shows a view of the Active Directory Sites and Services console.

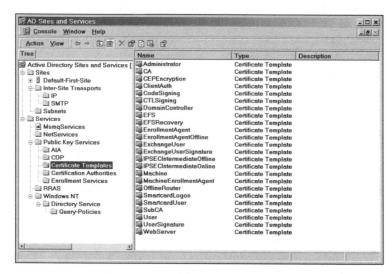

*Figure 3.4   The Active Directory Sites and Services console.*

# Dividing Your Network Into Sites

Sites are not part of the organizational structure of the domain itself, as is the case with organizational units and groups. Rather, the sites feature enables you to group computer systems to maximize performance and reduce traffic on your network.

It's important to understand the distinction between sites and domains. Sites define the physical structure of your network; domains define its logical structure. There need not be a correlation between the two. A site can contain clients from more than one domain and a domain can contain more than one site. Finally, there is no relationship between the namespaces of the site and the domain.

In most cases, sites are created for groups of computers in a remote location, such as a branch office. Each site has at least one domain controller. For replicating the Active Directory, the first controller in the site is linked to the main controller of the parent domain. Subsequent controllers within a site, however, are linked to the site's first controller, not to the main domain controller.

The basic building block of a site is the subnet mask assigned to each computer within the site. All systems within a subnet share the same subnet mask. A site can contain more than one subnet.

Although the method for assigning a subnet mask to a client depends on the client's operating system, the setting is often found in the dialog used to assign an Internet Protocol (IP) address to the client computer. Think of the subnet mask as the ZIP or postal code for the client system.

Here are the main advantages of a site, particularly if it is in a remote location:

- *Fast authentication*—When users log onto your network, they must be authenticated by a domain controller. Windows 2000 Server first searches for a domain controller that is in the same site as the client system, which speeds the process and reduces bandwidth on the network. Within a site, users are likely to be connected to the domain controller over a high-speed local area network (LAN). If the LAN is part of a larger wide area network (WAN), the connection between the remote site and the rest of the network is likely to be over a slower and much more expensive connection, possibly even a dial-up connection.

- *Ease of replication*—Data for the Active Directory is replicated among domain controllers within a site, as well as among controllers at other locations. However, replication within a site occurs more frequently than replication among controllers that are outside of the site. This helps to maintain a balance between the need for up-to-date data in the local copies of the Active Directory and the need to control the amount of traffic on the network.

The main purpose of the Active Directory Sites and Services console is to help you manage the replication of information in the Active Directory. By creating sites within the Active Directory, you can define the physical (as opposed to logical) structure of your network.

When setting up your structure for replication within a site, the issue of bandwidth should be one of your primary concerns. Make sure that all of the systems on the subnet have reliable, fast connections with each other. This applies particularly to domain controllers because of the frequency of replication of Active Directory data.

You can customize the way that the Active Directory replicates information by posting inter-site connections, along with the cost of those connections, and by specifying a schedule for replication. When you enter the information pertaining to inter-site connections, the Active Directory then determines the most efficient way to connect with other controllers in the domain. Once it has determined the best connections to use, Active Directory then looks at the cost for each one. The higher the cost, the less often Active Directory will use it. You can also schedule replication for times when traffic on the network is low.

# Situations That Call For A Single Site

When planning for efficient replication of Active Directory data, begin with a simple site structure and add new sites when they are needed. If your configuration consists of a single LAN, and the connections throughout the network are fast, you may need only one site for the entire network.

In its online help for Windows 2000 Server, Microsoft recommends against creating more than one site within a location that has good connections, such as a single LAN. If a user logs on and there are no controllers available within their site, Active Directory searches the entire domain for an available controller. It does not try to determine which controller has the best connection to the client, so the connection that it chooses might not be a very good one. If you want to connect a workstation to a specific group of domain controllers, configure your site so that only those controllers are in the same site as the workstation (see "Associating A Site With A Subnet" in the Immediate Solutions section).

# Situations That Call For More Than One Site

If your domain controllers are not responding quickly enough to meet normal needs, you should consider this option. The more geographically separated the systems in a domain, the slower your network's performance is likely to be.

Suppose that your company has its headquarters in New York City, and branch offices in Chicago and Los Angeles. The Chicago office, although it has only five employees, is connected to your network in New York by a high-speed T1 line, whereas the Los Angeles office, with a dozen employees, has only a dial-up connection. Network performance between Chicago and New York might be adequate as is, but the Los Angeles office would be a definite candidate for a separate site.

When planning a new site, consider the need for maximizing the efficiency of your network within the site, as well as the connections between its domain controllers and those elsewhere on your network. Assign each workstation to a controller with which it has a fast, reliable connection by assigning the same subnet mask to each.

# Using Links Between Sites

Planning and developing multiple sites is not enough—you must also consider the way information will be exchanged among the sites. Although Active Directory automatically creates a link to another site when you create the first domain controller within a new site, you may want to fine-tune this link.

For example, you can create a link that supplements your principal replication channel or creates a bridge that joins a series of site links. When you link a new site to an existing one, Windows 2000 Server creates just one link automatically. Although a single link may be enough for your purposes, multiple links lead to a more reliable system.

# The Active Directory Schema

The Active Directory schema is a collection of definitions of objects in the Active Directory. These definitions determine the objects that can be stored in the directory and the types of data that can be stored in the objects. Within the schema itself, there are two types of objects:

- *Classes*—These are collections of attributes pertaining to an object.

- *Attributes*—These define the type of data that can be stored in the object. The definition of an attribute specifies the format of the information, such as an integer number or string of text, as well as other information, such as whether the attribute can have more than one value. This data can normally be found in the Properties dialog box for the Active Directory objects that use the attribute.

You will not find the Active Directory Schema (shown in Figure 3.5) among the consoles in the Administrative Tools program group. The Active Directory Schema is available only as a snap-in. To use it, you must first install the snap-in, and then either create a new management console or add the snap-in to an existing one. For information on how to do this, see the section on adding a snap-in in Chapter 2.

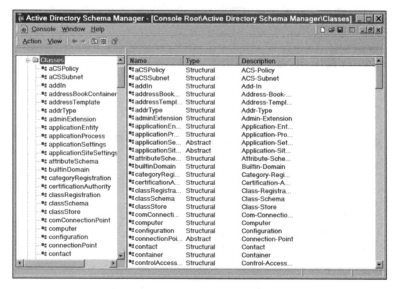

*Figure 3.5    The Active Directory Schema snap-in.*

It is possible to make some simple modifications to the schema by using the Active Directory Schema, although Microsoft recommends that this be done in a scripting or programming environment such as VBScript or Visual Basic. Most likely, you will need to add a class to the schema. You can do this by extending an existing class, deriving a subclass, or creating a new class.

## Extending An Existing Class

You extend an existing class by adding attributes or additional possible parents. For example, you may want to add the employeeID attribute to the user class. This is the method of choice when:

- The existing class meets your basic needs, but would be more useful to you with additional attributes.

- You do not need to make the extended class distinct from the existing one.

When modifying the user class, you should use this method whenever possible instead of deriving a subclass from the user class, even though having subclasses for distinct groups of users might seem to be a good idea. Once you create an object in the Active Directory, you cannot alter its class. For example, when you create an account for a new user, the user class is assigned to it, by default. Once the account is created, you cannot change the original class to a subclass.

## Deriving A Subclass

When you derive a subclass from an existing class, the new subclass inherits all of the attributes of the parent class, as well as any that you choose to add. Use this method when:

- The existing class meets your basic needs, but would be more useful to you with additional attributes.

- You need to create a distinct identify for the modified class.

## Creating A New Class

When you create a new class, you can build its list of attributes from scratch. Use this method only when none of the existing classes meet your requirements.

# The Schema Cache

The database for the Active Directory schema is stored in a cache. When Windows 2000 Server starts, it loads the schema into the cache, which is stored in system memory. When the schema is modified, the server saves the changes to the schema's database immediately. It waits for five minutes after the last change, however, before it re-loads the information in the database into the memory cache. If you attempt to perform certain actions during this five-minute waiting period, you may get an error message because the changed schema has not yet been loaded into the cache. The solution, explained in "Refreshing The Schema Cache" in the Immediate Solutions section that follows, is to force the Active Directory to reload the schema from disk as soon as you complete your modifications.

# Immediate Solutions

## Installing The Active Directory

By default, the Active Directory is installed only on domain controllers. Keep in mind that the data for the Active Directory must reside on a domain controller. Once you have completed the installation of the core Windows 2000 Server files, you need to promote your server to a domain controller in order to use the Active Directory.

The server-configuration procedure is fairly lengthy and involved. It's important that you get it right the first time because, in some cases, it is difficult (if not impossible) to make changes after the domain controller is configured. Therefore, I recommend that you do the following to prepare for the procedure:

- If you are creating a new domain, give careful consideration to how you plan to organize it. Although organization will not come into play until after you have configured the domain controller, it is important that you consider it at an early stage.

- Develop a good understanding of the DNS and TCP/IP protocols, and of the relationship between the Active Directory and DNS.

- If you are creating a new domain, be sure to register the domain name with the proper Internet naming authority, such as InterNIC, before you create the domain.

- Make sure that the partition you plan to use for the Active Directory has been formatted for NTFS. You cannot install the Active Directory on a FAT or FAT32 partition. The partition for the Active Directory need not be the same one that contains the Windows 2000 Server system files. During the configuration process, you can specify the drive or partition on which to store the Active Directory.

- Make sure that the TCP/IP protocol has been properly installed on the server. Be sure to specify a fixed IP address for the server. Make a note of the address, and keep it handy.

- Make sure that a DNS server is available. If this is to be the first domain controller on the network, and you have not yet installed DNS, the Configure Server Wizard will install it automatically. (The DNS server can be installed on the same system as the domain controller.)

- Record the full DNS name of the new domain. If you have a name that has been registered with an Internet naming authority, use it here.

- Record the NetBIOS name of the domain. Older workstation clients, such as Windows 95 and Windows NT 4 Workstation, will use it. If you are creating a new domain, use the first part of the domain name, before the period, up to 12 characters.

The following step-by-step exercises presume that you have a working knowledge of TCP/IP, DNS, and NetBIOS.

**WARNING!** *If you are creating a new domain, be sure to get the domain name right the first time. Windows 2000 Server has no way to check the name you entered against the domain names already on your network. Once the domain has been created, there is no way to change its name. If you find that you need to change the name, you need to demote the domain controller to an ordinary server, and then repeat the process of upgrading your server to a domain controller. When that happens, you will lose everything that you have done in the Active Directory, as well as your personalized custom settings on the Windows desktop. The reason is that in demoting your server, you also demote yourself. You will become the administrator of your local workstation and nothing more. Windows 2000 Server will consider you a different person from the administrator of the old domain.*

# Creating A Domain Controller

The first time you restart Windows 2000 Server after the installation is complete, you will see a Configure Server screen, as shown in Figure 3.6.

The configuration process has quite a few steps. I recommend that you read the following steps and study the accompanying screenshots, so that you will be familiar with the process before you begin. You also should make sure that you have all of the necessary information at hand.

If you have already installed Windows 2000 Server as a standalone server, there are two likely scenarios:

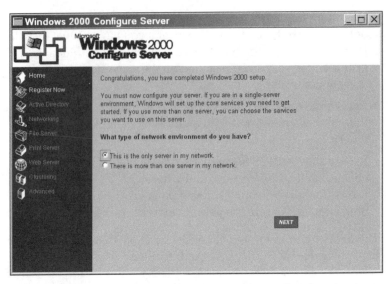

*Figure 3.6 The Configure Server screen displays the first time the server starts, following a successful installation.*

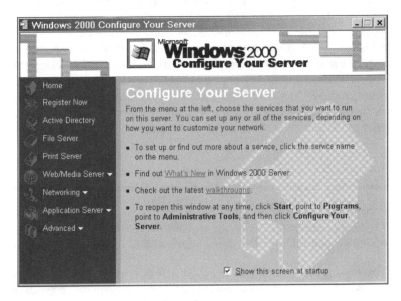

*Figure 3.7 The normal Configure Server screen.*

- If you still see a Configure Server screen after the network has started, it should look like Figure 3.7. To promote your server to a domain controller and install the Active Directory, click the Active Directory option in the menu at the left of the screen.

- If you do not see this screen, click Start|Run and enter the following command to start the Configure Server wizard:

```
dcpromo
```

The Configure Server Wizard offers a number of options, depending on whether the new domain will be the first or only domain on the network, or will instead be linked to other domains. The screenshots that accompany this systematic procedure demonstrate the configuration of a domain controller that was the first and only one on the network.

---

**NOTE:** *The process of promoting a server to a domain controller, as described here, was done using a late beta release of Windows 2000 Server. There may be slight differences between the dialog boxes displayed here and those in the shipping release.*

---

Are you ready to configure your server as a domain controller? Let's go through the process, step-by-step:

1. In the first screen, there are two radio buttons for indicating whether the server you are configuring is the only server in your network. Select the proper button and click Next at the bottom-right corner of the screen.

2. In the second screen, enter the name of the new domain, such as freedonia.com. Double-check your typing for accuracy, and then click Next. See Figure 3.8 for an example of this screen.

3. After a few minutes, a screen will inform you that you must restart the computer to continue the process. Click Next to continue.

   After Windows 2000 Server restarts, you will see another version of the Configure Server screen. This version is an HTML frameset appearing within Internet Explorer, with the main menu in the left frame. Figure 3.7 shows this screen, which will appear whenever you start Windows 2000 Server unless you uncheck the box at the bottom-right corner.

4. Now that your system has been promoted to a domain controller, you are ready to install the Active Directory. Click Active Directory in the main menu at the left of the screen.

5. The next screen introduces the Active Directory. If you need more information about the Active Directory before proceeding, click the Learn More hypertext link near the bottom of the

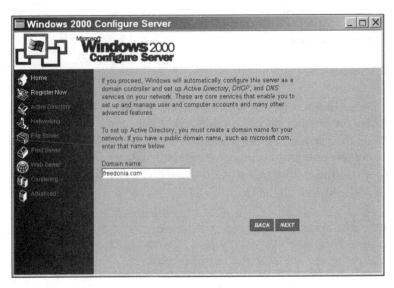

*Figure 3.8   The screen for entering the domain name.*

page at the right. To begin the installation process, click the Start link at the bottom of the page.

6. Next, you will see the opening Welcome screen of the Active Directory Installation Wizard. Click Next to continue.

7. In the Domain Controller Type screen, use the radio buttons to indicate whether you are creating a new domain with the server as the first domain controller, or configuring a replica domain controller in an existing domain. Use the first option to create a new child domain, domain tree, or forest. Use the second option to add the controller to an existing domain. Figure 3.9 shows this screen. Click Next to continue.

**WARNING!**   *Choosing the replica domain controller option will wipe out all of the local accounts on the server.*

The next few screens display when you create a new domain. If you are configuring your server as a replica domain controller, you will see a different set of screens with questions that are relevant to the domain you are replicating, such as the full DNS name of the domain. If you are setting up a replica domain controller, follow the prompts. When you get to the Database And Log Locations screen, pick up with Step 12. To continue with creating a new domain:

**Active Directory Installation Wizard** ☒

**Domain Controller Type**
Choose whether to create a new domain, or install a replica domain controller in an existing domain.

● New domain (this server will be the first domain controller)

Creating multiple domains on your network partitions your information, enabling Active Directory to scale up to very large organizations.

(Choose this option to create a new child domain, new domain tree, or new forest.)

○ Replica domain controller in existing domain

Installing additional domain controllers in a domain provides fault tolerance and improves performance.

Note: Choosing this option will cause all local accounts on this server to be deleted.

[< Back] [Next >] [Cancel]

*Figure 3.9    The Domain Controller Type screen.*

8. In the Create A Tree Or Child Domain screen, you are asked whether you want to create a new domain tree or a child domain. If you are creating the first domain on your network, or one whose namespace does not fit within the structure of an existing domain, select this option. To create a child domain whose namespace fits within the structure of an existing domain, select the second option. Click Next to continue.

---

**TIP:**   *If you are creating the first domain on your network, choose the first option. If you are creating an additional domain, you can go one of two ways. If the name of your principal domain is freedonia.com and the name of your new domain is huxley.com, choose the first option. If the name of your new domain is headquarters.freedonia.com or sales.freedonia.com, choose the second option.*

---

9. In the Create Or Join Forest screen, you are asked whether you want to create a new forest or join an existing one. If you are creating the first domain on your network, or if you want the new domain to be completely independent of other domains, select the option to create a new forest. If you want your users to be able to share resources with other domains (and vice versa), select the option to join an existing forest. Click Next to continue.

10. In the New Domain Installation screen, enter the full DNS name for the new domain. If you are creating a new domain, enter the same domain name that you entered in Step 2. Figure 3.10 shows an example. Click Next to continue.

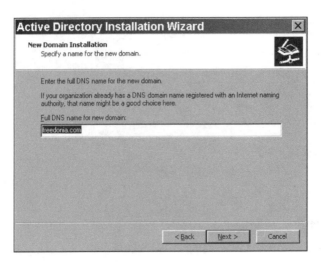

*Figure 3.10    The New Domain Installation screen.*

---

**TIP:**    *If you are configuring the first domain controller on your network, chances are that you don't have an available DNS server. While you are completing the next few steps, Windows 2000 Server will search your network for a nonexistent server. Eventually, you will see an error message, followed by a screen that asks you if you want to install and configure DNS on the server. Select Yes.*

---

11.  Next, enter the domain's NetBIOS name in the NetBIOS Domain Name screen. If you are creating a new domain, enter the first part of the domain name, up to 12 characters, without the period and extension (.com, .org, and so forth). For example, the DNS name of the demonstration network that I created for this book is "freedonia.com" while its NetBIOS name is simply "freedonia." Click Next to continue.

12.  In the Database And Log Locations screen, you can specify the locations of the Active Directory database and log. Both must be on an NTFS partition. Accept the default location for the database. If you have a second hard drive with an NTFS partition, put the log file there; otherwise, accept the default location. Figure 3.11 shows this screen. I had only one NTFS partition available, so do as I say, not as I do. Click Next to continue.

**Active Directory Installation Wizard** ☒

**Database and Log Locations**
Enter the location of the Active Directory database and log.

Note: For best performance and recoverability, place the database and the log on separate hard disks.

Where do you want to store the Active Directory database?

Database location:

C:\WINNT\NTDS     [ Browse... ]

Where do you want to store the Active Directory log?

Log location:

C:\WINNT\NTDS     [ Browse... ]

[ < Back ] [ Next > ] [ Cancel ]

*Figure 3.11   The Database And Log Locations screen.*

13. In the Shared System Volume screen, you can specify the directory to be shared as the system volume. Accept the default location unless you have a specific need to change it. Click Next to continue.

14. There's light at the end of the tunnel. You should now see the Confirmation screen, which shows you the key steps that you have taken so far. Review this information carefully because this is your last chance to make changes. If you need to correct anything, click the Back button. If not, click Next to continue.

15. Next, an informational screen informs you that the Active Directory is being configured. This is a good time to take a break.

16. After a few minutes, you should see the Completing The Active Directory Installation Wizard screen shown in Figure 3.12. Breathe a sigh of relief, and then click Finish.

17. You'll see the usual message that you must restart Windows 2000 Server for the changes to take effect. Click Restart Now.

**3. Managing Domains, Sites, And Schemas**

*Figure 3.12    The Completing The Active Directory Installation Wizard screen.*

# Managing Domains, Trees, And Forests

All of the procedures in this section use the Active Directory Domains and Trusts console in the Administrative Tools program group. To access the group, click Start|Programs|Administrative Tools|Active Directory Domains and Trusts.

You can use this console to do the following:

- Change the domain mode
- Create an explicit domain trust
- Add User Principal Name (UPN) suffixes to a domain

## Changing The Domain Mode

There are two types of modes for domain controllers: Mixed and Native. By default, when you create a domain controller, the Active Directory sets it up in Mixed mode, which enables it to coexist with backup controllers running Windows NT Server 4. However, this backward compatibility means that a small number of features of Windows 2000 Server, such as certain options for managing groups, are not available to you. If and when all of your servers are running Windows 2000, you may want to change all of your domain controllers to Native mode.

**WARNING!** *The only time you should change to Native is when all of your servers are running Windows 2000 Server, or when the controller is the only one in the domain. Once you have changed the controller to Native mode, you cannot change it back to Mixed mode.*

To change the domain mode from Mixed to Native, follow these steps:

1. Open the Active Directory Domains and Trusts console.

2. In the details pane, right-click on the domain whose mode you want to change, and select Properties.

3. On the General page of the dialog box, check the information under Domain Operation Mode in the middle of the page. If the controller is in Mixed mode, click the Change Mode button (see Figure 3.13).

4. At the warning and confirmation prompt, click the Yes button.

## Creating An Explicit Domain Trust

When you create a trust relationship between domains, the default setting is two-way transitive trust. Although there are many advantages to this type of trust, there may be occasions when you will need to create an explicit domain trust, the type used in Windows NT 4 Server. Here is how to do this:

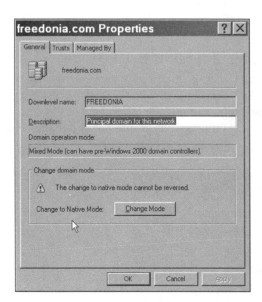

*Figure 3.13    Changing the domain mode.*

77

1. Open the Active Directory Domains and Trusts console.

2. In the details pane, right-click on the domain whose mode you want to change, and select Properties.

3. Select the Trusts page of the dialog box.

4. To configure the selected domain as a trusting domain, which allows users from another domain to have access to it, click the Add button to the right of the top window.

5. In the Add Trusted Domain screen, shown in Figure 3.14, enter the DNS name and the administrator password for the trusted domain (the domain to which you are granting access). Confirm the password, and then click OK. If you are only establishing a one-way trust, go to Step 8. If you are establishing a two-way trust, continue with Step 6.

6. To configure the selected domain as a trusted domain, which allows users from your domain to access another, click the Add button to the right of the bottom window.

7. In the Add Trusting Domain screen, enter the DNS name and the administrator password for the trusting domain (the domain to which your users have been granted access). Confirm the password, and then click OK.

8. Click OK to exit the dialog box.

9. Repeat the process on the other domain controller.

## Adding And Removing UPN Suffixes

The User Principal Name (UPN) is the friendly name used to identify a user on the network. An Internet email address is a good example of a UPN. The suffix to the UPN is simply the DNS name of the domain. My UPN on my hypothetical Freedonia domain is bob@freedonia.com, and freedonia.com is the suffix portion of my UPN.

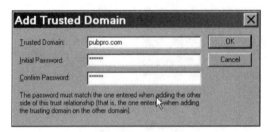

*Figure 3.14   Configuring an explicit trust relationship.*

There are times when you may have an alias for your DNS domain name, and want to add it to the list of UPN suffixes recognized on your domain. To add a UPN suffix:

1. Open the Active Directory Domains and Trusts console.

2. Right-click on the name of the snap-in at the console root in the console tree window. It should be Active Directory Domains and Trusts.

3. Select Properties.

4. Select the UPN Suffixes page.

5. To add a new suffix, enter the name in the edit box, and click the Add button.

6. To remove a suffix, select the suffix from the list of ones already entered, and click the Remove button.

7. Click OK to exit the dialog box.

# Managing Sites

You use the Active Directory Sites and Services console to manage sites within your domain, as well as certain server settings that relate to sites. You can use this console to do the following:

• Configure site settings

• Configure site connection settings

• Configure certain server settings—such as creating a bridgehead server, or repairing or removing a domain controller

To open the Active Directory Sites and Services, click Start|Programs| Administrative Tools|Active Directory Sites and Services.

## Creating A New Site

To create a new site:

1. Open the Active Directory Sites and Services console.

2. Expand the Sites folder.

3. Click the Action menu, and then select New Site.

4. In the New Object - Site dialog box, shown in Figure 3.15, enter a name for the new site.

5. Select a site link from the list in the window below the Name edit box.

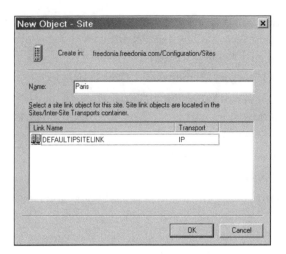

*Figure 3.15   The New Object - Site dialog box.*

6. Click OK to exit the dialog box.

7. Complete the steps in the "Associating A Site With A Subnet" section that follows.

8. Complete the steps in the "Configuring NT Directory Service Site Settings" section later in this chapter.

9. Complete the steps in the "Selecting A Licensing Computer" section later in this chapter.

10. Complete the steps in the "Delegating Control Of A Site" section later in this chapter.

## Associating A Site With A Subnet

To associate a site with a subnet:

1. Open the Active Directory Sites and Services console.

2. In the Sites folder, right-click on the Subnets folder and select New Subnet.

3. In the New Object - Subnet dialog box, shown in Figure 3.16, enter an IP address and a subnet mask for the site. Windows 2000 Server will automatically translate this information into the format that it needs.

4. In the list box that shows the existing sites in your domain, select the site that you want to associate with this subnet.

5. Click OK to exit the dialog box.

*Figure 3.16   The New Object - Subnet dialog box.*

## Configuring NT Directory Service Site Settings

To configure a site's NT Directory Service site settings:

1. Open the Active Directory Sites and Services console.

2. In the Sites folder, select the site to be configured.

3. In the details pane, right-click on NTDS Site Settings, and then select Properties.

4. In the Site Settings page of the dialog box, enter a description for the settings (see Figure 3.17).

5. You will see two options with checkboxes for disabling the automatic replication of Active Directory data. By default, these options should not be checked. Make sure that they are at their default, unchecked settings. See the section "Controlling Automatic Generation Of Replication Topology" later in this chapter for further information.

6. To change the security settings for this object, select the Security page, where you can add or remove groups, or change the permission settings for an assigned group.

7. Click OK to exit the dialog box.

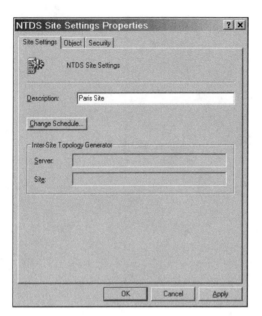

*Figure 3.17 The NTDS Site Settings Properties dialog box.*

## Selecting A Licensing Computer

To select a licensing computer:

1. Open the Active Directory Sites and Services console.

2. Expand the Sites folder.

3. Select the site that you want to modify.

4. In the details pane, right-click on Licensing Site Settings, and then select Properties.

5. In the Licensing Site Settings Properties dialog box, select the Licensing Settings page and enter a description for the settings.

6. The current licensing computer, if any, will be displayed at the bottom of the page. To set or change the licensing computer, click the Change button and select the appropriate computer from the list displayed.

7. To change the security properties for this object, select the Security page and modify the security options as needed.

8. Click OK to exit the dialog box.

## Delegating Control Of A Site

To delegate control over a site:

1. Open the Active Directory Sites and Services console.

2. Expand the Sites folder.

3. Right-click on the site that you want to modify and select Delegate Control. This opens the Delegation of Control Wizard.

4. On the Users Or Groups Selection page, click the Add button if the object that you want is not listed.

5. In the Select Users, Computers, Or Groups dialog box, shown in Figure 3.18, select the group or user to which you want to delegate control of the site, and click the Add button. The name of the object will appear in the bottom window. If you make a mistake, select the object in the bottom window and click the Remove button.

6. Repeat Step 5 to add other users or groups, if desired, and then click OK to return to the wizard, and then click Next.

7. On the Tasks To Delegate page, select one of the two radio buttons. If you select the Delegate The Following Common Tasks button, also select the groups of tasks that you want to delegate from the list in the main window. When you click Next, you will go directly to Step 10. If you select the Create A Custom Task To Delegate button, when you click Next you will continue with Step 8.

8. On the Active Directory Object Type page, use the two radio buttons to select whether you want to delegate control of the entire container to the selected groups or users, or only control of certain objects within the container. In the case of a site, there may not be any component objects shown.

**3. Managing Domains, Sites, And Schemas**

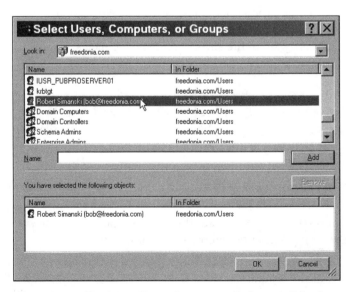

*Figure 3.18    The Select Users, Computers, Or Groups dialog box.*

9. Click Next to reach the Permissions page. Here, you can choose the permissions to be delegated and select options for filtering the list of displayed permissions.

10. Click Next. This will display a page that verifies the information that you have entered.

11. Click Finish to close the wizard.

## Modifying The Properties Of A Site

To modify the properties of a site:

1. Open the Active Directory Sites and Services console.

2. Expand the Sites folder.

3. In the details pane, right-click on the object whose properties you want to modify, and then select Properties. This opens the dialog box for the site's properties.

4. To add or change the description of the site, select the Site page. Enter or modify the description in the Description edit box.

5. To add or change location information, select the Location page. You can either enter the location in the Location edit box or browse your network to select the location from a list.

6. To change security options, select the Security page. Here, you can add or remove groups and users as needed, and modify the permissions assigned to each one.

7. To modify the group policy settings for the site, select the Group Policy page. Here, you can add or modify existing policies assigned to the site or create new policies.

8. Click OK to exit the dialog box.

Follow this same procedure to modify the properties of other objects in the Active Directory Sites and Services console. Right-click on the object and select Properties. The pages that appear in the dialog box depend on the nature of the object. In many cases, you will see only three or four pages:

- *General*—Here, you can enter a description of the object that will appear in the details pane.

- *Location*—Here, you can enter the network location of the object or select it from a list of computers on your network.

- *Object*—Displays information about the object. You cannot change this information.

• *Security*—Here, you can assign rights to groups and users, and modify the permissions assigned to each one.

## Assigning A Server To A Site

To assign a server to a site:

1. If necessary, add the server to the list of servers or domain controllers on your site. In Administrative Tools, open the Active Directory Users and Computers console. Add the server to the Computers or Domain Controllers folder, as appropriate, then close the console.

2. Open the Active Directory Sites and Services Manager.

3. Expand the Sites folder.

4. Expand the folder for the appropriate site.

5. Right-click on the Servers folder and select New|Server.

6. In the dialog box, enter the name of the server to be assigned to the site. You need to enter only the name of the computer—Windows 2000 Server appends the full network path to the name of the server.

7. Close the dialog box. The name of the server will now appear in the details pane.

8. Right-click on the new server object and select Properties. The Properties dialog box is shown in Figure 3.19. Modify the properties as needed.

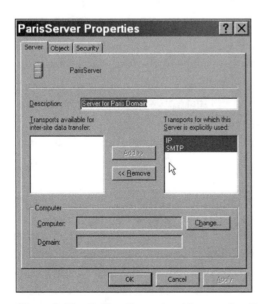

*Figure 3.19   Setting the protocol transport options for a site server.*

## Renaming A Site

To rename a site:

1. Open the Active Directory Sites and Services console.

2. Expand the Sites folder.

3. In the details pane, right-click on the server whose name you want to change, and then select Rename.

4. Enter the new name in the edit box.

## Creating A Link Between Two Sites

When you install the first domain controller on a site, Windows 2000 Server automatically generates a site link, connecting that controller to another on your network. It's called DEFAULTIPSITELINK. You'll find it in the IP folder under the Inter-Site Transports folder. This default link, however, might not be the most efficient one for your system.

The primary purpose of a site link is to provide for the efficient replication of Active Directory data. Therefore, you want to make sure that the site on which you're working has at least one link to a site on your network that has all of the latest Active Directory information for the entire network. The main site at corporate headquarters is probably a good candidate for a site link, so you may want to begin by creating a direct link to your headquarters site.

To create a link between two or more sites:

1. Open the Active Directory Sites and Services console.

2. Expand the Sites folder.

3. Expand the Inter-Site Transports folder. The details pane will show the available protocols.

4. Right-click on the protocol that you want to use for the link.

5. From the context-sensitive menu, select New Site Link. The New Object - Site Link dialog box will appear (see Figure 3.20).

6. In the dialog box, enter a descriptive name for the link in the Name edit box.

7. Below the Name edit box, you will see two lists of sites. The left list shows the sites that are available to be included and the right list shows the sites, if any, that are already included in the link. When you are creating a new link, this second list is empty.

*Figure 3.20    The New Object - Site Link dialog box.*

8. From the left list, select the sites to be included in the link and click the Add button. The selected sites will be added to the list in the right window. You must select at least two sites to create a link. If you make a mistake, highlight the site to be removed in the right window and click the Remove button.

9. Click OK to exit the dialog box.

## Changing The Sites In A Link

To change the sites in a link:

1. Open the Active Directory Sites and Services console.

2. Expand the Sites folder.

3. Expand the Inter-Site Transports folder. The details pane will show the available protocols.

4. Expand the folder for the protocol that contains the link to be modified. The links that are currently in use will be displayed in the details pane.

5. Right-click on the link that you want to modify. From the context-sensitive menu, select Properties.

6. To change the description, edit the text in the Name edit box.

7. To remove a site from the link, select the site in the right window under the Name edit box and click the Remove button. Remember that there must be at least two sites remaining in the link.

8. To add a site to the link, select the site in the left window and click the Add button.

9. Click OK to exit the dialog box.

## Creating A Bridge Between Site Links

At sites that have multiple site links, replication of the Active Directory can sometimes be sluggish. Creating a site link bridge that joins all of the multiple site links may help. To create a bridge between two or more site links:

1. Open the Active Directory Sites and Services console.

2. Expand the Sites folder.

3. Expand the Inter-Site Transports folder. The details pane will show the available protocols.

4. Right-click on the protocol containing the links to be bridged. The New Object - Site Link Bridge dialog box will appear (see Figure 3.21).

5. In the dialog box, enter a descriptive name for the bridge in the Name edit box.

6. Below the Name edit box, you will see two lists of site links. The left list shows the links that are available to be included and the right list shows the links, if any, that are already included in the bridge. When you are creating a new bridge, this second list will be empty.

*Figure 3.21   The New Object - Site Link Bridge dialog box.*

7. In the left window, select the links to be included in the bridge and click the Add button. The selected links will be added to the list in the right window. You must select at least two links. If you make a mistake, highlight the link to be removed and click the Remove button.

8. Click OK to exit the dialog box.

## Changing The Links In A Bridge

To change the links in a bridge:

1. Open the Active Directory Sites and Services console.

2. Expand the Sites folder.

3. Expand the Inter-Site Transports folder. The details pane will show the available protocols.

4. Expand the folder for the protocol that contains the bridge to be modified. The links and bridges that are currently in use will be displayed in the details pane.

5. Right-click on the bridge that you want to modify. From the context-sensitive menu, select Properties.

6. To change the description, edit the text in the Name edit box.

7. To remove a link from the bridge, select the link in the right window under the Name edit box and click the Remove button. Remember that there must be at least two links remaining in the bridge.

8. To add a link to the bridge, select the link in the left window and click the Add button.

9. Click OK to exit the dialog box.

## Modifying The Cost And Frequency Of Replication

As part of the process of providing the Active Directory with information about the available connections between the new site and existing ones, be sure to configure the site-link cost for each site link. This involves assigning a value for the cost of each connection used in replicating Active Directory data among sites. You assign ordinary numbers, not dollar values. The higher the number, the more costly the link. For example, you might assign a cost of 100 to an inexpensive link, 200 to a moderately expensive one, and 300 for a very costly link. As part of the process, you may also want to set the frequency of the replication. To accomplish these tasks:

1. Open the Active Directory Sites and Services console.

2. Expand the console tree to reveal the Sites and Services folders.

3. Expand the Sites and Inter-Site Transports folders. You will see subfolders for each of the protocols used, such as IP and SMTP.

4. Select the protocol that contains the link to be modified.

5. Right-click on the link that you want to modify and select Properties. The Link Properties dialog box will appear, as shown in Figure 3.22.

6. Select the General tabbed page. Near the bottom, you will see edit boxes for setting the cost and frequency. The default values are 100 for cost and 180 minutes for frequency.

7. For Cost, select or enter any number from 1 to 32,767. The higher the number that you select relative to the costs of other links, the higher the cost of the connection and the less frequently Active Directory is likely to use it for replication.

---

**NOTE:**    *You can set relative cost only for site links, not for site link bridges.*

---

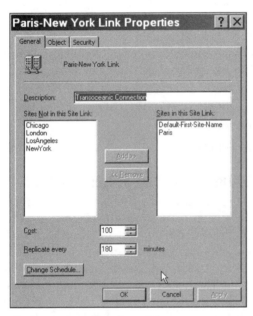

*Figure 3.22    Modifying a link's cost and replication settings.*

8. For Frequency, select or enter any integer multiple of 15 minutes, from 15 to 10,080.

9. To refine the replication schedule even further, click the Change Schedule button. In the screen that follows (shown in Figure 3.23), you'll find one row of 24 one-hour blocks for each day of the week. By default, each block is selected, meaning that replication is available during that hour. A group of two radio buttons allows you to select or deselect a block. To prevent replication during a specific one-hour block, left-click the block with your mouse, and then click the white radio button. To reverse the procedure, click the blue radio button.

10. Click OK to exit the schedule screen.

11. Click OK to exit the dialog box.

**WARNING!** *You should not modify the frequency of replication or the times when it is available unless you have a specific reason for doing so. When you create a link between sites, Active Directory configures replication automatically. Over time, it will reconfigure the topology to optimize performance. If you change the topology manually, you may prevent the Active Directory from optimizing the topology automatically, which may have a negative effect on the performance of your network. In a worst-case scenario, replication between sites may stop altogether.*

*This does not apply, however, to setting a relative cost for the connection. In fact, it's important that you establish relative costs among your links to help Active Directory in the optimization process.*

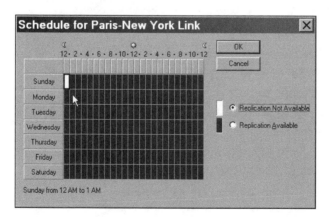

*Figure 3.23   Modifying the replication schedule for a link.*

## Changing Query Policy

To change the query policy for a server within a site:

1.  Open the Active Directory Sites and Services console.

2.  Expand the Sites folder.

3.  Expand the Servers folder for the selected site. The list of servers assigned to the site will appear in the details pane.

4.  Right-click on the server whose policy you wish to change and select Properties.

5.  On the General page of the Properties dialog box, enter a description for the setting in the Description edit box.

6.  In the Query Policy drop-down list box, select the policy that you wish to use. By default, the blank top line of the list box is selected. Clicking the down arrow displays the list of available policies. There should be at least one, called Default Query Policy.

7.  To disable query policies, select the blank entry at the top of the list box.

8.  Click on Apply to ratify your selections, and then click on OK to exit the dialog box.

## Enabling A Global Catalog Server

To enable a Global Catalog Server:

1.  Open the Active Directory Sites and Services console.

2.  Expand the Sites folder.

3.  Expand the Servers folder for the selected site. The list of servers assigned to the site will appear in the details pane.

4.  Expand the appropriate server.

5.  In the details pane, right-click on NTDS Settings and select Properties.

6.  On the General page of the Properties dialog box, enter a description for the setting in the Description edit box.

7.  Check the Global Catalog Server checkbox to enable this feature.

8.  Click on Apply to ratify your selections, and then click on OK to exit the dialog box.

## Specifying A Bridgehead Server

The domain controller that you intend to use for inter-site replication or transport should be configured as a bridgehead server. Here is how to do it:

1. Open the Active Directory Sites and Services console.

2. Expand the Sites folder.

3. Expand the Servers folder for the selected site. The list of servers assigned to the site will appear in the details pane.

4. In the details pane, right-click on the name of the server that you need to configure, and then select Properties. Be sure that you select a domain controller.

5. On the Server page of the Properties dialog box, enter a description of the server in the Description edit box, if you have not already done so.

6. Below the Description edit box, you will see two windows. In the left window, you will see a list of available protocols for inter-site transport. At a minimum, you should see IP and SMTP. In the right window, you will see a list of the protocols that have already been selected, if any. Select the protocols to be added and click the Add button.

7. To correct a mistake, select the protocol to be removed in the right window, and click the Remove button.

8. The name and domain of the server that you are modifying will appear near the bottom of the page. To change the server, click the Change button and select the new server from the list of systems on your network.

## Moving A Server Between Sites

To move a server to another site:

1. Open the Active Directory Sites and Services console.

2. Expand the Sites folder.

3. Expand the Servers folder for the selected site. The list of servers assigned to the site will appear in the details pane.

4. In the details pane, right-click on the name of the server that you need to move, and then select Move. The Move Server dialog box (shown in Figure 3.24) will appear.

5. The next screen will display a list of sites on your network. Select the site to which you want to move the server, then click OK to exit the dialog box.

**3. Managing Domains, Sites, And Schemas**

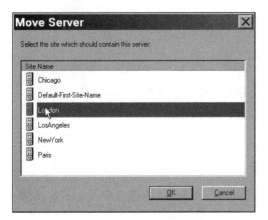

*Figure 3.24    The Move Server dialog box.*

## Removing An Inoperative Domain Controller

When you remove a domain controller from your network, you also need to remove it from the Active Directory. Here's how to do it:

1. Open the Active Directory Sites and Services console.

2. Expand the Sites folder.

3. Expand the Servers folder for the selected site.

4. In the details pane, right-click on the domain controller to be removed, and then select Delete.

5. Click Yes when prompted to verify your action.

# Managing The Schema

In order to use the Active Directory Schema snap-in, you first need to install it, and then either create a new Microsoft Management Console to contain it, or add it to an existing console. I recommend that you create a new console rather than add the snap-in to an existing one. You are not likely to use the snap-in very often, it takes a long time to generate the lists of classes and attributes, and there is no need to add this overhead to another console (see Chapter 2).

This section is divided into two types of tasks: working with the existing schema and modifying the schema itself. The procedures described in the first group are simple and safe, and do not directly modify the schema itself. Procedures in the first group include:

- Managing the membership of the schema administration group
- Viewing the contents of the schema
- Managing user and group schema permissions

Modifying the schema, on the other hand, should be done with great caution and only when necessary, because modifications can severely impact your Windows 2000 Server installation. Procedures in the second group include:

- Creating a new attribute
- Creating a new class
- Modifying the attributes assigned to a class
- Adding an auxiliary class to another class
- Refreshing the schema cache

## Installing The Active Directory Schema Snap-in

Before you can manage the Active Directory Schema, you must first install the snap-in from your Windows 2000 Server installation CD-ROM. Here is what you need to do:

1. Insert the Windows 2000 Server installation CD-ROM in your CD-ROM drive. At the opening menu, select Browse This CD-ROM.

2. Expand the i386 folder, then double-click on the Adminpak.msi Windows Installer file and follow the prompts.

3. Open the Microsoft Management Console in which you want to install the snap-in.

4. Select Console|Add/Remove Snap-in. This will open the Add/Remove Snap-in dialog box.

5. With the Console Root selected in the drop-down list box, select Add.

6. In the Add Standalone Snap-in dialog box, select Active Directory Schema, then click Add to return to the previous dialog box.

7. Click OK to save your changes and return to the main console window.

8. Save the console.

## Managing The Membership Of The Schema Administration Group

The Schema Admins group is one of the default security groups set up by Windows 2000 Server when you create a domain controller. For security reasons, the right to modify the schema should be limited to that group. Before you attempt to modify the Active Directory schema, you'll want to make sure that you are a member.

You cannot use the Active Directory Schema snap-in to modify the membership of this group; you have to use the Active Directory Users and Computers console instead. Here are the procedures that you need to follow:

1. Click Start|Programs|Administrative Tools|Active Directory Users and Computers.

2. Expand the console tree to show the included domains.

3. Expand the current domain.

4. Select the Users folder.

5. In the details pane, right-click on the Schema Admins group and select Properties.

6. In the dialog box, select the Members page to view the list of current members.

7. To remove a member, highlight the name and click the Remove button. If you are not adding any new members, proceed to Step 11.

8. To add a member, click the Add button.

9. In the next screen, you will see a list of people and computers in your domain. Select the first one to be added, and click the Add button in the middle of the screen. The object will appear in a window at the bottom of the screen. If you make a mistake, select the object in this screen, and click the Remove button.

10. Repeat Step 9 to add additional members. Click OK when you finish.

11. Click OK to exit the dialog box.

| Related solution: | Found on page: |
|---|---|
| Administering Groups | 164 |

## Viewing The Contents Of The Schema1

Even if you do not intend to modify the schema, you may want to
view its contents for your own information, as follows:

1. Open the console with the Active Directory Schema snap-in.

2. Expand the Classes folder. This may take some time.

3. Select a class in the console tree pane. The details pane will
   display all of the subclasses associated with the selected class,
   as well as all of the attributes associated with the parent class
   and its subclasses. You cannot modify any of the objects in the
   details pane.

4. Next, right-click on the class, and then select Properties.

5. In the dialog box, browse the General, Relationship, Attributes,
   and Security pages, but do not make any changes.

6. On the Security page, check to see if the Schema Admins group
   is listed. If not, you may have to add it here if you need to
   modify the class later.

7. Click the Advanced button on the Security page. The Permissions page of the Advanced dialog box shows an overview of
   the access control settings for the selected class. By selecting
   the View/Edit button, you can fine-tune the access control
   settings for any of the listed objects.

8. Click Cancel to exit the Advanced dialog box.

9. Click Cancel to exit the Properties dialog box.

10. Expand the Attributes folder. The attributes in the schema will
    be listed in the details pane.

11. Right-click on any attribute, and select Properties.

12. In the dialog box, you can see some information about the at-
    tribute. Although it may appear that some of the settings can be
    changed, do not attempt to do so unless you have already pre-
    pared your domain controller for modifying the schema. (See the
    section "Preparing To Modify The Schema" later in this chapter.)

## Managing User And Group Schema Permissions

You can manage permissions in the Active Directory Schema in two
ways: You can modify the security properties attached to the Active
Directory Schema itself or you can modify the security properties
attached to a specific class. We will cover each method in turn. Note
that modifications made to the Schema's security properties are not
automatically inherited by the classes in the schema.

### Modifying Permissions For The Active Directory Schema

To modify permissions for the Active Directory Schema, follow these steps:

1. Open the console containing the Active Directory Schema snap-in.

2. In the console tree pane, right-click on the Active Directory Schema, and then select Permissions.

3. The Permissions For Schema dialog box will appear, showing the names of people and groups on your network who can access the information in the schema (see Figure 3.25). To modify the permissions for an object on the list, highlight the object in the top window, and then change the associated permissions in the bottom window by checking or unchecking the boxes associated with each type of permission listed.

4. To remove a user or group from the list, highlight the object in the top window, and click the Remove button. If you do not need to add other objects to the list, proceed to Step 9.

5. To add a new user or group to the list, click the Add button to the right of the top window. This action opens the Select Users, Computers, Or Groups dialog box.

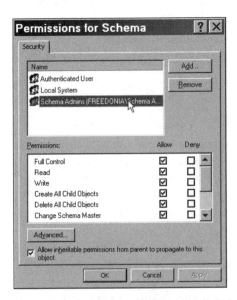

*Figure 3.25   Modifying Active Directory schema permissions in the Permissions For Schema dialog box.*

6. Select the user or group to be added in the top window, and then click the Add button. The name of the object will appear in the bottom window. If you make a mistake, select the object in the bottom window, and click the Remove button.

7. Repeat Steps 5 and 6 to add more users or groups.

8. Click OK to return to the previous dialog box.

9. To refine the settings for a user or group on the security list, select the item from the list, and click the Advanced button below the Permissions window. The Access Control Settings For Schema dialog box (shown in Figure 3.26) appears.

10. In the Access Control Settings dialog box, select the object and click the View/Edit button. The Permission Entry For Schema dialog box (shown in Figure 3.27) appears.

11. In the Permission Entry For Schema dialog box, modify the permissions as needed, and then click OK to return to the previous dialog box.

12. Repeat Steps 9 through 11 to modify additional items on the security list.

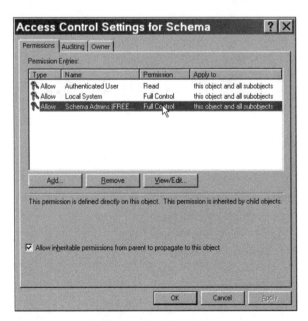

*Figure 3.26   Modifying permissions in the Access Control Settings For Schema dialog box.*

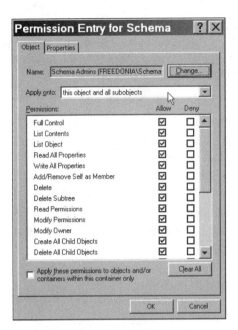

*Figure 3.27   Advanced refining of permissions in the Permission Entry For Schema dialog box.*

13. Click Apply, and then click OK to close the Access Control Settings dialog box and return to the Permissions For Schema dialog box.

14. Click Apply, and then click OK to exit the Permissions For Schema dialog box.

### Modifying Permissions For A Schema Class

Here is how to modify permissions for a class in the schema:

1. Open the console containing the Active Directory Schema snap-in.

2. Expand the Active Directory Schema.

3. Expand the Classes folder.

4. In the console tree pane, right-click on the class to be modified and select Properties.

5. In the Properties dialog box, select the Security page. The page will display the names of people and groups on your network who can access the information in the schema.

6. To modify the permissions for an object on the list, highlight the object in the top window, and then change the associated

permissions in the bottom window by checking or unchecking the boxes associated with each type of permission listed.

7. To remove a user or group from the list, highlight the object in the top window, and click the Remove button. If you do not need to add other objects to the list, proceed to Step 12.

8. To add a new user or group to the list, click the Add button to the right of the top window. This action opens the Select Users, Computers, Or Groups dialog box.

9. In the top window, select the user or group to be added, and then click the Add button. The name of the object will appear in the bottom window. If you make a mistake, select the object in the bottom window, and click the Remove button.

10. Repeat Step 9 to add more users or groups.

11. Click OK to return to the previous dialog box.

12. To refine the settings for a user or group on the security list, select the item from the list, and click the Advanced button below the Permissions window.

13. In the Access Control Settings dialog box, select the object, and then click the View/Edit button.

14. In the Permission Entry dialog box, modify the permissions as needed, and then click OK to return to the previous dialog box.

15. Repeat Steps 12 through 14 to modify additional items on the security list.

16. Click Apply, and then click OK to close the Access Control Settings dialog box and return to the Properties dialog box.

17. Click Apply, and then click OK to exit the dialog box.

## Preparing To Modify The Schema

An in-depth tutorial on making major modifications to the schema is beyond the scope of this book. However, in this chapter you will learn how to make simple changes by using the Active Directory Schema snap-in.

**WARNING!**  *Although the changes that you want to make to the Active Directory schema may be relatively simple, they should not be made unless you have a specific reason for doing so. Any changes that you make to an attribute, for example, may affect every object in the Active Directory that uses the attribute.*

*The relationship between the Active Directory schema and the Active Directory itself is much like the relationship between the Registry and recent versions of Microsoft Windows operating systems. The integrity of the schema is crucial to the integrity of the Active Directory itself. Break the schema and you might break the Active Directory.*

Before you can modify the Active Directory schema, you must take several preparatory steps:

1. Make sure that you are a member of the Schema Admins group. (See the section, "Managing The Membership Of The Schema Administration Group" earlier in the chapter.)

2. Back up everything on the server, in case something goes wrong.

3. If possible, take the controller offline.

4. Install the Active Directory Schema snap-in.

5. Open the console with the Active Directory Schema snap-in.

6. In the console tree, right-click on Active Directory Schema, and select Operations Master.

7. In the Change Operations Master dialog box (shown in Figure 3.28), check to make sure that your current controller is shown in the information windows. If your current controller is the only one in the domain, it is the Operations Master, by default. If another server is displayed in either of the information windows, click the Change button. Select the current controller from the ones listed, and click OK to return to the previous dialog box.

8. At the bottom of the dialog box, make sure that the box enabling the schema to be modified on the current server is checked.

9. Click OK to exit the dialog box.

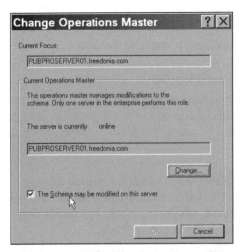

*Figure 3.28 Changing the Operations Master.*

10. Again, right-click on Active Directory Schema. This time, select Permissions, which opens a dialog box that lists the objects with security rights to the schema. If the Schema Admins group is listed, proceed to Step 13.

11. If the Schema Admins group is not on the list, click the Add button.

12. In the next dialog box, select the group from the list of users, computers, and groups on your network, click the Add button, and then click OK to return to the previous dialog box.

13. Highlight the Schema Admins group.

14. In the Permissions window, check the Full Control box in the Allow column.

15. Click the Advanced button to open the Access Control Settings dialog box.

16. Highlight the Schema Admins group, and click the View/Edit button.

17. In the Permission Entry dialog box, you'll see two pages: Object and Properties. On both pages, make sure that the following are done:

    • Apply Onto is set to This Object And All Subobjects

    • All of the boxes in the Allow column are checked

18. Click on OK to return to the previous dialog box.

19. In the Access Control Settings dialog box, click on Apply, and then click OK to return to the previous dialog box.

20. In the Permissions For Schema dialog box, click on Apply, and then click OK to exit.

## Creating A New Attribute

In the next few sections, you will learn how to create a new attribute and a new class, add the new attribute to the class, and make the new class a child of an existing class.

First, you will create two new attributes that enable you to add Social Security Number and salary fields to your user account data. Second, you will create a class to contain these attributes. Third, you will add the attributes to the new class. Finally, you will make the new class an auxiliary of the user class.

To create a new attribute, follow these steps:

1. Open the console containing the Active Directory Schema snap-in.

2. Expand the Active Directory Schema.

3. Right-click on the Attributes folder, and then select New| Attribute.

4. You should see a Schema Objects Creation warning message. Essentially, it cautions you that whatever object you create will become a permanent part of the schema that can be disabled, but not deleted. Click the Continue button.

5. In the Create New Attribute dialog box (shown in Figure 3.29), enter the data shown in Table 3.1.

---

**NOTE:**   *The minimum and maximum numbers apply to the length of the numerical string that may be entered—not to the content of the string. This range accommodates Social Security numbers that are entered both with and without hyphens, yet provides some protection against data entry errors. If you want to force your users to enter Social Security numbers one way or the other, adjust the range accordingly.*

---

6. Click OK when you are finished.

7. Repeat Steps 3 through 6 for the salary attribute, using the data shown in Table 3.2.

*Figure 3.29   Creating a new attribute.*

**Table 3.1    Specifications for the Social Security Number attribute.**

| Field | Data |
| --- | --- |
| Common Name | SocialSecurityAttribute |
| LDAP Display | SocialSecurityAttribute |
| Unique X500 Object ID | 1.2.840.113556.1.4.7000.141 |
| Syntax | Numerical String |
| Minimum | 9 |
| Maximum | 11 |
| Multi-Valued | (Do not check) |

**Table 3.2    Specifications for the salary attribute.**

| Field | Data |
| --- | --- |
| Common Name | SalaryAttribute |
| LDAP Display | SalaryAttribute |
| Unique X500 Object ID | 1.2.840.113556.1.4.7000.142 |
| Syntax | Integer |
| Minimum | (Leave blank) |
| Maximum | (Leave blank) |
| Multi-Valued | (Do not check) |

**NOTE:**   *The X.500 Object ID numbers used for these two new attributes were supplied by Microsoft for use in creating these practice attributes, and do not conflict with other Object ID numbers that may be in use on your system. When entering these numbers, do not add spaces between parts of the number. Use a period as the delimiter.*

8. Check the details pane to make sure that your new attributes were added.

9. Scroll to the top of the console tree, right-click on the Active Directory Schema, and select Reload The Schema. This ensures that the attributes that you just created will be immediately available to you.

## Creating A New Class

To create a new class, follow these steps:

1. Open the console containing the Active Directory Schema snap-in.

2. Expand the Active Directory Schema.

3. Right-click on the Classes folder, and then select New|Class.

4. You should see a Schema Objects Creation warning message. Essentially, it cautions you that whatever object you create will become a permanent part of the schema that can be disabled, but not deleted. Click the Continue button.

5. In the Create New Class dialog box (shown in Figure 3.30), enter the data shown in Table 3.3.

6. Click OK when you are finished.

7. Check the details pane to make sure that your new class was added.

8. Right-click on the Active Directory Schema, and select Reload The Schema. This action ensures that the class that you just created will be immediately available to you.

**Table 3.3   Specifications for the MoreUserInformation class.**

| Field | Data |
| --- | --- |
| Common Name | MoreUserInformation |
| LDAP Display | MoreUserInformation |
| Unique X500 Object ID | 1.2.840.113556.1.4.7000.17 |
| Parent Class | (Leave blank) |
| Class Type | Auxiliary |

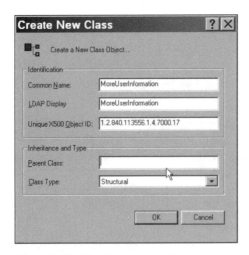

*Figure 3.30   Creating a new class.*

## Modifying The Attributes Assigned To A Class

There isn't much that you can do to modify the attributes of a class object that came with Windows 2000 Server, and you may not be able to do much more with the classes that you create yourself. Many of the attributes within a class are flagged as system-only once they are created, and hence cannot be modified. However, you can add attributes and change the security permissions. (See "Managing User And Group Schema Permissions" earlier in the chapter for an explanation of the latter.)

To add an attribute to a class, using the MoreUserInformation class as an example, follow these steps:

1. Open the console containing the Active Directory Schema snap-in.

2. Expand the Active Directory Schema.

3. Expand the Classes folder.

4. In the console tree pane, right-click on the MoreUserInformation class, and select Properties.

5. In the Properties dialog box, select the Attributes page. You will see separate lists of mandatory and optional attributes.

6. To remove an attribute, highlight it. If the attribute cannot be removed, you will see a message at the bottom of the window in which it is listed. If the attribute can be removed, click the Remove button next to the window. To confirm the removal, click Apply. If you do not intend to add any attributes, proceed to Step 11.

7. To add an attribute, click the Add button next to the appropriate window. I recommend that you add the attribute to the Optional window. In beta 3, whenever I attempted to add one to the Mandatory window, the attempt was rejected.

8. In the Select Schema Objects dialog box, select the SalaryAttribute object, click OK to return to the Properties dialog box, and then click Apply.

---

**TIP:** *You can wait until you have made all your changes before clicking the Apply button. After all, it takes a while for the Active Directory Schema to propagate the changes throughout the schema. However, I recommend that you do it after every major change when modifying the schema. The reason is that in some cases, the Schema rejects a change. The error message that you receive is not very helpful—if you made a series of changes, you won't know which change was rejected.*

---

3. Managing Domains, Sites, And Schemas

9. Repeat Steps 7 and 8 to add the SocialSecurityAttribute object.

10. The new attributes will appear at the top of the Optional list (see Figure 3.31). For some reason, you will see their X.500 Object ID numbers, rather than their common names. The next time that you open the Properties dialog box for the class, however, you should see the common names. I can't explain the reason why. Perhaps it has something to do with the delay in refreshing the copy of the schema in the memory cache.

11. Click OK to exit the Properties dialog box.

---

**NOTE:** *Even if you are able to add an attribute to a class, this does not mean that it will automatically show up in the Properties dialog boxes of objects that use the class. For example, you can add the employeeID, employeeNumber, and employeeType attributes to the user class. However, fields for entering this information will not automatically be added to the user account's Properties dialog box. You must still modify the component that generates the Properties dialog box to add the fields to it—a task that requires programming.*

---

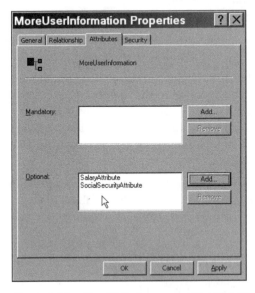

*Figure 3.31    The Attributes page of the MoreUserInformation class's Properties dialog box.*

## Adding An Auxiliary Class To Another Class

An auxiliary class shares all of the attributes of the class to which it is linked, as well as the attributes that you add to it. To link an auxiliary class to another class, using the MoreUserInformation class as an example, follow these steps:

1. Open the console containing the Active Directory Schema snap-in.

2. Expand the Active Directory Schema.

3. Expand the Classes folder.

4. In the console tree pane, right-click on the user class, and select Properties.

5. On the Relationship page (shown in Figure 3.32), click the Add button next to the Auxiliary Classes window.

6. In the Select Schema Objects dialog box, select the MoreUserInformation object, click OK to return to the Properties dialog box, and then click Apply.

7. Click OK to exit the Properties dialog box.

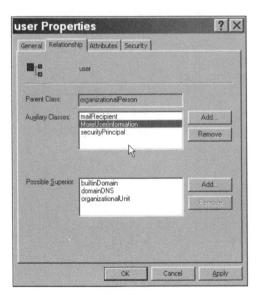

*Figure 3.32 The Relationship page of the user class's Properties dialog box.*

## Refreshing The Schema Cache

Whenever you modify the Active Directory schema, you should force Windows 2000 Server to refresh the version in memory as soon as you are finished, rather than wait for the Active Directory to do this five minutes later. To force the Active Directory to reload the schema:

1. If necessary, reopen the console containing the Active Directory Schema snap-in.

2. Right-click on the Active Directory Schema, and select Reload The Schema.

# Chapter 4

# Managing Computers, Users, And Domain Controllers

*(continued)*

# *In Brief*

In this chapter and the next, we get down to the practical details of using the new tools in Windows 2000 Server to make your everyday work easier. Here is where you will learn how to manage organizational units, groups, individual users, and computers—including domain controllers.

To accomplish the tasks in this chapter, you will use the Active Directory Users and Computers console in the Administrative Tools folder. In its default setting, the console has only one snap-in, Active Directory Users and Computers. To access it, click Start|Programs|Administrative Tools|Active Directory Users And Computers.

**NOTE:**   *To manage your domains and sites, use the Active Directory Domains and Trusts and Active Directory Sites and Services consoles that were covered in Chapter 3. To manage a computer that serves as a domain controller, on the other hand, use the Active Directory Users and Computers console covered in this chapter.*

When organizing your network, you begin by creating accounts for each user and each computer within your domain. Next, you create groups to contain these accounts. Finally, you assign groups to organizational units. You will look at managing user and computer accounts, including domain controllers, in this chapter. Groups and organizational units will be covered in Chapter 5.

# User And Computer Accounts

Before you can begin to manage the users and computers on your network effectively, you must create accounts for each one. Accounts are the starting points for creating security on your network, while allowing users and computers to log onto your network and gain access to the resources that they need.

Accounts help to authenticate the identity of the user or computer, permit access to network resources, check on the computer's files and critical hardware, and monitor certain actions of the user. Use Active Directory Users and Computers to manage these accounts.

*User accounts* provide users with security identities. When a user logs onto your network, Windows 2000 Server authenticates the user and provides the person with access to the resources that you have assigned to them.

The operating system installs two default user accounts: Administrator and Guest. The Administrator account—which you need to use the first time that you log on after installing Windows 2000 Server—includes all-encompassing rights and permissions, allowing you to do whatever you need to do. The Guest account, on the other hand, includes very limited rights and permissions. These accounts are designed to help you get started, but are not intended for regular use. The rights and permissions that you will want to assign to various users as you create new accounts for them will fall somewhere between these two extremes.

---

**NOTE:**    Additional default accounts may be present, depending on the Windows 2000 Server components that you have installed.

---

*Computer accounts* allow you to control security on individual systems and perform remote maintenance and software installation.

In order to make full use of the advanced computer-management features offered by Windows 2000 Server, however, you need to install Windows 2000 Professional on your client workstations. Earlier versions of Windows, including Windows NT 4 Workstation, do not have the advanced computer management features of Windows 2000 Professional.

# Domains

The subject of managing domains, particularly as they relate to other domains on the network, is covered in Chapter 3. The management of a specific domain, however, takes place within the Active Directory Users and Computers snap-in that is discussed in this chapter. The domain itself is at the top of the console tree.

The bulk of domain management revolves around managing objects, such as computers, users, groups, and organizational units, within the domain. In addition, you can perform several tasks at the domain level. Primary among them is the capability to set system-wide policy by using the Group Policy Editor. Also, you can delegate control of the domain, which might appeal to you if you have a large network with many domains. These tasks are covered briefly in this chapter, but a detailed discussion of managing group policy is deferred to Chapter 6.

*4. Managing Computers, Users, And Domain Controllers*

# Domain Controllers

A domain controller, in addition to being a server on the network, performs a number of special tasks. Thus, the Active Directory treats domain controllers separately from other computers on the network.

If a server is the only domain controller in a domain, it must perform many different roles, including several about which we tend to give little, if any, thought. On the other hand, if you have more than one domain controller in a given domain, you can spread this load among them.

For example, each domain in the Active Directory, even a one-tree forest with a single domain controller, must have servers that fulfill each of three roles: Relative ID (RID) Master, Primary Domain Controller (PDC) Emulator, and Infrastructure Master. In addition, each forest must have servers that fulfill two additional roles: Schema Master and Domain Naming Master. The Schema Master is selected in the Active Directory Schema snap-in, whereas the Domain Naming Master is selected in the Active Directory Domains and Trusts console. Here is the purpose of each role:

- *Schema Master*—The domain controller that hosts the Schema Master controls all updates and modifications to the schema. Each forest can have only one Schema Master (see Chapter 3).

- *Domain Naming Master*—The domain controller that hosts the Domain Naming Master controls the addition or removal of domains in the forest. Each forest can have only one Domain Naming Master.

- *Relative ID Master*—Each domain must have one Relative ID Master. This master allocates sequences of Relative IDs (RIDs) to each controller within the domain. Whenever you create a user, user account, or group, the domain controller assigns the object a unique security ID (SID). The SID consists of two components: a domain security ID that is the same for all SIDs created in the domain and an RID that is unique to each SID.

- *Primary Domain Controller Emulator*—Each domain must have a Primary Domain Controller (PDC) Emulator. If the domain includes computers that are not running Windows 2000 Professional client software or if it still uses Windows NT backup domain controllers, the emulator acts as a Windows NT primary domain controller. If all of the controllers are running Windows 2000 Server and the domain is operating in native mode, the emulator receives preferential treatment from other domain controllers within the domain. Password changes performed by other domain controllers are replicated first to the emulator. If a user logon fails on another domain controller because the controller cannot recognize a new password, the controller forwards the logon request to the emulator before rejecting it.

- *Infrastructure Master*—Finally, each domain must have an Infrastructure Master, which is responsible for updating group-to-user references whenever the membership of a group changes.

# *Immediate Solutions*

## Administering Computer Accounts

Use computer accounts to control security on individual systems and perform remote maintenance and software installation. Administer them with the Active Directory Users and Computers snap-in of the Active Directory Users and Computers console.

### Creating A New Computer Account

To create a new account:

1. Click Start|Programs|Administrative Tools|Active Directory Users And Computers.

2. Select the Computers folder in the console tree or the folder to which you want to add the new account.

3. Right-click on the folder. From the context-sensitive pop-up menu, select New|Computer.

4. Enter a name for the new computer.

5. Click OK.

---

**NOTE:** *Under the default domain policy, only members of the Domain Admins group can create a new computer account.*

---

### Joining A Computer Account To A Group

To join a computer account to an existing group:

1. Click Start|Programs|Administrative Tools|Active Directory Users And Computers.

2. Select the Computers folder in the console tree or the folder that contains the computer account.

3. Right-click on the computer name in the details pane. From the context-sensitive pop-up menu, select Properties.

4. In the Properties dialog box, select the Member Of page, and then click Add.

5. In the Select Groups dialog box (shown in Figure 4.1), you will see the available groups. Select the one that you want, and click Add. When you finish selecting groups, click OK.

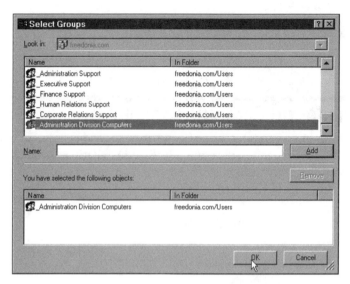

*Figure 4.1 Selecting a group for a computer account.*

## Removing A Computer Account

To delete a computer account:

1. Click Start|Programs|Administrative Tools|Active Directory Users And Computers.

2. Select the Computers folder in the console tree or the folder that contains the computer account.

3. In the details pane, right-click on the computer name. On the context-sensitive pop-up menu, select Delete.

4. In the confirmation prompt that follows, click Yes.

## Searching For A Computer Account

To find a computer account in the Active Directory:

1. Click Start|Programs|Administrative Tools|Active Directory Users And Computers.

2. To search the entire domain, right-click on the domain node at the top of the console tree. To limit the search to an organizational unit, right-click on the folder that contains the unit.

3. On the context-sensitive pop-up menu, select Find.

4. In the next dialog box, select Computers from the Find drop-down list.

5. Enter as much information as you can in the fields on the Computers page, and then click Find Now. The search results, if any, will appear in the bottom pane. (See Figure 4.2.)

6. To view the properties of a found computer, double-click on its name in the bottom pane. To access its context-sensitive menu, right-click on the name.

7. Close the Find Computers dialog box.

---

**TIP:** *Whenever you use the Find feature, use wildcard symbols, such as the asterisk (\*) and the question mark (?), if you are not sure of the exact name of the object. For example, "administra\*" will find objects whose names begin with either "administrative" or "administration." Unfortunately, the Find feature does not seem to support Boolean operators such as AND or OR.*

---

## Accessing The Computer Management Console

If a computer in your domain is running a version of Windows 2000, you can manage it remotely by accessing the Computer Management console through Active Directory Users and Computers. This does not work, however, if the computer is running an earlier version of

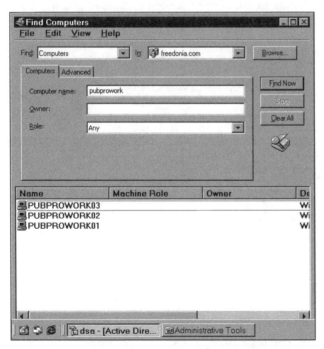

*Figure 4.2    The Find Computers dialog box, with the results of a search.*

Windows. To access the Computer Management console from within Active Directory Users and Computers:

1. Click Start|Programs|Administrative Tools|Active Directory Users And Computers.

2. Select the Computers folder in the console tree or the folder that contains the computer account.

3. In the details pane, right-click on the computer name. On the context-sensitive pop-up menu, select Manage. This action opens the Computer Management console (see Figure 4.3), which includes the Computer Management snap-in, in a second window. The tasks that you can perform here are beyond the scope of this book.

4. To return to Active Directory Users and Computers, close the Computer Management console.

## Viewing Or Modifying The General Properties Of A Computer Account

The General page of the Properties dialog box for computer accounts contains information about the selected computer, including its description. The description appears in the Active Directory's details

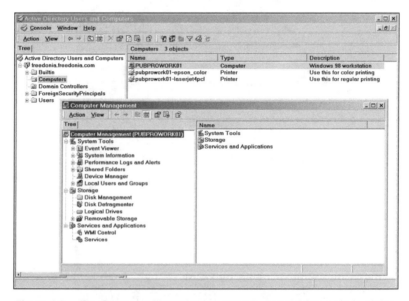

*Figure 4.3    The Computer Management console, opened from within Active Directory Users and Computers.*

pane, and in other places as well. It's the only descriptive information item on the page that you can change. To do so:

1. Click Start|Programs|Administrative Tools|Active Directory Users And Computers.

2. Select the Computers folder in the console tree or the folder that contains the computer account.

3. In the details pane, right-click on the computer name. On the context-sensitive pop-up menu, select Properties.

4. Select the General tab.

5. Edit the text in the Description field.

6. Click Apply to confirm your changes, and then click OK to exit the dialog box.

## Viewing A Computer's Operating System Properties

In certain circumstances, you can view operating-system information for computers on your network. This appears to work only with computers running Windows 2000 Professional or Windows NT 4 Workstation. To view a computer's operating system information:

1. Click Start|Programs|Administrative Tools|Active Directory Users And Computers.

2. Select the Computers folder in the console tree or the folder that contains the computer account.

3. In the details pane, right-click on the computer name. On the context-sensitive pop-up menu, select Properties.

4. Select the Operating System tab to view the available information.

5. Click OK to exit the dialog box.

## Adding A Computer To A Group Through Its Properties Settings

To add a computer to a group through its Properties settings:

1. Click Start|Programs|Administrative Tools|Active Directory Users And Computers.

2. Select the Computers folder in the console tree or the folder that contains the computer account.

3. In the details pane, right-click on the computer name. On the context-sensitive pop-up menu, select Properties.

4. Select the Member Of page.

5. Click Add.

6. In the Select Groups dialog box (shown in Figure 4.4), select the group that you want to add from the list in the top pane, and then click Add. The selected group appears in the bottom pane.

7. When you are finished, click OK to return to the Member Of page.

8. Click Apply to confirm your changes, and then click OK to exit the dialog box.

## Removing A Computer From A Group

To remove a computer from a group:

1. Click Start|Programs|Administrative Tools|Active Directory Users And Computers.

2. Select the Computers folder in the console tree or the folder that contains the computer account.

3. In the details pane, right-click on the computer name. On the context-sensitive pop-up menu, select Properties.

4. Select the Member Of page.

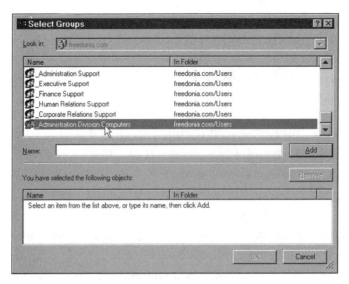

*Figure 4.4   Assigning a computer to a group.*

5. Select the group to be removed, and then click the Remove button.

6. When you are finished, click OK to return to the Member Of page.

7. Click Apply to confirm your changes, and then click OK to exit the dialog box.

## Viewing Or Modifying A Computer's Network Location Properties

Sometimes, it is useful to record the location of a specific computer on your network. To change the network location information for a computer:

1. Click Start|Programs|Administrative Tools|Active Directory Users And Computers.

2. Select the Computers folder in the console tree or the folder that contains the computer account.

3. In the details pane, right-click on the computer name. On the context-sensitive pop-up menu, select Properties.

4. Select the Location page to view the computer's network location properties. If you do not need to make any changes, click OK to exit the dialog box.

5. To change the location properties, enter the network location of the computer in the edit box manually or click Browse. If you entered the location manually, skip to Step 9.

6. Click Browse to open the Browse For Location dialog box, which displays a layout of your network. Select the location of the computer.

7. When you are finished, click OK to return to the Location page. The change that you have made should be displayed.

8. Click Apply to confirm your changes, and then click OK to exit the dialog box.

## Viewing Or Modifying Information About The Computer's Manager

You can assign responsibility for a given computer to a user, although this is not mandatory. To view or change the "Managed By" information for a computer:

1. Click Start|Programs|Administrative Tools|Active Directory Users And Computers.

2. Select the Computers folder in the console tree or the folder that contains the computer account.

3. In the details pane, right-click on the computer name. On the context-sensitive pop-up menu, select Properties.

4. Select the Managed By page. This page displays basic information about the currently assigned manager, if any.

5. To view more information about the current manager, click the View button, which opens the Properties dialog box for the person. You can edit the information in this dialog box. (See "Administering User Accounts" later in this chapter.)

6. If you make any changes to the user's properties, click Apply to confirm them.

7. Click OK to return to the Managed By page. (See Figure 4.5.)

8. If you do not need to change the currently assigned manager, click OK to exit the dialog box.

9. To change the currently assigned manager, click the Change button to open the Select User Or Contact dialog box.

10. Select the appropriate user from the displayed list, or enter the person's name in the edit box.

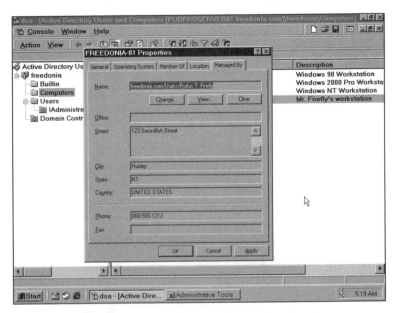

*Figure 4.5    The Managed By page in the Properties sheet for a computer account.*

11. When you are finished, click OK to return to the Managed By page.

12. Click Apply to confirm your changes, and then click OK to exit the dialog box.

---

**NOTE:** *You can assign a manager to many different types of objects in the Active Directory. However, selecting a user in the Managed By Properties page of the object does not delegate any specific rights or permissions to the user. Moreover, assigning a manager is not mandatory. The Managed By Properties page is nothing more than a convenient place for you to record information about a user when you assign or delegate responsibilities for an object to them. In the Active Directory, you can formally delegate authority only at the domain, site, or organizational unit level.*

---

## Moving A Computer Account

At times, you may need to move a computer account to another folder within the domain. For example, you might have created it in the Users folder, but now need to move it to an organizational unit. To move a computer account:

1. Click Start|Programs|Administrative Tools|Active Directory Users And Computers.

2. Select the Computers folder in the console tree or the folder that contains the computer account.

3. In the details pane, right-click on the computer name. On the context-sensitive pop-up menu, select Move. This opens the Move dialog box, with a tree showing only the name of the domain at the root.

4. Expand the tree by clicking on the plus boxes until you can select the new folder for the account. (See Figure 4.6.)

5. Select the appropriate folder, and then click OK.

## Resetting A Computer Account

To reset a computer account:

1. Click Start|Programs|Administrative Tools|Active Directory Users And Computers.

2. Select the Computers folder in the console tree or the folder that contains the computer account.

3. In the details pane, right-click on the computer name. On the context-sensitive pop-up menu, select Reset.

If the account has been reset successfully, you will get a confirmation message.

*Figure 4.6   Selecting a folder in which to move a computer.*

# Administering User Accounts

Create user accounts to authenticate the identity of the user, permit access to network resources, and monitor certain actions of the user. Administer user accounts with the Active Directory Users and Computers snap-in of the Active Directory Users and Computers console.

*NOTE: Late in the development of Windows 2000 Server, Microsoft added four new pages to the Properties sheets for user accounts. These pages—Environment, Sessions, Remote Control, and Terminal Services Profile—are related to the Terminal Services feature in Windows 2000. You will see these pages in the screen shots for viewing and managing the properties of user accounts. The Terminal Services feature is not covered in this book, however, and thus these pages are not covered in the Immediate Solutions that follow.*

## Creating A User Account

To create a user account:

1. Click Start|Programs|Administrative Tools|Active Directory Users And Computers.

2. In the console tree, right-click on the Users folder or the folder in which the account exists.

3. On the context-sensitive pop-up menu, select New|User.

4. In the New Object - User dialog box, enter the required data, and then click Next. (See Figure 4.7.)

5. Enter and confirm a password for the user, and then select the appropriate password options in the checkboxes. Note the checkbox to disable the account.

*Figure 4.7    Entering information for a new user account.*

6. Click Next to bring up a confirmation screen with some of the information that you entered.

7. If some of the information is incorrect, click Back to correct the entry, and then work your way back to this screen.

8. Click Finish to create the account.

---

**NOTE:**  *This procedure does not take you through all of the pages and fields in the Properties dialog box. Be sure to go back and modify the account properties to add more information about the user and assign him to the proper groups.*

---

### Viewing Or Modifying The General Properties Of A User Account

Information that you can enter on this page includes the user's first and last names, as well as their user logon name and domain. To view or modify general properties in a user account:

1. Click Start|Programs|Administrative Tools|Active Directory Users And Computers.

2. Select the Users folder in the console tree or the folder in which the account exists.

3. In the details pane, right-click on the user account. On the context-sensitive menu, select Properties.

4. Select the General page (shown in Figure 4.8). Edit the information on this page, as needed.

5. Click Apply to confirm your changes, and then click OK to exit the dialog box.

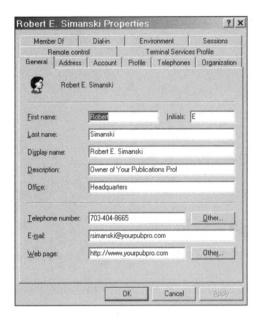

*Figure 4.8 Modifying general information in a user account.*

### Viewing Or Modifying The Address Properties Of A User Account

The properties of a user account can contain a substantial amount of information about a user, including their mailing address and telephone numbers. To view or modify address information in a user account:

1. Click Start|Programs|Administrative Tools|Active Directory Users And Computers.

2. Select the Users folder in the console tree or the folder in which the account exists.

3. In the details pane, right-click on the user account. On the context-sensitive menu, select Properties.

4. Select the Address page. Edit the information on this page, as needed.

5. Click Apply to confirm your changes, and then click OK to exit the dialog box.

### Viewing Or Modifying The Account Properties Of A User Account

Account properties include the user's logon name, restrictions (if any) on logon hours and workstations, password options, and expiration date (if any). To view or modify account properties in a user account:

1. Click Start|Programs|Administrative Tools|Active Directory Users And Computers.

2. Select the Users folder in the console tree or the folder in which the account exists.

3. In the details pane, right-click on the user account. On the context-sensitive menu, select Properties.

4. Select the Account page (shown in Figure 4.9). Edit the settings, as needed.

5. To set or change the user's allowable logon hours, select the Logon Hours button.

6. In the Logon Hours screen, you will see a grid consisting of one-hour increments for every day in the week. Logon is permitted around the clock, by default. To prohibit the user from logging on during certain hours, select the hours and click the Logon Denied radio button. (See Figure 4.10.)

7. Click OK to return to the Account page.

8. To restrict the user to certain workstations, click the Logon To button.

9. In the Logon Workstations dialog box, the user is allowed to log on to all workstations, by default. To restrict the user to a specific workstation, enter the workstation's NetBIOS name in the edit window, and then click Add. (For some reason, there is no Browse function in this dialog box.)

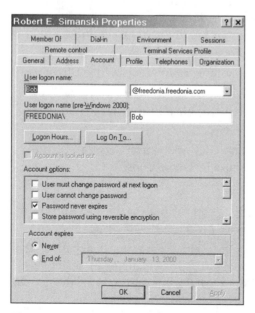

*Figure 4.9   The Account page in the user account Properties dialog box.*

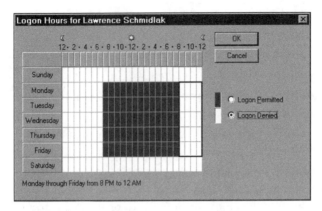

*Figure 4.10   Restricting a user's logon hours.*

10. Repeat Step 9, as needed.

11. To remove a workstation from the list, highlight the name of the workstation and click Remove.

12. Click Close to return to the Account page.

13. Click Apply to confirm your changes, and then click OK to exit the dialog box.

### Viewing Or Modifying The User Profile Properties Of A User Account

Information that you can enter in this dialog box includes the user's profile path, logon script name, home directory location, and shared documents folder. To view or modify user profile information in a user account:

1. Click Start|Programs|Administrative Tools|Active Directory Users And Computers.

2. Select the Users folder in the console tree or the folder in which the account exists.

3. In the details pane, right-click on the user account. On the context-sensitive menu, select Properties.

4. Select the Profile page.

5. In the User Profile area, enter the path to the user's profile and the name of the applicable logon script, if any.

6. In the Home directory area, either enter the local path on the user's workstation, or create a drive mapping by selecting a drive letter in the drop-down list box and entering the network path to the user's home directory.

7. In the Shared Documents Folder area, enter the network path to the user's shared folder.

8. Click Apply to confirm your changes, and then click OK to exit the dialog box.

### Viewing Or Modifying The Telecommunications Information In A User Account

Information that you can enter in this dialog box includes telephone numbers for the user's home phone, pager, mobile phone, fax, and IP phone. There is also a field for adding comments. (The user's work phone is entered on the General page of the Properties dialog box.) To view or modify this information:

1. Click Start|Programs|Administrative Tools|Active Directory Users And Computers.

2. Select the Users folder in the console tree or the folder in which the account exists.

3. In the details pane, right-click on the user account. On the context-sensitive menu, select Properties.

4. Select the Telephones page in the dialog box.

5. Enter the appropriate information.

6. Click Apply to confirm your changes, and then click OK to exit the dialog box.

### Viewing Or Modifying The Organization Properties Of A User Account

Information that you can enter on this page includes the user's title, department, company, the manager to whom the user reports, and the names of employees who report directly to the user. To view or modify organization information in a user account:

1. Click Start|Programs|Administrative Tools|Active Directory Users And Computers.

2. Select the Users folder in the console tree or the folder in which the account exists.

3. In the details pane, right-click on the user account. On the context-sensitive menu, select Properties.

4. Select the Organization page.

5. Enter the appropriate information.

6. To select or change the name of the user's manager, click the Change button and select the appropriate person from the list of network users.

7. To view information about the user's manager, click the View button. This action displays the Properties dialog box for the manager.

8. When you are ready, close the manager's Properties dialog box to return to the Organization page.

9. Click Apply to confirm your changes, and then click OK to exit the dialog box.

### Viewing Or Modifying The Group Membership Properties Of A User Account

On this Properties page, you can change the groups of which the user is a member. To view or modify group memberships in a user account:

1. Click Start|Programs|Administrative Tools|Active Directory Users And Computers.

2. Select the Users folder in the console tree or the folder in which the account exists.

3. In the details pane, right-click on the user account. On the context-sensitive menu, select Properties.

4. Select the Member Of page.

5. To add the user to a group, click Add.

6. In the Select Groups dialog box, choose the desired group from the list in the top pane, and click Add. The name of the selected group will appear in the bottom pane. If you make a mistake, highlight the group and click the Remove button.

7. Repeat Step 6 to add more groups, as needed.

8. Click OK to close the dialog box and return to the Member Of window.

9. To cancel the user's membership in a group, select the group, and then click the Remove button.

10. Click Apply to confirm your changes to the Member Of page, and then click OK to exit the dialog box.

### Viewing Or Modifying The Remote Access Properties Of A User Account

On this Properties page, you can configure the user's dial-in permission, callback options, and other remote access information. To view or modify remote access properties in a user account:

1. Click Start|Programs|Administrative Tools|Active Directory Users And Computers.

2. Select the Users folder in the console tree or the folder in which the account exists.

3. In the details pane, right-click on the user account. On the context-sensitive menu, select Properties.

4. Select the Dial-in page. (See Figure 4.11.)

5. Select the appropriate remote access permission.

6. If the user is required to call in from a specific telephone number, check the Verify Caller-ID box, and enter the phone number in the edit box.

7. Select the appropriate callback options. If a specific phone number is required for callback, select the Always Callback To radio button, and enter the phone number in the edit box.

8. To assign a static IP address to the user when he calls in, select the Assign A Static IP Address checkbox, and enter the IP address in the edit box.

9. To apply static routes to the caller, select the Apply Static Routes checkbox, and then click the Static Routes button. This opens the Static Routes dialog box that shows the available static routes.

10. To add a route, click the Add Route button. In the Add A Static Route dialog box, enter the destination and network mask, select the number of hops, and click OK to return to the previous dialog box.

**4. Managing Computers, Users, And Domain Controllers**

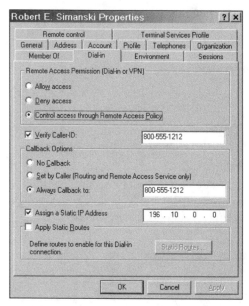

*Figure 4.11    The Dial-in Properties page.*

11. To remove a static route from the available list, select the route in the Static Routes dialog box, and click the Delete Route button.

12. Click OK to return to the Dial-in page.

13. Click Apply to confirm your changes, and then click OK to exit the dialog box.

## Searching For A User Account

To search for a user account:

1. Click Start|Programs|Administrative Tools|Active Directory Users And Computers.

2. In the console tree, right-click on the domain node or the organizational unit in which the account exists.

3. On the context-sensitive menu, select Find.

4. In the next dialog box, make sure that Find Users, Contacts, And Groups and the correct domain have been selected in the drop-down lists at the top.

5. Enter as much information as you can in the Name and Description fields. Wildcard symbols can be used. (See Figure 4.12.)

6. Click the Find Now button. The results will be displayed in the bottom pane.

7. To modify the properties of a found user, right-click on the object.

8. To close the dialog box, click the X at the top right of the window.

## Disabling A User Account

To disable a user account:

1. Click Start|Programs|Administrative Tools|Active Directory Users And Computers.

2. Select the Users folder in the console tree or the folder in which the account exists.

3. In the details pane, right-click on the user account. On the context-sensitive menu, select Disable Account. You should see a message confirming that the account is disabled.

**NOTE:** *This menu option is a toggle. If the account is already disabled, the option will read Enable Account.*

*Figure 4.12    Finding a user in the Active Directory.*

## Re-enabling A Disabled User Account

To re-enable a disabled user account:

1. Click Start|Programs|Administrative Tools|Active Directory Users And Computers.

2. Select the Users folder in the console tree or the folder in which the account exists.

3. In the details pane, right-click on the user account. On the context-sensitive menu, select Enable Account.

---

**NOTE:** *This menu option is a toggle. If the account is already enabled, the option will read Disable Account.*

---

## Removing A User Account

To remove a user account:

1. Click Start|Programs|Administrative Tools|Active Directory Users And Computers.

2. Select the Users folder in the console tree or the folder in which the account exists.

3. In the details pane, right-click on the user account. On the context-sensitive menu, select Delete.

4. You will see a warning message, asking you to confirm the deletion. Click Yes to confirm the action.

## Moving A User Account

This feature enables you to move a user account to another folder in the console tree. For example, you can move a user account from the main Users folder to the folder for an organizational unit. To move a user account to another folder:

1. Click Start|Programs|Administrative Tools|Active Directory Users And Computers.

2. Select the Users folder in the console tree or the folder in which the account exists.

3. In the details pane, right-click on the user account. On the context-sensitive menu, select Move.

4. In the Move dialog box, expand the folder tree and select the desired folder.

5. Click OK to complete the move and exit the dialog box.

## Renaming A User Account

To rename a user account:

1. Click Start|Programs|Administrative Tools|Active Directory Users And Computers.

2. Select the Users folder in the console tree or the folder in which the account exists.

3. In the details pane, right-click on the user account. On the context-sensitive menu, select Rename.

4. The account name will appear in an edit box. Edit the name, as needed, and then click outside the edit box to confirm the change. If you make a mistake, press Escape while the edit box is still open.

If you need to modify more name-related items than the account name, here is an alternate method:

1. With the account name highlighted, press Delete, and then press Enter. This will open the Rename User dialog box.

2. Modify the user's first, last, and logon names as needed. You can also change the user's logon domain here.

3. Click OK to confirm your changes and exit the dialog box.

## Changing A User's Password

To change a user's password:

1. Click Start|Programs|Administrative Tools|Active Directory Users And Computers.

2. Select the Users folder in the console tree or the folder in which the account exists.

3. In the details pane, right-click on the user account. On the context-sensitive menu, select Reset Password.

4. In the Reset Password dialog box, enter and confirm the new password. If appropriate, select the checkbox to force the user to change the password at her next logon.

5. Click OK to exit the dialog box.

## Changing A User's Primary Group

A primary group is the group with which a Macintosh user normally shares documents stored on a server. When a user creates a folder on the server, his primary group, by default, becomes the folder's associated group. To change a user's primary group:

1. Click Start|Programs|Administrative Tools|Active Directory Users And Computers.

2. Select the Users folder in the console tree or the folder in which the account exists.

3. In the details pane, right-click on the user account. On the context-sensitive menu, select Properties.

4. Select the Member Of page.

5. Select the group that you want to make the primary group for the user.

6. Click the Set Primary Group button.

7. Click Apply to confirm your changes, and then click OK to exit the dialog box.

## Adding A User To A Group

You can add a user to a group without having to open the Properties dialog box, although you can only select one group at a time in this case. To do so:

1. Click Start|Programs|Administrative Tools|Active Directory Users And Computers.

2. Select the Users folder in the console tree or the folder in which the account exists.

3. In the details pane, right-click on the user account. On the context-sensitive menu, select Add To Group.

4. This opens the Select Group dialog box, with a list of available groups. Select the desired group, and then click OK.

## Opening A User's Home Page

If the user has a home page on the Internet or on a local intranet, and the home page is listed in the properties for her account, you can access the page through the Active Directory. To do so:

1. Click Start|Programs|Administrative Tools|Active Directory Users And Computers.

2. Select the Users folder in the console tree or the folder in which the account exists.

3. In the details pane, right-click on the user account. On the context-sensitive menu, select Open Home Page. This action passes the URL to your default Web browser. (Internet Explorer 5 ships with Windows 2000 Server.)

## Sending Email To A User

If the user has an email account and that account is listed in the properties for his account, you can send him an email message from the Active Directory. To do so:

1. Click Start|Programs|Administrative Tools|Active Directory Users And Computers.

2. Select the Users folder in the console tree or the folder in which the account exists.

3. In the details pane, right-click on the user account. On the context-sensitive menu, select Send Mail. This action opens your default mail reader. (Microsoft Outlook 5 ships with Windows 2000 Server.)

## Creating A New Contact

*Contacts* are individuals who do not have user rights and permissions in your domain, but who are often in frequent contact with your users. An example is an outside vendor with whom your company does business regularly. Establishing a contact account enables you to enter information about them in the Active Directory, so that users can contact them easily and include them in mail distribution groups.

To create a contact:

1. Click Start|Programs|Administrative Tools|Active Directory Users And Computers.

2. In the console tree, right-click on the Users folder or the folder in which you wish to create the account.

3. Select New|Contact.

4. In the New Object - Contact dialog box, enter the naming information. (See Figure 4.13.)

5. Click OK to exit the dialog box.

### Viewing Or Modifying The General Properties Of A Contact Account

Information that you can enter on this page includes the contact's first and last names, as well as a description. To view or modify general properties in a contact account:

1. Click Start|Programs|Administrative Tools|Active Directory Users And Computers.

2. Select the Users folder in the console tree or the folder in which the account exists.

3. In the details pane, right-click on the contact account. On the context-sensitive menu, select Properties.

4. Select the General page. Edit the information on this page, as needed. (See Figure 4.14.)

5. Click Apply to confirm your changes, and then click OK to exit the dialog box.

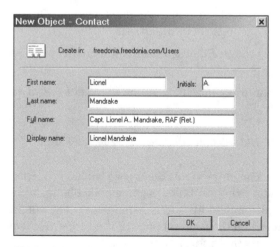

*Figure 4.13   The dialog box for creating a new contact.*

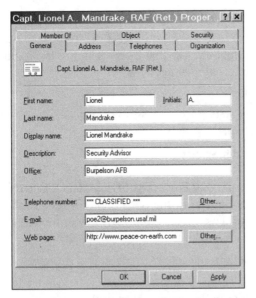

*Figure 4.14   Modifying the general information for a contact account.*

### Viewing Or Modifying The Address Properties Of A Contact Account

To view or modify address information in a contact account:

1. Click Start|Programs|Administrative Tools|Active Directory Users And Computers.

2. Select the Users folder in the console tree or the folder in which the account exists.

3. In the details pane, right-click on the contact account. On the context-sensitive menu, select Properties.

4. Select the Address page. Edit the information on this page, as needed.

5. Click Apply to confirm your changes, and then click OK to exit the dialog box.

### Viewing Or Modifying The Telecommunications Properties Of A Contact Account

Information that you can enter in this dialog box includes telephone numbers for the contact's home phone, pager, mobile phone, fax, and IP phone. There is also a field for adding comments. (The contact's work phone is entered on the General page of the Properties dialog box.) To view or modify this information:

1. Click Start|Programs|Administrative Tools|Active Directory Users And Computers.

2. Select the Users folder in the console tree or the folder in which the account exists.

3. In the details pane, right-click on the contact account. On the context-sensitive menu, select Properties.

4. Select the Telephones/Notes page in the dialog box.

5. Enter the appropriate information.

6. Click Apply to confirm your changes, and then click OK to exit the dialog box.

### Viewing Or Modifying The Organization Properties Of A Contact Account

Information that you can enter on this page includes the contact's title, department, company, the manager to whom the contact reports, and the names of employees who report directly to the contact. To view or modify this information:

1. Click Start|Programs|Administrative Tools|Active Directory Users And Computers.

2. Select the Users folder in the console tree or the folder in which the account exists.

3. In the details pane, right-click on the contact account. On the context-sensitive menu, select Properties.

4. Select the Organization page.

5. Enter the appropriate information.

6. To select or change the name of the contact's manager, click the Change button and select the appropriate person from the list of network users. If the person is outside of your organization, enter the manager's name in the Name edit box.

7. To view information about the contact's manager, click the View button. This will bring up the Properties dialog box for the manager, provided that the manager also has a user or contact account on your network.

8. When you are ready, close the manager's Properties dialog box to return to the Organization page.

9. Click Apply to confirm your changes, and then click OK to exit the dialog box.

**4. Managing Computers, Users, And Domain Controllers**

### Viewing Or Modifying The Group Membership Properties Of A Contact Account

On this page, you can change the groups of which the user is a member. To view or modify group memberships in a user account:

1. Click Start|Programs|Administrative Tools|Active Directory Users And Computers.

2. Select the Users folder in the console tree or the folder in which the account exists.

3. In the details pane, right-click on the contact account. On the context-sensitive menu, select Properties.

4. Select the Member Of page.

5. To add the contact to a group, click Add.

6. In the Select Groups dialog box, select the desired group from the list in the top pane and click Add. The name of the selected group will appear in the bottom pane. If you make a mistake, highlight the group and click the Remove button.

7. Repeat Step 6 to add more groups, as needed.

8. Click OK to close the dialog box and return to the Member Of window.

9. To cancel the contact's membership in a group, select the group, and then click the Remove button.

10. Click Apply to confirm your changes to the Member Of page, and then click OK to exit the dialog box.

---

**NOTE:** *The security provisions of Windows 2000 Server do not apply to contacts. For example, you cannot assign a password or user logon name to a contact. If you assign a contact to a security group, the rights and permissions of that group will not apply to him. To make it easier for you to administer contact accounts, it is best to confine them to distribution groups, such as those that are set up for email purposes.*

---

### Viewing The Object Properties Of A Contact Account

You can view—but not modify—the object properties of a contact account, including its Update Sequence Numbers (USNs). The USNs are used to track changes to Active Directory objects. To view the object properties:

1. Click Start|Programs|Administrative Tools|Active Directory Users And Computers.

2. Select the Users folder in the console tree or the folder in which the account exists.

3. In the details pane, right-click on the contact account. On the context-sensitive menu, select Properties.

4. Select the Object page.

5. When you are finished, click Cancel to exit the Properties dialog box.

### Viewing Or Modifying The Security Properties Of A Contact Account

On this page, you can modify the security properties of a contact account. You cannot grant the contact account any of the normal security privileges. However, you can use the settings on this page to control how the contact account can be managed by members of other security groups. To access the security properties page:

1. Click Start|Programs|Administrative Tools|Active Directory Users And Computers.

2. Select the Users folder in the console tree or the folder in which the account exists.

3. In the details pane, right-click on the contact account. On the context-sensitive menu, select Properties.

4. Select the Security page. You will see a list of groups with assigned security permissions for the account.

5. To add a group to the list, click Add. Select the group in the Select Users, Computers, Or Groups dialog box, then click OK to return to the Security page.

6. To modify the permissions for a group listed on the page, select the group in the Name window and modify the permissions as needed by checking or unchecking the boxes in the Permissions window.

7. For additional security options, select the Advanced button, which will open the Access Control Settings dialog box for the contact account. Edit the settings as needed, then click OK to return to the Security page.

8. Click Apply to confirm your changes, then click OK to exit the Properties dialog box.

# Administering Domains

In addition to managing the objects within a domain, such as computer and user accounts, groups, and organizational units, you can perform several administrative tasks at the domain level itself. They include changing the focus to another domain, modifying the properties of the domain, and delegating control of the domain to someone else.

## Changing The Focus To Another Domain

To change the focus to another domain:

1. Click Start|Programs|Administrative Tools|Active Directory Users And Computers.

2. Right-click on the domain node at the top of the console tree.

3. On the context-sensitive menu, select Connect To Domain.

4. In the Connect To Domain dialog box, enter the name of the domain or click Browse to select a domain from the Browse For Domain dialog box.

5. If necessary, click OK to close the Browse For Domain dialog box.

6. Click OK to confirm your selection and exit the Change Domain dialog box.

## Viewing Or Modifying The General Properties Of A Domain

To view or modify the General properties of a domain:

1. Click Start|Programs|Administrative Tools|Active Directory Users And Computers.

2. Right-click on the domain node at the top of the console tree.

3. On the context-sensitive menu, select Properties.

4. Select the General page. The only item that you can change here is the description of the domain.

5. Edit the description, as needed.

6. Click Apply to confirm your changes, and then click OK to exit the dialog box.

## Viewing Or Modifying Information About A Domain's Manager

To view or modify the Managed By properties of a domain:

1. Click Start|Programs|Administrative Tools|Active Directory Users And Computers.

2. Right-click on the domain node at the top of the console tree.

3. On the context-sensitive menu, select Properties.

4. Select the Managed By page.

5. To change the current manager, click Change.

6. In the Select User Or Contact dialog box, select the name of the new manager, and then click OK.

7. To view more information about the current manager, click View. This will open the Properties dialog box for the user's account.

8. Close the Properties dialog box for the user's account to return to the Managed By page.

9. Click Apply to confirm your changes, if any, and then click OK to exit the dialog box.

## Viewing The Object Properties Of A Domain

You can view—but not modify—the object properties of a domain, including its Update Sequence Numbers (USNs). The USNs are used to track changes to Active Directory objects. To view the object properties:

1. Click Start|Programs|Administrative Tools|Active Directory Users And Computers.

2. Select the root folder in the console tree.

3. In the details pane, right-click on the domain whose properties you want to view. On the context-sensitive menu, select Properties.

4. Select the Object page.

5. When you are finished, click on Cancel to exit the Properties dialog box.

## Viewing Or Modifying The Security Properties Of A Contact Account

On this page, you can modify the security properties of a contact account. You cannot grant the contact account any of the normal security privileges. However, you can use the settings on this page to control how the contact account can be managed by members of other security groups. To access the security properties page:

1. Click Start|Programs|Administrative Tools|Active Directory Users And Computers.

2. Select the root folder in the console tree.

3. In the details pane, right-click on the domain whose properties you want to view. On the context-sensitive menu, select Properties.

4. Select the Security page. You will see a list of groups with assigned security permissions for the domain.

5. To add a group to the list, click Add. Select the group in the Select Users, Computers, Or Groups dialog box, then click on OK to return to the Security page.

6. To modify the permissions for a group listed on the page, select the group in the Name window and modify the permissions as needed by checking or unchecking the boxes in the Permissions window.

7. For additional security options, select the Advanced button, which will open the Access Control Settings dialog box for the domain. Edit the settings as needed, then click on OK to return to the Security page.

8. Click Apply to confirm your changes, then click on OK to exit the Properties dialog box.

## Viewing Or Modifying The Group Policy Properties Of A Domain

The subject of managing group policies is a complex one that is beyond the scope of this chapter. In this section, you get an overview of how to use the group policy features of a domain.

### Creating A New Policy For A Domain

To create a new policy for a domain:

1. Click Start|Programs|Administrative Tools|Active Directory Users And Computers.

2. In the console tree, right-click on the name of the domain.

3. On the context-sensitive menu, select Properties.

4. Select the Group Policy page. The Default Domain Policy is listed, as well as any other policies that are attached to the domain.

5. To create a new policy for the domain, click New, and then edit the name of the new policy, which defaults to New Group Policy Object.

6. Click Apply to confirm your changes, and then click OK to exit the dialog box.

After you create the new group policy, you need to edit the policy, set its options, and review its properties.

### Setting Options For A Group Policy For A Domain

To set options for a policy:

1. Click Start|Programs|Administrative Tools|Active Directory Users And Computers.

2. In the console tree, right-click on the name of the domain.

3. On the context-sensitive menu, select Properties.

4. Select the Group Policy page.

5. To set options for a policy, select the policy, and then click Options. You can select either or both of two options for a selected policy:

   - *No Override*—By default, policy settings for a lower-level object in the Active Directory override equivalent settings in policies set at a higher level. For example, policies set for an organizational unit would override the Default Domain Policy. Checking the No Override box prevents a lower-level policy from overriding the selected one.

   - *Disabled*—Checking this box disables the selected policy for the current container (in this case, the domain).

6. Make your selections, and then click OK to return to the Group Policy page.

7. Click Apply to confirm your changes, and then click OK to exit the dialog box.

### Adding A Link To An Existing Policy In A Domain

If you have a group policy, perhaps for another organizational unit, that closely meets the needs of the current unit, you can create a link to it. To add a link to an existing policy:

1. Click Start|Programs|Administrative Tools|Active Directory Users And Computers.

2. In the console tree, right-click on the name of the domain.

3. On the context-sensitive menu, select Properties.

4. Select the Group Policy page. The Default Domain Policy will be listed, as well as any other policies that are attached to the domain.

5. To link another policy to the domain, click Add, and then select from the lists of available policies in the Add A Group Policy Object Link dialog box. There are separate lists of policies for domains and organizational units, sites, and the entire network.

6. Make your selection, and then click OK to return to the Group Policy page.

7. Click Apply to confirm your changes, and then click OK to exit the dialog box.

### Deleting A Group Policy Link Or Object In A Domain

On the Group Policy properties page, you can delete a link to a policy or even the policy itself. To do this:

1. Click Start|Programs|Administrative Tools|Active Directory Users And Computers.

2. In the console tree, right-click on the name of the domain.

3. On the context-sensitive menu, select Properties.

4. Select the Group Policy page. The Default Domain Policy will be listed, as well as any other policies that are attached to the organizational unit.

5. Select the policy or link that you wish to remove and click Delete. You will see a Delete dialog box with two radio buttons:

   • Remove The Link From The List

   • Remove The Link And Delete The Group Policy Object

6. Select the appropriate option, and then click OK to return to the Group Policy page. (If you select the second option, you will see a Delete Group Policy Object dialog box. Click Yes to confirm the deletion.)

7. Click Apply to confirm your changes, and then click OK to exit the dialog box.

### Editing A Group Policy Linked To A Domain

To edit a group policy linked to a domain:

1. Click Start|Programs|Administrative Tools|Active Directory Users And Computers.

2. In the console tree, right-click on the name of the domain.

3. On the context-sensitive menu, select Properties.

4. Select the Group Policy page. The Default Domain Policy will be listed, as well as any other policies that are attached to the organizational unit.

5. Select the policy that you want to edit and click Edit. This will load the Group Policy Editor in a separate console. Depending on the size of the group policy, the editor may take a while to load.

6. Make your changes in the Group Policy Editor, and then close its console to return to the Group Policy properties page.

7. Click Apply to confirm your changes, and then click OK to exit the dialog box.

### Viewing The Properties Of A Group Policy Linked To A Domain

To view the properties of a group policy linked to a domain:

1. Click Start|Programs|Administrative Tools|Active Directory Users And Computers.

2. In the console tree, right-click on the name of the domain.

3. On the context-sensitive menu, select Properties.

4. Select the Group Policy page.

5. Select the policy whose properties you want to view and click Properties. This will open the Properties dialog box for the selected group policy. Because this dialog box is covered in detail in Chapter 6, it is not discussed here.

6. When you finish, close the Properties dialog box for the group policy object to return to the Group Policy properties page for the organizational unit.

7. Click OK to exit the Properties dialog box for the organizational unit.

### Modifying The Hierarchy Of Group Policies In A Domain

There is a hierarchy of group policies in the Active Directory, beginning with the Default Domain Policy. Settings in lower-level policies override the equivalent settings in higher-level policies. If you have more than one domain-wide policy, you will want to make sure that the group policies follow the hierarchy that you intend for them.

To modify the hierarchy of group policies linked to a domain:

1. Click Start|Programs|Administrative Tools|Active Directory Users And Computers.

2. In the console tree, right-click on the name of the domain.

3. On the context-sensitive menu, select Properties.

4. Select the Group Policy page. The policies that apply to the domain will be shown in their current hierarchy, usually with the Default Domain Policy at the top.

5. To change the position of a group policy, select the policy, and click the Up and Down buttons as needed.

4. Managing Computers, Users, And Domain Controllers

6.  Click Apply to confirm your changes, and then click OK to exit the Properties dialog box.

| Related solution: | Found on page: |
| --- | --- |
| Viewing And Modifying The Properties Of A Group Policy | 207 |

## Delegating Control Of A Domain

Just as you can delegate control of an organizational unit, you can also delegate control of a domain. To do so:

1.  Click Start|Programs|Administrative Tools|Active Directory Users And Computers.

2.  Right-click on the domain node at the top of the console tree.

3.  On the context-sensitive menu, select Delegate Control. This will open the Delegation of Control Wizard.

4.  At the opening page, click Next to continue.

5.  On the Users Or Groups page, the names of groups or users, if any, who currently have administrative authority over the domain are displayed. If you need to remove any of them, select the name and click Remove.

6.  Click Add to add a new group or user to the list.

7.  In the Select Users, Computers, Or Groups dialog box, select the users or groups to be added and click Add.

8.  When you are ready, click OK to return to the Users Or Groups page. The domain and logon name for each user will be added to the list.

9.  Click Next to continue.

10. On the Tasks To Delegate page, select one of the two radio buttons. If you select the Delegate The Following Common Tasks button, also select the groups of tasks that you want to delegate from the list in the main window. When you click Next, you will go directly to Step 13. If you select the Create A Custom Task To Delegate button, when you click Next you will continue with Step 11.

11. On the Active Directory Object Type page, you will find two radio buttons, with a scrolling list of object types under the second one:

    • *Delegate Control Of The Folder*—To give the administrators wide-ranging control of the domain, select this button. This is the default selection. The scrolling list is grayed-out when this is selected.

• *Delegate Control Of The Following Objects In The Folder*—
  To limit administrators' control, select this second radio
  button. When this button is selected, the checkbox options in
  the list of object types become available. By default, none of
  the checkboxes are selected, so you will have to decide on
  each one.

12. Click Next to continue.

13. On the Permissions page, you will find a scrolling list of permis-
    sions that can be delegated. Underneath the list is a group of
    filter options. After you select your permissions, click Next to
    continue.

14. On the Completing The Delegation Of Control Wizard page, you
    will see a confirmation of the selections that you have made.
    Click Back to change a selection, Cancel to abort the process,
    or Finish to confirm your choices and close the wizard.

# Administering Domain Controllers

A domain controller performs many different roles on a Windows 2000
network. By default, these roles fall to the first controller in the domain. As you set up additional controllers, you can spread the load
among them by transferring some of these roles to them.

## Changing The Focus To Another Domain Controller

To change the focus to another domain controller:

1. Click Start|Programs|Administrative Tools|Active Directory
   Users And Computers.

2. Right-click on the domain node at the top of the console tree.

3. On the context-sensitive menu, select Change Domain Controller.

4. In the Change Domain Controller dialog box, select from the
   list of available controllers.

5. Click OK to confirm your selection and exit the dialog box.

## Transferring The Relative ID Master Role To Another Controller

To transfer the Relative ID Master role to another domain controller:

1. Click Start|Programs|Administrative Tools|Active Directory
   Users And Computers.

2. Right-click on Active Directory Users And Computers.

3. On the context-sensitive menu, select Operations Masters.

4. In the Operations dialog box, select the RID Pool page. The name of the current RID server will be displayed. (See Figure 4.15.)

5. Click Change to select from a list of available servers, and then click OK to return to the Operations dialog box.

6. Click OK to confirm your selection and exit the dialog box.

## Transferring The PDC Emulator Role To Another Controller

To transfer the PDC emulator role to another domain controller:

1. Click Start|Programs|Administrative Tools|Active Directory Users And Computers.

2. Right-click on Active Directory Users And Computers.

3. On the context-sensitive menu, select Operations Masters.

4. In the Operations dialog box, select the PDC page. The name of the current PDC server will be displayed.

5. Click Change to select from a list of available servers, and then click OK to return to the Operations dialog box.

6. Click OK to confirm your selection and exit the dialog box.

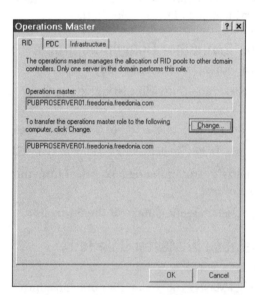

*Figure 4.15   The Operations dialog box with the RID Pool page selected.*

## Transferring The Infrastructure Master Role To Another Controller

To transfer the Infrastructure Master role to another domain controller:

1. Click Start|Programs|Administrative Tools|Active Directory Users And Computers.

2. Right-click on Active Directory Users And Computers.

3. On the context-sensitive menu, select Operations Masters.

4. In the Operations dialog box, select the Infrastructure page. The name of the current Infrastructure server will be displayed.

5. Click Change to select from a list of available servers, and then click OK to return to the Operations dialog box.

6. Click OK to confirm your selection, and exit the dialog box.

## Transferring The Domain Naming Master Role To Another Controller

To transfer the Domain Naming Master role to another domain controller:

1. Click Start|Programs|Administrative Tools|Active Directory Domains And Trusts.

2. Right-click on Active Directory Domains And Trusts.

3. On the context-sensitive menu, select Operations Masters.

4. In the Change Operations Master dialog box, the name of the current server will be displayed.

5. Click Change to select from a list of available servers, and then click OK to return to the Operations dialog box.

6. Click OK to confirm your selection and exit the dialog box.

## Transferring The Schema Master Role To Another Controller

To transfer the Schema Master role to another domain controller:

1. Open the management console to which you have added the Active Directory Schema snap-in or add the snap-in to an existing console.

2. Right-click on Active Directory Schema.

3. On the context-sensitive menu, select Schema Masters.

4. In the Change Schema Master dialog box, the name of the current server will be displayed.

4. Managing Computers, Users, And Domain Controllers

5. Click Change to select from a list of available servers, and then click OK to return to the Schema Master dialog box.

6. Click OK to confirm your selection and exit the dialog box.

# Chapter 5

# Managing Groups And Organizational Units

# *In Brief*

Within the Active Directory, the hierarchy of a given domain, top to bottom, consists of sites, domains,organizational units, groups, users, and computers. If you use Windows NT 4 Server, you are already familiar with the concepts of groups, users, and computers as you use them within a domain. Organizational units, however, are new to Windows 2000 Server, and fall between domains and groups in the NT 4 hierarchy. Many of the tasks that you perform at the domain level in NT 4, such as creating system policies, you can now perform more appropriately at the organizational unit level in Windows 2000 Server. Although organizational units are not mandatory, you will find that they offer many benefits, particularly in larger networks.

To accomplish the tasks in this chapter, you will use the Active Directory Users and Computers console in the Administrative Tools folder. In its default setting, the console has only one snap-in, Active Directory Users and Computers. To access it, click Start|Programs|Administrative Tools|Active Directory Users and Computers.

## Groups

*Groups* are containers for users, contacts, computers, and even other groups. You can use them to manage access to resources on your network, filter group policy, and create email distribution lists. (Contacts are people who do not have access to your network, but may have frequent dealings with your organization. You can add their contact information to the Active Directory so that your users can find it easily, and you can add them to groups that you set up solely as email distribution lists.)

Instead of assigning permissions to each individual user account, you can set them once for a group, and then assign users and computers to the group. Each member of a group inherits the permissions assigned to the group.

In addition, you can nest groups within other groups. By default, a child group inherits the permissions of the parent group. You can filter these permissions—that is, enable, disable, or modify them—by making selections in the security properties of the child group. For example, you can set up a master group that has all of the permissions that most users might need, and then add child groups in which you can disable some of those permissions.

Groups can be created in the root domain of a forest, in any other domain within a forest, or within an organizational unit. Where you place a group can affect the scope of a domain. Make your decision based on the administrative requirements of the group. If you divide your domain into organizational units and delegate administration of an organizational unit to another person, place groups that you want that person to administer within their organizational unit rather than directly under the domain. You can even nest one group within another.

Suppose, for example, that you have established several organizational units along the lines of your company's departmental structure, including one for administration. You could create a master global group for the administration unit, with all of the permissions needed by employees of the administration department. Assume that you might not want support staff to have access to some of the resources used by managers—for example, shared folders with confidential files. You could create separate global groups for managerial and support staff, and nest them within the master administration group. Your designated administrator would be able to manage each of the groups within the unit.

In addition, you might want to be able to apply some security controls or permissions outside of the structure of the organizational unit itself. To accomplish this, you could nest the master administration group within a larger global or universal group.

## Group Types

There are two basic types of groups in Windows 2000 Server:

- *Security groups*—Most of the time, you will create these types of groups. Security is enabled, so these groups can be assigned permissions to resources on your network. They also serve as email distribution lists. When you send an email message to the group, it goes to every user in the group.

- *Distribution groups*—With these groups, there is no enabled security. They are suited primarily for email distribution.

You can add outside contacts to either type of group. If you add them to a security group, however, they do not inherit its rights and permissions.

---

**NOTE:**   *If your domain controller is operating in native mode (the preferred mode if you do not have a mix of Windows 2000 and Windows NT 4 domain controllers), you can convert groups to and from either type. This option is not available if your domain controller is operating in mixed mode, which is the mode that is required if you have a mix of both types of controllers.*

---

# Group Scopes

Groups are also characterized by their scope, which defines their boundaries. They can be universal, global, or local to the domain. Here are the characteristics of group scopes for domain controllers operating in native mode:

- *Universal groups*—These groups can include user and computer accounts, global accounts, and even other universal groups. They can be from any Windows 2000 domain in the same forest. You can grant them permissions in any domain within that forest. Universal groups cannot bridge multiple forests, however.

- *Global groups*—These groups can contain only user accounts and other global groups from the same domain. You can assign them permissions to any domain within their forest.

- *Domain local groups*—These groups can include user accounts, universal groups, global groups, and other domain local groups from the same domain. You can assign them permissions only for their own domain.

If your domain controller is operating in mixed mode, these options apply only to distribution groups. For security groups, your options are more limited. Global groups can contain only user accounts, and domain local groups can contain only user accounts and global groups.

Here are some suggestions for using the three scopes of groups:

- Use domain local groups to manage access to resources within a specific domain. Suppose, for example, that you need to give the staff of your administration department access to a network printer. You could create a global group for the users in the department, create a domain local group with access rights to that specific printer, and then place the global group within it. If you later need to change or add a printer, you only need to do it once—in the domain local group.

- Use global groups for Active Directory objects that need to be maintained frequently, such as user and computer accounts. Because the groups are not replicated to other domains through the global catalog, the changes that you make do not severely affect network traffic outside of their own domain.

- Limit universal groups to objects that do not change frequently because changes to these groups are replicated to every global catalog server in the forest. Universal groups are useful when you need to consolidate users across more than one domain. For example, suppose you have a European division with its own domain. Both your headquarters operation and the European division have their own marketing departments, and users in these departments need access to shared folders in the root domain. You could create global groups for each marketing department, and then join them to a universal group that provides the members of each global group with access to these folders. Changes to either of the global groups do not cause replication of the universal group.

---

**NOTE:** *You may wonder why I have not made any reference to the Group Policy Editor in this section. The reason is that you cannot create a group policy for a specific group! You can filter only inherited policies that exist at a higher level. The lowest level at which you can create a group policy is the organizational unit, which is discussed later in this chapter. (For more information about the Group Policy Editor, see Chapter 6.)*

# Builtin Groups

Windows 2000 Server installs several default security groups when you create a domain controller. In Active Directory Users and Computers, you will find them in the Builtin and Users folders. These groups contain sets of commonly used rights and permissions to help you get started. The default domain local groups are in the Builtin folder and the global groups are in the Users folder. You can move them to other folders later, as needed. (See Figures 5.1 and 5.2.)

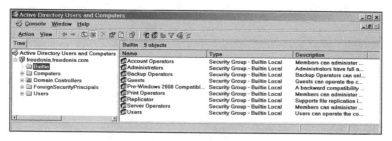

*Figure 5.1    The Active Directory Users and Computers snap-in, with the default domain local security groups displayed.*

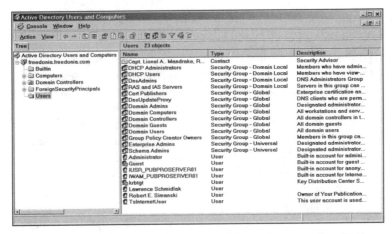

*Figure 5.2    The Active Directory Users and Computers snap-in, with the default global security groups displayed.*

Tables 5.1 and 5.2 list each default group and its function.

The following global groups are likely to be of most interest to you:

- *Domain Users*—By default, any time that you create a user account, Windows 2000 Server automatically adds it to the Domain Users global group, which in turn is a member of the

*Table 5.1    Default local groups in Windows 2000 Server.*

| Built-in Local Groups | Functions |
| --- | --- |
| Account Operators | Administers domain user and group accounts |
| Administrators | Fully administers the computer or domain |
| Backup Operators | Bypasses file security to backup files |
| Guests | Accesses the computer or domain |
| Pre-Windows 2000 Compatible Access | Used for backward compatibility; allows read access for all users and groups in the domain |
| Print Operators | Administers domain printers |
| Replicator | Supports file replication in a domain |
| Server Operators | Administers domain servers |
| Users | Ordinary users |
| **Domain Local Groups** | **Functions** |
| DHCP Administrators | Administrative access to DHCP service |
| DHCP Users | View-only access to DHCP service |
| DnsAdmins | DNS administrative group |
| RAS and IAS Servers | Remote access properties of users |

**Table 5.2    Default global and universal groups in Windows 2000 Server.**

| Global Groups | Members |
|---|---|
| Cert Publishers | Enterprise certification and renewal agents |
| Domain Admins | Designated administrators of the domain |
| Domain Computers | All workstations and servers joined to the domain |
| Domain Controllers | All domain controllers in the domain |
| Domain Guests | All domain guests |
| Domain Users | All domain users |
| **Universal Groups** | **Members** |
| Enterprise Admins | Designated administrators of the enterprise |
| Schema Admins | Designated administrators of the schema |

Users domain local group. If you want every user to have access to a specific resource, such as a network printer, you can assign the necessary permissions to the group.

- *Domain Admins*—This group is a member of the broader Administrators group; it is a good place to assign users who need extensive administrative privileges.

- *Domain Guests*—By default, this group contains the default Guest user account and is, in turn, a member of the Guests domain local group.

# Organizational Units

Organizational units, a new feature of Windows 2000 Server, are Active Directory containers (or folders, if you prefer). They can contain user and computer accounts, groups, and even other organizational units. When you create an organizational unit, it appears as a folder under the Users folder in Active Directory Users and Computers.

Organizational units offer some of the features of domains, as implemented in Windows NT 4, and are much easier to administer. For example, you can create a group policy or delegate administrative responsibility for an organizational unit.

In most cases, you probably want to create organizational units that reflect the structure of your own organization, then create groups of users and place the groups in the appropriate units. This enables you to delegate responsibility for managing a unit to the appropriate person. For example, if your company has separate divisions for administration, marketing, and operations, you can create an organizational unit for each one and delegate responsibility for managing it to an appropriate person within the division.

As with groups, you can nest organizational units within other units. For example, your company's administration division might have departments for executive administration, finance, human relations, and corporate relations. You can create organizational units for each department and nest them within the administration division's unit.

# Strategies For Creating Effective Organizational Units

To use organizational units effectively, you need to give careful thought to how you want to organize your domain and the best way to group your users in order to take advantage of organizational units.

Previously, the most common way of dividing a large domain into more-manageable administrative units was to create additional domains. Dividing your network into domains or sites is still the method of choice if your organization is highly decentralized or if portions of your domain are connected by very slow links. In other circumstances, organizational units offer a good alternative. Here are some examples of when organizational units would be helpful:

- When you want to organize your domain according to your company's structure.

- When you need to delegate administrative responsibilities.

- When the organizational structure of your company is likely to change in the near future. (Organizational units give you much more flexibility than domains in this regard.) At the same time, be sure to organize your domains so that you will not have to move or split them frequently in the future.

Here are some other points to keep in mind:

- The organizational unit is the lowest level, within the structure of the domain, at which you can create a separate group policy or delegate responsibility. Windows 2000 Server installs a default policy that covers the entire domain. All that you can do at the group level is filter the specific provisions of that policy by enabling or disabling them. You may find that you need to establish a custom policy to meet specific needs that the default domain policy does not cover. In that case, you may want to create an organizational unit for the policy and add the necessary groups of users to it. The policy that you create will apply to every object within the unit. As with the domain policy, you can filter it at the group level.

- Unlike groups, organizational units cannot span domains. You cannot use them to manage security at the user and computer account level. Primarily, they help you to organize objects within a domain. You still need groups to grant rights and permissions to users.

# Delegating Authority Over Organizational Units

If you administer a network of any substantial size, you no doubt have to juggle many different tasks and responsibilities. Windows 2000 Server gives you the opportunity to delegate some of your responsibilities easily and tailor those delegated responsibilities very carefully.

The default security policy for a domain defines many specific permissions and rights. You can use them to set tight parameters on what a designated administrator for an organizational unit can and cannot do. For example, you can give them considerable latitude in managing groups and user accounts in their unit, but limit their ability to manage files and folders on a network server.

You can also nest authority. For example, if you have a large division with several departments, you could create a master organizational unit for the division with nested child units for each department within the division. Each departmental unit could have its own administrator, whose authority would be limited to that unit. On the other hand, you could give the administrator of the divisional unit authority over the departmental units, as well as over the groups and other objects in their own unit.

# *Immediate Solutions*

## Administering Groups

Use groups to manage access to resources on your network, filter group policy, and create email distribution lists. Administer groups with the Active Directory Users and Computers console.

### Creating A New Group

To create a new group:

1. Click Start|Programs|Administrative Tools|Active Directory Users and Computers.

2. Right-click on the Users folder in the console tree or the folder in which you want to add the group.

3. On the context-sensitive menu, click New|Group.

4. In the New Object - Group dialog box, enter the name of the new group, and then select its scope and type. (See Figure 5.3.)

5. Click OK to create the group and exit the dialog box.

The New Object - Group dialog box contains only a subset of the information that can be entered in the Properties settings for a group. After you create the group, you will want to right-click on the name of

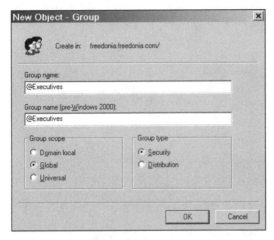

*Figure 5.3    The dialog box for creating a new group.*

the group in the results pane and select Properties to complete the process of configuring your new group. Each of the individual Properties pages is covered later in this chapter.

---

**TIP:** *To help separate groups, organizational units, and other objects that you create in the Active Directory from the rest of the pack, use the at (@) sign, the number (#) sign, or an underscore (_) as the first character in the name. Every Microsoft operating system released to date sorts names one character at a time, and it places these characters (and the others on the top row of the standard keyboard) ahead of the alphanumeric characters. Sort the list of objects in the results pane by name by clicking on the Name heading at the top of the column. Objects that you name in this way appear together at or near the top of the column. (The order of precedence is @, #, and _.) You can also use the exclamation point (!). Be aware, however, that this does not work with the Windows 2000 Server Find feature.*

---

## Removing A Group

To remove a group:

1. Click Start|Programs|Administrative Tools|Active Directory Users and Computers.

2. Select the Users folder in the console tree or the folder in which the group is installed.

3. In the details pane, right-click on the name of the group.

4. On the context-sensitive menu, select Delete.

5. In the confirmation message box, click Yes.

## Searching For A Group

To search for a group:

1. Click Start|Programs|Administrative Tools|Active Directory Users and Computers.

2. In the console tree, right-click on the domain node or the organizational unit in which the group exists.

3. On the context-sensitive menu, select Find.

4. In the next dialog box, make sure that Find Users, Contacts, And Groups and the correct domain are selected in the drop-down lists at the top.

5. Enter as much information as you can in the Name and Description fields. Wildcard symbols may be used.

6. Click the Find Now button. The results will be displayed in the bottom pane.

**5. Managing Groups And Organizational Units**

7. To modify the properties of a found group, right-click on the object and select the Properties option.

8. To close the Find feature's dialog box, click the X at the top right of the window.

## Viewing Or Modifying The General Properties Of A Group

The General page of the Properties dialog box for a group includes information about the group, including its type and scope. To view or modify the general properties of a group:

1. Click Start|Programs|Administrative Tools|Active Directory Users and Computers.

2. Select the Users folder in the console tree or the folder in which the group is installed.

3. In the details pane, right-click on the name of the group.

4. On the context-sensitive menu, select Properties.

5. Select the General page. Here, you can edit the description and download name of the group, enter an email address for it, or add a comment. You can also change the group's type and scope.

6. Click Apply to confirm your changes, and then click OK to exit the dialog box.

## Converting A Group From One Type To Another

By default, groups that you create are security groups. If you do not wish the members of the group to have rights and permissions on your network, or if you are using the group for email purposes only, you can change the group type to distribution. To convert a group from one type to another:

1. Click Start|Programs|Administrative Tools|Active Directory Users and Computers.

2. Select the Users folder in the console tree or the folder in which the group is installed.

3. In the details pane, right-click on the name of the group.

4. On the context-sensitive menu, select Properties.

5. Select the General page.

6. Select the radio button for the group type that you want (either security or distribution). (See Figure 5.4.)

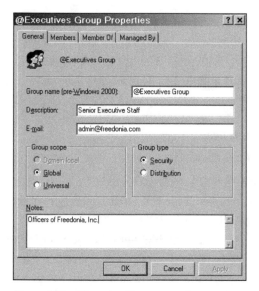

**Figure 5.4** *Changing the scope of a group.*

7. Click Apply to confirm your changes, and then click OK to exit the dialog box.

## Changing The Scope Of A Group

To change the scope of a group:

1. Click Start|Programs|Administrative Tools|Active Directory Users and Computers.

2. Select the Users folder in the console tree or the folder in which the group is installed.

3. In the details pane, right-click on the name of the group.

4. On the context-sensitive menu, select Properties.

5. Select the General page.

6. Select the radio button for the scope that you wish to change to. If you originally assigned the Domain Local scope to the group, the Global option is grayed-out. If you originally created the group as a Global group, the Domain Local option is grayed-out. In either case, the only other option is Universal. (See Figure 5.4)

7. Click Apply to confirm your changes, and then click OK to exit the dialog box.

## Viewing Or Modifying The Membership Of A Group

You can add users, computers, printers, and other groups to the membership of a group. To view or modify a group's membership:

1. Click Start|Programs|Administrative Tools|Active Directory Users and Computers .

2. Select the Users folder in the console tree or the folder in which the group is installed.

3. In the details pane, right-click on the name of the group.

4. On the context-sensitive menu, select Properties.

5. Select the Members page (see Figure 5.5). The members of the group will be displayed in the Members window.

6. To remove a member of the group, highlight the member in the list and click the Remove button.

7. To add a member to the group, click the Add button to open the Select Users, Contacts, Computers, Or Groups dialog box.

8. Select the objects that you want to add to the group and click the Add button.

9. When you have made all of your selections, click OK to exit the selection dialog box and return to the Members page of the Properties dialog box.

10. When you are ready, click OK to exit the Properties dialog box.

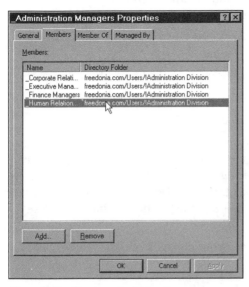

*Figure 5.5   The membership of a group.*

# Viewing Or Modifying A Group's Membership In Other Groups

You can join a group to another group. To view or modify a group's membership in other groups:

1. Click Start|Programs|Administrative Tools|Active Directory Users and Computers.
2. Select the Users folder in the console tree or the folder in which the group is installed.
3. In the details pane, right-click on the name of the group.
4. On the context-sensitive menu, select Properties.
5. Select the Member Of page.
6. To join a group to another group, click Add.
7. In the Select Groups dialog box, select the groups that you wish to join, and click Add. When you finish, click OK to return to the Member Of page.
8. Click Apply to confirm your changes, and then click OK to exit the dialog box.

# Viewing Or Modifying Information About A Group's Manager

It is possible to assign a user to manage a group. To view or modify information about the group's assigned manager:

1. Click Start|Programs|Administrative Tools|Active Directory Users and Computers.
2. Select the Users folder in the console tree or the folder in which the group is installed.
3. In the details pane, right-click on the name of the group.
4. On the context-sensitive menu, select Properties.
5. Select the Managed By page.
6. To add a manager or change the current one, click Change.
7. In the Select User Or Contact dialog box, select the user whom you wish to manage the group from the scrolling list, or enter the person's name in the edit box.
8. Click OK to return to the Managed By page.
9. Some information about the person will be displayed on the page. To view or modify the Properties settings in the user's

account, click View. When you are finished, click OK, exit the Properties dialog box, and return to the Managed By page.

10. Click Apply to confirm your changes, and then click OK to exit the dialog box.

## Adding A Member To A Group

You can add users, computers, printers, and other groups to a group. To add a member to a group:

1. Click Start|Programs|Administrative Tools|Active Directory Users and Computers.

2. Select the Users folder in the console tree or the folder in which the group is installed.

3. In the details pane, right-click on the name of the group.

4. On the context-sensitive menu, select Properties.

5. Select the Members page. (Refer to Figure 5.5, earlier in the chapter.)

6. To add a member, click Add.

7. In the Select Users, Contacts, Computers, Or Groups dialog box, select the member that you want to add to the group, and click Add. After you have added all of the members that you want, click OK to return to the Members page.

8. Click Apply to confirm your changes, and then click OK to exit the dialog box.

## Removing A Member From A Group

To remove a member from a group:

1. Click Start|Programs|Administrative Tools|Active Directory Users and Computers.

2. Select the Users folder in the console tree or the folder in which the group is installed.

3. In the details pane, right-click on the name of the group.

4. On the context-sensitive menu, select Properties.

5. Select the Members page. (Refer to Figure 5.5, earlier in the chapter.)

6. To remove a member, select the member from the list on display and click Remove.

7. Click Apply to confirm your changes, and then click OK to exit the dialog box.

## Renaming A Group

To rename a group:

1. Click Start|Programs|Administrative Tools|Active Directory Users and Computers.

2. Select the Users folder in the console tree or the folder in which the group is installed.

3. In the details pane, right-click on the name of the group.

4. On the context-sensitive menu, select Rename. This action opens an edit box with the name of the group in it.

5. Edit the name, and then click outside of the edit box to confirm the change. If you make a mistake, press Esc while your cursor is still in the edit box.

---

**NOTE:** *Windows 2000 Server issues a unique Security Identifier (SID) to each user, group, and computer account when you first create it. Certain processes use the account's SID rather than its name. If you delete an account and then create a new one with the same name, it will have a different SID than the first account. Therefore, the new account will not inherit the rights and permissions that had been granted to the old one. When you rename an account, however, it retains its original SID.*

---

## Moving A Group

There may be occasions when you want to move a group, particularly one that you have created. For example, you may want to move the root of the Users folder to a folder for an organizational unit. To move a group:

1. Click Start|Programs|Administrative Tools|Active Directory Users and Computers.

2. Select the Users folder in the console tree or the folder in which the group is installed.

3. In the details pane, right-click on the name of the group.

4. On the context-sensitive menu, select Move.

5. In the Move dialog box, expand the tree and select the folder to which you want to move the group.

6. Click OK to exit the dialog box.

## Sending Email To A Group

To send email to a group:

1. Click Start|Programs|Administrative Tools|Active Directory Users and Computers.

2. Select the Users folder in the console tree or the folder in which the group is installed.

3. In the details pane, right-click on the name of the group.

4. On the context-sensitive menu, select Send Mail. This will open a new message in your default mail reader with the email address of the group filled in.

# Administering Organizational Units

Organizational units can contain user and computer accounts, groups, and even other organizational units. Administer organizational units with the Active Directory Users and Computers console.

## Creating An Organizational Unit

To create a new organizational unit:

1. Click Start|Programs|Administrative Tools|Active Directory Users and Computers.

2. Right-click on the domain node in the console tree or the folder in which the organizational unit is to be installed. Selecting a folder that contains an organizational unit will nest the new unit within the existing one.

3. Select New|Organizational Unit from the context-sensitive menu.

4. In the New Object - Organizational Unit dialog box, enter the name of the new unit. (See Figure 5.6.)

5. Click OK to create the unit and exit the dialog box.

*TIP:    Keep in mind that the organizational unit is the lowest level at which you can create or customize group policy, and that policies are inherited by the objects within the unit. If you want to establish a policy for a division and make modifications to that policy for each department within the division, consider creating an organizational unit for the division as well as for each department, and then placing the department units within the division unit.*

## Removing An Organizational Unit

To remove an organizational unit:

1. Click Start|Programs|Administrative Tools|Active Directory Users and Computers.

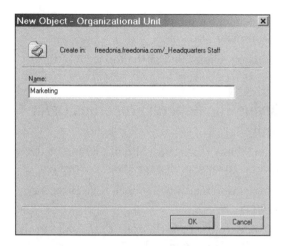

*Figure 5.6    The dialog box for creating a new organizational unit.*

2. Select the Users folder in the console tree or the folder in which the organizational unit is installed.

3. In the details pane, right-click on the name of the organizational unit.

4. On the context-sensitive menu, select Remove.

5. In the confirmation message box, click OK.

## Searching For An Organizational Unit

To search for an organizational unit:

1. Click Start|Programs|Administrative Tools|Active Directory Users and Computers.

2. In the console tree, right-click on the domain node or the organizational unit in which the group exists.

3. On the context-sensitive menu, select Find.

4. In the Find Users, Contacts, And Groups dialog box, select Organizational Units in the drop-down list at the top left. Make sure that the correct domain is selected in the drop-down list at the top right.

5. Enter as much information as you can in the Name field. Wildcard symbols can be used.

6. Click the Find Now button. The results will be displayed in the bottom pane.

7. To modify the properties of a found organizational unit, right-click on the object in the bottom pane, select Properties from

the context-sensitive menu, and modify the properties as described in the following sections.

8. To close the dialog box, click the X at the top right of the window.

## Viewing Or Modifying The General Properties Of An Organizational Unit

The General Properties of an organizational unit include its description and mailing address. To view or change these properties:

1. Click Start|Programs|Administrative Tools|Active Directory Users and Computers.

2. Select the Users folder in the console tree or the folder in which the organizational unit is installed.

3. In the details pane, right-click on the name of the organizational unit.

4. On the context-sensitive menu, select Properties.

5. Select the General page. (See Figure 5.7.)

6. Edit the information, as needed.

7. Click Apply to confirm your changes, and then click OK to exit the dialog box.

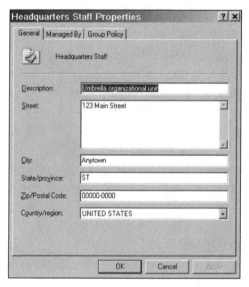

*Figure 5.7    The General Properties page for an organizational unit.*

## Viewing Or Modifying Information About An Organizational Unit's Manager

It is possible to assign a user to manage an organizational unit. To view or modify information about a unit's assigned manager:

1. Click Start|Programs|Administrative Tools|Active Directory Users and Computers.

2. Select the Users folder in the console tree or the folder in which the organizational unit is installed.

3. In the details pane, right-click on the name of the organizational unit.

4. On the context-sensitive menu, select Properties.

5. Select the Managed By page.

6. To add a manager or change the current one, click Change.

7. In the Select User Or Contact dialog box, select the user whom you wish to manage the organizational unit from the scrolling list, or enter the person's name in the edit box.

8. Click OK to return to the Managed By page.

9. Some information about the user will be displayed on the page. To view or modify the Properties settings in the user's account, click View. When you are finished, click OK, exit the Properties dialog box, and return to the Managed By page.

10. Click Apply to confirm your changes, and then click OK to exit the dialog box.

## Viewing Or Modifying The Group Policy Properties Of An Organizational Unit

An organizational unit inherits the default domain group policy, by default. You can customize the provisions of that policy for an organizational unit.

The subject of managing group policies is a complex one that is beyond the scope of this chapter. This section gives you an overview of how to use the group policy features of an organizational unit. (For detailed information on creating and modifying group policies, see Chapter 6.)

### Creating A New Policy For An Organizational Unit

To create a new policy for an organizational unit:

1. Click Start|Programs|Administrative Tools|Active Directory Users and Computers.

2. Select the Users folder in the console tree or the folder in which the organizational unit is installed.

3. In the details pane, right-click on the name of the organizational unit.

4. On the context-sensitive menu, select Properties.

5. Select the Group Policy page. The Default Domain Policy will be listed, as well as any other policies that have been attached to the organizational unit. (See Figure 5.8.)

6. To create a new policy for the organizational unit, click New, and then edit the name of the new policy, which defaults to New Group Policy Object.

7. Click Apply to confirm your changes, and then click OK to exit the dialog box.

After you create the new group policy, you will need to edit the policy, set its options, and review its properties.

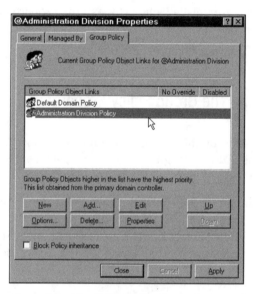

*Figure 5.8    The Group Policy Properties page for an organizational unit.*

### Setting Options For A Group Policy In An Organizational Unit

To set options for a policy:

1. Click Start|Programs|Administrative Tools|Directory Users and Computers.

2. Select the Users folder in the console tree or the folder in which the organizational unit is installed.

3. In the details pane, right-click on the name of the organizational unit.

4. On the context-sensitive menu, select Properties.

5. Select the Group Policy page. The Default Domain Policy will be listed, as well as any other policies that are attached to the organizational unit.

6. To set options for a policy, select the policy, and then click Options. (See Figure 5.9.) You can select either or both of the following two options for a selected policy:

   • *No Override*—By default, policy settings for a lower-level object in the Active Directory override equivalent settings in policies set at a higher level. For example, policies set for an organizational unit override the Default Domain Policy. Checking the No Override box prevents a lower-level policy from overriding the selected one.

   • *Disabled*—Checking this box disables the selected policy for the current container (in this case, an organizational unit).

7. Make your selections, and then click OK to return to the Group Policy page.

8. Click Apply to confirm your changes, and then click OK to exit the dialog box.

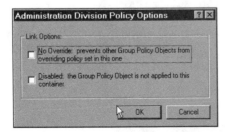

*Figure 5.9    The Options dialog box for a group policy.*

### Adding A Link To An Existing Policy In An Organizational Unit

If you have a group policy, perhaps for another organizational unit, that closely meets the needs of the current unit, you can create a link to it. To add a link to an existing policy:

1. Click Start|Programs|Administrative Tools|Directory Users and Computers.

2. Select the Users folder in the console tree or the folder in which the organizational unit is installed.

3. In the details pane, right-click on the name of the organizational unit.

4. On the context-sensitive menu, select Properties.

5. Select the Group Policy page. The Default Domain Policy will be listed, as well as any other policies that are attached to the organizational unit.

6. To link another policy to the organizational unit, click Add, and then select from the lists of available policies in the Add A Group Policy Object Link dialog box. There are separate lists of policies for domains and organizational units, sites, and the entire network. (See Figure 5.10.)

7. Make your selection, and then click OK to return to the Group Policy page.

8. Click Apply to confirm your changes, and then click OK to exit the dialog box.

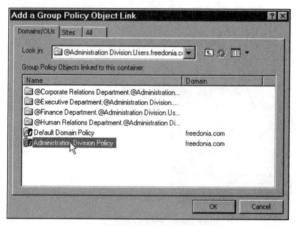

*Figure 5.10 The Add A Group Policy Object Link dialog box.*

### Deleting A Group Policy Link Or Object In An Organizational Unit

On the Group Policy properties page, you can delete a link to a policy or even the policy itself. To do this:

1. Click Start|Programs|Administrative Tools|Directory Management to open the Active Directory Users and Computers console.

2. Select the Users folder in the console tree or the folder in which the organizational unit is installed.

3. In the details pane, right-click on the name of the organizational unit.

4. On the context-sensitive menu, select Properties.

5. Select the Group Policy page. The Default Domain Policy will be listed, as well as any other policies that are attached to the organizational unit.

6. Select the policy or link that you wish to remove, and click Delete. You will see a Delete dialog box with two radio buttons:

   • Remove The Link From The List

   • Remove The Link And Delete The Group Policy Object

7. Select the appropriate option, and then click OK to return to the Group Policy page. (If you select the second option, you will see a Delete Group Policy Object dialog box. Click Yes to confirm the deletion.)

8. Click Apply to confirm your changes, and then click OK to exit the dialog box.

---

**TIP:** *Think of a link to a group policy object as being similar to a shortcut on the Windows desktop. Think of the group policy object itself as a file. If you delete a link to a group policy object, you delete only the link, not the object to which it points. The group policy object continues to exist, and you can create another link to it at any time. If you delete the object itself, however, you are deleting a file—and it is gone forever.*

---

### Editing A Group Policy Linked To An Organizational Unit

To edit a group policy linked to an organizational unit:

1. Click Start|Programs|Administrative Tools|Directory Users and Computers.

2. Select the Users folder in the console tree or the folder in which the organizational unit is installed.

*5. Managing Groups And Organizational Units*

3. In the details pane, right-click on the name of the organizational unit.

4. On the context-sensitive menu, select Properties.

5. Select the Group Policy page. The Default Domain Policy will be listed, as well as any other policies that are attached to the organizational unit.

6. Select the policy that you want to edit, and click Edit. This will load the Group Policy Editor in a separate console. (See Figure 5.11.) Depending on the size of the group policy, the editor may take a while to load.

7. Make your changes in the Group Policy Editor, and then close its console to return to the Group Policy properties page.

8. Click Apply to confirm your changes, and then click OK to exit the dialog box.

### Viewing The Properties Of A Group Policy Linked To An Organizational Unit

To view the properties of a group policy linked to an organizational unit:

1. Click Start|Programs|Administrative Tools|Directory Users and Computers.

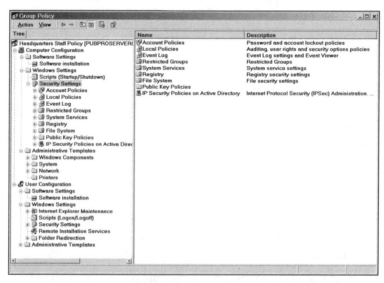

*Figure 5.11   The Group Policy Editor, with the policy options for an organizational unit. The console tree has been partially expanded to give you an idea of the number of areas covered in the policy.*

2. Select the Users folder in the console tree or the folder in which the organizational unit is installed.

3. In the details pane, right-click on the name of the organizational unit.

4. On the context-sensitive menu, select Properties.

5. Select the Group Policy page.

6. Select the policy whose properties you want to view, and click Properties. This action opens the Properties dialog box for the selected group policy. This dialog box is covered in detail in Chapter 6, so I will not go into detail here.

7. When you are finished, close the Properties dialog box for the group policy object to return to the Group Policy properties page for the organizational unit.

8. Click OK to exit the Properties dialog box for the organizational unit.

### Modifying The Hierarchy Of Group Policies In An Organizational Unit

There is a hierarchy of group policies in the Active Directory, beginning with the Default Domain Policy. Settings in lower-level policies, such as those that you create for an organizational unit, override equivalent settings in higher-level policies. If you have nested organizational units, each with its own group policy, you want to make sure that the group policies used by each organizational unit follow the hierarchy that you intend for them.

To modify the hierarchy of group policies linked to an organizational unit:

1. Click Start|Programs|Administrative Tools|Directory Users and Computers.

2. Select the Users folder in the console tree or the folder in which the organizational unit is installed.

3. In the details pane, right-click on the name of the organizational unit.

4. On the context-sensitive menu, select Properties.

5. Select the Group Policy page. The policies that apply to the organizational unit will be shown in their current hierarchy, usually with the Default Domain Policy at the top.

6. To change the position of a group policy, select the policy, and click the Up and Down buttons as needed.

**5. Managing Groups And Organizational Units**

7. Click Apply to confirm your changes, and then click OK to exit the Properties dialog box.

| Related solutions: | Found on page: |
|---|---|
| Managing Group Policies Assigned To Active Directory Objects | 196 |
| Viewing And Modifying The Properties Of A Group Policy | 207 |

## Moving An Organizational Unit

If the structure of your organizational units parallels the organizational structure of your company, there may be times when you need to move an organizational unit to another folder. Moving a unit to the home folder of another organizational unit causes the moved unit to be nested within it.

To move an organizational unit:

1. Click Start|Programs|Administrative Tools|Directory Users and Computers.

2. Select the Users folder in the console tree or the folder in which the organizational unit is installed.

3. In the details pane, right-click on the name of the organizational unit.

4. On the context-sensitive menu, select Move.

5. In the Move dialog box, expand the tree and select the folder to which you want to move the unit.

6. Click OK to exit the dialog box.

## Renaming An Organizational Unit

To rename an organizational unit:

1. Click Start|Programs|Administrative Tools|Directory Users and Computers.

2. Select the Users folder in the console tree or the folder in which the organizational unit is installed.

3. In the details pane, right-click on the name of the organizational unit.

4. On the context-sensitive menu, select Rename. This opens the name of the organizational unit in an edit box.

5. Edit the name, and then click outside of the edit box to confirm the change. If you make a mistake, press Esc while your cursor is still in the edit box.

# Delegating Administration Of An Organizational Unit

One of the advantages of organizational units is the capability to delegate the administration of a unit to a qualified user. If the structure of your organizational units mirrors the structure of your company, you can delegate the administration of a unit to a responsible executive or manager in the department served by the unit. If you have nested organizational units, each child unit can have its own administrator. Whether or not these child units are also the responsibility of the administrator of the parent unit is up to you. In any case, you can exercise very fine control over the rights and permissions that you give to your designated administrators.

---

**NOTE:** *You can also delegate administration at the domain and site levels.*

---

To delegate control of an organizational unit:

1. Click Start|Programs|Administrative Tools|Directory Users and Computers.

2. Select the Users folder in the console tree or the folder in which the organizational unit is installed.

3. In the details pane, right-click on the name of the organizational unit.

4. On the context-sensitive menu, select Delegate Control. This will open the Delegation Of Control Wizard. (See Figure 5.12.)

5. At the opening page, click Next to continue.

5. Managing Groups<br>And Organizational Units

*Figure 5.12   The Delegation Of Control Wizard.*

6.  On the Group Or User Selection page, the names of groups or users, if any, who currently have administrative authority over the organizational unit will be displayed. If you need to remove any of them, select the name, and click Remove.

7.  Click Add to add a new group or user to the list.

8.  In the Select Users, Computers, Or Groups dialog box, select the users or groups to be added and click Add.

9.  When you are ready, click OK to return to the Users Or Groups Selection page. The domain and logon name for each user will be added to the list. (See Figure 5.13.)

10. Click Next to continue.

11. On the Tasks To Delegate page, select one of the two radio buttons. If you select the Delegate The Following Common Tasks button, also select the groups of tasks that you want to delegate from the list in the main window. When you click Next, you will go directly to Step 16. If you select the Create A Custom Task To Delegate button, when you click Next you will continue with Step 12.

12. On the Active Directory Object Type page, you will find two radio buttons, with a scrolling list of object types under the second one.

    • To give the administrators wide-ranging control of the organizational unit, select the first radio button: Delegate Control Of The Folder. This is the default selection. The scrolling list is grayed-out when this is selected.

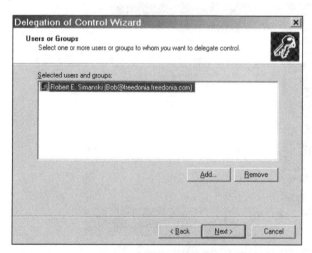

*Figure 5.13    The Users Or Groups Selection page showing the logon names of currently assigned administrators.*

- To limit their control, select the second radio button: Delegate Control Of The Following In The Folder. When this button is selected, the checkbox options in the list of object types become available. By default, none of the checkboxes are selected, so you have to decide on each one.

---

**NOTE:**   *The object types include many features of Windows 2000 Server, and explaining each one is beyond the scope of this book. You need to have a solid working knowledge of Windows 2000 Server to make full use of this feature. Therefore, I recommend that you limit your choices to those objects with which you are already familiar, such as organizational units and computer objects.*

---

13. Click Next to continue.

14. On the Permissions page, you will find a scrolling list of permissions that can be delegated. Underneath the list is a group of filter options. By default, only the first filter option, General, is selected. I recommend that you select the other two filters as well, so that you see all of the permissions available. The list of permissions is straightforward. If you select the first one, Full Control, all of the other boxes will be checked as well. The permissions that you select here apply only to those objects that you have already selected on the previous page. (See Figure 5.14.)

15. Click Next to continue.

16. On the Completing The Delegation Of Control Wizard page, you'll see a confirmation of the selections that you made. Click Back to change a selection, Cancel to abort the process, or Finish to confirm your choices and close the wizard.

5. Managing Groups And Organizational Units

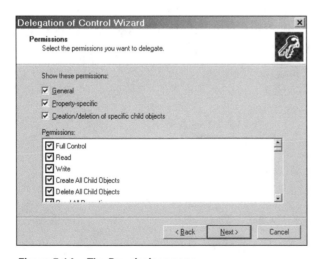

*Figure 5.14    The Permissions page.*

**Chapter 6**

# Using The Group Policy Editor

# *In Brief*

Group policies enable you to manage and control important aspects of the Windows settings and desktop environments of the users and computers on your network. These aspects include:

- Software installation settings
- Security settings
- Use of scripts at startup, shutdown, logon, and logoff
- Folder redirection
- Windows components such as Internet Explorer, Windows Explorer, Control Panel, the Windows desktop, Task Scheduler, Microsoft Management Console, and Windows Installer
- System options, including startup and logon
- Options for offline files and network and dial-up connections
- Printer management options

When you install Windows 2000 Server or Professional on a computer, the installation routine automatically creates a Local Computer Policy that affects only that local computer. Every Windows 2000 system, whether it is running the Server or Professional version of Windows 2000, has a Local Computer Policy. When you promote a server to a domain controller, Windows 2000 adds the Default Domain Policy, which affects the entire domain. Where there is a conflict, the Default Domain Policy takes precedence over the Local Computer Policy. If the server is the default controller for the domain, a third policy—the Default Domain Controller Policy—is also installed. The Default Domain Controller Policy affects only that controller. By default, all of its settings are unconfigured, so it has no effect unless you choose to configure one or more of its policies.

You can also create your own policies and apply them at the site, domain, or organizational-unit level. In addition, you can modify the order in which the policies attached to that level are applied. (See "The Order In Which Policies Are Applied," later in this chapter.)

The Microsoft Management Console tool that you use to create and modify group policies is the Group Policy snap-in. This snap-in uses the Group Policy Editor, which takes the place of the System Policy Editor in Windows NT 4 Server. The snap-in is installed as an extension to other snap-ins in the Active Directory Sites and Services and Active Directory Users and Computers consoles.

Normally, you access the Group Policy snap-in by opening the Group Policy page of the Properties dialog box for the selected site, domain, domain controller, organizational unit, or local computer. This is where you can apply group policies to the object in question, create new policies, or edit existing ones. Selecting an existing policy for editing opens the Group Policy Editor.

Group Policy can also be installed as a standalone snap-in. In that case, it is attached to a specific policy that you select. Thus, you can install more than one instance of Group Policy in the same console.

In this chapter, you will learn how to create and manage group policies, and you will become familiar with the Group Policy Editor. Most of the remaining chapters of this book also make extensive use of group policies and the Group Policy Editor.

# Structure Of A Group Policy

Each group policy is divided into two main sections: Computer Configuration and User Configuration. Computer Configuration policies are applied when a computer starts up, and User Configuration policies are applied when a user logs onto the network.

Each of these sections has three child folders: Software Settings, Windows Settings, and Administrative Templates. Although the two sets of child folders share the same names, and in some cases, similarly named child folders, their content varies. For example, the Windows Settings folder under Computer Configuration has many more security settings than the similarly named folder under User Configuration.

In some cases, the same setting appears under both Computer Configuration and User Configuration. However, it is often necessary to change both settings for the change to take effect.

All policies, including the ones that you create, have the same default structure and content, regardless of their purpose. The Default Domain Policy serves as a model for all group policies.

Detailed information about the structure of a group policy and the locations of all of the settings that it contains can be found in Appendix A. See Figures A.1 and A.2 in that appendix for the structures of the Computer Configuration and User Configuration sections, respectively.

# The Order In Which Policies Are Applied

When it starts up, Windows 2000 Server applies group policies in this order:

1. NT 4-style policies contained in the file ntconfig.pol. This affects only those systems that are still using Windows NT 4. When you upgrade a system to Windows 2000, these policies are discarded.

2. The Local Group Policy Object for the specific system being used.

3. Site-wide policies, in the order that you specify. Sites come before domains because sites can bridge more than one domain.

4. Domain-wide policies, in the order that you specify.

5. Organizational-unit policies, in the order that you specify. If there are nested organizational units, the policies for the parent unit are applied first, then the child units, and so on. Within each organizational unit, you can specify the order in which policies are applied.

By default, policies that are applied later override those applied earlier when there is a conflict. Let's say, for example, that you have enabled a specific setting in the Default Domain Policy and disabled the same setting in a policy that you have created for an organizational unit. The setting will be disabled for the members of that organizational unit and enabled for everyone else.

This is where the "Not Configured" or "Not Defined" option for group policy settings becomes very important. (The two terms are used interchangeably by Microsoft.) Because each group policy has essentially the same structure and policy settings, it is very easy to inadvertently create conflicts. For this reason, most of the settings in the Default Domain Policy, and all of the settings in both the Default Domain Computer Policy and new policies that you create, are unconfigured by default. See the section called "A Strategy For Using Group Policies," later in this chapter, for suggestions on how to avoid problems with conflicting policies.

---

***TIP:*** *If you find yourself making extensive use of group policies, I strongly recommend that you create your own custom Microsoft Management Console for group policies. After you create the console, install one instance of the snap-in for each policy that you want to manage with this tool. This will make it much easier and faster for you to access and modify all of your group policies, compare settings in different policies, and resolve conflicts between policies that are applied early in the startup process (such as the Default Domain Policy) and those that are applied later (such as policies for organizational units). See Chapter 2 for information on creating a custom console.*

---

# Attaching Group Policies To Active Directory Objects

As noted earlier, you can apply group policies at the site, domain, and organizational-unit levels. As we have seen, Windows 2000 also applies two policies—the Local Computer Policy and the Default Domain Controller Policy—to specific computers. Although you can modify these policies, you do not have the option of creating and applying new ones at the computer level. Policies apply to computers and users within the level to which the policy is attached. Thus, the Default Domain Policy applies to all computers and users within the domain, whereas a policy created for an organizational unit applies only to computers and users who are members of that unit.

You cannot attach a group policy to a group. Although the term "group policy" may be a confusing misnomer, security groups are still important to the effective use of group policies. The reason is that a group policy must be specifically applied to an Active Directory object— such as a group, computer, or user—before it will have any effect on that object.

You apply a group policy to an object by adding that object to the Security properties of the specific group policy. Groups are among the types of objects that you can add. Although group policies apply only to users and computers, it is much easier to add a user to a group, and then add the group to the Security list of a group policy, than it is to add each individual user to the list.

For example, when you create a new user, that user automatically becomes a member of the domain to which you have added him. In addition, Windows 2000 Server automatically adds the new user to the built-in Authenticated Users group. The group is already on the Security list of the Default Domain Policy and the policy has already been applied to that group. Because of this, every new user added to the domain is automatically affected by the settings in the policy.

Suppose that you want to create a group policy that prevents certain users from modifying certain aspects of their Windows environments. You would begin by creating and populating a security group that contains those users to whom the policy should apply. Next, you would create the new policy, add the group to the policy's Security list, and select the option to apply the policy to that group. (See the Immediate Solutions section of this chapter for instructions on how to do this.)

To implement the policy, you must now add it to the appropriate level in the Active Directory. If you add it to the domain level, the policy will apply to all users in the domain who are members of the new group.

On the other hand, you might want the policy to apply to members of only two out of three organizational units. In that case, you would first move the appropriate members of the group from the Users folder to the folders for their appropriate organizational units, if you have not already done so. Next, you would attach the policy to the two organizational units to which you want it to apply.

In this latter case, the policy would affect only those members of the group who belong to the organizational units to which you had attached the new policy. Group members who were in the third organizational unit, to which you had not attached the policy, would not be affected by it. However, if you should move a group member from the third unit to one of the other two units, she would be affected by the policy after you moved her account. The reverse would happen if you were to move a group member from one of the first two units to the third one.

Also, even though the policy would be attached to an organizational unit, members of the unit who were not members of the security group to which the policy had been applied would not be affected by it. Thus, you could attach several group policies to the organizational unit, each affecting only those members of the unit who were also members of groups to which the policies have been applied. This means, for example, that you could have a very liberal group policy for directors and senior staff, a more-restrictive policy for middle managers, and a very restrictive policy for support staff.

# A Strategy For Using Group Policies

In order to use group policies effectively, you must keep in mind the order in which they are applied. (See "The Order In Which Policies Are Applied" earlier in the chapter.) Also, whereas you can control the order in which most policies are applied, you cannot control the fact that the Local Group Policy attached to the computer that you are using is applied before any of the other Windows 2000 group policies.

Because of this, you may find that attempting to override certain policy settings in the Local Group Policy with opposite settings in other policies, such as the Default Domain Policy, does not always work. For example, if you create a logon message in the Local Group Policy attached to a specific computer and then configure the same setting in the Default Domain Policy to not use a logon message, you may find that you still get the logon message when that particular computer starts up. Hopefully, this bug will be corrected in the shipping release of Windows 2000. Perhaps the reason is that the logon message setting is implemented fairly early in the startup process, before all of the network connections needed to implement the additional policies have been made.

Because the Default Domain Policy affects everything in your domain and is executed ahead of most other policies, I recommend that you begin by reviewing each of the settings in the policy. Most of the settings, by default, are not configured; those that are configured, such as the default maximum lifetime of user passwords, should not cause you any great problems.

Nevertheless, because the Default Domain Policy serves as a baseline policy, you may want to enable or modify those settings that can safely be applied to your entire domain. For example, you might want to set a minimum length for passwords or enable settings relating to features that you intend to use, such as user profiles and offline files. Be aware that some settings must be enabled in both the Computer Configuration and User Configuration areas before they will take effect.

Be judicious when changing the settings in this policy. If in doubt, it is best to leave them unconfigured or unchanged from their defaults. Also, be aware that with settings that require you to configure them after you have enabled them (by setting one or more default parameters, for example), selecting the "Not Configured" option does not disable the settings altogether. Rather, it means that they will use their default parameters. Therefore, always be sure to read the help text in the Explain tab that appears in many Group Policy Editor dialog boxes.

New policies that you create, such as those that are attached to organizational units, are normally applied after the Default Domain Policy. By default, all settings in a new policy are unconfigured, so that they will not cause a conflict with existing policies.

Use these policies primarily to enable or disable settings that are unconfigured in the Default Domain Policy. As much as possible, avoid overriding settings that are configured in the latter policy. Try to keep potential conflicts to a minimum. Be particularly careful when it comes to security settings.

In the Default Domain Policy, the settings in the Administrative Templates areas in the Computer Configuration and User Configuration sections are unconfigured by default. Therefore, you can modify their settings in policies that are applied after the Default Domain Policy without having to worry about conflicts. These areas deal with the user interface, among other things, and contain most of the settings that you are likely to want to modify.

# Local Computer Policy

Although configuring the Default Domain Policy to meet the needs of your domain is important, you must not overlook the Local Computer Policy that is installed on each Windows 2000 computer in your system. The reason is that although most of the settings in the Default Domain Policy are unconfigured, many of the settings in the default Local Computer Policy, especially those related to security, are configured by default.

The reason that this is of concern is that the Local Computer Policy is applied when the computer is started, before the Default Domain Policy. Therefore, even if you leave these settings unconfigured in the Default Domain Policy (allowing those that have parameters to use their defaults), you may find that the settings are still enabled because the Not Configured option in the Default Domain Policy settings allows the configured settings of the Local Computer Policy to remain in effect.

Furthermore, when you install Windows 2000 on a system, it automatically creates default groups for the local computer, as well as a default administrator account. One of these groups, Power Users, is not among the default built-in groups installed on a domain controller. Access to the computer is automatically granted to specific groups. Users who are not members of those groups may have difficulty logging onto the computer.

Obviously, you need to exercise tight control over the users who can log onto a domain controller or other server. Therefore, the groups permitted by default to log onto a system running Windows 2000 Server are probably adequate for most purposes. When it comes to workstations, however, you probably want to allow liberal access, particularly if you are using roaming profiles where the user's Windows settings are available on any compatible computer.

This would not be a concern if Windows 2000 Professional included Authenticated Users among the default groups that are granted access to the workstation on which it is installed. When I attempted to log on as a domain user who was not a member of any of the workstation's default groups, in order to test the group policies that I had created, I was unsuccessful. Before I could log on, I had to add the user to the local users and groups permitted to use the workstation. Eventually, I created a Microsoft Management Console, added the Group Policy snap-in, attached it to the Local Computer Policy, and added the Authenticated Users group to the groups allowed to log onto the system.

Fortunately, the results panes that show the settings available in each part of the Local Computer Policy display both the local policy and the effective policy for each setting. Where there is a conflict, the effective policy—that is, the one applied last—overrides the local policy. If the setting has not been configured in a "later" policy, however, the setting in the Local Computer Policy remains in effect.

**6. Using The Group Policy Editor**

# *Immediate Solutions*

## Managing Group Policies Assigned To Active Directory Objects

You can use the Properties pages of a domain, site, or organizational unit to assign existing group policies to the object, create new policies, edit policies assigned to the object, delete policies, or view the properties of an assigned policy.

### Assigning An Existing Group Policy To An Active Directory Object

To assign a group policy to a compatible Active Directory object:

1. Click Start|Programs|Administrative Tools|Active Directory Users And Computers.
2. Expand the console tree to expose the object to which you want to attach a policy.
3. Right-click on the object. On the context-sensitive menu, select Properties.
4. Select the Group Policy page. (See Figure 6.1.)
5. Click the Add button to open the Add A Group Policy Object Link dialog box.
6. In the Look In window, select a domain, site, or organizational unit that already contains the group policy that you want. If in doubt, select the All tab to view a list of all available policies. (See Figure 6.2.)
7. Click OK to add the selected policy to the current object.
8. If there are several policies assigned to the current object and you need to change the order in which they are applied, select the policy to be moved, and click the Up or Down buttons as needed.
9. Click Apply to confirm your changes, and then click OK to exit the Properties dialog box.

| Related solutions: | Found on page: |
|---|---|
| Opening A Preconfigured System Administration Console | 33 |
| Opening A Custom Administrative Tool | 34 |

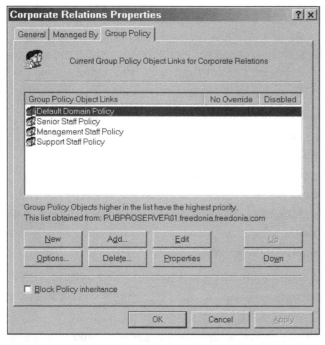

Figure 6.1    *The Group Policy page of the Properties dialog box for an organizational unit.*

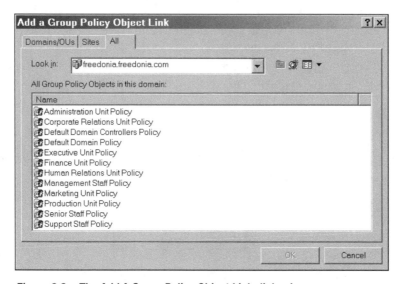

Figure 6.2    *The Add A Group Policy Object Link dialog box.*

## Setting Options For An Assigned Policy

Using the Options dialog box on the Group Policy Properties page, you can prevent other group policies from overriding the settings in the selected policy or prevent the policy from being applied to the current object.

To access the Options dialog box:

1. Click Start|Programs|Administrative Tools|Active Directory Users And Computers.

2. Expand the console tree to expose the object to which the policy has been attached.

3. Right-click on the object. On the context-sensitive menu, select Properties.

4. Select the Group Policy page.

5. Select the policy for which you want to set options.

6. Click the Options button to open the Options dialog box for the selected policy. (See Figure 6.3.)

7. Select the No Override checkbox to prevent other policies from overriding the settings in the selected policy.

8. Select the Disabled checkbox to disable the policy in the current object.

9. Click OK to confirm your selections and return to the Group Policy Properties page.

10. Click Apply to confirm your changes, and then click OK to exit the Properties dialog box.

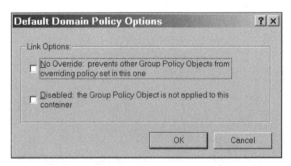

*Figure 6.3    The Options dialog box for the Default Domain Policy.*

## Creating A New Group Policy For An Active Directory Object

From the Group Policy Properties page, you can create a new group policy and apply it to the current Active Directory object. To create a new group policy for an Active Directory object:

1. Click Start|Programs|Administrative Tools|Active Directory Users And Computers.

2. Expand the console tree to expose the object to which you want to attach a policy.

3. Right-click on the object. On the context-sensitive menu, select Properties.

4. Select the Group Policy page.

5. Click the New button to create a new policy and assign it to the object. Its default name will be New Group Policy Object.

6. Change the default name to a more-suitable one.

7. By default, the new policy will be disabled; that is, it will not be applied to the current object. To enable the policy, click the Options button, uncheck the Disabled box, and click OK to return to the Group Policy Properties page.

8. If there are several policies assigned to the current object and you need to change the order in which they are applied, select the policy to be moved and click the Up or Down buttons as needed.

9. Click Apply to confirm your changes, and then click OK to exit the Properties dialog box.

**NOTE:** *By default, all of the settings in your new policy will be unconfigured; therefore, you will need to edit the policy. See "Editing A Group Policy Assigned To An Active Directory Object" later in this chapter.*

## Deleting A Policy From An Active Directory Object

From the Group Policy Properties page, you can delete a link to an assigned group policy or even delete the policy itself from the Active Directory. To delete the link to a policy from an Active Directory object:

1. Click Start|Programs|Administrative Tools|Active Directory Users And Computers.

2. Expand the console tree to expose the object that contains the policy that you want to delete.

**6. Using The Group Policy Editor**

3. Right-click on the object. On the context-sensitive menu, select Properties.

4. Select the Group Policy page.

5. Select the policy that you want to delete and click the Delete button. This will open the Delete dialog box. (See Figure 6.4.)

6. Choose the appropriate radio button for the action that you want. The first option, removing the link to the policy from the current list, is like deleting a shortcut on the Windows desktop. Only the shortcut is deleted, not the object to which it is linked. The second option not only removes the link from the list, but also deletes the group policy entirely. You are deleting the file itself, not just the shortcut to it.

7. Click OK to confirm your selection and return to the Group Policy Properties page.

8. Click Apply to confirm your changes, and then click OK to exit the Properties dialog box.

## Editing A Group Policy Assigned To An Active Directory Object

From the Group Policy Properties page, you can edit a group policy that has been assigned to the current Active Directory object. To edit a group policy assigned to an Active Directory object:

1. Click Start|Programs|Administrative Tools|Active Directory Users And Computers.

2. Expand the console tree to expose the object to which you have attached the policy.

3. Right-click on the object. On the context-sensitive menu, select Properties.

4. Select the Group Policy page.

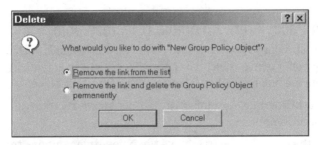

*Figure 6.4   The Delete dialog box, which is used for removing a group policy from the current object.*

5. Select the policy that you want to edit and click the Edit button. This will open the policy in the Group Policy Editor.

6. In the console tree pane, expand the tree until the first setting that you want to edit appears in the results pane. (See Figure 6.5.)

7. In the results pane, double-click on the setting that you want to edit.

8. Follow the instructions in the dialog box, make your changes, and return to the main Group Policy Editor window.

9. Repeat Steps 7 and 8 to make other changes, as needed.

10. When you finish, click Console|Exit to close the Group Policy Editor and return to the Group Policy Properties page.

11. Click OK to exit the Properties dialog box.

## Working With Dialog Boxes In The Group Policy Editor

With the hundreds, if not thousands, of settings that are available in every group policy, it is impossible to provide instructions for them all in a book of this size. You will find, however, that the dialog boxes, for the most part, are relatively simple and straightforward. This section covers some of the commonly used types.

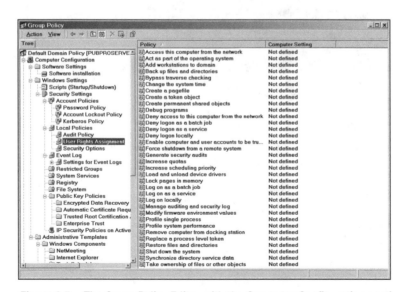

*Figure 6.5    The Group Policy Editor with the Computer Configuration section fully expanded.*

Many dialog boxes, such as the one in Figure 6.6, consist simply of Enabled and Disabled radio buttons, and a checkbox for excluding the setting from the current configuration.

By default, the box is usually unchecked, causing the radio buttons and their options to be grayed-out. To reveal the radio button options, check the box. The option that you choose (Enabled, Disabled, or not configured) will appear under the Stored Template Setting column for the selected setting.

Other dialog boxes, such as the one in Figure 6.7, require you to set one or more parameters if you enable the option. To set configuration parameters, check the Define This Policy Setting In The Template checkbox, and then follow the instructions in the dialog box.

A few dialog boxes, such as the one in Figure 6.8, are more involved. They require you to add something, such as a user or group, to a list. Clicking the Add button opens a second dialog box, such as the familiar Select Users Or Groups dialog box.

Some dialog boxes, such as the one in Figure 6.9, require you to create or modify parameter strings. This dialog box is typical of the ones

*Figure 6.6    A simple dialog box for enabling or disabling a setting, or leaving it unconfigured.*

*Figure 6.7    A dialog box that requires a configuration parameter.*

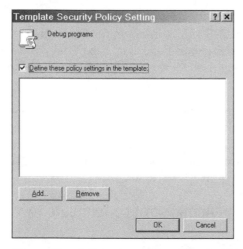

*Figure 6.8    A dialog box with options to add or remove objects in a list.*

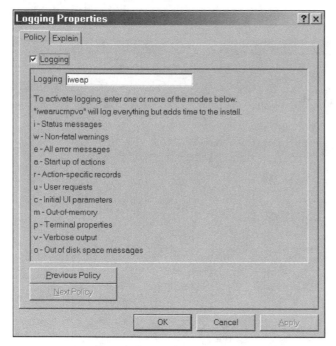

*Figure 6.9    A dialog box commonly used for Administrative Templates settings.*

used for Administrative Templates settings. They often have an Explain tab page with applicable help information for the setting, as in Figure 6.10. Also, they have Previous Policy and Next Policy buttons to help you navigate quickly through the other settings in the same window.

In the case of the Administrative Templates dialog boxes, where you are simply enabling or disabling a setting, or leaving it unconfigured, you will find only a checkbox instead of radio buttons and a checkbox. Clicking the box toggles through the enabled (checked), disabled (unchecked), or unconfigured (grayed-out) state.

## Adding Or Removing An Administrative Template To A Group Policy

You cannot modify the content of the Software Settings or Windows Settings folders, or of their child folders and branches. However, you can modify the content of the Administrative Templates folders by

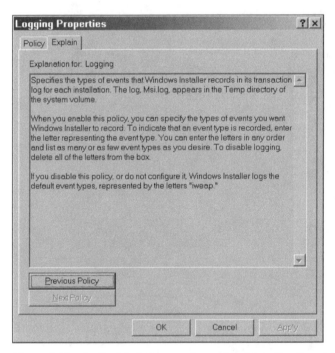

*Figure 6.10   An Explain help page for an Administrative Templates dialog box.*

adding templates. Administrative templates are ASCII text files with .adm extensions.

By default, Windows 2000 Server installs two templates, system.adm and inetres.adm. Windows 2000 Server also includes nine other templates. Most of them, however, are essentially empty shells, with few if any settings. They appear to be intended for use as starting points for developing your own templates, and have little, if any, value in their default state.

Administrative templates directly modify keys in the Windows 2000 Registry. Creating or modifying a template requires that you understand both basic programming concepts and the Registry. These subjects are beyond the scope of this book.

If you want to add an administrative template to a group policy, here is how to do it:

1. Open the policy, as described in the "Editing A Group Policy Assigned To An Active Directory Object" section earlier in the chapter.

2. Expand the tree to expose the Administrative Templates folder in the Computer Configuration section. (Templates added here will also apply to the Administrative Templates area under the User Configuration section.)

3. Right-click on the folder and select Add/Remove Templates from the context-sensitive menu. This opens the Add/Remove Templates dialog box with a list of installed templates.

4. To add a template, click the Add button, which will show you a list of template files in the \WINNT\Inf folder. (See Figure 6.11.) Select the templates that you want to install (multiple selections are allowed) and click the Open button.

5. When you return to the main Add/Remove Templates dialog box, click Close to return to the Group Policy Editor. The content of the Administrative Templates folder will change to reflect the new template.

6. To remove an installed template, repeat Steps 1 through 3, select the template to be removed, click the Remove button, and then click Close.

**6. Using The Group Policy Editor**

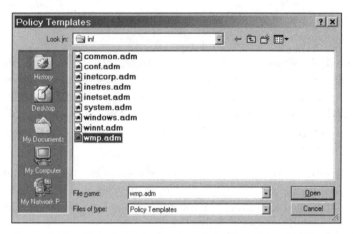

*Figure 6.11    The administrative templates that ship with Windows 2000 Server.*

## Preventing Higher-Level Policies From Being Applied To The Current Object

You can prevent higher-level policies from being applied to the current object. For example, if the current object is an organizational unit, you can prevent policies assigned at the site or domain level from affecting the unit. To do this:

1. Click Start|Programs|Administrative Tools|Active Directory Users And Computers.

2. Expand the console tree to expose the appropriate object.

3. Right-click on the object. On the context-sensitive menu, select Properties.

4. Select the Group Policy page.

5. Select the Block Policy Inheritance checkbox at the bottom left of the page.

6. Click Apply to confirm your action, and then click OK to close the Properties dialog box.

**WARNING!**   *Microsoft discourages the use of this feature in its documentation for Windows 2000 Server because of the problems that it can cause in tracing Group Policy-related conflicts. I mention it here mainly because you are bound to see it and wonder about its purpose.*

# Viewing And Modifying The Properties Of A Group Policy

Group policies, as with other features of the Active Directory, are considered objects. Each one has its own Properties page. On these pages, you can modify the security and access control properties of the selected group policy.

## Viewing The Properties Of A Group Policy

To view or modify the properties of a group policy:

1. Click Start|Programs|Administrative Tools|Active Directory Users And Computers.

2. Select an object to which the group policy has been attached. It can be a site, domain, or organizational unit.

3. Right-click on the object. On the context-sensitive menu, select Properties.

4. Select the Group Policy page. The Default Domain Policy will be listed, as well as any other policies that are attached to the object.

5. Select the policy that you want and click the Properties button. This will open a Properties dialog box with three pages: General, Links, and Security.

   - *General*—Displays a brief revision history of the policy. It also includes two checkboxes that enable you to disable the computer- and user-configuration settings in the policy. This should be done only if these settings are not needed. Disabling them may help to improve system performance.

   - *Links*—Enables you to search for other sites, domains, and organizational units that use the policy.

   - *Security*—Displays the groups whose members have permissions relating to the group policy. (See Figure 6.12.) This page holds the most interest for us. The actions that you can take on it are described in the next two Immediate Solutions.

**6. Using The Group Policy Editor**

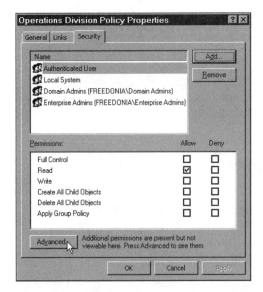

*Figure 6.12    The Security properties page for a group policy.*

## Viewing And Modifying The Basic Security Properties Of A Group Policy

To modify the basic security properties of a group policy object:

1. Click Start|Programs|Administrative Tools|Active Directory Users And Computers.

2. Select an object to which the group policy has been attached. It can be a site, domain, or organizational unit.

3. Right-click on the object. On the context-sensitive menu, select Properties.

4. Select the Group Policy page. The Default Domain Policy will be listed, as well as any other policies that are attached to the organizational unit.

5. Select the policy that you want and click the Properties button. This will open a Properties dialog box with three pages: General, Links, and Security.

6. Select the Security page. You will see a list of groups with security permissions for the group policy object.

7. To modify the permissions for a group, select the group in the top pane, and use the checkboxes in the lower pane to change the settings.

8. To add a group to the list, click Add. In the Select Users, Computers, Or Groups dialog box, make your selection and click Add. (Multiple selections are allowed.) When you are finished, click OK to return to the Security Properties page.

9. To remove a group from the list, select the group and click Remove.

10. To modify the hierarchy of the group policies on the list, select the policy to be moved, and click the Up or Down button as needed. Settings in a lower-level policy will override those of a higher-level policy.

11. When you are finished, click Apply to confirm your changes, and then click OK to exit the Properties dialog box.

## Viewing And Modifying The Access Control Settings Of A Group Policy

You can fine-tune the security settings that apply to users and groups that have permissions to modify a group policy object. By using advanced security features, you can modify the settings in the Access Control List. To view or modify these settings:

1. Click Start|Programs|Administrative Tools|Active Directory Users And Computers.

2. Select an object to which the group policy has been attached. It can be a site, domain, or organizational unit.

3. Right-click on the object. On the context-sensitive menu, select Properties.

4. Select the Group Policy page.

5. Select the desired policy and click Properties. This will open a dialog box with three pages: General, Links, and Security.

6. Select the Security page, and then click Advanced to open the Access Control Settings dialog box. (See Figure 6.13.)

7. This dialog box has three pages that list the permissions, auditing, and owner settings for the group policy. On each page, you can view or edit the specific settings for each group.

8. To view or edit the permission settings for a group, switch to the Permission page, select the group, and click View/Edit. This will display the Permission Entry dialog box, with separate pages for the object itself and its properties. (See Figure 6.14.)

**6. Using The Group Policy Editor**

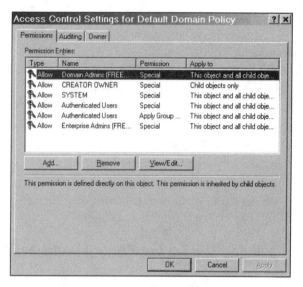

*Figure 6.13    The Access Control Settings dialog box for a group policy.*

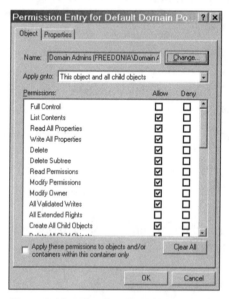

*Figure 6.14    The Permission Entry dialog box for the Domain Admins*
*security group.*

9. Use the checkboxes to make your changes, and then click OK
   to return to the Access Control Settings dialog box.

10. Switch to the Auditing page, and repeat Steps 8 and 9 to view
    the auditing settings for a group. The Auditing Entry dialog box
    is essentially similar to the Permissions Entry dialog box.

11. To view or change the owner of the group policy object, switch to the Owner page. The name of the current owner (usually the system administrator or one of the administrative security groups) will be displayed, along with other users and groups with the required security permissions. To change the owner, select the appropriate user or group, and click Apply.

12. Click OK to return to the Access Control Settings dialog box.

13. Click Apply to confirm your changes to the advanced settings and return to the Security Properties page.

14. Click Apply to confirm all changes to the properties of the group policy object, and then click OK to exit the Properties dialog box.

# Creating Your Own Group Policy Administrative Tool

You'll find it much easier to edit group policies if you create your own custom group policy administrative tool using the Microsoft Management Console. Refer to Chapter 2 for detailed information on creating custom consoles. To create your own group policy manager:

1. Click Start|Run and enter this command to open a new empty console:

```
mmc /a
```

2. Click Console|Save. This will open the Save As dialog box.

3. Navigate to the system32 folder, which contains all of the preconfigured consoles that ship with Windows 2000 Server.

4. Name the file using the MS-DOS 8+3 naming convention, and be sure to use an .msc extension.

---

**NOTE:** *Microsoft Management Console 1.2 shipped with beta 3, release candidate 1, which was used during the writing of this chapter. In this version, the default extension is .msc. Earlier versions used an .mmc extension. Some of the consoles that shipped with the beta were created in the earlier version. If you save one of these consoles, you'll get a message informing you that it was created with the earlier version of the software. This message will give you the option of saving the file in the new format. You can safely allow this.*

---

6. Using The Group Policy Editor

5. Click Save to return to the new console.

6. Click Console|Options, and then click the Console tab.

7. In the top window, give the console a meaningful name, such as "Group Policy Admin Tool".

8. Click Apply, and then click OK to return to the main console window.

9. Click Console|Add/Remove Snap-in to begin populating the console.

10. Select the Standalone page and make sure that Console Root is selected in the Snap-in Added To drop-down list box.

11. Click Add to open the Add Standalone Snap-in dialog box.

12. Select Group Policy, and then click Add. This will open the Select Group Policy Object dialog box.

13. Select the group policy that you want to add to your console. For now, accept the default selection, Local Computer.

14. Click Finish to return to the Add Standalone Snap-in dialog box.

15. Repeat Step 12.

16. In the Select Group Policy Object dialog box, click the Browse button. This will open the Browser for a Group Policy Object dialog box.

17. Select the All page, which will show you a list of all available policies.

18. Select the Default Domain Policy, click OK to return to the Select Group Policy Object dialog box, and then click Finish.

19. Repeat Steps 12, 16, 17, and 18 to add the Default Domain Controller policy.

20. Repeat Steps 12, 16, 17, and 18 for each additional policy that you want to manage, substituting the desired policy in Step 18.

21. When you have finished, click Close to close the Add Standalone Snap-in dialog box and return to the Add/Remove Snap-in dialog box.

22. Select one of the policies that you just installed, and then select the Extensions page.

23. Make sure that the Add All Extensions box is checked, so that all extensions that can be added to the Group Policy snap-in will be installed. The box is checked by default, so if it is checked for

one policy, it will be checked for all of them. If the box is checked, click Cancel to return to the previous dialog box, and then go to Step 26.

24. If the box is not checked, check it, and then click OK to return to the previous dialog.

25. Repeat Steps 22, 23, and 24 for all other policies.

26. Click OK to close the Add/Remove Snap-in dialog box and return to the main console window.

27. Click Console|Save to save the new configuration.

The policies that you have added will appear in the console tree pane. Your new tool should look something like Figure 6.15. Expand each policy as needed until the desired setting appears in the results pane.

| Related solutions: | Found on page: |
|---|---|
| Customizing A Console | 38 |
| Adding A Snap-in | 39 |
| Creating A Console From Scratch | 43 |

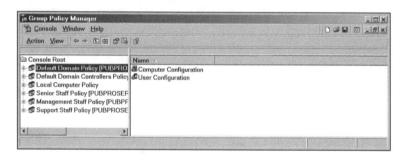

*Figure 6.15   A custom console for editing group policies.*

6. Using The Group Policy Editor

# Managing User Profiles

# In Brief

The first time that you log onto a computer running Windows 2000 or Windows NT 4, the operating system creates a custom user profile for you. This user profile contains your custom Windows work environment, such as your display settings and your network and printer connections. As you modify your environment, the operating system updates your user profile automatically.

Windows 98 and 95 also support user profiles; however, you must specifically enable the feature if you want to allow each user to have his own custom settings. The default is for all users to share the same settings. (See "Enabling User Profiles In Windows 98 And Windows 95" in the "Immediate Solutions" section of this chapter.)

## Advantages Of User Profiles

User profiles offer a number of advantages to both your users and to you as an administrator. Here are some of the advantages to users:

- Several users can share the same computer. Each user can create her own Windows environment without affecting the environments of other users. When a user logs on, her custom settings are loaded.

- User profiles can be stored on a server as well as on a local workstation, enabling them to roam with the user from one workstation to another. When a user logs onto any computer running Windows 2000, Windows NT 4, Windows 98, or Windows 95, her profile is downloaded to the local workstation. Changes that she makes to her Windows environment are saved to the network copy of the profile when she logs off.

---

**TIP:**   *In order for roaming profiles to work properly, either the video hardware on the various workstations must be similar or the profile must use lowest-common-denominator settings. For example, if the profile calls for a display resolution of 1024x768 pixels per inch and a color depth of 24-bit true color, then all of the systems that the user normally uses must support these settings. If the user were to log onto a system that did not support these settings, serious display problems would occur and, in some cases, the monitor could be damaged. Therefore, in creating a roaming user profile, you should make certain that the settings are compatible with all of the workstations that the user is likely to use.*

*In addition, you may want to modify the appropriate group policy to prevent the user from modifying these settings. Open the appropriate group policy and expand the User Configuration, Administrative Templates, Windows Components, Control Panel, and Display folders in the console tree pane. In the results pane, enable either Hide The Settings Tab or Prohibit User From Running Display Control Panel. See Chapter 6 for more information on creating and editing group policies.*

As an administrator, you can do the following:

- Create user profiles that are geared to the needs of specific users or groups of users.

- Create mandatory profiles that the user cannot modify. Mandatory profiles are stored on the network and downloaded to the local computer when the user logs on. Although users might change the settings during a session, these changes will not be saved when they log off.

- Specify defaults for all user profiles.

# Types Of User Profiles

There are three types of user profiles: local, roaming, and mandatory:

- *Local user profiles*—Local profiles are stored on the local hard drive of the user's current workstation. Changes to the local user profile affect only that workstation.

- *Roaming user profiles*—Roaming profiles are created by administrators and stored on a server. You define the location of the profile in the Properties settings for the user's account. When the user logs onto a workstation, the profile is downloaded from the server and copied to the workstation. If the workstation already contains a local profile for the user, it is updated. Any changes made to the profile are copied back to the server when the user logs off.

- *Mandatory user profiles*—Mandatory profiles are roaming profiles that cannot be permanently changed by the user. You can use mandatory profiles for groups of users, as well as for individual users. Although a user can change settings temporarily during a session, the changes are not copied to the server or saved to the local hard drive when the user logs off. Only system administrators can change a mandatory profile.

The operating system creates a local profile automatically the first time that you log onto a workstation. Roaming and mandatory profiles are created manually by network administrators.

# Roaming Profiles

From the standpoint of reducing your administrative workload, roaming profiles (the mandatory variety, in particular) have great potential. With a roaming profile, the user can log onto any Windows 2000, Windows NT 4, Windows 98, or Windows 95 system in your domain. When a user logs onto the network for the first time after you have created his roaming profile, the Active Directory authenticates the user and his profile. Once it has been authenticated, the copy of the profile stored on the server is downloaded to his workstation. This includes all of the user's settings and documents that have been stored on the server.

**TIP:**   If the workstation has a local profile for the user that was created before you implemented the roaming profile, the user will be asked to choose between the two. Be sure to instruct the user to select the network version.

When the user logs off, a copy of his profile is saved to both the local workstation and the network server. The next time the user logs onto the network, if he already has a local user profile on the current workstation, it is compared with the profile on the network and updated, if necessary.

# Cached Profiles

Roaming profiles are an important part of IntelliMirror, which provides for the synchronized caching of user files on both the network and the local system. (See Chapter 13 for more information.)

If the server is not available, and there is a cached copy of the user's profile on the workstation, the local copy is used. If the user has never logged onto that particular workstation, the operating system creates a new local user profile. In this case, the network copy of the roaming profile is not updated when the user logs off, even if the server becomes available before then.

**NOTE:**   If the local user profile is created or used because the network copy is not available, it becomes the more recent of the two copies. If the user logs onto the same workstation in her next network session, she will be asked to specify whether to use the newer local copy of her user profile or the older one on the network. If you have set up the original user profile, you may prefer that she choose the older version on the network. The user must take care, however, to make sure that files in the My Documents and My Pictures folders are not overwritten with earlier versions. (She will be given the option of preserving the newer versions during the copying process.)

**7. Managing User Profiles**

# Makeup Of A User Profile

In general, you create user profiles—including ones designed to serve as templates for other profiles—on a local workstation. If a profile is to be a roaming or mandatory profile, you then copy it to the server where it is to be stored. Generally, you place them under a shared folder that you designate for user profiles—for example, c:\profiles.

When they generate a user profile, Windows 2000 and Windows NT 4 (as well as Windows 98 and 95, to a lesser extent) create a hierarchy of folders to contain the user's custom settings. The name of the main folder is the same as the user's logon name. This main folder contains one of the key components of each user profile—a file that contains the Registry portion of the profile. On Windows 2000 and Windows NT 4 workstations, the file is called ntuser.dat. On Windows 98 and Windows 95 workstations, the file is called user.dat.

Under the main folder for the specific user profile is a tree of child folders. Table 7.1 contains a list of the folders created on Windows 2000, Windows NT 4, Windows 98, and Windows 95 workstations.

*Table 7.1 Folders in a user profile.*

| Folder | Content | Platform |
| --- | --- | --- |
| Application Data | Data created and used by application programs. For example, the folder might contain a custom dictionary used by a word processor. | Windows 2000 only; in Windows NT 4, this folder is not part of the user profiles |
| Cookies | Files created by Internet Explorer. | All |
| Desktop | Items found on the user's desktop, including files, shortcuts, and folders. | All |
| Favorites | Shortcuts to bookmarked pages on the Internet. | Windows 2000 only |
| My Documents | Default folder for the user's document files. | Windows 2000 only |
| My Pictures | Default folder for the user's graphics files. A child folder of My Documents. | Windows 2000 only |
| Nethood | Shortcuts to items and locations on your network. | All |
| Printhood | Shortcuts to printer folder items. | Windows 2000 and Windows NT 4 only |
| Recent | Shortcuts to recently used documents and folders. | All |

*7. Managing User Profiles*

*(continued)*

**Table 7.1    Folders in a user profile** (continued).

| Folder | Content | Platform |
|--------|---------|----------|
| SendTo | Shortcuts to document-oriented utilities. | Windows 2000 and Windows NT 4 only |
| Start Menu | Shortcuts to programs. | All |
| Templates | User templates. | Windows 2000 only |

**TIP:**  In Windows 2000, the Nethood, Printhood, Recent, and Templates folders are hidden by default. To view these folders and their contents, click on Start|Programs|Accessories|Windows Explorer. In Windows Explorer, click on View|Options, and then click on the Show All Files checkbox to make these folders visible.

# Inherited Program Groups

Windows 2000 supports two types of program groups:

- *Common program groups*—These groups are always available on the local computer, no matter who is logged onto the system. An example is the Accessories group of Windows utilities. These utilities are installed by default. If the system is running Windows 2000 with the NTFS file system, the only users who can modify the common program groups are members of the Administrators group.

- *Personal program groups*—These groups are available only to the user who created them. They appear in the Start Menu section of the user's custom profile.

Each user profile inherits the common groups for the current workstation. These groups are found in the All Users folder, which also contains common settings for the Desktop and Start Menu. In Windows 2000, the All Users folder is found under the Documents and Settings folder, the root folder for user profiles. In Windows NT 4, the default folder for profiles is c:\winnt\profiles; however, this will depend on how the operating system was installed. In Windows 9x, it is found under the main Windows folder (generally c:\windows).

# Settings Included In A User Profile

A user profile contains the user's configuration preferences and options. This includes options for specific applications, such as Microsoft Word, that are saved to the Application Data folder. Table 7.2 lists the items that are saved in a user profile.

**Table 7.2** *Information saved in a user profile.*

| Category | Saved Information |
| --- | --- |
| Windows Explorer | All user-definable settings. |
| My Documents folder | Documents created or placed here by the user. |
| My Pictures folder | Graphics created or placed here by the user. |
| Favorites folder | Shortcuts to bookmarked pages on the Internet. |
| Mapped network drives | User-created drive mappings. |
| My Network Places folder | Links to other systems on your network. |
| Desktop | Items stored on the desktop. |
| Screen colors and fonts | All user-definable settings. |
| Application data and registry hive | Application data and user-defined configuration settings. |
| Printer settings | Connections to network printers. |
| Control Panel | All user-defined settings. |
| Accessories | User-specific settings in utilities, such as Calculator, Clock, Notepad, and Paint. |
| Windows 2000-based programs | Programs written for Windows 2000 can track their settings on a per-user basis and save this information to the user's profile. |
| Online help files | User-created bookmarks in the Windows 2000 help system. |

**NOTE:** *Profiles are attached to accounts, not to users. If the user has separate workstation and domain user accounts, or more than one domain user account, the profile for the account under which he has logged on is the one that will be used, and changes will be saved to that account only.*

# Using Master Profiles

Unlike working with group policies, creating and modifying user profiles can be very time-consuming. Much of the work must be done at a workstation, not on a server. In order to create a user profile—even a master profile that you will use as a basis for other new profiles—you must perform a number of distinct procedures:

1. Create a user account if one does not already exist. If you are creating a master profile, you must first create a dummy user account for it.

2. Define the network location of the user profile in the Properties settings for the user account.

3. Log onto a workstation as the user.

4. Configure all of the settings for that user, including application-specific settings where appropriate.

5. Copy the user profile folders from the workstation to a shared folder on a network server.

---

**NOTE:** *A master profile is my term for a roaming user profile that you apply to many different users. You will not find it in Microsoft's documentation.*

---

If yours is a small network or one where your users work more or less autonomously at the same workstation each time, taking the time to create custom user profiles might not be cost-effective for you. On the other hand, you may be administering a relatively large network with groups of users who perform similar or identical tasks. In this case, it may be worth your while to create a master profile for each group and copy the profile for each member of the group. When combined with the effective use of group policies, user profiles can give you a high level of control over the Windows environments of your users and help you to prevent problems.

For example, your company might be organized into administrative, marketing, and production departments. Each department might have large groups of users who perform identical or similar tasks. You could create master profiles for each department by creating a dummy user for each master profile, logging onto a workstation as that user, customizing the Windows environment, copying the profile to the main profile folder of each user who will use it, and adding the network location of each profile to the properties of each user's account.

# Immediate Solutions

## Enabling User Profiles In Windows 98 And Windows 95

In Windows 2000 and Windows NT, custom user profiles are enabled by default. In Windows 98 and Windows 95, on the other hand, the default setting is for all users to share the same profile.

To enable custom user profiles in Windows 98 or Windows 95, do the following:

1. Click on Start|Settings|Control Panel, or open My Computer and double-click on Control Panel.

2. Double-click on the Passwords utility to open the Passwords Properties dialog box.

3. Click on the User Profiles tabbed page.

4. At the top of the page, select the second radio button, Users Can Customize Their Preferences And Desktop Settings. (See Figure 7.1.)

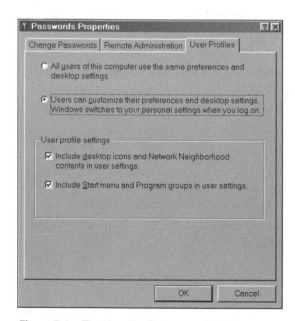

Figure 7.1   The User Profiles page of the Passwords Properties dialog box.

5. Check both boxes in the User Profile Settings section of the page.

6. Click on OK to confirm your choices and exit the dialog box.

# Creating A Shared Folder For Roaming User Profiles

For roaming profiles to work, the folders containing them must be shared. The simplest way to ensure this is to create a root folder for profiles on a network server and make it a shared folder. The user profiles that you create later will be copied to this folder.

To create a shared folder, follow these steps:

1. Log onto the server that will contain the shared folders as administrator.

2. Click on Start|Programs|Accessories|Windows Explorer.

3. In the left window, expand the My Computer folder, and then expand the folder for the local drive that is to contain the shared folder for profiles.

4. With the selected drive highlighted, place your cursor in the right window and right-click on an empty area.

5. In the context-sensitive pop-up menu, select New|Folder.

6. With the new folder highlighted, press F2 to edit the default name, "New Folder." Change the name to Profiles or some other meaningful term.

7. Right-click on the folder and select Sharing.

8. On the Sharing page of the folder's Properties dialog box, select the Share This Folder radio button.

9. Enter a share name for the folder, as well as a comment describing the purpose of the folder. Leave the other options on the page at their default settings. (See Figure 7.2.)

10. Click on Apply to confirm your choices, and then click on OK to exit the dialog box.

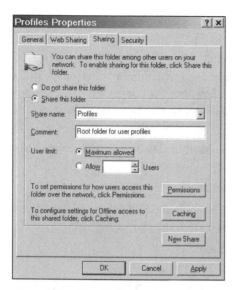

*Figure 7.2    The Sharing page of a shared folder's Properties dialog box.*

# Working With Roaming User Profiles

In this section, you will learn how to create a roaming user profile from scratch, work with existing profiles, and use master profiles.

## Creating A Roaming User Profile

To create a roaming user profile for a user account, you must first create a local user profile on a system running Windows 2000 Professional or Windows NT Workstation. (If a local user profile on a compatible workstation already exists, you can use that instead.)

To create a roaming user profile from scratch, do the following:

1. If you have not already done so, create the user account to which the profile will be attached.

2. Log onto the server that will contain the network copy of the profile and create a folder for the user. It should be a child of the shared folder that you have created to contain roaming profiles. The name of the folder must be exactly the same as the user name for the account.

3. As the user, log onto the user's workstation, or one that has a hardware and software configuration similar to the computer on which the user normally works. The workstation should be

running Windows 2000 Professional. The operating system will create a local user profile for the user if one does not already exist.

4. Customize the user's Windows environment, as needed. Do not overlook options and preferences for commonly used applications such as Internet Explorer or the various components of Microsoft Office.

5. Log off the system. The customized settings will be saved to the local user profile on the workstation.

6. Log onto the same system as administrator.

7. Click on Start|Settings|Control Panel|System. This will open the System Properties dialog box.

8. Select the User Profiles page.

9. In the Profiles Stored On This Computer window, select the profile that you have just created and click on the Copy To button. (See Figure 7.3.)

10. In the Copy To dialog box, enter the full network path to the main folder for the user's roaming profile or click on the Browse button to navigate to the desired folder.

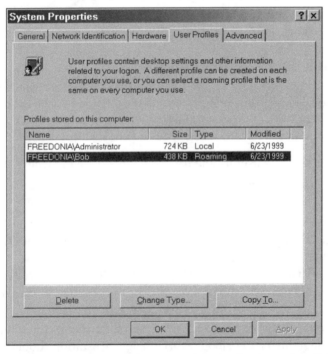

*Figure 7.3    The User Profiles page of the System Properties dialog box.*

11. When you are ready, click on OK to exit the Copy To dialog box and return to the User Profiles page. The copying process will begin.

---

**NOTE:** *The copying process may take awhile. Watch your hard drive activity light and listen for disk activity for indications as to when it has finished.*

---

12. Click on the Change Type button, and then select the Roaming Profile radio button. When there is a slow network connection, you can select the Use Cached Profile On Slow Connections checkbox to use a locally cached copy of the profile in place of the network copy. (See Figure 7.4.) Click on OK to close the Change Type dialog box.

13. Click on OK to close the System Properties dialog box.

14. Log off the workstation.

15. Log onto a Windows 2000 server to access the Active Directory Users and Computers management console.

16. Click on Start|Programs|Administrative Tools|Active Directory Users And Computers to open the console. You will need to add the profile path to the appropriate user account.

17. In the console tree pane, select the Users folder or the folder containing the user account that you want to modify.

18. In the results pane, right-click on the user account. On the context-sensitive pop-up menu, select Properties.

19. Select the Profile page.

20. In the Profile Path edit box, enter the full network path to the main profile folder. In place of the user name for the account, you can enter the environmental variable %username%. For example, the line might read "\\pubproserver01\Profiles\ %username%". (See Figure 7.5.)

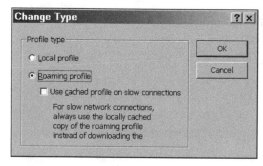

*Figure 7.4    The Change Type dialog box.*

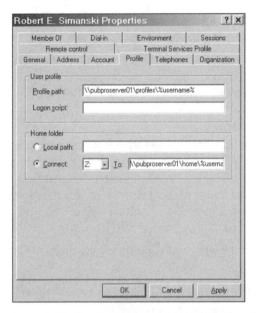

*Figure 7.5   The Profile page of the Properties dialog box for a user account.*

21. Click on Apply to confirm your entry. When you do, Windows 2000 Server will change "%username%" to the correct user name for the account.

22. Click on OK to exit the account's Properties dialog box and return to the Active Directory Users and Computers console.

23. Click on Console|Exit to exit the console.

| Related solution: | Found on page: |
|---|---|
| Creating A User Account | 126 |

## Converting A Roaming User Profile To Mandatory Status

A normal roaming user profile can be modified by the user, at least to the extent permitted by the applicable group policy. To prevent a user from modifying his profile, you can convert it to mandatory status. In effect, you are making the policy read-only. The process is very simple. Follow these steps:

1. Create a roaming user profile, as described in the preceding section.

2. As administrator, log onto the server that contains the profile.

3. Click on Start|Programs|Accessories|Windows Explorer.

4. Navigate to the main folder for the profile and look for a file called ntuser.dat.

5. Change the name of the file to ntuser.man.

## Copying An Existing Profile To A Server

There may be circumstances when you will not need to create a roaming user profile from scratch. For example:

- A user may have an existing local user profile on her workstation that does not need to be modified.

- You may have created a master profile that needs to be copied to the profile folders of several users.

To copy an existing profile to a server, follow these steps:

1. If you have not already done so, log onto the server that will contain the network copy of the profile and create a folder for the user. It should be a child of the shared folder that you have created to contain roaming profiles. The name of the folder must be exactly the same as the user name for the account.

2. Log onto the workstation that contains the local user profile as administrator.

3. Click on Start|Settings|Control Panel|System. This will open the System Properties dialog box.

4. Select the User Profiles page.

5. In the Profiles Stored On This Computer window, select the profile that you have just created and click on the Copy To button.

6. In the Copy To dialog box, enter the full network path to the main folder for the user's roaming profile or click on the Browse button to navigate to the desired folder.

7. When you are ready, click on OK to exit the Copy To dialog box and return to the User Profiles page. The copying process will begin.

8. When the copying process has finished, click on the Change Type button, and then select the Roaming Profile radio button. When there is a slow network connection, you can select the Use Cached Profile On Slow Connections checkbox to use a locally cached copy of the profile in place of the network copy.

9. Click on OK to close the System Properties dialog box.

10. Log off the workstation.

11. Add the profile path to the user's account. (See the next section.)

**7. Managing User Profiles**

## Adding A Profile Path To A User Account

For roaming user profiles to work, you must define the path to the main folder of the network copy of the profile. This is done in the Properties dialog box for the user account to which the profile is attached. As noted in the "Creating A Roaming User Profile" section, it is best to create the local user version of the profile and copy the profile to the server before adding the profile path to the properties of the account.

To add the path to a roaming user profile to the properties of a user account, do the following:

1. Click on Start|Programs|Administrative Tools|Active Directory Users And Computers. This opens the Active Directory Users and Computers management console.

2. In the console tree pane, select the Users folder or the folder containing the user account that you want to modify.

3. In the results pane, right-click on the user account. On the context-sensitive pop-up menu, select Properties.

4. Select the Profile page.

5. In the Profile path edit box, enter the full network path to the main profile folder. In place of the user name for the account, you can enter the environmental variable %username%. For example, the line might read "\\pubproserver01\Profiles\ %username%".

6. Click on Apply to confirm your entry. When you do, Windows 2000 Server will change "%username%" to the correct user name for the account.

7. Click on OK to exit the account's Properties dialog box and return to the Active Directory Users and Computers console.

## Testing A Roaming User Profile

While you are learning how to use roaming user profiles (and later, when you create a particularly important profile), you will want to test your profiles before you make them available to their intended users. The best way to test a profile is to log onto a workstation as the user, make a change to a Windows environment setting, log off, and then log onto another workstation as the user.

Microsoft recommends a good test in the Beta 3 Technical Walkthrough, *User Data and User Settings Management*. It involves the creation of a custom bitmap for use as Windows wallpaper. This offers a good test because the custom bitmap will not exist on any other computer. Here is how it works:

1. Log onto a workstation as the user. You should see the customized environment that you created earlier.

2. Click on Start|Programs|Accessories|Paint.

3. Click on File|Open, and then navigate to the root folder for the Windows installation files (usually c:\winnt).

4. Open one of the BMP files installed by Windows 2000 for use as background images. (Other BMP files may be too large for this purpose.)

5. Save the file to the same folder under another name, and then modify it in some way.

6. When you are finished, save the file, and then exit Paint.

7. Click on Start|Settings|Control Panel|Display, and then select the Background page.

8. In the list of available background pictures, select your new BMP file and click on OK. The new bitmap should appear on the Windows desktop.

9. Log off the workstation.

10. Log onto another workstation as the same user. The new background image should appear.

11. Click on Start|Settings|Control Panel|Display, and then select the Background page again.

12. Revert to your previous setting for the background image and click on OK.

13. Log off the system.

## Adding A Home Directory To A Profile

You can assign a home directory to each user and add it to their profile. (Although recent versions of Windows create default directories such as My Documents and My Pictures, which are used by many Microsoft applications, they do not replace the user's home directory.)

To define a home directory and add it to a user profile, follow these steps:

1. Log onto a Windows 2000 server as administrator, and click on Start|Programs|Administrative Tools|Active Directory Users And Computers. This opens the Active Directory Users and Computers console.

2. In the console tree pane, select the Users folder or the folder containing the first user account that you want to modify.

3. In the results pane, right-click on the user account. On the context-sensitive pop-up menu, select Properties.

4. Select the Profile page.

5. In the Home Directory section, you can either specify a local path on the user's workstation or map a network drive to a folder on a server. Select the appropriate radio button and fill in the required information.

6. Click on Apply to confirm your changes, then click on OK to exit the dialog box and return to the console.

7. Click on Console|Exit to exit the console.

## Using Master Profiles

A master profile is a roaming user profile that you apply to many different users. (The term is mine; you won't find it in Microsoft's documentation.) Here is how I would use one:

1. Create the necessary folders on the server for each user account that will use the master profile.

2. Create a fictitious user account to which you will attach the profile.

3. As the fictitious user, log onto a system that is running Windows 2000 Professional. The operating system will create a local user profile for the fictitious account.

4. Customize the Windows environment, as needed.

5. Log off the system. The customized settings will be saved to the local user profile on the workstation.

6. Log onto the same system as administrator.

7. Click on Start|Settings|Control Panel|System. This opens the System Properties dialog box.

8. Select the User Profiles page.

9. In the Profiles Stored On This Computer window, select the profile that you just created and click on the Change Type button.

10. In the Change Type dialog box, select the Roaming Profile radio button. Click on OK to return to the User Profiles page.

11. Next, click on the Copy To button. In the Copy To dialog box, enter the full network path to the main folder for the first user to be assigned the profile or click on the Browse button to navigate to the desired folder.

12. When you are ready, click on OK to exit the Copy To dialog box and return to the User Profiles page. The copying process will begin.

13. Repeat Steps 11 and 12 for each copy needed.

14. Click on OK to close the System Properties dialog box.

15. Log off the workstation.

16. Log onto a Windows 2000 server to access the Active Directory Users and Computers management console. You will need to add the appropriate profile path to each user account in the group.

17. Click on Start|Programs|Administrative Tools|Active Directory Users And Computers to open the console.

18. In the console tree pane, select the Users folder or the folder containing the first user account that you want to modify.

19. In the results pane, right-click on the user account. On the context-sensitive pop-up menu, select Properties.

20. Select the Profile page.

21. In the Profile path edit box, enter the full network path to the main profile folder. In place of the user name for the account, you can enter the environmental variable %username%. For example, the line might read "\\pubproserver01\Profiles\%username%".

22. Click on Apply to confirm your entry. When you do, Windows 2000 Server will change "%username%" to the correct user name for the account.

23. Click on OK to exit the account's Properties dialog box and return to the Active Directory Users and Computers console.

24. Repeat Steps 18 through 23 for each user account to be modified.

25. When you are finished, click on Console|Exit to exit the console.

# Setting Group Policies That Apply To Profiles

By using the Group Policy Editor, you can exclude specified directories from roaming user profiles and limit the size of each profile.

## Excluding Folders From Roaming User Profiles

There may be times when you want to exclude some of the folders that are normally associated with roaming user profiles from a group of profiles. You can do this by using the Group Policy Editor discussed in Chapter 6. To exclude folders from roaming user profiles, follow these steps:

1. Open the group policy that applies to the users whose profiles will be affected.

2. In the console tree pane, expand the User Configuration, Administrative Templates, and System folders, and then select the Logon/Logoff folder.

3. In the results pane, double-click on Exclude Directories In Roaming Profile.

4. On the Policy page of the dialog box, check the Enabled radio button.

5. In the edit box that will be revealed, several folders are listed by default. Add the required folders, separating them with semi-colons.

6. Click on Apply to confirm your changes, and then click on OK to exit the dialog box.

7. Exit the Group Policy Editor.

| Related solution: | Found on page: |
|---|---|
| Editing A Group Policy Assigned To An Active Directory Object | 200 |

## Limiting The Size Of Profiles

The folders in a roaming user profile can get quite large, particularly if they include user-created documents. You may find it necessary to limit the size of each profile, particularly if you have many users or are running short on disk space.

To limit the size of profiles, do the following:

1. Open the group policy that applies to the users whose profiles will be affected.

2. In the console tree pane, expand the User Configuration, Administrative Templates, and System folders, and then select the Logon/Logoff folder.

3. In the results pane, double-click on Limit Profile Size.

4. On the Policy page, check the Enabled radio button.

5. This will reveal options for setting a size limit, including or excluding the Registry-related settings in the size limit, and sending a message to a user when he has exceeded the limit. Accept the default settings or modify them, as needed.

6. Click on Apply to confirm your selections, and then click on OK to exit the dialog box.

7. Exit the Group Policy Editor.

**7. Managing User Profiles**

# Chapter 8

# Managing Disk Quotas

# In Brief

Disk quotas enable you to monitor and control the amount of disk space on any given volume that users can take up with files that they own. Quotas are assigned on a per-user and per-volume basis, and can be applied to both local and remote volumes.

You can manage disk quotas as tightly or as loosely as necessary. For example, you can set default quotas for all users, and then override them with smaller or larger quotas for specific users. You can regulate quotas tightly by having Windows 2000 Server send users a warning message when their quotas are almost used up. If they fail to heed the warning, you can configure Windows 2000 Server to prevent them from exceeding their quotas. On the other hand, you can choose not to send warnings and allow users to exceed their quotas and simply track the amount of space that each person is using.

---

**NOTE:**   *In most cases, a volume is the same as a drive partition. It is possible, however, for a volume to span more than one drive. For example, if you have two physical drives in your system, and each is formatted with a Windows 2000-compatible file system, then the operating system sees them as volumes C and D (or whatever you chose to name them). Later, if you were to add a third physical drive, you could choose to either configure it as volume E or extend volume D by spanning it onto the new drive. Be aware that you cannot span the volume that contains the Windows 2000 system files (normally installed on drive C). Also, the physical drive that is being spanned onto another disk must have at least 1MB of unpartitioned space. Finally, often it is not possible to extend a volume already in use unless you first delete the existing volume. When you do this, the data on the volume is lost. In such cases you need to back up your data, delete the existing volume, then re-create a new volume that spans the desired partitions.*

---

There are several advantages to using disk quotas:

- If you have several users working on the same system, you can ensure that no one user consumes so much disk space that he prevents other users from doing their work.

- You can prevent individual users from monopolizing the available disk space on your network file servers.

- If you share folders on your local workstation with others on the network, you can make sure that no one uses an excessive amount of disk space on your system.

In short, disk quotas help you to manage the hard drive storage resources on your network. This can be particularly useful if you are running tight on disk space and your budget does not permit you to add storage capacity right away.

# Options For Managing Disk Quotas

Disk quotas are managed through the Quota page in the Properties dialog box for each disk volume. On this page, you can:

- Enable or disable disk quotas for the selected volume.
- Set the default disk space limit for new users (those who do not yet have any files on the volume).
- Set the default warning level. When a user reaches that level, she receives an automatic warning message.
- Prevent users from adding new data to the volume when they reach their limit.
- View disk quota information for each person who is using the volume.
- Set custom limits for individual users.
- Create a record in your event log whenever users exceed their warning levels or quota limits. Later, you can view these events in Event Viewer.

For example, you might establish a default quota limit of 50MB on a volume and set the warning trigger point to 45MB. Perhaps your default limit might be appropriate for most users, but not for someone working with large graphics. You could override the default limit by selecting that person from a list of users and setting a more appropriate limit for him.

# Understanding How Disk Quotas Work

In understanding how disk quotas work, there are a number of small but important points to keep in mind. I have grouped them by category, as shown in the following sections.

## Requirements For Enabling Disk Quotas

There are two basic requirements for enabling disk quotas:

- The volume that you want to manage must be formatted for the NTFS version 5 file system, which is new with Windows 2000.

**8. Managing Disk Quotas**

Volumes formatted for NTFS version 4, used by Windows NT 4, are upgraded automatically when you upgrade the system to Windows 2000.

- You must be a member of the Administrators group for the system in which the drive is installed.

If the volume has not been formatted for NTFS version 5 or if you are not a member of the appropriate Administrators group, the Quota page will not appear in the Properties dialog box for the volume.

---

**TIP:** *Being a member of the Administrators group for the domain does not automatically make you a member of the local Administrators group for a given workstation. When Windows 2000 Professional is installed on a workstation, the operating system creates a local Administrator account. That account is assigned to the local Administrators group. Whoever does the installation must create a password for the local Administrator account. To make things easier for yourself, you might want to create a common password to be used for all local Administrator accounts. Needless to say, this could present a security problem, so be sure to use a password that only you will know and that others could not guess. One good option might be a combination of your mother's maiden name and birthday.*

---

# Relationship To Volumes

Quotas apply to volumes, not to physical drives, even if a volume spans more than one drive. For example, the system that you are managing might have two physical drives, C and D, each with only one volume. You might limit a given user to 50MB on each volume. If he were to use up his quota on volume C, he could not borrow capacity from volume D to add a new file to C. He would have to save the file to volume D. Later, you might add a new drive to the system and span volume C onto that drive. The user would still be limited to 50MB on volume C, even though the volume would be much larger.

# Relationship To Individual Users

Quotas are assigned to individual users. If one user exceeds his quota, this has no effect on other users. In addition, quotas are based on the total size of the files owned by the user, regardless of where they are located on the volume. If a user moves a file from one folder to another on the same volume, his available disk space is not affected. On the other hand, if he copies the file to another folder on the same volume, his available space is reduced by the size of the file.

# Relationship To File Ownership

Normally, the person who creates or installs a file is the owner of the file. If one user takes over ownership of a file from another, the new owner's available space is reduced and the previous owner's available space is increased by the size of the file. On the other hand, suppose that one user edits a file owned by another, changing its size, but does not take over ownership of the file. In that case, the quota for the owner of the file is the one that is affected by the change in file size.

Software program files, including the Windows 2000 system files, are assigned to the person who installs them. Administrators, however, are not limited by disk quotas, even if you have assigned quotas to them. For this reason—among many others, I am sure—it is usually best to have an administrator install new software on any volume where you have enabled disk quotas.

---

**NOTE:** *Administrators can take ownership of a file but cannot reassign it to another user, even if they have taken ownership of the file first. Microsoft claims that it did this to keep administrators from abusing the privilege! In my opinion, this compromises the usefulness of the ownership feature. I hope that Microsoft will reconsider and change the feature in an early service pack update.*

---

This is not always possible, of course. You may need to ask someone who is not an administrator to install Windows 2000 or a major application on a volume where they have been assigned a disk quota. In this case, you may want to give them a very high quota or perhaps remove their quota altogether.

Roaming user profiles, incidentally, do not seem to have an effect on a user's quota. This is true even if files that the user has created and placed in his My Documents folder are copied to a server on which he has a quota limit. The ownership of the files in the server-based copy of the folder is assigned to the Administrators group.

---

**NOTE:** *In the versions of the NTFS file system used by both Windows 2000 and Windows NT 4, the ownership of a file is stored along with other information about the file. The FAT and FAT32 file systems used by other operating systems, however, do not store ownership information. The operating system itself owns all of the files. If you convert a FAT or FAT32 volume to NTFS, ownership of the files in it will be assigned to the Administrator account.*

---

## Should You Enforce Disk Quota Limits?

The decision to enforce disk quota limits might seem to be a no-brainer. If you don't intend to enforce limits, why set them at all?

The answer is that a considerable amount of information is generated when you enable disk quotas, even if you choose not to enforce them. You can use them to track disk space consumption on a per-user basis and monitor disk quota-related events in Event Viewer. Enabling disk quotas can provide you with the information you need to build a historical track record, document the need for additional hard drive storage capacity, and notify those users who have exceeded their limits. This may be all that you need to accomplish your goals.

On the other hand, when you enforce quota limits, users who attempt to exceed their limits get a Disk Full error message. The exact message depends on how the application that they are using handles disk-full situations. Your decision to enforce disk-quota limits strictly could create some internal relations problems for you, so consider it carefully and make sure that your users understand what you have done and why you have done it.

Keep in mind that if users get a Disk Full error message, they will lose their work unless they know how to take appropriate action. Be sure that your users know how to save a file to an alternate location, and how to move or delete files in order to free up disk space. I have encountered many people who have used personal computers for years and still do not know how to perform these basic tasks.

*WARNING!  Some applications, such as Microsoft Word 97, save backup files to the same folder as the file being edited. These backup files—unlike Word's auto-recover files—remain on the disk and can quickly deplete available disk space. In Word 97, at least, there is unfortunately no way to route these files to another location. Although I normally recommend enabling the option to create backup files, you may want to disable the option if the situation requires it. In Word 97, click on Tools|Options|Save and make sure that the Always Create Backup Copy box is unchecked.*

## Other Considerations

Here are some other points to keep in mind in managing disk quotas:

- Enabling disk quotas causes a slight increase in overhead, and therefore a slight performance hit on the system in question.
- File compression is not a factor. Quotas are based on uncompressed file sizes.

Finally, a word of caution: Before you invest a substantial amount of your time in working with disk quotas, I recommend that you check out several limitations that I found. I hope that they will be corrected in the shipping release or an early service pack update:

- Files generated by a user on a Windows 98 workstation and saved to a volume with disk quotas were assigned to the Administrators group, even though the user was assigned a specific custom quota. This was the case with a new file that was saved directly to the volume. It was also the case with a file originally saved on the workstation and then saved on the volume being tested. This would seem to rule out the fact that the workstation was using FAT32 as a factor.

- Specific disk quota information for users working on a Windows 2000 Professional workstation did not update properly when the users copied files to the managed volume. Ownership of these files was also assigned to the Administrators group.

For all practical purposes, then, the disk quota feature may work only with users who are working on systems running Windows 2000. Even in these cases, it may not work as you expect.

8. Managing Disk Quotas

# Immediate Solutions

## Accessing And Viewing Disk Quota Settings

The methods of accessing the Quota page in the Properties dialog box are slightly different for local and remote computer systems. Rather than repeat each method in the steps for each of the solutions in the rest of this chapter, I will describe them here.

Keep in mind that disk quotas work only on volumes formatted for the NTFS version 5 file system, which limits the feature's use to systems running Windows 2000. It will not work on systems running Windows NT, Windows 9x, or Windows 3.x.

### Accessing And Viewing Disk Quota Settings On A Local System

To access the disk quota settings for a volume on a local system, do the following:

1. Double-click on the My Computer icon on your Windows desktop.

2. Right-click on the drive that you want to manage.

3. Select the Quota page of the Properties dialog box (see Figure 8.1).

4. When you are finished, click on Cancel to close the Properties dialog box for the drive and return to the My Computer window.

### Accessing And Viewing Disk Quota Settings On A Remote System

To access the disk quota settings for a volume on a remote system:

1. Double-click on the My Network Places icon on your Windows desktop.

2. Double-click on the Entire Network icon.

3. Double-click on the Microsoft Windows Network icon.

4. In the next window, you will see icons for each domain on your network. Double-click on the icon for the domain that contains the appropriate remote system.

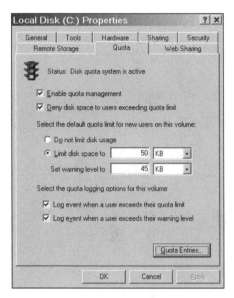

*Figure 8.1*    *The Quota page of the Properties dialog box for a local drive.*
*Disk quota management and event logging have been*
*enabled and default quota limits and warning trigger levels*
*have been set.*

5. This next window will show you all of the computers within the domain. Double-click on the icon for the computer that you want to manage.

6. In this last window, you will see icons for each of the volumes on the selected system. Right-click on the volume that you want to manage. On the context-sensitive pop-up menu, select Map Network Drive.

7. In the Map Network Drive dialog box, select a drive letter to represent the volume in My Computer and Windows Explorer. If you intend to access the drive frequently, make sure that the Reconnect At Logon box is checked (see Figure 8.2).

8. Click on Finish to exit the dialog box. This will open a My Computer window on the selected drive.

9. Close all open windows.

10. Double-click on the My Computer icon on your Windows desktop.

11. Right-click on the network drive that you have just mapped.

**8. Managing
Disk Quotas**

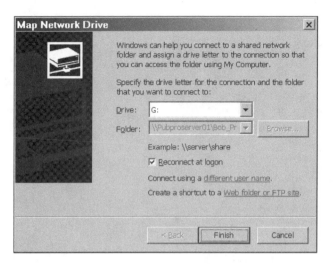

*Figure 8.2   The Map Network Drive dialog box.*

12. Select the Quota page of the Properties dialog box. Here you
    will be able to view the disk quota settings for the volume.

13. When you are finished, click on Cancel to close the Properties
    dialog box for the drive and return to the My Computer window.

---

**NOTE:**   *You can access the Properties dialog box for a volume by right-clicking on its icon, as
specified in Step 6, making it appear that it is not necessary to complete the remaining steps in
the procedure. Microsoft's online documentation, however, specifies these additional steps.*

---

# Working With Default Disk Quota Settings

Almost everything that you need to do in working with disk quotas
for a given volume can be done on the Quota page of the Properties
dialog box for the volume. From here, you can enable or disable disk
quotas for the volume, enter default settings for quota levels and warning trigger points, or override the default settings for individual users. You will learn how to do each of these tasks in this section.

You can also monitor disk space usage for individual users, generate
usage reports, and transfer settings for individual users between volumes. These topics are covered in the section called "Working With
Disk Quota Entry Information," which is near the end of this chapter.

## Enabling Disk Quotas

By enabling disk quotas, you can gain control over the hard-drive storage resources of your network and prevent individual users from monopolizing those resources. The best time to enable disk quotas is before any of your users have begun to copy or save files to the volume that you are managing. When you enable disk quotas on a volume that already contains files, Windows calculates the disk space used by everyone who has files on the volume at that point in time. It uses that information to generate quota limits and warning levels for each of the current users, as well as the default settings for users who do not yet have files on the volume.

This is not a problem if all of the files on the volume belong to an Administrator account because usage by administrators is not factored into the calculations. If other users already have files on the volume, however, the automatically generated settings may not be appropriate, so you will need to change them manually.

To enable quotas for a volume, follow these steps:

1. Access the Quota page of the volume's Properties dialog box, as described earlier in the "Accessing And Viewing Disk Quota Settings" section.
2. Check the Enable Quota Management checkbox (refer to Figure 8.1 earlier in the chapter).
3. Accept the default settings and click on Apply. This opens a message box asking you to confirm your decision.
4. Click on OK to continue and return to the Quota page.
5. Click on OK to exit the Properties dialog box and return to the My Computer window.

## Disabling Disk Quotas

There may be circumstances where you find that you no longer need disk quotas on a volume on which you have enabled them. This might occur, for example, when you have added capacity to a volume, either by replacing the physical drive that it is on or spanning the volume across more than one drive.

To disable disk quotas for a volume, do the following:

1. Access the Quota page of the volume's Properties dialog box. (Refer to the "Accessing And Viewing Disk Quota Settings" section earlier in the chapter.)

**8. Managing Disk Quotas**

2. Uncheck the Enable Quota Management checkbox.

3. Click on Apply. This will open a message box asking you to confirm your decision.

4. Click on OK to continue and return to the Quota page.

5. Click on OK to exit the Properties dialog box and return to the My Computer window.

## Assigning Default Quota Limits And Warning Trigger Levels

The most important step that you will take, once you have decided to enable disk quotas, is to assign default quota limits and warning trigger levels. These values will apply to new users (those who do not yet have files on the volume), but not to existing users.

To set the default values, do the following:

1. Access the Quota page of the volume's Properties dialog box. (See "Accessing And Viewing Disk Quota Settings" earlier in the chapter.)

2. Check the Enable Quota Management box if disk quotas have not yet been enabled.

3. By default, the Do Not Limit Disk Usage radio button is selected. To enable default quota limits, select the Limit Disk Space To radio button, instead. This will open edit windows in which you can enter the numbers for the size limit and warning trigger level, as well as drop-down list boxes in which you can select the appropriate acronyms (such as KB, MB, or GB).

4. Enter the desired settings. The values that you enter cannot exceed the maximum capacity of the volume (refer to Figure 8.1).

*WARNING! If there are no users with files on the volume except for administrators, the default limits will be 1KB, which is patently absurd. This means that the first time a new user attempts to save a file to the volume, she will get a Disk Full error message. Be sure to change the settings to realistic ones.*

5. Click on Apply. This will open a message box asking you to confirm your decision.

6. Click on OK to continue and return to the Quota page.

7. Click on OK to exit the Properties dialog box and return to the My Computer window.

8. Managing Disk Quotas

## Denying Space To Users Who Exceed Their Quotas

If you are intent on managing your hard-drive storage resources as tightly as possible, simply setting quota limits and sending messages to users when they have exceeded their warning trigger levels may not be sufficient. You may need to go one step further and deny space to users who exceed their quotas.

To prevent users from exceeding their disk quota limits, do the following:

1. Access the Quota page of the volume's Properties dialog box. (Refer to "Accessing And Viewing Disk Quota Settings" earlier in the chapter.)

2. Check the Enable Quota Management box if disk quotas have not yet been enabled.

3. If you have not already done so, select the Limit Disk Space To radio button and enter the desired settings for disk quota limits and warning trigger levels. (See "Assigning Default Quota Limits And Warning Trigger Levels" earlier in the chapter.)

4. Check the Deny Disk Space To Users Exceeding Quota Limit checkbox (refer to Figure 8.1).

5. Click on Apply. This opens a message box, asking you to confirm your decision.

6. Click on OK to continue and return to the Quota page.

7. Click on OK to exit the Properties dialog box and return to the My Computer window.

## Logging Disk Quota Events

Once you have enabled disk quota limits and warning trigger levels, you may want to log events when users exceed either or both. To enable logging of these events, do the following:

1. Access the Quota page of the volume's Properties dialog box (see "Accessing And Viewing Disk Quota Settings").

2. Check the Enable Quota Management box if disk quotas have not yet been enabled.

3. If you have not already done so, select the Limit Disk Space To radio button and enter the desired settings for disk quota limits and warning trigger levels (see "Assigning Default Quota Limits And Warning Trigger Levels" earlier in the chapter).

4. At the bottom of the screen are checkboxes for logging events when users exceed their quota limits or warning trigger levels. Select the appropriate box or boxes (refer to Figure 8.1).

5. Click on Apply. This opens a message box, asking you to confirm your decision.

6. Click on OK to continue and return to the Quota page.

7. Click on OK to exit the Properties dialog box and return to the My Computer window.

## Viewing Disk Quota Events In Event Viewer

Event Viewer is one of the administrative tools that comes with Windows 2000. If you have enabled logging of disk quota events, it creates a record of which users have exceeded their limits and when they did so.

To view these events, follow these steps:

1. Click on Start|Programs|Administrative Tools|Event Viewer to open the Event Viewer management console.

2. In the console tree pane at left, select Application Log.

3. With Application Log highlighted, select View|Filter to open the Filter page of the Application Log Properties dialog box (see Figure 8.3).

4. In the Source drop-down list box, select DiskQuota.

5. Select additional filter options as appropriate, and then click on Apply to confirm your selections.

6. Click on OK to close the Application Log Properties dialog box and return to the Event Viewer console window.

---

**NOTE:**   *Event Viewer presents a historical, chronological record of events that were logged. It does not show you an up-to-date list, however, of users who have currently exceeded their limits or warning trigger levels. If a user receives a warning message and then frees up some of his allotted space on the volume, for example, the warning event will be reported in the log, but not the fact that the user responded to it and is once again below the warning trigger level. For an accurate view of current standings, follow the steps under "Viewing Disk Quota Entries" in the next section.*

---

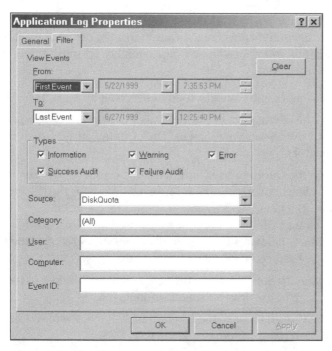

*Figure 8.3   The Filter page of the Application Log Properties dialog box.*

# Working With Disk Quota Settings For Individual Users

In addition to setting default disk quota settings that will apply to all new users, you can view the disk space usage for each person with files on the volume and override the default settings for individual users, as needed.

## Viewing Disk Quota Entries

If you have enabled disk quotas on a given volume, you can monitor the amount of space used by every individual with files on that volume. This is done through the Quota Entries option on the Quota page of the Properties pages of the volume.

The first time that you select this option, it will take some time for the information to appear. The reason is that each user's unique security ID, not their user account name, is used in recording disk usage. The disk quota feature must obtain the user account names and match them against the security IDs before it can display the required information. The account names are then saved to a file on the volume, so the information will appear much more quickly the next time that you access the feature.

To view disk quota entry details, follow these steps:

1. Access the Quota page of the volume's Properties dialog box (refer to "Accessing And Viewing Disk Quota Settings" earlier in the chapter).

2. Click on the Quota Entries button at the bottom right of the page. This will open the Quota Entries window for the selected volume. The name of each user with files on the volume will be listed, along with the amount of space used, their assigned quota limit, their warning trigger level, and the percent of their limit that has been used (see Figure 8.4).

3. When you are finished, close the Quota Entries window to the Quota page of the drive's Properties dialog box.

4. Click on Cancel to close the Properties dialog box and return to the My Computer window.

---

**TIP:**   *Changes that you make to your user accounts list after viewing quota entries for the first time may not be picked up automatically the next time that you use the feature. To update the list, open the Quota Entries window and press F5. As with the first time that you view quota entries for a volume, it may take some time for the information to appear.*

---

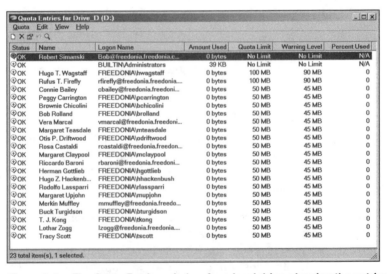

**8. Managing Disk Quotas**

*Figure 8.4    The Quota Entries window for a local drive, showing the entries for users with quota assignments on the drive.*

## Adding Disk Quota Entries

At times, you may need to add a user to the Quota Entries for a given volume before the user begins to place files on the volume. This would be appropriate, for example, if you needed to override the default quota limit and warning trigger level settings for the user.

To add a quota entry to a volume, do the following:

1. Access the Quota page of the volume's Properties dialog box (refer to "Accessing And Viewing Disk Quota Settings" earlier in the chapter).

2. Click on the Quota Entries button at the bottom right of the page. This will open the Quota Entries window for the selected volume.

3. Click on Quota|New Quota Entry. This will open the familiar Select Users dialog box (see Figure 8.5).

4. Select the name of the user that you want, and then click on Add.

5. When you are ready, click on OK. This will open the Add New Quota Entry dialog box, shown in Figure 8.6.

6. To cancel all disk quota limits for the new entry, select the Do Not Limit Disk Usage radio button, and then skip to Step 9.

7. To set a custom quota limit and warning trigger level for the new entry, select the Limit Disk Space To radio button. This will open a group of edit boxes and drop-down lists for the disk

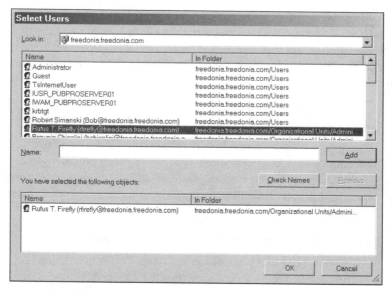

*Figure 8.5   The Select Users dialog box.*

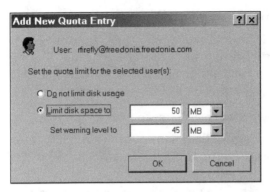

*Figure 8.6    The Add New Quota Entry dialog box, with the default quota
limit and warning trigger level shown.*

quota limit and warning trigger level, with the current default
settings shown. Modify the settings, as needed. The values that
you enter cannot exceed the maximum capacity of the volume.

8. Click on OK to confirm your settings. The new entry will be
   added to the list, and then you will be returned to the Quota
   Entries window.

9. Click on Quota|Close to close the Quota Entries window and
   return to the Quota page of the drive's Properties dialog box.

10. Click on OK to exit the Properties dialog box and return to the
    My Computer window.

---

**TIP:**   *If you want to apply the same settings to a group of users, select all of the users in one
batch. To select more than one user in the Select User dialog box (refer to Step 4), hold down the
Ctrl key while you left-click on each name to highlight it, and then click on Add and continue with
Step 5. The settings that you specify in the Add New Quota Entry dialog box will apply to each of
the selected users.*

---

## Deleting Disk Quota Entries

When a user no longer needs to use a volume for which you have set
disk quotas—for example, when a user leaves the company—you can
delete his quota entry. Before you can do this, however, you must
either remove all of his files from the volume or assign their ownership to someone else.

To delete a quota entry from a volume, do the following:

1. Access the Quota page of the volume's Properties dialog box
   (refer to "Accessing And Viewing Disk Quota Settings" earlier in
   the chapter).

2. Click on the Quota Entries button at the bottom right of the page. This will open the Quota Entries window for the selected volume.

3. Click on Quota|Delete Quota Entry. This will open a message box asking to confirm your action.

4. Click on OK to continue.

5. If the user still has files on the system, you will now see a Disk Quota dialog box with a list of each file belonging to the user (see Figure 8.7). For each file, you have three options: permanently delete the file, take ownership of the file yourself, or move the file to another location. To select multiple files for the same action, hold down the Ctrl key as you highlight each one.

6. To delete a file, click on the file name to highlight it, and then click on Delete. You will see a message box asking you to confirm your action. Click on OK to delete the file and return to the Disk Quota dialog box.

7. To take ownership of a file, click on the file name in the list to highlight it, and then click on Take Ownership. (There is no confirmation message box for this action.)

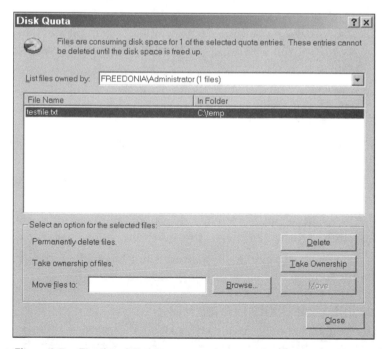

*Figure 8.7    The list of files for a user whose quota entry is about to be deleted.*

8. To move a file, click on the file name to highlight it. Either enter the full path of the new destination in the Move Files To edit box or click on Browse to select the destination from a folder tree, and then click on Move.

9. Click on OK to return to the Quota Entries window. The selected quota entry will be removed from the list.

10. Click on Quota|Close to close the Quota Entries window and return to the Quota page of the drive's Properties dialog box.

11. Click on OK to exit the Properties dialog box and return to the My Computer window.

## Modifying Disk Quota Entries

From time to time, you will need to modify the disk quota settings for a specific user. For example, you might have a user who has been governed by the default limit, but who is now working with very large graphics or database files and needs more space.

To modify the quota entry for a given user, do the following:

1. Access the Quota page of the volume's Properties dialog box (refer to "Accessing And Viewing Disk Quota Settings" earlier in the chapter).

2. Click on the Quota Entries button at the bottom right of the page. This will open the Quota Entries window for the selected volume.

3. Double-click on the name of the user in the Quota Entries window. This will open the Quota Settings dialog box for the user (see Figure 8.8).

4. Modify the disk space limit and warning trigger level as needed, and click on Apply to confirm your new settings.

5. Click on OK to exit the Quota Settings dialog box and return to the Quota Entries window.

6. Click on Quota|Close to close the Quota Entries window and return to the Quota page of the drive's Properties dialog box.

7. Click on OK to exit the Properties dialog box and return to the My Computer window.

## Finding Disk Quota Entries

If the volume has only a relatively small number of users—two dozen or so—you can easily find a specific user by scrolling through the list in the Quota Entries window. However, if it has a large number of users, you may find it faster to use the window's Find feature.

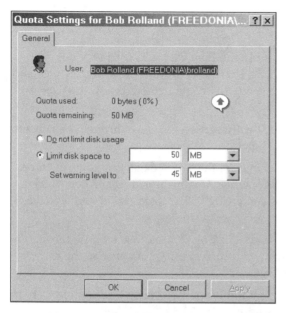

*Figure 8.8    The Quota Settings dialog box for the selected user.*

Here is how to use this feature:

1. Access the Quota page of the volume's Properties dialog box (see "Accessing And Viewing Disk Quota Settings" earlier in the chapter).

2. Click on the Quota Entries button at the bottom right of the page. This will open the Quota Entries window for the selected volume.

3. Click on Edit|Find to open the Find Quota Entry dialog box (see Figure 8.9).

4. Enter the user's logon name. Depending on how you have entered it in the Properties for their user account, it will normally be in one of two forms: *domain_name\user_name* or *user_name@domain_name* (for example:freedonia\

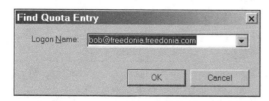

*Figure 8.9    The Find Quota Entry dialog box.*

pcarrington, pcarrington@freedonia.com, or pcarrington@sales. freedonia.com).

5. Click on OK to close the Find Quota Entry dialog box and return to the Quota Entries window. If the search is successful, the name of the user will be highlighted. If not, you'll get an error message.

6. To find additional entries, repeat Steps 3 through 5. Each entry will remain highlighted.

7. To modify the settings for the selected entry or group of entries, click on Quota|Properties. Modify the settings, as described in Steps 4 and 5 of "Modifying Disk Quota Entries" earlier in the chapter.

8. When you are ready, click on Quota|Close to close the Quota Entries window and return to the Quota page of the drive's Properties dialog box.

9. Click on OK to exit the Properties dialog box and return to the My Computer window.

## Sorting Disk Quota Entries

By default, quota entries are sorted by amount used, and then by quota limit. You can also sort the entries by the folder that contains the user account, network domain, user name, status, warning level, or percent used.

To sort the entries in the Quota Entries window, do the following:

1. Click on the heading at the top of each column to sort by that heading. Clicking a second time toggles between ascending and descending order.

   As an alternative, you can click on View|Arrange Items and select the desired sort order.

2. When you are ready, click on Quota|Close to close the Quota Entries window and return to the Quota page of the drive's Properties dialog box.

3. Click on OK to exit the Properties dialog box and return to the My Computer window.

---

**TIP:**   By default, the column for folders containing the user accounts is not displayed. To add this column to the display, click on View|Containing Folder. Note, however, that the name of the containing folder is displayed only when the logon name is in the format domain_name\ user_name. If the logon name is in the format user_name@domain_name, the name of the containing folder is not displayed.

---

8. Managing Disk Quotas

## Moving Columns In The Disk Quota Entries Display

In addition to changing the sort order of the items displayed in the Quota Entries window, you can change the order of the columns in that window. To do so, follow these steps:

1. Access the Quota page of the volume's Properties dialog box (see "Accessing And Viewing Disk Quota Settings" earlier in the chapter).

2. Click on the Quota Entries button at the bottom right of the page. This will open the Quota Entries window for the selected volume.

3. Click on the heading of the column that you want to move, and drag it to its new position.

4. When you are ready, click on Quota|Close to close the Quota Entries window and return to the Quota page of the drive's Properties dialog box.

5. Click on OK to exit the Properties dialog box and return to the My Computer window.

# Working With Disk Quota Entry Information

In addition to using quota entries to configure custom settings for individual users, you can use the information in the Quota Entry window to generate reports, and you can exchange quota entry settings between volumes.

---

**TIP:** *If you are using disk quotas solely to generate information and not to enforce your settings, you can reduce the overhead on your network that is created when you enable disk quotas. Enable disk quotas just long enough for Windows 2000 Server to generate the information that you need—for example, to monitor disk space usage or to determine which users are close to exceeding their limits. When you have the required information, disable the feature until you need it again. You can also control event logging through the Event Viewer settings in a group policy. The Default Domain Policy would seem to be the best place to do this. See Chapter 6 and Appendix A for more information.*

---

**8. Managing Disk Quotas**

## Creating Disk Quota Entry Reports

You can drag and drop the information in the Quota Entries window into another application, such as Microsoft Excel or even WordPad. (You can also copy and paste the data, if you prefer.) In most cases, at least, the data will retain its column and entry order, although this will depend on the application that you are using.

To import quota entry data into another application, do the following:

1. Access the Quota page of the volume's Properties dialog box (see "Accessing And Viewing Disk Quota Settings" earlier in the chapter).

2. Click on the Quota Entries button at the bottom right of the page. This will open the Quota Entries window for the selected volume.

3. Click on Edit|Select All to highlight all of the data in the window.

4. Open the application into which you want to import the data. Start a new file or open the file into which you want to import the data, and position your cursor where you want the data to appear.

5. Arrange the windows on your screen so that both the document in your target application and the data in the Quota Entries window are easily accessible.

6. Using your mouse or other pointing device, drag-and-drop the data from the Quota Entries window into your target application. (See Figure 8.10.)

7. When you are ready, click on Quota|Close to close the Quota Entries window and return to the Quota page of the drive's Properties dialog box.

8. Click on OK to exit the Properties dialog box and return to the My Computer window.

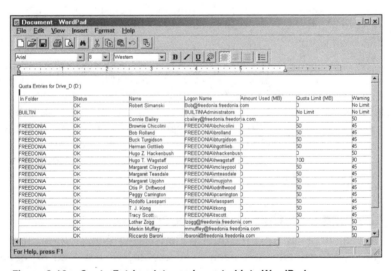

Figure 8.10   Quota Entries data, as imported into WordPad.

## Transferring Disk Quota Entries Between Volumes

After you configure the quota entries the way you want them for a specific volume, you can use those entries in other volumes as well. You do this by exporting the desired entries from the first volume to a file, and then importing the file into the second volume.

---

**TIP:** *You can import data into a volume that does not have disk quotas enabled. If you later decide to enable disk quotas, the settings for the quota entries that you have imported will override the default settings that you configure for the volume.*

---

To transfer quota entries between volumes, do the following:

1. Access the Quota page of the Properties dialog box of the first volume. This is the volume that contains the entries that you want to export (see "Accessing And Viewing Disk Quota Settings" earlier in the chapter).

2. Click on the Quota Entries button at the bottom right of the page. This will open the Quota Entries window for the selected volume.

3. Click on Edit|Select All to highlight all of the data in the window, or select the individual entries that you want to export.

4. Click on Quota|Export. This will open the Export Quota Settings dialog box. (See Figure 8.11.)

5. Select the folder to contain the exported file and enter a file name in the File Name edit window. Ignore the Save As Type drop-down list box, which is empty, and simply add an appropriate extension to the file name.

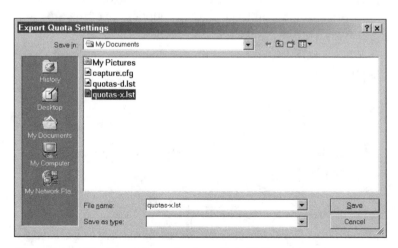

*Figure 8.11    The Export Quota Settings dialog box.*

6. Click on Save to export the data, close the Export Quota Settings dialog box, and return to the Quota Entries window.

7. When you are ready, click on Quota|Close to close the Quota Entries window and return to the Quota page of the drive's Properties dialog box.

8. Click on OK to exit the Properties dialog box and return to the My Computer window.

9. Right-click on the volume to which you want to import the data, and select Properties from the context-sensitive pop-up menu.

10. Select the Quota page and click on the Quota Entries button.

11. Click on Quota|Import to open the Import Quota Settings dialog box.

12. Navigate to the folder containing the file to be imported, select the file, and click on Open to import the data.

13. The current volume may already have settings for one or more of the quota entries in the data to be imported. If so, you will see a message box, as shown in Figure 8.12, asking if you want to replace the current settings with the ones in the import file. Click on Yes to import the entry's disk space limit and warning trigger level settings. Click on No to retain the settings in the current volume. You can also apply your choice to all other duplicate entries.

14. You will be returned to the Quota Entries window. New entries will be added to the window and existing entries will be updated if you have specified this.

15. When you are ready, click on Quota|Close to close the Quota Entries window and return to the Quota page of the drive's Properties dialog box.

16. Click on OK to exit the Properties dialog box and return to the My Computer window.

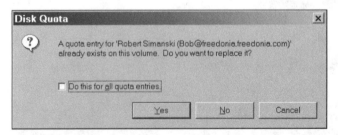

Figure 8.12    A Disk Quota message box, asking the user how to handle a duplicated quota entry.

# Chapter 9

# Using Security Templates

# In Brief

This is the first of two chapters devoted to what I like to call the Security Configuration Tool Set. This tool set is the successor to the Security Configuration Editor, a Microsoft Management Console snap-in developed for Windows NT 4. These tools make it easier for you to analyze and configure the security settings that are in effect on a local computer and to modify the security sections in group policies that can be applied throughout your domain.

---

**NOTE:** *In order to use the security settings discussed in these chapters, Windows 2000 must be installed on an NTFS partition. You cannot apply these settings if it is installed on a FAT partition, including FAT32.*

---

## Overview Of The Security Configuration Tool Set

The Security Configuration Tool Set includes four components: two standalone snap-ins that can be added to a Microsoft Management Console, a command-line utility, and an extension to the Group Policy snap-in:

- *Security Templates standalone snap-in*—The Security Templates snap-in allows you to create and modify template files that can be used to help manage the security settings on the current local system. Security templates can also be imported into a group policy. Windows 2000 comes with a number of predefined templates. These templates cover a wide range of scenarios, from basic security on workstations to very tight security on domain controllers. You must add the Security Templates snap-in manually to a Microsoft Management Console. This snap-in replaces the Security Configuration Editor developed for Windows NT 4.

- *Security Configuration and Analysis standalone snap-in*—The Security Configuration and Analysis snap-in uses security templates to analyze and configure the security settings of the current system. As with the Security Templates snap-in, you must add it manually to a console. This tool replaces the Security Configuration Manager snap-in that was used with the Windows NT 4 Security Configuration Editor.

- *secedit.exe*—This command-line version of the Security Configuration and Analysis snap-in also uses security templates. It can be run in scripts and batch files in circumstances where the GUI version is not appropriate. For example, you can use it in logon scripts or in batch files that you run after normal working hours.

- *Security Settings extension snap-in*—The Security Settings snap-in is used as an extension to the Group Policy Editor snap-in. This extension is installed by default in consoles that use the Group Policy Editor discussed in Chapter 6.

In this chapter, we'll cover security templates and the Security Templates snap-in used to manage them. In Chapter 10, we'll cover the Security Configuration and Analysis snap-in and the secedit.exe command-line utility in detail. We will also take a brief look at the Security Settings extension to the Group Policy Editor. See Chapter 6 and Appendix A for more information about security settings in the Group Policy Editor.

The subject of network security in a Windows 2000 environment is worthy of a book of its own and is beyond the scope of this one. Before using any of the components of the Security Configuration Tool Set, you should have a basic understanding of the various types of policies that can be modified with these tools. You should also be familiar with such security-related subjects as access control lists, authentication, authorization, data protection, and user rights and permissions.

In addition, I am writing these chapters under the assumption that you are already familiar with the Group Policy Editor, covered in Chapter 6 and Appendix A. If you have not read them, please do so first.

I see the Security Configuration Tool Set as a supplement to the Group Policy Editor. The security policies that are included in security templates are the same ones that appear in the Computer Configuration section of every group policy.

In order to become familiar with the Security Templates and the Security Configuration and Analysis snap-ins, you need to either create a new console to contain them or add them to an existing console. See Chapter 2 for information on how to create a custom console or add a snap-in to an existing console.

If you have created the Group Policy Manager console that I suggested in Chapter 6, I recommend that you add them to that console. This

9. Using Security Templates

will make it easier for you to create or modify a template, import it into a group policy, and compare the new settings in the policy with those in the template.

Table 9.1 lists the categories of policies included in a security template. For lists of the specific policies within each category, see Tables A.1 through A.4 in Appendix A.

# Overview Of The Security Templates Snap-in

Security templates are text files that contain settings for each of the types of policies listed in Table 9.1. They do not add any new policies or parameters to those already present by default in every group policy. Instead, in conjunction with the Security Templates snap-in, they provide you with a convenient means of configuring a set of security policies and capturing them to a template. Later, together with the Security Configuration and Analysis snap-in and the Group Policy Editor, you can use your template to perform the following tasks:

- Compare your custom settings against the actual settings in use on a local system.

- Apply your custom settings to a local system, which is especially useful when the system is not part of a domain.

- Apply your settings to groups of computers by importing them into a group policy.

*Table 9.1    Categories of policies included in a security template.*

| Category | Types Of Policies |
| --- | --- |
| Account Policies | Password, account lockout, and Kerberos |
| Local Policies | Auditing, user rights, and security options |
| Event Log | Event Log settings; for example, maximum sizes of the Application, Security, and System logs |
| Restricted Groups | Restricted Groups (none are specified in the default setting) |
| System Services | System services settings; for example, Application Management, Computer Browser, and Indexing Service |
| Registry | Registry security settings (none are specified in the default setting) |
| File System | File security settings for designated folders and files; for example, the %windir% folder (such as c:\winnt) or the file explorer.exe |

Note that these settings apply only to computers, not to users. There is no equivalent feature in Windows 2000 that covers user-related security settings.

Security templates are stored in the folder %windir%\security\templates, where %windir% is the parent folder for the Windows 2000 system files (for example, c:\winnt). The best way to access them is through the Security Templates snap-in, which you must add manually to an existing Microsoft Management Console. When you expand the Security Templates folder in the console tree pane, the snap-in displays child folders for each of the templates that it finds. (See Figure 9.1.) You expand each folder until the specific policy that you want to modify appears in the results pane.

When you edit a policy, you see the same dialog box used for the policy in the Group Policy Editor. See Chapter 6 for information about the various types of dialog boxes that you are likely to encounter.

Windows 2000 Server comes with a number of predefined templates that can serve as excellent starting points. The Windows 2000 installer itself uses some of these templates, depending on the purpose of the system on which the operating system is being installed. You can use the Security Templates snap-in to modify these templates or create your own. If you modify a predefined template, be sure to save it under another name.

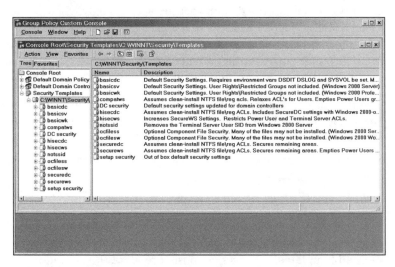

*Figure 9.1   The Security Templates snap-in with the preconfigured security templates that are included in Windows 2000.*

---

**TIP:**    *Because security templates are ASCII text files with an .inf extension, they can be opened in a text editor such as Notepad. Their format is similar to that of an INI file. Nevertheless, for safety reasons, I recommend that whenever possible, you use the Security Templates snap-in, rather than a text editor, to edit the templates. This will help to avoid syntax errors. If a template becomes corrupted, however, you may not be able to use it with the Security Configuration and Analysis snap-in. In that case, you may be able to determine and correct the problem by opening the template in a text editor.*

---

Predefined templates for use on workstations include basicwk, compatws (which can also be used on a server), securews, and hisecws. The basicsv template is intended for servers other than domain controllers. Templates for use on domain controllers include basicdc, securedc, and hisecdc.

The predefined templates are further divided into two types: default and incremental. In addition, there are other templates that are installed for special purposes and are not intended for general use.

---

**NOTE:**    *There is an inconsistency in the way Microsoft refers to workstations in the names of these policies. Both "wk" and "ws" stand for workstation.*

---

# Default Security Templates

When you install Windows 2000 on either a server or a workstation, the installer applies the default security settings only when you do a clean install on an NTFS partition. If you upgrade from Windows NT 4 or earlier, and the operating system is installed on an NTFS partition, your current security settings are not modified. (As noted previously, security settings cannot be applied at all to any FAT-based partition.)

The default templates enable you to apply the default security settings that the installer normally uses during a clean install. There are two common circumstances when you might want to do this:

- When you want to replace your Windows NT security settings with those of Windows 2000

- When you have converted a partition from a FAT-based file system to NTFS

One thing that you cannot do effectively by using any of the predefined templates, however, is to restore all of the computer security policies in a group policy to their default states. You might want to do this if you have configured settings that were not configured originally. The reason this does not work is that security templates contain data only for policies that have been configured. If a policy shows up as not configured when you view a template with the Security Templates snap-in, this means that the template does not contain a setting for that policy. If you were to import the template into a group policy, the only settings that would change would be those contained in the template.

Table 9.2 lists the default security templates that ship with Windows 2000.

**WARNING!** *The basicdc.inf template that came with Release Candidate 3 of Windows 2000 Server (the final release before the shipping version) was flawed. When I attempted to import the template for use with the Security Configuration and Analysis snap-in, I got an error message, saying that the data was invalid. I then opened the file in a text editor, along with a template that I had been able to use, and compared the two. I found and corrected a number of errors in basicdc.inf, after which I was able to use it. If you get a similar error message with the version in the shipping release of Windows 2000, you may want to do likewise.*

# Incremental Security Templates

The incremental security templates that ship with Windows 2000 are designed to be applied to systems that have already been configured with the basic default settings. They are intended to modify settings that are not included in the default templates and do not duplicate any of the policy settings in those templates. These templates are designed to increase the security levels of the systems to which they are applied.

If you have done a clean install of Windows 2000 on the current system, you do not need the default template for that system and can go directly to the appropriate incremental template. If you have upgraded from Windows NT or converted the system partition from FAT to NTFS, you should first apply the appropriate default template.

*Table 9.2   Default security templates in Windows 2000.*

| File Name | Purpose |
|---|---|
| basicwk.inf | For systems running Windows 2000 Professional. Default security settings. Does not include user rights or restricted groups. |
| basicsv.inf | For systems running Windows 2000 Server. Default security settings. Does not include user rights or restricted groups. Should not be used on domain controllers. |
| basicdc.inf | For domain controllers running Windows 2000 Server. |

9. Using Security Templates

**Table 9.3   Incremental security templates in Windows 2000.**

| File Name | Purpose |
|---|---|
| compatws.inf | For use on workstations and servers. Offers backward-compatiblity with legacy applications. |
| securews.inf | Secure configuration for workstations and servers. Can be used in a mixed-mode environment. |
| securedc.inf | Secure configuration for domain controllers. Can be used in a mixed-mode environment. |
| hisecws.inf | Highly secure configuration for workstations and servers. Can only be used in a native Windows 2000 environment. |
| hisecdc.inf | Highly secure configuration for domain controllers. Can only be used in a native Windows 2000 environment. |

Table 9.3 lists the incremental security templates that come with Windows 2000.

### compatws

The compatws.inf template can be used on either workstations or servers. It should not be used on domain controllers, however, because it does not create a sufficiently secure environment. Here is why you might want to use it:

When a new user logs onto a Windows 2000 workstation for the first time, he is assigned to the Power Users group for the local system. The members of this group have a considerable amount of latitude. For example, they can create, modify, and delete user accounts; create local groups, then add and remove members; and remove members from the Power Users, Users, and Guests groups on the local system.

This may be more latitude than you want to give them. You might prefer to make them members of the Users group instead. Although members of the Users group can create or modify local groups, they cannot create or modify user accounts or remove members from groups that they have not created. Also, they cannot share folders or create local printers.

The problem is that the limitations on the user rights and permission of the members of the Users group may prevent some legacy applications, including Microsoft Office 97, from working properly. For example, these applications may add to or modify files in system folders to which a member of the Users group does not have write permission. The template compatws.inf solves the problem by modifying those default permissions for the Users group that might keep these applications from running correctly.

### securews And securedc

The template securews.inf provides a secure configuration for workstations or servers, whereas securecd.inf does the same for domain controllers. These templates are added to the basic configuration. Because they assume that the basic security settings are already in effect, they do not modify the access control lists. These templates provide increased security for areas of the operating system that are not covered by explicit permissions (such as account policy, auditing, and certain Registry keys that are related to security).

### hisecws And hisecdc

The template hisecws.inf is designed for workstations and servers, whereas hisecdc.inf is designed for domain controllers. They provide highly secure configurations for Windows 2000 systems that are operating in a native Windows 2000 environment. They cannot be used in mixed-mode environments, such as those that include systems running Windows NT 4 or earlier, Windows 98, Windows 95, Windows 3.1, or non-Windows operating systems. In their highly secure environments, all network communications must be digitally signed and encrypted at a level that is provided only by Windows 2000. In this setting, a Windows 2000 system can communicate only with another Windows 2000 system.

# Special-Purpose Security Templates

In addition to the default and incremental security templates, you will find several special-purpose templates, including DC security and setup security. Although DC security and setup security are not intended for general use, they appear in the Security Templates snap-in, so you need to be aware of them. The template file DC security.inf includes default security settings that have been updated for domain controllers, whereas setup security.inf provides the out-of-box security settings used during the installation process.

**9. Using Security Templates**

# *Immediate Solutions*

## Adding The Security Templates Snap-in To A Console

The Security Templates snap-in is not installed by default in any of the administrative tools that ship with Windows 2000. In order to use it, you must either create a console for it or add it to an existing console.

### Creating A New Console For The Security Templates Snap-in

Here is how to create a new console for the Security Templates snap-in:

1. Click Start|Run.

2. Enter the following command to open a new console:

```
mmc /a
```

   You will see a blank, empty console in Author mode, called Console1 by default.

3. Click Console|Save. Make sure that the Save dialog box is open to the My Administrative Tools folder.

4. Give the file a meaningful name and save it. Windows 2000 Server will automatically add the .MSC extension.

5. Click Console|Add/Remove Snap-ins. This will open the Add/Remove Snap-in dialog box.

6. You will see a list of all the available standalone snap-ins that are installed on your system. Click Add to open the Add Standalone Snap-in dialog box. (See Figure 9.2.)

7. Select Security Templates, click Add, and then click Close to return to the previous dialog box. The Security Templates snap-in should now appear on the list of installed snap-ins. The snap-in does not use extensions, so you need not be concerned about adding any.

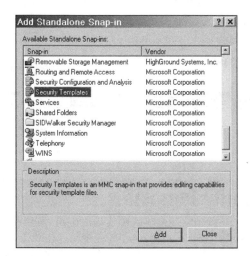

*Figure 9.2   The Add Standalone Snap-in dialog box.*

8. Click OK to return to the console window. The Security Templates snap-in should appear in the console tree pane.

9. Click Console|Save to save the new console.

## Adding The Security Templates Snap-in To An Existing Console

Rather than create a new console for the Security Templates snap-in,
you may prefer to add it to an existing console, such as the Group
Policy Manager that you created in Chapter 6. Follow these steps to
add the snap-in (if the existing console is not in the Administrative
Tools folder, you will need to adapt these steps to allow for this):

1. Click Start|Programs|Administrative Tools and select the name
   of the console to which you want to add the snap-in.

2. Click Console|Add/Remove Snap-ins. This will open the Add/
   Remove Snap-in dialog box.

3. You will see a list of all the available standalone snap-ins that
   are installed on your system. Click Add to open the Add
   Standalone Snap-in dialog box.

4. Select Security Templates, click Add, and then click Close
   to return to the previous dialog box. The Security Templates
   snap-in should now appear on the list of installed snap-ins. The
   snap-in does not use extensions, so you need not be concerned
   about adding any.

5. Click OK to return to the console window. The Security Templates snap-in should appear in the console tree pane.

6. Click Console|Save to save the modified console.

| Related solution: | Found on page: |
|---|---|
| Customizing A Console | 38 |

# Working With Security Templates

After you add the Security Templates snap-in to a Microsoft Management Console, you can use it to view and modify existing templates or create new ones.

## Viewing The Contents Of A Security Template

To view the contents of a security template, follow this procedure:

1. Open the console in which you have installed the Security Templates snap-in.

2. In the console tree pane, locate the Security Templates folder.

3. Expand the folder to expose the template path folders (for example, c:\winnt\security\templates).

---

**NOTE:** *It is possible to have templates in different folders. For the sake of simplicity and safety, however, I recommend that you stay with the default folder. One reason is that the default folder has adequate security protection. By default, only administrators have full control over this folder. If you should place additional templates in another folder, be sure to review the security settings for the default folder and apply the same settings to the new folder.*

---

4. Expand the template path folder that contains your template to expose the folder for the template that you need to view.

5. Expand the template folder to expose the categories of security settings covered by the template.

6. Expand each of the category folders until the security settings are displayed in the results pane. (See Figure 9.3.)

## Saving A Security Template Under Another Name

Before modifying an existing security template, particularly one of the preconfigured templates that ship with Windows 2000, you may want to save it under another name. Here is how to do it:

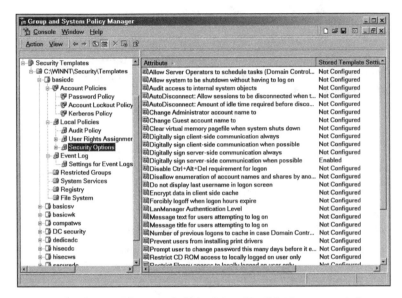

*Figure 9.3   The basicdc security template with all folders expanded.*

1. Open the console in which you have installed the Security Templates snap-in.

2. In the console tree pane, locate the Security Templates folder.

3. Expand the folder to expose the template path folders (for example, c:\winnt\security\templates).

4. Expand the template path folder that contains your template to expose the folder for the template that you need to view.

5. Right-click on the template folder and select Save As from the context-sensitive pop-up menu. This will open the Save As dialog box.

---

**NOTE:** *By default, the dialog box should be open to the default templates folder. If it is not, navigate to the %windir%\security\templates folder, where %windir% is the main folder for the Windows 2000 system files (c:\winnt, for example).*

---

6. Enter a new name for the template, using the DOS 8+3 naming convention. Windows 2000 will add the appropriate extension, so you need not add one yourself.

7. Click Save to save the template, exit the dialog box, and return to the console.

8. If the new name does not appear in the list of templates, right-click on the template path folder that contains your new template and choose Refresh from the context-sensitive pop-up menu.

## Creating A New Security Template

The preconfigured security templates that ship with Windows 2000 will probably meet your needs with little or no modification. If they do not, however, you can create your own template from scratch. Here is how to do it:

1. Open the console in which you have installed the Security Templates snap-in.
2. In the console tree pane, locate the Security Templates folder.
3. Expand the folder to expose the template path folder that will contain your new template (for example, c:\winnt\security\ templates).
4. Right-click on the template path folder and select New Template from the context-sensitive pop-up menu. This will open a dialog box, in which you can enter a name and description for the new template. (See Figure 9.4.)
5. Enter a name of up to eight characters following the DOS 8+3 naming convention. Windows 2000 will add the proper extension.
6. Enter a description. This will be added to the body of the template file.
7. Click OK to close the dialog box and return to the console window. The name of your new template will be added to the list.
8. Expand the categories folders to view the contents of your new template. By default, none of the security settings will be configured.

## Refreshing The Security Templates List

In most cases, when you add a new template using the Security Templates snap-in, the template will appear under the appropriate template path folder as soon as you create it. If you add a template by

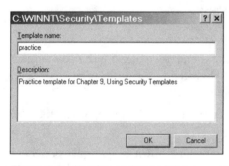

*Figure 9.4   Naming and describing a new template.*

another means, however—such as creating one with a text editor or using Windows Explorer to copy a template from another source to the default templates folder—the new template might not appear right away. Here is how to refresh the list:

1. Open the console in which you have installed the Security Templates snap-in.

2. In the console tree pane, locate the Security Templates folder.

3. Expand the folder to expose the template path folder that contains your new template (for example, c:\winnt\security\ templates).

4. Right-click on the template path folder and select Refresh from the context-sensitive pop-up menu. This will force the snap-in to reload the template files in the path folder.

## Modifying A Security Template

I recommend that you work with the unmodified versions of the preconfigured security templates before creating your own custom templates. The sets of preconfigured templates intended for use on specific types of systems—namely workstations, servers, and domain controllers—are designed to complement each other and should work well together.

However, many security settings are not configured in any of these templates because they must be tailored to specific needs. Examples include settings relating to restricted groups or the local file system. You may need to modify some of these settings to address your specific needs. If you decide to modify one of the preconfigured templates, be sure to save it under another name and modify the copy.

Here is the basic procedure for modifying a security setting, followed by some practical examples:

1. Open the console in which you have installed the Security Templates snap-in.

2. In the console tree pane, locate the Security Templates folder.

3. Expand the folder to expose the template path folders (for example, c:\winnt\security\templates).

4. Expand the template path folder that contains your template to expose the folder for the template that you need to view.

5. Expand the template folder to expose the categories of security settings covered by the template.

**9. Using Security Templates**

6.  Expand each of the category folders until the security settings are displayed in the results pane.

7.  Double-click on the policy that you want to modify. This will open the appropriate dialog box for that policy—the same dialog box used for the equivalent policy in the Group Policy Editor. See Figure 9.5 for an example.

8.  If necessary, check the Define This Policy Setting In The Template box to enable you to modify the settings. (If you need to reverse a previously configured setting and want to leave the setting unconfigured, uncheck the box.)

9.  Make your changes, follow the prompts to confirm your changes, and close the various dialog boxes.

10. In the console tree pane, right-click on the main folder for the security template and select Save from the context-sensitive pop-up menu.

| *Related solution:* | *Found on page:* |
|---|---|
| Working With Dialog Boxes In The Group Policy Editor | 201 |

### Practical Example: Displaying A Custom Logon Message

Here is how to display a custom logon message. The message will be seen by everyone who logs onto the system:

1.  Open the console in which you have installed the Security Templates snap-in.

2.  In the console tree pane, locate the Security Templates folder.

3.  Expand the folder to expose the template path folders (for example, c:\winnt\security\templates).

4.  Expand the template path folder that contains your template to expose the folder for the template that you need to modify.

*Figure 9.5    An example of a dialog box for modifying a setting in a security template.*

5. Expand the template folder to expose the categories of security settings covered by the template.

6. Expand the Local Policies folder, and then select Security Options.

7. In the results pane, double-click on Message Text For Users Attempting To Log On. This will open a dialog box in which you can enter the desired text. (See Figure 9.6.)

8. Check the Define This Policy Setting In The Template checkbox to enable the feature.

9. Enter the desired text in the edit window, and then click OK to return to the console.

10. If you also want a title for the message box, double-click on Message Title For Users Attempting To Log On.

11. Enter the desired text in the edit window, and then click OK to return to the console.

### Practical Example: Creating A Policy For Restricted Groups

A policy for restricted groups allows you to define who should—and who should not—belong to a specific group. When you apply a template or policy that defines a restricted group to the local system, the Security Configuration Tool Set adds and removes members from the group as needed. This is done to make sure that the membership is consistent with the settings in the template or policy.

In the following example, you will define a policy for the Administrators group on the local system. By doing so, you will ensure that only the Administrator of the local system can belong to the local Administrators group, once the policy is applied to the system. When it reconfigures the local system, the Security Configuration Tool Set will remove all other users who belong to the local Administrators group and add the Administrator, if that user is not already a member. Keep in

*Figure 9.6 Creating a user logon message.*

mind that this policy will affect only the local Administrators group, not the Administrators group defined in the Active Directory.

Here is the procedure for creating a restricted group policy:

1. Open the console in which you have installed the Security Templates snap-in.

2. In the console tree pane, locate the Security Templates folder.

3. Expand the folder to expose the template path folders (for example, c:\winnt\security\templates).

4. Expand the template path folder that contains your template to expose the folder for the template that you need to modify.

5. Expand the template folder to expose the categories of security settings covered by the template.

6. Right-click on the Restricted Groups folder and select Add Group from the context-sensitive pop-up menu. This will open the Add Group dialog box. (See Figure 9.7.)

7. In the edit window, enter the name Administrators, and then click OK to close the dialog box and return to the console. The Administrators group will now appear in the results pane for the Restricted Groups folder. You will now need to define the membership of the group.

8. Double-click on Administrators in the results pane. This will open the Configure Membership For Administrators dialog box, which has two windows. The top window displays the members of the group and the bottom window displays the names of other groups, of which the current group is a member. Because this restricted group has not yet been configured, each of the windows will be empty.

9. Click Add next to the top window to add members to the group. This will open the Select Users Or Groups dialog box. (See Figure 9.8.)

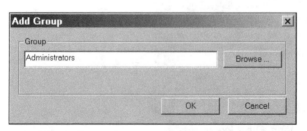

*Figure 9.7   Adding a group to the restricted groups folder.*

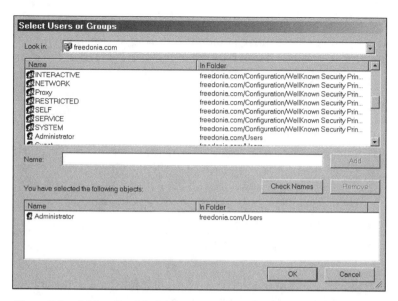

*Figure 9.8    Adding the Administrator to the local Administrators group.*

10. Select Administrator, click Add, and then click OK to return to the Administrators dialog box.

11. You do not need to add the local Administrators group to any other group, so click OK to close the dialog box and return to the console. The name Administrator will now appear in the Membership column of the results pane.

### Practical Example: Configuring Permissions For A Folder

You can use a security template to configure permissions for folders in the local computer's file system. As an example, we will use the %windir%\repair folder, where %windir% is the main folder for the Windows 2000 system files (for example, c:\winnt). Here is the procedure:

1. Open the console in which you have installed the Security Templates snap-in.

2. In the console tree pane, locate the Security Templates folder.

3. Expand the folder to expose the template path folders (for example, c:\winnt\security\templates).

4. Expand the template path folder that contains your template to expose the folder for the template that you need to modify.

5. Expand the template folder to expose the categories of security settings covered by the template.

6. Right-click on the File System folder and select Add File from the context-sensitive pop-up menu. This will open the Add A File Or Folder dialog box, with folder trees for each drive on the system. (See Figure 9.9.)

7. Expand the folder for the drive that contains your system files (typically drive C:), and then expand the %windir% folder and select the repair subfolder.

8. Click OK. This will open the Template Security For %windir%\ repair dialog box, which displays the members of the Access Control List for the folder and the permissions available to each. By default, only one group, Everyone, will be listed.

9. Select the Everyone group and click Remove.

10. Click Add to open the Select Users, Computers, Or Groups dialog box.

11. Select the Administrators group, click Add, and then click OK to return to the previous dialog box.

12. In the Permissions window, select the Full Control checkbox in the Allow column. (See Figure 9.10.)

13. Uncheck the Allow Inheritable Permissions From Parent To Propagate To This Object checkbox.

14. Click OK. This will open the Template Security Policy Setting dialog box. (See Figure 9.11.)

*Figure 9.9   Adding a file or folder to File System security settings in a template.*

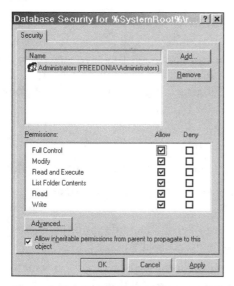

*Figure 9.10    Giving the Administrator full control over the %windir%\
repair folder.*

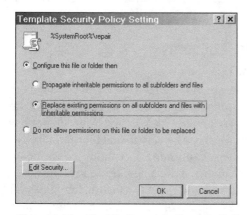

*Figure 9.11    The File Template Security Policy Setting dialog box.*

15. This dialog box has several radio buttons that control the way
    security is applied to this folder and its child folders. Select
    Configure This File Or Folder, and then select Replace Existing
    Permissions. This will prevent the folder from inheriting the
    permissions of its parent. Also, administrators will have full
    control over its child folders, if any.

16. Click OK to exit the dialog box and return to the console.

17. In the console tree pane, right-click on the main folder for the
    template that you have just modified and select Save from the
    context-sensitive pop-up menu.

**9. Using Security
Templates**

**283**

## Deleting A Security Template

If you use security templates, no doubt you will create your own templates for practice and experimentation. Eventually you may want to reduce the clutter by deleting those that you no longer need. (I do not recommend deleting any of the preconfigured templates that come with Windows 2000.) Here is how to delete a template:

1. Open the console in which you have installed the Security Templates snap-in.

2. In the console tree pane, locate the Security Templates folder.

3. Expand the folder to expose the template path folders (for example, c:\winnt\security\templates).

4. Expand the template path folder that contains your template to expose the folder for the template that you need to view.

5. Right-click on the main folder for the template that you want to remove and select Delete from the context-sensitive pop-up menu. This will open a message box with a confirmation request.

6. Click Yes to confirm the deletion and return to the console. The list of templates will be refreshed.

## Creating Or Modifying A Security Template's Description

Template descriptions appear in the results pane when you select the template path folder in the console tree pane. They are optional, and even some of the templates that ship with Windows 2000 do not have them. Nevertheless, descriptions can be very useful for reminding you of the purpose of a template or cautioning you about its use. Therefore, I recommend that you always write a description when you create a new template, and that you add them to existing templates that lack descriptions. You can also modify an existing description to make it more useful to you.

Here is how to add a new description to a template or modify an existing one:

1. Open the console in which you have installed the Security Templates snap-in.

2. In the console tree pane, locate the Security Templates folder.

3. Expand the folder to expose the template path folders (for example, c:\winnt\security\templates).

4. Expand the template path folder that contains your template to expose the folder for the template that you need to view.

5. Right-click on the main folder for the template that you want to describe and select Set Description from the context-sensitive pop-up menu. This will display the Security Template Description dialog box. (See Figure 9.12.)

6. Enter your description and click OK to return to the console. Your new description will appear in the results pane.

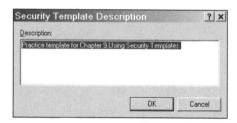

*Figure 9.12    Editing the description of a security template.*

# Chapter 10

# Managing Security Configuration And Analysis

# *In Brief*

This is the second of two chapters devoted to the Security Configuration Tool Set, which is the successor to the Security Configuration Editor in Windows NT 4. In Chapter 9, I covered security templates and the Security Templates snap-in used to manage them. Please read that chapter first, if you have not already done so.

In this chapter, I will cover the Security Configuration and Analysis snap-in and the secedit.exe command-line utility in detail. I will also take a brief look at the Security Settings extension to the Group Policy Editor. See Chapter 6 and Appendix A for more information about security settings in the Group Policy Editor.

In addition, I am assuming that you are already familiar with the Group Policy Editor, which is covered in Chapter 6 and Appendix A. If you have not read Chapter 6, please do so before reading this chapter. Also, if you have not already added the Security Templates and Security Configuration and Analysis snap-ins to a Microsoft Management Console, as suggested in Chapter 9, please do so now.

# Overview Of The Security Configuration And Analysis Snap-in

The Security Configuration and Analysis snap-in enables you to use system templates to analyze and configure the current local system. As with the Security Templates snap-in, you must add it manually to an existing console.

The snap-in uses the information stored in a database to compare the currently effective security settings on your local system against the settings in the template or templates stored in the database. The databases are stored in the %windir%\security\database folder, in which %windir% is normally the c:\winnt folder.

Whenever you use the snap-in to configure or analyze your system, it creates a log in which it records the actions taken, and whether they were successes or failures. At the beginning of the process, you will see a dialog box with the default path name of the log. You can edit the path name, as needed. By default, the logs are stored in the %windir%\security\logs folder.

# Using The Snap-in

Normally, the first time that you access it in a session, the Security Configuration and Analysis snap-in opens your last-used custom database. The very first time that you use the snap-in, however, no such custom database will exist. The only database that you will see is secedit.sdb. This database contains critical information and cannot be opened. You will get an "Access Denied" message if you attempt to use it. What you need to do, instead, is to create a new database and import one or more of the preconfigured templates. See "Creating A New Database," in the Immediate Solutions section of this chapter.

A database can contain more than one template. For example, if you want to create a composite template that shows all of the settings for a highly secure domain controller, you can import the basicdc, securedc, and hisecdc templates into one database. If you do this, be sure to import them in the order given; that is, start with the basic template and work up. When you add a template to an existing database, some settings in the new template may conflict with those in a previously installed template. If you import them in the order that I have suggested, you can select the option to overwrite the previous settings with the newer ones. This makes it easy for you to build a composite template that will give you a true picture of what all of the security settings for a highly secure domain controller should be.

Once you have created your database, you can analyze your current security settings against the ones in the stored template in your new database. The Security Configuration and Analysis snap-in uses marks to flag both consistencies and inconsistencies between the template stored in the database and the settings on the analyzed system. A green mark indicates that the settings are consistent with each other, whereas a red mark indicates an inconsistency. (See Figure 10.1.) If there is no mark, it means that the policy is not configured in the database's stored settings. You can modify the settings in the stored template by double-clicking on a policy in the results pane and making the required changes. Changes that you make to the stored template in the database do not affect the source templates that you imported into the database.

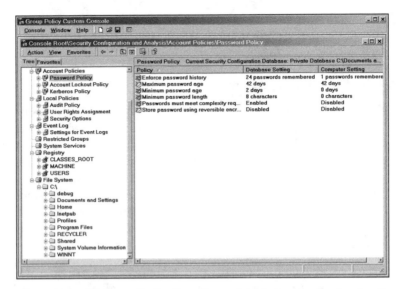

*Figure 10.1    The Security Configuration and Analysis snap-in, showing the results of an analysis using the securedc security template.*

You can use the settings in the stored template to configure the local system or export the stored template to a new file that you can import into a group policy. If you save the new template to the same folder as the preconfigured templates, it will be added to the list in the Security Templates snap-in, where you can modify it further. Remember that the stored template is part of the database file, so save the database from time to time, as well. See the Immediate Solutions section later in this chapter for instructions on how to perform each of these procedures.

# A Word Of Warning

When using this snap-in to configure the security settings for a local system—as opposed to simply analyzing them—you need to exercise extreme caution. The most important precaution that you can take is to give yourself a means of restoring your previous settings. The best way to do this is to export your current settings as a template, and then add that policy to a database. To do this, you will need to open the Local Computer Policy in the Group Policy Editor. See "Backing Up Your Current Security Settings" in the Immediate Solutions section for the step-by-step procedure. This backup should supplement, not replace, your regular tape backups. In an emergency, you can use the secedit command line utility to restore your original policy quickly.

When you use the Local Computer Policy to export your settings to a template, you will be asked what settings to export. You can export either the local settings contained in the policy or the actual policies that are in effect at the time, which may have been set in another policy that overwrites the local computer policy. I recommend that you export two templates, one for the local policy and another for the effective policy, although the latter is probably the more important of the two.

Be sure to experiment with security templates on a test system, not a production system. If you should run into a problem, and you have created a backup template as suggested, you will have an escape hatch. Get to a command prompt and use the command-line utility secedit.exe to restore your previous configuration. This utility is covered in detail elsewhere in this chapter. To avoid potential problems with long file names, I recommend that you observe the DOS 8+3 convention when assigning file names to your templates and databases.

---

**TIP:** *If you do not have a system that you can dedicate to testing, I recommend that you buy some inexpensive hard drives, and outfit at least two systems (one server and one workstation) with removable drive caddies. The caddies can be bought for about $40 per set, and are available for both IDE and SCSI drives. Each set comes with both a caddy and a dock that you install in an available 5.25-inch drive bay. This approach makes it very easy to switch between different installations on the same computer. Just remember to run your BIOS's IDE hard-drive detection routine whenever you switch drives if you are using IDE drives that are not identical. Setting the drive's configuration to auto in the first setup screen, which forces the BIOS to determine the drive type each time that you boot the system, caused problems with some of the earlier beta versions of Windows 2000 Server.*

---

# Overview Of The secedit Command-Line Utility

This command-line version of the Security Configuration and Analysis snap-in also uses security templates. It can be run in scripts and batch files, in circumstances in which the GUI version is not appropriate. For example, you can use it in logon scripts or in batch files that you run after normal working hours. The utility can also be used in conjunction with other administrative tools, such as Microsoft Systems Management Server or the Windows 2000 Task Scheduler. Figure 10.2 shows a screen of help information for the basic functions performed by the utility.

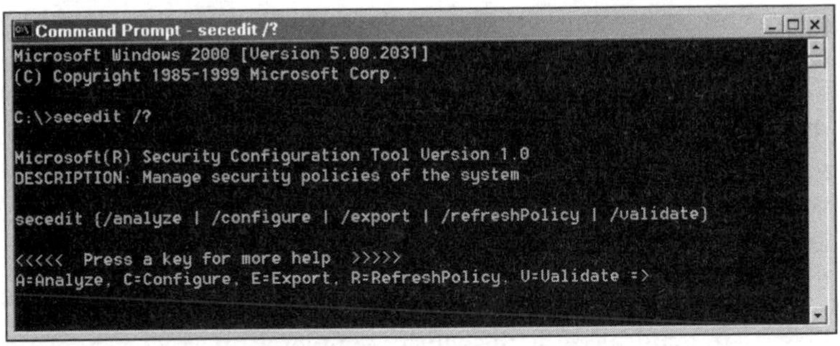

```
Command Prompt - secedit /?                                        _□x
Microsoft Windows 2000 [Version 5.00.2031]
(C) Copyright 1985-1999 Microsoft Corp.

C:\>secedit /?

Microsoft(R) Security Configuration Tool Version 1.0
DESCRIPTION: Manage security policies of the system

secedit {/analyze | /configure | /export | /refreshPolicy | /validate}

<<<<<  Press a key for more help  >>>>>
A=Analyze, C=Configure, E=Export, R=RefreshPolicy, V=Validate =>
```

*Figure 10.2    The secedit.exe command-line utility, with a help screen
showing the basic functions available.*

You can use this utility to perform the following tasks, some of which
are not available in the Security Configuration and Analysis snap-in:

- *Analyze and configure system security*—These tasks corre-
  spond to similar functions in the snap-in. You must still use the
  snap-in, however, to view the results of an analysis.

- *Export a stored template in a database to a security template file*—
  This corresponds to the Export Template function in the snap-in.

- *Refresh a group policy object by reapplying security settings
  to it*—This option enables you to trigger a group policy event that
  propagates changes in security settings whenever the system
  boots, periodically thereafter, and whenever local security
  policies are modified using the Security Settings extension to the
  Group Policy Editor. There is also a command-line switch to
  force a refresh.

- *Validate the syntax in a security template file before importing
  it into a database*—This option validates the syntax of each line
  in the template. Apparently, however, it does not check the
  accuracy of the data itself. For example, it did not identify or
  repair the problems in the basicdc template that were preventing
  me from using it with the Security Configuration and Analysis
  snap-in.

If you use the utility to analyze system security, it will generate a log
file. You will need to open the Security Configuration and Analysis
snap-in to view the results of the analysis. See "Using The secedit.exe
Command-Line Utility" in the Immediate Solutions section later in
this chapter for instructions on how to use this program.

# Notes On The Security Settings Extension To The Group Policy Editor

The Security Settings snap-in is used as an extension to the Group Policy Editor snap-in. This extension is installed by default in consoles that use the Group Policy Editor, discussed in Chapter 6 and Appendix A.

To access the security settings for a group policy, open the policy in the Group Policy Editor. In the console tree, expand the Computer Configuration Windows Settings folders to expose the Security Settings folder.

It is beyond the scope of this book to discuss the various security settings in detail. I will point out simply that by right-clicking on the Security Settings folder and selecting Import Policy, you can import any of the security templates on your system. This includes both the preconfigured templates that ship with Windows 2000 and any custom ones that you may have created. Also, if you have selected the Local Computer Policy, you can export its settings to a template.

# Strategies For Using The Security Configuration Tool Set

As I delved into my research for these chapters on the Security Configuration Tool Set, a nagging question began to come up in the back of my mind. If group policies were as powerful as I had described them in Chapter 6, what was the need for the Security Configuration Tool Set? Was it a vestige of Windows NT that Microsoft had left in for the benefit of current users, or did it serve an important purpose in Windows 2000?

I have concluded that these tools are a useful addition to Windows 2000. However, they need to be used judiciously as a supplement to the Group Policy Editor, not as a replacement for it. Here are my suggestions for when—and when not—to use these tools.

## Managing Local Computer Policy

As good as the group policy features are in Windows 2000, there are two areas in which they leave much to be desired. These areas include the difficulty of applying a consistent Local Computer Policy to a large number of systems and the near impossibility of restoring any group policy to its default state. The Security Configuration Tool Set can be very useful in addressing the Local Computer Policy issue. The Local Computer Policy is created automatically when you install Windows 2000 on any system. Here are some of the drawbacks to this feature, as I see them:

- Because the Local Computer Policy applies only, and specifically, to the local system, you cannot apply or manage it remotely. If you need to modify the local policy on a specific system, you must log onto the system and edit the policy there. Moreover, you must do this for every local policy that you want to change.

- In theory, you can overwrite the settings in the Local Computer Policy by modifying the settings in a group policy, such as the Default Domain Policy, which is applied after the local policy. In practice, this is not always a good idea because settings that might be appropriate for a workstation would not be appropriate for a server or domain controller.

- Certain specific policies are implemented when the system is started, before the user logs on and the network connections have been completed. Therefore, overriding them in the Default Domain Policy, for example, has no effect.

You could use the features in the Security Configuration Tool Set to create a Local Computer Policy template that you could apply to other systems, as needed. You would do this by configuring the Local Computer Policy on a reference system, exporting the settings to a template, and copying the template to a shared folder on your network or even to a floppy disk. When you needed to modify the Local Computer Policy on another system, you could import the template into the policy. Although security templates apply only to computer security settings, most of the remaining settings in the Local Computer Policy are unconfigured, by default.

---

**NOTE:**   *Microsoft, in its Beta 3 Technical Walkthrough, Using The Security Configuration Tool Set, recommends using security templates to modify the Local Computer Policy only on systems that are not part of a domain, and hence not covered by other group policies. Although security templates would be particularly useful in that situation, I have found that they can also be useful on systems that are part of a domain, when it comes to policies that are implemented before the other applicable group policies can be accessed over the network. For example, when I was doing research on group policies, I enabled the default logon message on one system. Later, I decided that I no longer wanted it. Even though I disabled the policy in every applicable group policy, including the Local Group Policy, I kept getting the message. This remained until I imported an appropriate template into the policy, after which I no longer got the message.*

---

# Upgrading Security On A System

When you install Windows 2000, it implements the basic security settings appropriate to the way the local system is being used—as a workstation, server, or domain controller. Moreover, they are implemented only during a clean installation on an NTFS partition. If you are upgrading over Windows NT or installing Windows 2000 on another type of partition, these settings are not implemented at all.

Later, you will probably want to upgrade the system's security settings. For example, you might want to apply the basic settings after converting a partition to NTFS or upgrade the default settings to a more secure level.

I would use the appropriate preconfigured templates to modify the Local Computer Policy, but only if you have not already substantially modified that policy yourself. Because a security template contains only those policies that have been specifically configured in it, the template has no effect on policies that it does not contain. If you import a security template into a Local Computer Policy that you have already modified, you may find that your modifications have been overwritten and you could very well wind up with a mess on your hands.

This caution applies only when it comes to using templates to configure security settings or importing a template into a group policy. It does not apply to using templates to analyze current settings. In fact, this can be very useful in helping you to plug security holes and to compare your modifications with the recommended settings.

# Modifying A Network-Based Group Policy

Yes, you can import a security template into a network-based group policy, such as the Default Domain Policy or a custom policy that you have created. The question is why you would want to do it.

Keep in mind that the preconfigured templates that ship with Windows 2000 are designed to be used on local systems—to apply appropriate security levels to a server or domain controller, for example. Security templates affect only computer-related security policies, not user-related ones. Security settings that are appropriate for one type of system may not be appropriate for another.

The main value of network-based group policies is that they enable you to manage user-related policies. In the Default Domain Policy, most of the computer-related security settings and virtually all of the user-related settings are not configured, by default. This enables you to apply security settings at a lower level, such as a policy for an organizational unit, without having to worry about conflicts.

One reason to import a security template into a network-based group policy would be to work around the problem of restoring the policy's default settings. Suppose that you had made many modifications to the security settings in the Default Domain Policy, and then decided that you wanted to restore the group policy to its default state. If you had followed my suggestion to export your Local Computer Policy settings to templates before using the Security Configuration Tool Set to modify your system's configuration, you might be able to do it. See "Restoring Your Original Security Settings" in the Immediate Solutions section that follows.

# *Immediate Solutions*

## Using The Security Configuration And Analysis Snap-in

The Security Configuration and Analysis snap-in is a very powerful management tool. With it, you can:

- Analyze the computer-oriented security settings on a local system.
- Compare the current settings with recommendations in preconfigured templates designed for the same type of system.
- Reconfigure the current system, using either a preconfigured security template or one that you have created.

The snap-in is a database driver. To use the snap-in for the first time, you must create a database that contains the templates that you want to use to analyze and configure your system.

The template within the database is called the stored template. You can modify the settings in the stored template and export the settings to a new, separate security template. In addition, you can import more than one template into the database. When you do so, the templates are merged into one.

The Security Configuration and Analysis snap-in is not installed by default in any of the administrative tools that ship with Windows 2000. In order to use it, you must either create a Microsoft Management Console for it or add it to an existing console. Hopefully, you have already created a console for the Security Templates snap-in (described in Chapter 9) or added the Security Templates snap-in to the Group Policy Manager console (described in Chapter 6). If so, I recommend that you add this snap-in to either one of those consoles.

### Creating A New Console For The Security Configuration And Analysis Snap-in

Here is how to create a new console for the Security Templates snap-in:

1. Click on Start|Run.

**10. Managing Security Configuration And Analysis**

2. Enter the following command to open a new console:

```
mmc /a
```

You will see a blank, empty console in Author mode. By default, it will be called Console1.

3. Click on Console|Save. Make sure that the Save dialog is open to the My Administrative Tools folder.

4. Give the file a meaningful name and save it. Windows 2000 Server will automatically add the .msc extension.

5. Click on Console|Add/Remove Snap-ins. This will open the Add/Remove Snap-in dialog box.

6. You will see a list of all the available standalone snap-ins that have been installed on your system. Click on Add to open the Add Standalone Snap-in dialog box. (See Figure 10.3.)

7. Select Security Configuration And Analysis, click on Add, and then click on Close to return to the previous dialog box. The Security Configuration and Analysis snap-in should now appear on the list of installed snap-ins. The snap-in does not use extensions, so you need not be concerned about adding any.

8. Click on OK to return to the console window. The Security Configuration and Analysis snap-in should appear in the console tree pane.

9. Click on Console|Save to save the new console.

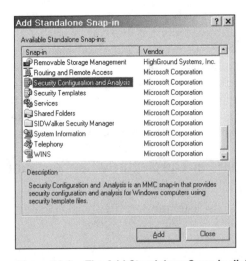

*Figure 10.3  The Add Standalone Snap-in dialog box.*

## Adding The Security Configuration And Analysis Snap-in To An Existing Console

Rather than create a new console for the Security Configuration and Analysis snap-in, you may prefer to add it to an existing console, such as the Group Policy Manager that we created in Chapter 6. Here is how to do it (if the existing console is not in the Administrative Tools folder, you will need to adapt these steps to allow for this):

1. Click on Start|Programs|Administrative Tools and select the name of the console to which you want to add the snap-in.

2. Click on Console|Add/Remove Snap-ins. This will open the Add/Remove Snap-in dialog box.

3. You will see a list of all the available standalone snap-ins that have been installed on your system. Click on Add to open the Add Standalone Snap-in dialog box.

4. Select Security Configuration And Analysis, click on Add, and then click on Close to return to the previous dialog box. The Security Configuration and Analysis snap-in should now appear on the list of installed snap-ins. The snap-in does not use extensions, so you need not be concerned about adding any.

5. Click on OK to return to the console window. The Security Configuration and Analysis snap-in should appear in the console tree pane.

6. Click on Console|Save to save the modified console.

| *Related solution:* | *Found on page:* |
|---|---|
| Customizing A Console | 38 |

## Creating A New Database

To use the Security Configuration and Analysis feature, you must first create a new custom database that includes the security templates that you want to use to analyze or configure your system.

Normally, you would expect to see a New command on the Action and context-sensitive pop-up menus for a snap-in. However, this command was not on the menus for the Security Configuration and Analysis snap-in. In order to create a new database, you must select the Open command, and then enter the name of the database that you want to create. Here is what you need to do:

1. Open the Microsoft Management Console in which you have installed the Security Configuration and Analysis snap-in.

2. In the console tree pane, right-click on the Security Configuration and Analysis folder, and then select Open Database from the context-sensitive pop-up menu. You will see the Open Database dialog box. (See Figure 10.4.)

3. Do not select any of the existing databases. Instead, enter a file name for your new database. I recommend that you adhere to the DOS 8+3 naming convention to avoid potential problems with long file names when using the secedit.exe command-line utility. The extension must be .sdb.

4. After you have entered the file name, click on Open. Because the database does not yet include any security templates, this will open the Import Template dialog box. Select the template that you want to use. (See Figure 10.5.)

5. Click on Open to import the template and return to the console. The template will be imported into your new database. You will see a help message in the results pane.

## Opening An Existing Database

Once you have created a custom database, you can use it at any time. To open an existing database, do the following:

1. Open the Microsoft Management Console in which you have installed the Security Configuration and Analysis snap-in.

2. In the console tree pane, right-click on the Security Configuration and Analysis folder, then select Open Database from the

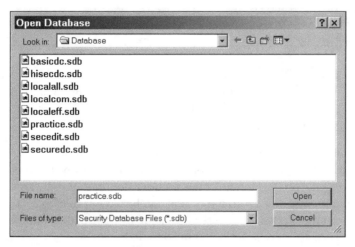

*Figure 10.4    The Open Database dialog box. Be sure to enter a new name if you are creating a new database.*

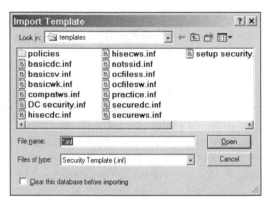

*Figure 10.5    Importing a security template into a database.*

context-sensitive pop-up menu. You will see the Open Database dialog box.

3. Select the database that you want to use and click on Open. This will return you to the console, where you can use the stored template in the database to analyze or configure your system.

## Importing A Template Into An Existing Database

As you gain experience with the Security Configuration Tool Set, you may want to add to the stored template in a database. Perhaps you may have started out by importing one of the basic default templates when you created the database. Later, you may need to increase the security level of a local system. The best way to do this is to add the next incremental template to your database.

For example, on a domain controller, you may have created a database that uses the basicdc security template. To bring security on the system to the next level, you would add the securedc template to your database. Later, if necessary, you could add the hisecdc template.

Here is how to import a template into an existing database:

1. Open the Microsoft Management Console in which you have installed the Security Configuration and Analysis snap-in.

2. In the console tree pane, right-click on the Security Configuration and Analysis folder, and then select Open Database from the context-sensitive pop-up menu. You will see the Open Database dialog box.

3. Select the database that you want to use and click on Open. This will return you to the console, where you can use the stored template in the database to analyze or configure your system.

4. In the console tree, right-click on the parent Security Configuration and Analysis folder and select Import Template from the context-sensitive pop-up menu. This will open the Import Template dialog box.

5. Select the template that you want to import. If you want all of the settings in this template to overwrite conflicting settings (if any) in the existing stored template, check the Clear The Database Before Importing option at the bottom of the dialog box. You might want to check it, for example, if you are importing an incremental template to increase the security level of the local system. If you do not want to overwrite all of them, leave the box unchecked, and you will have an opportunity to approve each instance individually.

6. Click on Open to import the template. If there are conflicts with existing settings and you have not selected the Overwrite option, you will be asked to resolve each conflict individually. When the import has been completed, you will be returned to the console.

---

**NOTE:** *If you click on Open without selecting a template, absolutely nothing will happen. You won't even get an error message. You must select a template to get out of the dialog box.*

---

## Exporting A Stored Template From A Database

You can export the stored template in a database to a separate security template that you can use elsewhere. You might want to do this, for example, if you have merged several templates into the stored templates in a database or have modified some of the settings in the stored template.

Here is how to export the stored template to a separate file:

1. Open the Microsoft Management Console in which you have installed the Security Configuration and Analysis snap-in.

2. In the console tree pane, right-click on the Security Configuration and Analysis folder, and then select Open Database from the context-sensitive pop-up menu. You will see the Open Database dialog box.

3. Select the database that you want to use and click on Open. This will return you to the console, where you can use the stored template in the database to analyze or configure your system.

4. In the console tree, right-click on the Security Configuration and Analysis folder and select Export Template from the context-sensitive pop-up menu. This will open the Export Template To dialog box. (See Figure 10.6.)

5. Enter a file name for your template. I recommend that you adhere to the DOS 8+3 naming convention to avoid potential problems with long file names when using the secedit.exe command-line utility.

6. Click on Save to complete the export, close the dialog box, and return to the console.

## Analyzing Security Settings On A Local System

After you have created a database and imported the template or templates that you want to use, you can analyze the computer-related security settings on the local system. Here is how to do it:

1. Open the Microsoft Management Console in which you have installed the Security Configuration and Analysis snap-in.

2. In the console tree pane, right-click on the Security Configuration and Analysis folder, and then select Open Database from the context-sensitive pop-up menu. You will see the Open Database dialog box.

3. Select the database that you want to use and click on Open. This will return you to the console, where you can use the stored template in the database to analyze your system.

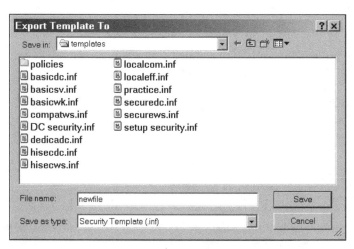

*Figure 10.6    The Export Template To dialog box.*

**10. Managing Security Configuration And Analysis**

4. In the console tree pane, right-click again on the Security Configuration and Analysis folder and select Analyze System Now from the context-sensitive pop-up menu. This will open the Perform Analysis dialog box, in which you can specify the path and name of the error log file that the snap-in will generate. (See Figure 10.7.)

5. Accept the default path name and click on OK. You will see an Analyzing System Security progress meter. When the analysis is complete, you will be returned to the console.

6. In the console tree pane, expand the Security Configuration and Analysis folder until you see the settings in which you are interested in the results pane. Next to the name of the setting, you will see two columns that show the settings in the stored template and the effective settings on the analyzed system. Where there is a serious conflict between the two settings, there will be a red mark next to the name of the setting. (See "Modifying A Setting In A Stored Template" section for instructions on changing a setting in a stored template.)

## Modifying A Setting In A Stored Template

You can modify the settings in a database's stored template. You may want to do this, for example, if an analysis shows a serious discrepancy between a setting in a stored template and one that is in effect on the local system, and you prefer the latter setting. You will only be modifying the stored template, not the source template that you imported into the database.

Here is how to modify a setting in a stored template:

1. Open the Microsoft Management Console in which you have installed the Security Configuration and Analysis snap-in.

*Figure 10.7    The Perform Analysis dialog box, with the full path name of the log file to be generated.*

2. In the console tree pane, right-click on the Security Configuration and Analysis folder, and then select Open Database from the context-sensitive pop-up menu. You will see the Open Database dialog box.

3. Select the database that you want to use and click on Open. This will return you to the console.

4. In the console tree pane, expand the Security Configuration and Analysis folder until you see the setting that you want to modify in the results pane.

5. Double-click on the setting and change it as needed. (See Figure 10.8.)

6. When you are returned to the console, right-click on the Security Configuration and Analysis folder and select Save from the context-sensitive pop-up menu.

## Preventing A Setting From Being Analyzed

You may find that some of the settings in a stored template are not relevant to your needs. To save time and avoid problems, you may want to prevent them from being analyzed or, more importantly, from being included in a reconfiguration of the system. Here is how to exclude a setting from analysis:

1. Open the Microsoft Management Console in which you have installed the Security Configuration and Analysis snap-in.

2. In the console tree pane, right-click on the Security Configuration and Analysis folder, and then select Open Database from the context-sensitive pop-up menu. You will see the Open Database dialog box.

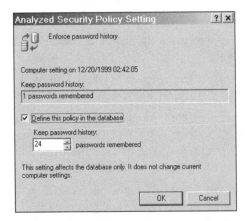

*Figure 10.8    Modifying a setting in a stored template.*

3. Select the database that you want to use and click on Open. This will return you to the console.

4. In the console tree pane, expand the Security Configuration and Analysis folder until you see the setting that you want to exclude in the results pane.

5. Double-click on the setting and uncheck the Define This Policy In The Database checkbox. (Refer to Figure 10.8 for an example of the checkbox.)

6. Click on OK to return to the console. In the results pane, the setting in the stored template should now read Not Configured.

7. Right-click on the Security Configuration and Analysis folder and select Save from the context-sensitive pop-up menu.

---

**TIP:**   *If you want to disable a setting in the source security template itself, open the template in the Security Templates snap-in, expose the setting in the results pane, and execute the previous Steps 5 and 6. When you return to the console, right-click on the template's parent folder in the console tree and select Save from the context-sensitive pop-up menu.*

---

## Configuring Security Settings On A Local System

You can use the Security Configuration and Analysis snap-in to reconfigure the computer-related security settings on a local system. You should do this only after you have analyzed your system with the database that you plan to use and fine-tuned the settings in the database to meet your specific needs.

In addition, before you reconfigure your system, I strongly recommend that you back up your current configuration, as explained in "Backing Up Your Current Security Settings" later in this chapter. This may save you much grief and aggravation if something should go wrong.

Here is how to reconfigure your system by using the Security Configuration and Analysis snap-in:

1. Open the Microsoft Management Console in which you have installed the Security Configuration and Analysis snap-in.

2. In the console tree pane, right-click on the Security Configuration and Analysis folder, and then select Open Database from the context-sensitive pop-up menu. You will see the Open Database dialog box.

3. Select the database that you want to use and click on Open. This will return you to the console, where you can use the stored template in the database to analyze your system.

4. In the console tree pane, right-click again on the Security Configuration and Analysis folder and select Analyze System Now. This will open the Perform Analysis dialog box, in which you can specify the path and name of the error log file that the snap-in will generate.

5. Accept the default path name and click on OK. You will see an Analyzing System Security progress meter. When the analysis is complete, you will be returned to the console.

6. In the console tree pane, expand the Security Configuration and Analysis folder until you see the various settings in the results pane. If you need to modify a setting in the stored template, double-click on the setting and modify it as needed.

7. In the console tree pane, right-click once again on the Security Configuration and Analysis folder. If you have modified the settings, select Save from the context-sensitive pop-up menu before proceeding. Otherwise, select Configure System Now from the same menu. You will see a Security Templates message box, reminding you that the settings in your custom configuration might be overwritten by conflicting settings elsewhere.

8. Click on OK to continue. This will open the Configure System dialog box, in which you can specify the full path name of the error log file that the snap-in will generate.

9. Accept the default path name and click on OK. You will see a Configuring System Security progress meter. When the analysis is complete, you will be returned to the console.

10. Your new settings will not take effect until you restart your system. Click on Console|Exit to close the console, and then close any other open applications. When you are ready, click on Start|Shut Down|Restart to restart Windows 2000.

# Using The secedit.exe Command-Line Utility

The command-line utility secedit.exe enables you to perform many of the functions of the Security Configuration and Analysis snap-in in scripts and batch files. The utility can also be used in conjunction with other administrative tools. It includes some features that do not exist in the snap-in.

You can use the utility to perform the following tasks:

- Analyze the security settings on a system
- Configure the security settings on a system
- Export the settings in a stored template to a separate security template file
- Refresh system security settings periodically
- Validate the syntax of a security template

Please keep the following points in mind as you study the Immediate Solutions that follow for analyzing and configuring a system, exporting a stored template, refreshing security policy, and validating the syntax of a security template:

- In each of the examples, the command line is built cumulatively. Enter the commands and separate each command-line parameter with a space, but do not press Enter until you have read the entire example.
- We will use the securedc security template and database for the sake of example. Feel free to substitute a template or database that is more suitable for your needs.
- For the %windir% environmental variable, substitute the drive and path to your main Windows folder (for example, c:\winnt).

## Using Command-Line Parameters

The utility secedit.exe is controlled by command-line parameters. Table 10.1 shows the basic command-line parameters used with the command.

*Table 10.1   Basic command-line parameters used with secedit.exe.*

| Parameter | Function |
|---|---|
| **/?** (or no parameter at all) | Displays help information. |
| **/analyze** | Analyzes the security settings on the local system. |
| **/configure** | Configures the security settings on the local system. |
| **/export** | Exports the security settings in a stored template to a separate security template file. |
| **/refreshPolicy** | Forces the Security Settings extension to the Group Policy Editor to refresh the security settings on the local system at specified occurrences and intervals. |
| **/validate** | Validates the syntax of a security template. |

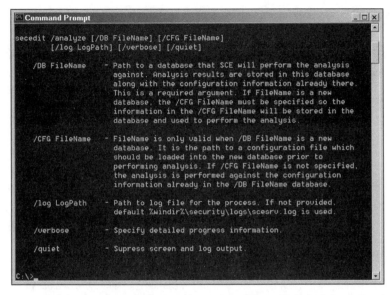

*Figure 10.9    The secedit.exe command-line utility with help information for the /analyze function.*

The utility also uses function-dependent command-line parameters following the basic command-line parameter, as shown in Figure 10.9.

Table 10.2 lists the function-dependent command-line parameters and the functions with which they may be used.

*Table 10.2    Optional command-line parameters used with secedit.exe.*

| Parameter | Used With | Purpose |
| --- | --- | --- |
| **/DB** *file name* | **/analyze**, **/configure**, **/export** | Specifies the path to the database that contains the stored template to be used in performing an analysis or configuration or to be exported. Required. If **file name** specifies a new database that has yet to be configured, then the **/CFG file name** parameter must also be used. |
| **/CFC** *file name* | **/analyze**, **/configure**, **/export** | When used with the **/DB file name** parameter, it indicates the path to the security template that will be imported into the database and either used for the analysis or configuration or exported. If this switch is not used, then it is assumed that the database specified in the **/DB file name** parameter is a configured database. In that case, the stored template in that database will be used. |

**Table 10.2   Optional command-line parameters used with secedit.exe (continued).**

| Parameter | Used With | Purpose |
|---|---|---|
| /overwrite | /configure | Can be used only with the **/CFG *file name*** parameter. Indicates that the security template specified in the **/CFG *file name*** parameter should overwrite, rather than be appended to, the template stored in the database. If this switch is not specified, the security template specified in the **/CFG *file name*** parameter will be appended to the stored template. Note that the **/overwrite** parameter is available only with the **/configure** parameter, not with the **/analyze** or **/export** parameters. |
| /area *areas* | /configure, /export | Specifies the security area or areas whose settings will be applied or exported. If none are specified, the settings in all areas will be applied. Areas include: **SECURITYPOLICY**—Local policy and domain policy for the system; for example, account or audit policies **GROUP_MGMT**—Restricted group settings for any groups specified in the security template **USER_RIGHTS**—User logon rights and granted privileges **REGKEYS**—Security for local-system Registry keys **FILESTORE**—Security for local file storage **SERVICES**—Security for all defined services |
| /log *logpath* | /analyze, /configure, /export | The path to the log file that will be created. |
| /verbose | /analyze, /configure, /export | Directs the utility to produce detailed progress information during the analysis, configuration, or export. |
| /quiet | /analyze, /configure, /export | Suppresses screen and log output. However, you will still be able to view the results of the process with the Security Configuration and Analysis snap-in. |

*(continued)*

*Table 10.2   Optional command-line parameters used with secedit.exe (continued).*

| Parameter | Used With | Purpose |
|---|---|---|
| **machine_policy** | **/refreshpolicy** | Refreshes the security settings for the local policy. |
| **user_policy** | **/refreshpolicy** | Refreshes the security settings for the user account currently logged onto the system. |
| **Enforce** | **/refreshpolicy** | Refreshes the security settings, even if there have been no changes to the settings of the group policy object. |
| **/mergedPolicy** | **/Export** | Merges and exports domain and local policy security settings. |
| *file name* | **/validate** | The file name of the security template to be verified. |

## Opening A Command Prompt Window

To use the secedit command-line utility, you will need to get to a command prompt. From within the Windows 2000 graphical user interface, you can open a command prompt window in one of two ways:

- Click on Start|Programs|Command Prompt.
- Click on Start|Run. In the Run dialog box's edit window, enter the following command, and then click on OK:

```
cmd
```

**TIP:** *You will find it easier to use the secedit utility if you maximize the command-prompt window. The help information, in particular, often fills an entire window. By maximizing the window, you will also be able to read the messages that the utility displays upon completion more easily.*

## Viewing Help Information

The utility secedit.exe includes embedded help information. To view this information, do the following:

1. Open and maximize a command prompt window.
2. Enter the following command at a command prompt, without any command-line parameters:

```
secedit
```

**NOTE:** *You can also use the /? command-line parameter if you are in the habit of doing so.*

3. At the next prompt, select the particular feature for which you need help, and then press Enter.

4. If necessary, use the scrollbar to view information that has scrolled off the screen.

5. Close the command prompt window to return to the Windows 2000 desktop.

## Analyzing A System's Security Settings

You can use secedit.exe to analyze the security settings of the current local system. Later, you can view this information in the Security Configuration and Analysis snap-in.

To analyze security settings with secedit.exe, follow these procedures:

1. Open and maximize a command prompt window.

2. Change to the %windir%\security\database folder.

3. Begin to build the command line by entering the following at the command prompt:

```
secedit /analyze
```

4. Add the name of the database that you want to use for the analysis. For example:

```
/DB securedb.sdb
```

5. If you are creating a new database or adding another template to an existing database, add the name of the security template to be imported into the database (if not, skip to Step 6):

```
/CFG %windir%\security\templates\securedb.inf
```

6. Optional: Add the full path name for the log that will be created. (If you do not enter this parameter, a default file will be created.) For example:

```
/log %windir%\security\logs\mysecure.log
```

7. Optional: If you want detailed progress information during the analysis process, add the following parameter:

```
/verbose
```

8. Optional: If you want to suppress screen and log output, add the following parameter instead:

```
/quiet
```

9. Check your command line against this sample, which uses the **/verbose** parameter. The command is divided among several lines below but you should enter it on one continuous line. (See Figure 10.10 for an example.)

```
secedit /analyze /DB securedb.sdb /CFG
%windir%\security\templates\securedb.inf
/log %windir%\security\logs\mysecure.log /verbose
```

10. When you are ready, press Enter.

11. When you are finished, close the command prompt window to return to the Windows 2000 desktop.

## Configuring A System's Security Settings

You can use secedit.exe to configure the security settings of the current local system. Later, you can view the changes in the Security Configuration and Analysis snap-in.

To configure security settings with secedit.exe, follow these procedures:

1. Open and maximize a command prompt window.

2. Change to the %windir%\security\database folder.

3. Begin to build the command line by entering the following at the command prompt:

```
secedit /analyze
```

4. Add the name of the database that you want to use for the configuration. For example:

```
/DB securedb.sdb
```

*Figure 10.10    The secedit **/analyze** function with a full set of command-line parameters.*

5. If you are creating a new database or adding another template to an existing database, add the name of the security template to be imported into the database (if not, skip to Step 7):

```
/CFG %windir%\security\templates\securedb.inf
```

6. Optional: If you want the settings in the imported security template to overwrite any conflicting settings in the stored template of the existing database, add the **/overwrite** parameter. (If you do not specify this parameter, the settings in the imported template will be appended to the settings in the stored template and existing settings will not be overwritten.):

```
/overwrite
```

7. If you want to specify the security areas in the database that will be applied to the current system, use the **/area** parameter. Specify the area or areas to be applied and separate each with a space. (If you do not specify this parameter, all areas will be applied.) The following example lists all of the available areas: They must all be entered on one line. (The line has been divided here for readability.)

```
/area SECURITYPOLICY GROUP_MGMT USER_RIGHTS
REGKEYS FILESTORE SERVICES
```

8. Optional: Add the full path name for the log that will be created. (If you do not enter this parameter, a default file will be created.) For example:

```
/log %windir%\security\logs\mysecure.log
```

9. Optional: If you want detailed progress information during the configuration process, add the following parameter:

```
/verbose
```

10. Optional: If you want to suppress screen and log output, add the following parameter instead:

```
/quiet
```

11. Check your command line against this sample, which uses the
**/quiet** parameter. The command is divided among several lines,
but you should enter it on one continuous line:

```
secedit /configure /DB securedb.sdb
/CFG %windir%\security\templates\securedb.inf /overwrite
/area SECURITYPOLICY GROUP_MGMT USER_RIGHTS
REGKEYS FILESTORE SERVICES
/log %windir%\security\logs\mysecure.log /quiet
```

12. When you are ready, press Enter.

13. When you are finished, close the command prompt window to
return to the Windows 2000 desktop.

## Exporting Security Settings From A Stored Template

You can use secedit.exe to export the security settings in the stored
template of a database to a separate security template that you can
use elsewhere.

To export security settings with secedit.exe, follow these procedures:

1. Open and maximize a command prompt window.

2. Change to the %windir%\security\database folder.

3. Begin to build the command line by entering the following at
the command prompt:

```
secedit /export
```

4. Use the **/CFG** parameter, shown here, to specify the name of
the security template to be created:

```
/CFG %windir%\security\templates\securedb.inf
```

***WARNING!*** *Microsoft's online help for secedit.exe indicates that this is an optional
parameter. This is incorrect. The parameter is mandatory. If you enter the command
without specifying the name of the template file, you will get the utility's help screen,
indicating that something was wrong with the command line.*

5. Optional: Use the **/DB** parameter, shown here, to add the name
of the database that has the stored template that you want to
export. If you do not specify this parameter, the stored template
in the system policy database, called secedit.sdb, will be used:

```
/DB securedb.sdb
```

6. Optional: Use the **/mergedPolicy** parameter, shown here, if you want to export both the domain and local policy settings:

```
/mergedPolicy
```

---

**NOTE:**   *Microsoft does not state what happens if you do not use this parameter.*

---

7. Optional: If you want to specify the security areas in the database that will be exported to the template, use the **/area** parameter. Specify the area or areas to be applied and separate each with a space. (If you do not specify this parameter, all areas will be applied.) The following example lists all of the available areas:

```
/area SECURITYPOLICY GROUP_MGMT USER_RIGHTS
REGKEYS FILESTORE SERVICES
```

8. Optional: Use the **/log** parameter, shown here, to add the full path name for the log that will be created. (If you do not enter this parameter, a default file will be created.):

```
/log %windir%\security\logs\mysecure.log
```

9. Optional: If you want detailed progress information during the configuration process, add the following parameter:

```
/verbose
```

10. Optional: If you want to suppress screen and log output, add the following parameter instead:

```
/quiet
```

11. Check your command line against this sample, which uses neither the **/verbose** nor the **/quiet** parameter. The command is divided among several lines, but you should enter it on one continuous line:

```
secedit /export /DB securedb.sdb
/CFG %windir%\security\templates\securedb.inf
/area SECURITYPOLICY GROUP_MGMT USER_RIGHTS
REGKEYS FILESTORE SERVICES
/mergedPolicy /log %windir%\security\logs\mysecure.log
```

12. When you are ready, press Enter.

13. When you are finished, close the command prompt window to return to the Windows 2000 desktop.

# Refreshing A System's Security Settings

You can use secedit.exe to refresh system security by reapplying the security settings to the local group policy object.

To refresh security settings with secedit.exe, follow these procedures:

1. Open and maximize a command prompt window.

2. Change to the %windir%\security\database folder.

3. Begin to build the command line by entering the following at the command prompt:

```
secedit /refreshpolicy
```

4. Add either **machine_policy** or **user_policy** to the command line, but not both at the same time. The **machine_policy** parameter refreshes the policy for the local machine, whereas the **user_policy** parameter refreshes the policy for the currently logged-on user. Enter them as follows, without a slash:

```
machine_policy
user_policy
```

5. Optional: Use the **/enforce** parameter, shown here, to refresh the security settings, even if they have not been changed:

```
/enforce
```

6. Check your command line against this sample, which uses the **machine_policy** parameter:

```
secedit /refreshpolicy machine_policy /enforce
```

7. When you are ready, press Enter.

8. When you are finished, close the command prompt window to return to the Windows 2000 desktop.

Regardless of the parameters that you have selected, if the command has been executed, you will see a message informing you that group policy propagation has been initiated. The message will remind you that the process may take a few minutes and that you should check the Application Log for any errors that might have occurred. (Use Event Viewer to check the log.) If the command has not been executed because of an error in the command line, you will see a help screen with the proper syntax for the **/refreshpolicy** function. (See Figure 10.11.)

## Validating The Syntax Of A Security Template

You can use secedit.exe to validate the syntax of a security template. Here is how to do so:

1. Open and maximize a command prompt window.

2. Change to the %windir%\security\templates folder.

3. Begin to build the command line by entering the following at the command prompt:

```
secedit /validate
```

4. Enter the name of the security template that you want to validate. For example:

```
securedc.inf
```

5. Check your command line against this sample:

```
secedit /validate securedc.inf
```

6. When you are ready, press Enter.

7. When you are finished, close the command prompt window to return to the Windows 2000 desktop.

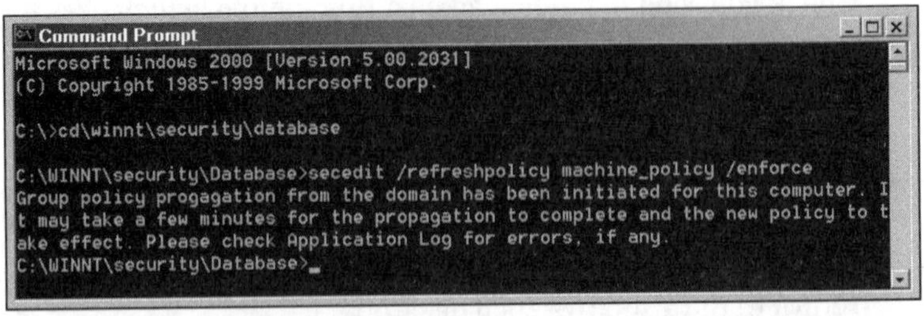

*Figure 10.11*   *The secedit **/refreshpolicy** function, with the message that follows the execution of the command.*

**WARNING!** *I used the /validate function to check the basicdc.inf template, which I had been unable to import into a database because it apparently contained invalid data. The function failed to report any problems with the template, and I continued to be unable to import it. Therefore, I would not rely solely on this function to correct problems with security templates.*

# Using The Security Settings Extension Snap-in

In the context of the Security Configuration Tool Set, the main purpose of the Security Settings extension snap-in for the Group Policy Editor is to enable you to import and export security templates. This snap-in extension is installed by default.

You can import security templates to any group policy. However, you can only export them from the Local Computer Policy. In both cases, the context-sensitive pop-up menu will say "Policy" instead of "Template," but the effect is the same.

The procedures for backing up and restoring your current configuration, also covered in this section, make use of both the Security Settings extension snap-in to the Group Policy Editor and the Security Configuration and Analysis standalone snap-in. You must install the latter manually in a Microsoft Management Console.

## Importing Policies From A Security Template

You can import a security template into any group policy. When you do so, the configured settings in the templates will overwrite the settings in the group policy. Settings that are not configured in the template will not be affected.

Because you are most likely to be importing templates into the Local Computer Policy, we will use that one as an example. Here is how to do it:

1. If you have created the Microsoft Management Console for group policies, suggested in Chapter 6, click on Start|Programs, select the program group that contains the shortcut to the console, select the console, and then skip to Step 3.

2. If you have not created the Group Policy Management console, suggested in Chapter 6, click on Start|Run and enter this command to open the Local Computer Policy in the Group Policy Editor:

```
gpedit.msc
```

3. In the console tree pane, expand the Local Computer Policy folder to expose the Computer Configuration folder. Expand this folder, then expand the Windows Settings folder to expose the Security Settings folder.

4. In the console tree pane, right-click on the Security Settings folder. Select Import Policy from the context-sensitive pop-up menu. This will open the Import Policy From dialog box. (See Figure 10.12.)

5. Select the template that you want to import and click on Open. This will import the settings in the template into the group policy and return you to the Group Policy Editor.

## Exporting Policies To A Security Template

You can only export templates from the Local Computer Policy. When you do, you will be asked whether to export the settings in the Local Computer Policy itself or the currently effective settings on the local system. If you choose the latter, you will be including some settings that have been configured elsewhere, such as in the Default Domain Policy. Unless you are sure of which version you need, I recommend that you do it both ways, just to be safe.

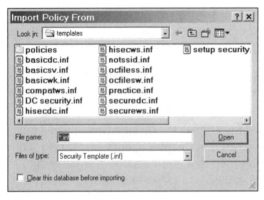

*Figure 10.12    The Import Policy From dialog box.*

In naming your policy, be sure to give it an .inf extension. I recommend that you use the DOS 8+3 naming convention. This will help to avoid potential problems with long file names if you need to use the policy with the secedit.exe command-line utility.

Also, in order to be able to export a security template from the Local Computer Policy, you must change one of the computer-oriented security settings in the policy. After you have made this change, you can change it back to the default setting before exporting the policy.

Here is how to export policy settings from the Local Computer Policy:

1. If you have created the Microsoft Management Console for group policies, suggested in Chapter 6, click on Start|Programs, select the program group that contains the shortcut to the console, select the console, and then skip to Step 3.

2. If you have not created the group policy management console suggested in Chapter 6, click on Start|Run and enter this command to open the Local Computer Policy in the Group Policy Editor:

```
gpedit.msc
```

3. In the console tree pane, expand the Local Computer Policy folder to expose the Computer Configuration folder. Expand this folder, and then expand the Windows Settings folder to expose the Security Settings folder.

4. If you have already made at least one modification to the Local Computer Policy, skip to Step 7. (You must make at least one change before you will be able to export the security settings.) If you have not made any changes, expand the Security Settings folder, followed by the Account Policies folder, and select Password Policy.

5. In the results pane, double-click on Minimum Password Age, change the default setting from 0 to 1, and click on OK. You will now be able to export the security settings to a template.

6. Double-click on the policy setting again and change the default setting back to 0.

7. In the console tree pane, right-click on the Security Settings folder, and select Export Policy from the context-sensitive pop-up menu. Select either Local Policy or Effective Policy

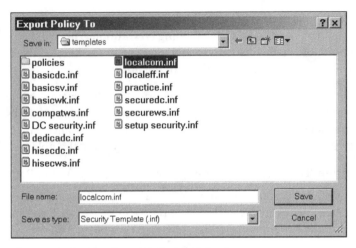

*Figure 10.13    The Export Policy To dialog box.*

from the fly-out menu. This will open the Export Policy To dialog box. (See Figure 10.13.) By default, the dialog box should be open to the default folder for security templates. If not, navigate to that folder.

8. In the File Name edit window, enter a name for your template, and click on Save. You will be returned to the console.

## Backing Up Your Current Security Settings

Before using either the Security Configuration Tool Set or the Group Policy Editor to modify the security settings for a local computer, you can back up the current settings by exporting them to a set of two security templates. Later, if you modify the settings and then have a problem, you can use these templates to restore your original configuration.

The procedure for backing up your current security settings will accomplish two purposes:

- It will provide you with a means of recovery if you decide to modify the security settings on the local system and then experience some problems. In case it is necessary to use the command-line utility secedit.exe to restore your original settings, I recommend that you use the DOS 8+3 naming convention when creating your backup templates.

- By importing your exported templates into databases, you will be able to use them as a baseline to compare with any changes that you make later.

This procedure calls for you to export two templates from the Local Computer Policy. The first, localcom.inf, will contain the settings in the policy itself. The second, localeff.inf, will contain the currently effective settings, which may have been implemented by other group policies that were applied after the Local Computer Policy. In many cases, this will be the Default Domain Policy. In restoring the configuration, you would import the first policy into the Local Computer Policy and the second into either the Default Domain Policy or whatever other policy contained the overriding settings.

Here is how to back up your current configuration:

1. Follow the procedures under the "Exporting Policies To A Security Template" section. Export both the local policy, with a file name of localcom.inf, and the effective policy, with a file name of localeff.inf.

2. If the current console does not contain the Security Configuration and Analysis snap-in, close the current console and open the one containing the snap-in.

3. Follow the procedures from the "Creating A New Database" section. Name the new database localcom.sdb, and import the localcom.inf template into it.

4. Repeat Step 3, but call the database localeff.sdb, and import the localeff.inf template instead.

## Restoring Your Original Security Settings

If you decide to restore your original configuration, you have two basic options:

- If you can access the Group Policy Editor, you can import your backup security templates into the appropriate group policy. This procedure is covered here. It is preferable to using either the Security Configuration and Analysis snap-in or the secedit.exe command-line utility to modify the local security settings because those settings could be overridden by a group policy.

- If you cannot access the Group Policy Editor, but can at least get to a command prompt, you can use the command-line utility, secedit.exe, to apply the templates to the local system. See the section on secedit.exe for information on using that utility to apply a policy.

The procedure described below tells you not only how to restore your configuration but also how to double-check its effectiveness and take additional steps to return the computer-related security settings in the Default Domain Policy to their default states. Here are the steps to follow:

1. As a precaution, export your current settings as described under "Exporting Policies To A Security Template" earlier in the chapter. Do this for both your local and effective policies. Be careful not to overwrite your previous backup templates.

2. In the console tree pane, expand the Computer Configuration section of the Local Computer Policy until you expose the Security Settings folder. Right-click on the folder and select Import Policy from the context-sensitive pop-up menu. This will open the Import Policy From dialog box.

3. Select the localcom.inf template and click on Open. This will import the settings in the template into the group policy and return you to the Group Policy Editor.

4. Open the Default Domain Policy or whatever policy contained the overriding "effective" settings when you created the backup templates. If you have been using the Group Policy Manager console, suggested in Chapter 6, it should be in your current console. If not, you will have to open the Active Directory Users and Computers administrative console, select an object to which you have applied the policy, and access the policy through the Group Policy page of the object's Properties dialog box.

5. In the console tree pane, expand the folders under Computer Configuration to expose the Security Settings folder. Right-click on the folder and select Import Policy from the context-sensitive pop-up menu. This will open the Import Policy From dialog box.

6. Select the localeff.inf template and click on Open. This will import the settings in the template into the group policy and return you to the Group Policy Editor.

7. The changes that you have made will not take effect until you restart the local computer. Click on Console|Exit to close the Group Policy Editor, exit any dialog boxes that may still be open, and close all open applications. When you are ready, select Start|Shut Down|Restart.

8. After Windows 2000 has restarted, open the Microsoft Management Console that contains the Security Configuration and Analysis snap-in. The purpose here is to make sure that your restoration has taken effect properly.

9. In the console tree pane, right-click on the Security Configuration and Analysis folder, and then select Open Database from the context-sensitive pop-up menu. You will see the Open Database dialog box.

10. Select the localeff.sdb database that you created when you backed up your configuration, and click on Open. This will open the database and return you to the console. You will see a help page in the results pane.

11. Right-click on the parent Security Configuration and Analysis folder, and select Analyze System Now from the context-sensitive pop-up menu. This will open the Perform Analysis dialog box.

12. The Error Log File Path edit window enables you to specify the name and location of the error log that the snap-in will generate as it analyzes your system. Accept the default location and click on OK. You will see an Analyzing System Security progress message box. When the analysis is complete, you will be returned to the console.

13. Expand all of the folders under Security Configuration and Analysis. Drill down to the folders that contain actual policy settings. In the results pane, you will see the name of the policy, the setting in the stored template in the selected database, and the effective setting on the current system. If your restoration has been successful, all—or at least most—of the security settings should be identical. If not, then you will see those settings that may need to be modified in other policies or templates.

14. Open a console that contains both the Local Computer Policy and the Default Domain Policy (or whatever policy into which you imported the localeff.inf template).

15. In the console tree, expand each of the two policies so that you can view all of the computer-related policy settings.

16. Compare the settings in the Local Computer Policy with the ones in the second policy. Where a setting has been configured in the Local Computer Policy, change the setting to Not Configured in the second policy. To do this, double-click on the setting in the results pane and check the Exclude This Setting From Configuration checkbox. By performing this step, you will return the second policy to something that is very close, if not identical, to its default state.

# Managing Software

# In Brief

Throughout this book, I have frequently referred to new features of Windows 2000 that worked only—or at least worked best—with other Windows 2000 servers or workstations. If you still need a compelling reason to justify upgrading your Windows NT and Windows 9x workstations to Windows 2000 Professional, the new software management features in Windows 2000 should give you the ammunition that you need.

Software management in Windows 2000 makes it easy for you to manage business productivity applications and service-pack upgrades of operating system software on remote workstations over the entire life cycle of the software. To accomplish this, it uses the Active Directory, Group Policy, the Windows Installer, and the Add/Remove Programs utility in Control Panel.

By using the software settings in a group policy, you can assign managed software to computers or users affected by the policy. If you assign a managed program to users who are affected by the policy, it is available to them, regardless of the Windows 2000 workstation that they are using. At the same time, it is not available to other users who have not been assigned the application, even if the application has already been installed on the workstation for use by someone else. If you use a group policy to assign a managed program to a computer, on the other hand, it is available to everyone who uses that computer.

---

**NOTE:**   *Software management—the remote management and installation of business productivity applications and operating system upgrades—should not be confused with the Remote Installation Services feature of Windows 2000. The latter is used for the remote first-time installation of the Windows 2000 Professional operating system on workstations, and is covered in Appendix B.*

---

## Overview Of Software Management

Software management allows you to set up an application once in a shared network folder, instead of having to install the application manually on every workstation where it might be needed. In some cases, all you have to do is make a few simple modifications to a group policy. From that point on, the software will be available to every user who is affected by that policy the next time that they log onto the network.

You can choose between two installation options:

- *You can assign an application.* If you assign the application, its icon will be added to the Start menu. The first time that an authorized user clicks on the icon or attempts to open a file type associated with the application, the program will be installed on the workstation. If the user later logs onto a different workstation that is also running Windows 2000 Professional, the application also will be installed on that workstation the first time that they need it.

**NOTE:** *In this context, "authorized user" means a user who has been given access to the application through a group policy, not simply an authenticated user with an account on your network.*

- *You can publish the application.* In this case, it will simply be added to the list of available programs in the Control Panel's Add/Remove Programs utility. The user can install the application by selecting it from the list. If the user later logs onto a different workstation that is also running Windows 2000 Professional, the application will be available to the user on that workstation as well.

If two or more users who are allowed to install the software use the same workstation, the first user to install the application goes through the normal installation process. When the second user installs the application, the process goes much more quickly because the installer only has to generate the custom files and folders that are required for the new user.

You can also use software management to deploy upgrades of existing applications and service packs for current applications and operating systems. Finally, when an application is no longer needed, you can use software management to block new deployments or even uninstall the application from every workstation where it has been deployed.

The Add/Remove Programs utility in Control Panel plays an important role in software management. When you publish an application, it appears as an option when an assigned user runs the utility. That

**11. Managing Software**

user can also use Add/Remove Programs to add new features that she passed up the first time around or repair an application that is not working properly.

What makes the software management features of Windows 2000 even more attractive is that managed software is self-healing. The user does not have to initiate the process. If a critical file is deleted, the Windows Installer will automatically repair the application the next time an authorized user attempts to run it. Even if a user deletes an application from a workstation, the application will be automatically reinstalled when another authorized user attempts to run it. If the application has been assigned rather than published, it will be reinstalled the next time that any authorized user, including the one who uninstalled it, selects a file or shortcut that requires the application.

The fact that an application on a local workstation has been uninstalled by a user has no effect on the application's settings in the group policy that contains its software package. When a user attempts to run an application that has been uninstalled, the Windows Installer sees that the person is authorized to use the software but the files from the previous installation have been removed. It then proceeds to reinstall the application, even if the person is the user who uninstalled the application in the first place.

---

**TIP:**   *If one user deletes an application that is used by another on the same system, this can be very disconcerting to the second user, even though she can reinstall the program. To prevent users from uninstalling a program without preventing them from being able to install it at all, try this: Open the group policy that contains the settings for the managed software. In the console tree, expand the User Configuration, Administrative Templates, and Control Panel folders. Under Control Panel, highlight Add/Remove Programs. In the results pane, double-click on "Hide Change or Remove Programs page." This will open a dialog box with three radio buttons. Select the Enabled button, click on Apply, and then click on OK.*

*This will help to prevent users from uninstalling software while still enabling them to install it. It is not foolproof, however. If an application comes with its own uninstaller, and a user knows how to access it, he can still uninstall the program.*

---

# Prerequisites For Using Software Management

There are several prerequisites for using the software management features in Windows 2000:

- You must be using a Windows 2000 domain controller. (See Chapter 3.)
- You must be using the Active Directory. (See Chapter 3.)

- You must be familiar with the Group Policy Editor. (See Chapter 6 and Appendix A.)

- If you intend to make the managed software available to a limited number of users, rather than to everyone on your network, you must first create the necessary groups, policies, and sites or organizational units. (See Chapter 5.)

- The installation files for the software to be managed must be in a shared folder on a Windows 2000 server. The folder must be on an NTFS volume and have the appropriate permission settings. If you have a large network with multiple domains, Microsoft recommends that you use the Distributed File System to make it easy for authorized users to access the folders, regardless of the location of their workstation.

- Each application that you want to manage must have a Windows Installer package file that is compatible with Windows 2000.

The package file, which has an .msi extension, is a relational database that contains installation information for many different scenarios. Here are some examples of typical scenarios:

- *Installation on different platforms*—The installation process on a system running Windows 95, for example, is different from that on a system running Windows 2000 Professional. This is due primarily to differences in the Windows Registry.

- *Installation on systems with different sets of previously installed products and features*—Let's say that you authorize a user for Microsoft Word. Later, you also authorize the user for Microsoft Excel. Both are components of the Microsoft Office applications suite. When the user installs Word on her workstation, certain files that are shared by more than one application in the suite will be copied to a common folder on her hard drive. Later, when the user adds Excel, those files will already be present and the installer will not need to copy them again.

- *Upgrading over an earlier version of the application*—The installer must be able to distinguish between a first-time installation and an upgrade as well as between different earlier versions of the application.

- *Using different default locations*—The default location for the application's main files is normally on drive C. Perhaps drive C is relatively full, however, and the system has another drive with more space. The person installing the application may prefer that the files be copied to the second drive. The installation process must be able to adjust to this change.

11. Managing Software

The file may also include a reference to the location where the files to be installed reside. If the application is relatively small, the package file may even include the files to be installed themselves.

You cannot modify a package file with a text editor. Windows 2000 Server includes the Veritas Software Console with the Windows Installer Package Editor, a third-party utility that you can use for this purpose. This program, formerly marketed by Seagate, is also known as WinINSTALL Limited Edition and WinINSTALL LE. For the sake of brevity, we will refer to it as WinINSTALL LE. (See Chapter 12.) If an application's installation files do not include a compatible package file, you can use the Discover utility that comes with WinINSTALL LE to create one.

**NOTE:**  *In the context of software management, the terms "managed software," "application," "application package," and simply "package" are used interchangeably. Applications that you add to the software settings of a group policy are called packages in the Group Policy Editor.*

You can also create a transform file, which has an .mst extension, to customize the package file without having to edit the package file itself. Transform files can be used to solve problems such as support for multiple languages and for different levels of installation, such as minimal, complete, run from the CD-ROM, or run from the network. You can also use a transform file to include custom templates or installation options for specific users. For example, you could use a transform file to make a legal dictionary and legal forms for Microsoft Word available to your legal staff without also making them available to other users of Word.

**NOTE:**  *Unfortunately, WinINSTALL LE cannot open a transform file or save a file in that format. While writing this book, I was not able to find any sample transform files. I have since learned that Office 2000 comes with a Custom Installation Wizard that allows you to create transform files for as many scenarios as you need. You can use the Wizard with other applications as well, but with certain limitations.*

# Organizing Your Network For Effective Software Management

In order to make effective use of software management, your network must be structured in an appropriate way. The software management features in Windows 2000 are closely tied to other features of the network operating system, such as the Active Directory and the Group Policy Editor. Be sure that you have a thorough understanding of the material in Chapters 3 through 6 and Appendix A, which cover these subjects.

One of the goals of software management is to help you ensure that every user who is authorized to use a particular application has it available at all times. Similarly, you also want to ensure that unauthorized users do not have access to the application, even if it has been installed on the workstation that they are using. By using software management, you can minimize the number of software licenses that you need for each application.

To illustrate how this might work, I will use as examples several popular Microsoft applications: Word, Excel, PowerPoint, Access, Publisher, and FrontPage. Let us assume that everyone on your network needs Word. You could add that package to the software settings of the Default Domain Policy or to a custom policy that you have created and applied at the domain level. In addition to Word, some of your users need other applications. For example:

- Your financial and executive staffs need Excel and Access, and your executive staff needs PowerPoint as well.

- Your marketing staff needs PowerPoint, but not Excel or Access.

- Your public relations department needs PowerPoint, Publisher, and FrontPage.

To organize the structure of your network to provide for everyone's software needs, try this approach:

- Create organizational units for executive staff, finance, marketing, and public relations, and move the appropriate user and computer accounts to those units. (See Chapter 5.)

- Create new group policies for each of these units. Keep in mind that whenever you create a new policy, each setting is unconfigured by default, so you do not have to worry about settings in the new policy unintentionally overriding those in an existing policy. (See Chapter 6.)

- Assign each unit the applications that it needs by adding them to the software settings of the appropriate group policy.

11. Managing Software

# Immediate Solutions

## Preparing To Implement Software Management

To use software management effectively, begin by making sure that your network, by way of the Active Directory, is organized appropriately. Before you can begin to use the software management features in Windows 2000, you must create the necessary sites and organizational units, if appropriate, as well as the group policies to which you will add the software settings. (See "Organizing Your Network For Effective Software Management" in the In Brief section of this chapter.)

### Preparing The Shared Folders And Installation Files

Once you have organized the structure of your network for software maintenance, you need to prepare the necessary shared network folders and set up the installation files for each application to be managed. Follow these steps:

1. Decide on the applications to be managed and determine the amount of disk space that you will need to hold their installation files. Plan to copy all of the files from each installation CD-ROM. In some cases you will not need to copy every file, but by including all of them in your calculations, you will leave yourself a safety margin.

2. Decide on the Windows 2000 server that will contain the installation files. The volume on which the files will be installed must be formatted for the NTFS file system. For best performance, consider dedicating the entire volume to the installation files.

3. Create a shared folder that will serve as the root for the installation files, and then create child folders for each of the applications to be managed. (See "Creating A Network Shared Folder" in this Immediate Solutions section.)

4. If yours is a large network with more than one domain, you may have users in other domains who will need access to the installation files. If so, consider creating a new root volume in your network's Distributed File System, using the root folder

that you have just created. Among other benefits, this will make it easier for you to find the package file when you install the application in a group policy.

5. For applications that come with Windows 2000-compatible package files, copy the appropriate installation files to the appropriate child folder.

---

**TIP:** *Many CD-ROM installation disks include extras that are not covered by the package file and must be installed manually. Often they are contained in folders with names such as VALUADD, BONUSPAK, or EXTRAS. You need not copy these files unless you plan to allow users to install them manually from the network share.*

---

6. Right-click on the package file, select Properties, and uncheck the read-only attribute. You are now ready to implement software maintenance for these applications.

---

**NOTE:** *If you have a CD-ROM server for your network and you can permanently dedicate a drive to the application's installation CD-ROM, it might seem tempting to leave the disk in the server and make the drive shareable. Although this would appear to save you time and effort, I do not recommend that you do it.*

*When I tried to do this myself, my attempt to add the package to the software settings of the group policy failed, showing a message saying that there was a problem with the package file. I believe that this happened because the file on the CD-ROM was read-only, even though the Software Settings snap-in does not modify the file. When I copied all of the installation files to a shared network folder on my hard drive and removed the read-only attribute from the package file, the process went smoothly.*

*Even if you could get the CD-ROM server idea to work, I am not sure that it would be advisable. I would be reluctant to put original installation disks to that kind of heavy use. Also, in most cases at least, installations would take much longer when done from a CD-ROM than from a hard drive.*

---

7. For applications that do not come with Windows 2000-compatible package files, use the WinINSTALL LE Windows Installer Package Editor or an appropriate third-party application to create the required file. (See Chapter 12.)

## Creating A Network Shared Folder

The installation files for managed software must be installed in a network shared folder. Follow these steps to make the root folder for your installation files shareable:

1. Click on Start|Programs|Accessories|Windows Explorer.
2. Expand the folder tree to expose the folder to be shared.

3. Right-click on the folder and select Properties from the context-sensitive pop-up menu.

4. In the Properties dialog box, select the Sharing page. (See Figure 11.1.)

5. By default, the folder will not be shared. Select the Share This Folder radio button to expose the sharing options.

6. In the appropriate edit boxes, enter a name for the shared folder and a descriptive comment.

7. Click on Permissions to open the Permissions dialog box for the folder. The names and permissions of all groups and users with specific permissions for the folder will be displayed.

8. Select the Everyone group. In the list of permissions for this group, uncheck Full Control and Change in the Allow column, leaving only the Read permission checked.

9. If the Administrators group is listed, make sure that it has been granted Full Control. (See Figure 11.2.) Skip to Step 12.

10. If the Administrators group is not shown, click on Add to open the Select Users, Computers, Or Groups dialog box. Select the Administrators group, as well as any other groups or users that you want to add, and then click on OK to close the dialog box.

11. By default, the users and groups that you have added will have only Read permission. Select the Administrators group and assign it Full Control. Modify the other permissions, as needed.

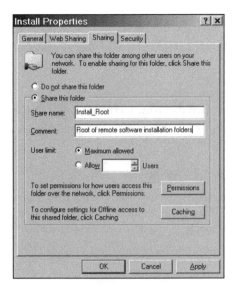

*Figure 11.1   The sharing page of a folder's Properties dialog box.*

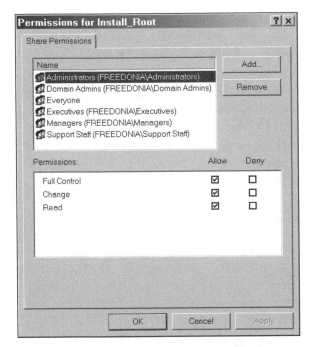

*Figure 11.2    Setting permissions for the Administrators group.*

12. Click on Apply to confirm your changes, and then click on OK to exit the Permissions dialog box and return to the Sharing page.

13. Click on Apply to confirm your changes, and then click on OK to close the Properties dialog box and return to Windows Explorer.

14. Click on File|Close to exit Windows Explorer.

---

**NOTE:** *The child folders for the individual applications will inherit the sharing and permission settings of the root folder. Therefore, you need not make them individually shareable.*

---

## Creating A Distributed File System Root Volume

In its Software Installation and Maintenance Walkthrough, Microsoft recommends that if you have a large network, you should add the root folder for your software installation files to the Distributed File System. To add the folder, follow these steps:

1. Click on Start|Programs|Administrative Tools|Distributed File System to open the Distributed File System Microsoft Management Console.

2. In the console tree, right-click on the Distributed File System folder. Select New Dfs Root from the context-sensitive pop-up menu. This will open the New Dfs Root Wizard. Click on Next to continue.

3. In the Select Dfs Root Type dialog box, you can create either a domain Dfs root or a standalone root. (See Figure 11.3.) Accept the domain choice, and then click on Next to continue.

4. In the Select The Host Domain For The Dfs Root dialog box, select the domain in which the installation files are located, and then click on Next to continue.

5. In the Select The Host Server For The Dfs Root dialog box, enter the network path name of the server or click on Browse to open the Find Computers dialog box. The Find Computers feature will automatically search for all of the computers in the current domain and list them in a window at the bottom of the screen. If the server that you need is listed, double-click on its name to select it, and close the dialog box. If not, enter the appropriate search criteria in the appropriate fields, select Find Now, and then select the server from the resulting list.

6. When the information in the Select Server To Host Dfs dialog box is correct, click on Next to continue.

7. In the Select The Dfs Root Share dialog box, you can either specify an existing share or create a new one. To select an existing share, click on the arrow in the drop-down list box next to the radio button. This will display a list of all of the

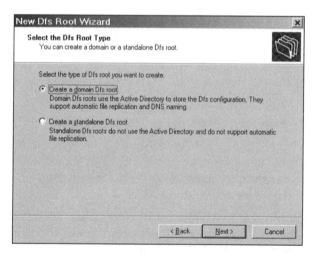

*Figure 11.3   Selecting the Dfs root type in the Create New Dfs Root Wizard.*

shared folders on the selected server. To create a new share, enter the path to the share and the share name in the appropriate edit boxes. When you are ready, click on Next to continue.

8. In the Name The Dfs Root dialog box, enter a name for the Dfs root or accept the default name, which will be the same as the name of the folder. Add a comment if you like. Click on Next to continue.

9. In the Completing The New Dfs Root Wizard dialog box, double-check the displayed information. Click on Back to correct an entry or Finish to close the wizard.

10. The new root will be added to the console tree. Right-click on the new root and select Properties from the context-sensitive pop-up menu.

11. In the Properties dialog box, select the Security page. You will see the names of the security objects with permissions for the folder. Click on Add to open the Select Users, Computers, Or Groups dialog box. Select the groups or users who will be using the managed software, and then click on OK to return to the previous dialog box.

12. On the security page, modify the permissions of each security object, as needed. For the groups or users mentioned in Step 11, the Read permission should be sufficient. Click on Apply to confirm your changes, and then click on OK to close the Properties dialog box.

13. Close the Distributed File System console.

## Accessing The Software Installation Settings In A Group Policy

To use software management, you must edit the appropriate group policy. Because there are several ways to open a policy in the Group Policy Editor, we will cover them once here, rather than repeat the instructions in each of the other Immediate Solutions in this section.

1. This step assumes that you have created the Microsoft Management Console for group policies (suggested in Chapter 6) and added the appropriate group policies to that console. If so, click on Start|Programs, select the program group that contains the shortcut to the console, select the console, select the policy to be edited, and then skip to Step 5.

2.  If you have not created the console mentioned in Step 1, click on StartIProgramsIAdministrative Tools. Depending on where you have applied the group policy, select either Active Directory Users and Computers or Active Directory Sites and Services.

3.  Expand the console tree to expose the Active Directory object to which you have applied the policy that you want to edit. Right-click on the object and select Properties from the context-sensitive pop-up menu.

4.  In the Properties dialog box, select the Group Policy page, and then select the policy to be edited. Click on Edit to open the policy in the Group Policy Editor.

5.  If the managed software is to be assigned to users affected by the policy, expand the User Configuration folder. If it is to be assigned to computers, expand the Computer Configuration folder.

6.  Expand the Software Settings folder and select Software Installation in the console tree. (See Figure 11.4.)

7.  Follow the procedures described in this Immediate Solutions section to manage software. When you are finished, click on ConsoleIExit to close the Group Policy Editor.

8.  If you have accessed the policy from the Properties dialog box of an Active Directory object, click on OK to close the dialog box, and then exit the open console.

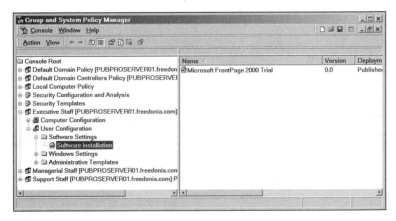

*Figure 11.4   The Software Installation leaf in a group policy.*

| Related solutions: | Found on page: |
| --- | --- |
| Managing Sites | 79 |
| Administering Organizational Units | 172 |
| Editing A Group Policy Assigned To An Active Directory Object | 200 |
| Creating Your Own Group Policy Administrative Tool | 211 |

# Setting Options For Software Installation

You can set certain options for software installation, even before you install a software package in a group policy. For example, you can set installation defaults, create categories that can be applied to the applications that you are deploying, and configure automatic installation options.

## Setting Software Installation Defaults

Using software installation defaults, you can do the following:

- Set the default location for Windows Installer package files.
- Determine the deployment options that the Software Settings snap-in presents to you when you add a new package.
- Set the default interface options presented to the end user during installation.
- Force the uninstallation of managed software when the group policy no longer applies to a specific user or computer previously covered by the policy.

To set software installation defaults, follow these steps:

1. Open the group policy for editing, as described in "Accessing The Software Installation Settings In A Group Policy" earlier in this Immediate Solutions section.

2. In the console tree pane, right-click on the Software Installation leaf and select Properties from the context-sensitive pop-up menu.

3. On the General page of the Software Installation Properties dialog box, locate the Default Package Location edit box at the top. (See Figure 11.5.) Here, you can enter the network path to the default folder in which the Software Settings snap-in will look for package files when you add software to be managed. This is an optional setting that you can leave blank.

11. Managing Software

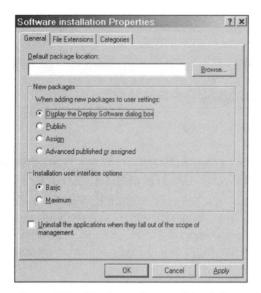

*Figure 11.5    The General page of the Software Installation Properties
dialog box.*

---

**TIP:**   *Although Windows 2000 Server allows you to specify a default folder for the package
files, it is best to keep the files in the same relative location to where they are found on the
original installation disk. In many cases, this will be the root folder for the installation files—in
other words, the folder that you have created for the specific application. The reason is that the
relative location of other files to the package file is often hard-coded in the package file.*

*Even if you do not plan to place the package files in a common folder, however, it is a good idea
to enter the path to the root folder for all installation files. That way, when you browse for the
package file that you need, you will only have to drill down one level in most cases.*

---

4.  In the New Packages area of the dialog box, select the action
    that you want the Software Settings snap-in to take when you
    add a new package:

    • *Display The Deploy Software Dialog Box*—This is the default
      setting. When you add a new package, it will ask whether you
      want to publish the application, assign it, or configure its
      properties. I recommend that you keep this as the default
      setting while you are becoming familiar with adding software
      packages because it gives you the most flexibility of the four
      options described here.

    • *Publish*—Select this option if you expect to publish most
      packages and do not expect to be modifying their installa-
      tions with transform files. When you publish an application,

it is added to the list of available applications in the Control Panel's Add/Remove Programs utility, but it is not installed automatically. You can publish an application only to users, not to computers.

- *Assign*—Select this option if you plan to assign most applications and do not expect to be modifying their installations with transform files. When you assign an application, its icon is added to the Start menu and the application is installed the first time that the user selects the icon. In addition, when a user double-clicks on a file with an associated extension, the installation process begins automatically. You can assign applications to either users or computers.

- *Advanced Published Or Assigned*—Select this option if you expect to be customizing the properties of most packages before deploying them, particularly if you expect to be modifying their installations with transform files. This will open the package's Properties dialog box when you add a new package. You can choose to publish or assign an application from the Deployment page of its Properties dialog box.

**WARNING!** *You must apply transform files before the package is deployed. If you expect to be modifying installations with transform files, do not select the Publish or Assign options in Step 4.*

5. In the Installation User Interface Options area, select one of the following options:

- *Basic*—With this option, all that the user will see during the installation is a progress window with a Cancel button. Use this option when you want to prevent the user from making any changes to the default installation options or the custom settings that you have created in a transform file.

- *Maximum*—This option is the default selection. The user will see all of the normal installation messages and dialog boxes.

6. To automatically uninstall the application when the group policy no longer applies to a specific user or computer, enable the "Uninstall the applications..." checkbox at the bottom of the page.

7. Click on Apply to confirm your choices, and then click on OK to close the Properties dialog box and return to the Group Policy Editor.

*11. Managing Software*

## Matching Applications To File Extensions

Occasionally, you may have a situation in which two or more managed applications are associated with the same file extension. For example, you might want to make both Adobe Photoshop and a simpler, "quick and dirty" image editor available to your graphic designers or Web site developers. Both applications would normally be associated with JPEG files. If an authorized user attempts to open a file with a .jpg extension and the appropriate software has not already been installed on her workstation, Windows 2000 needs to know which managed application to install.

To control the order that Windows 2000 follows in selecting the application to be installed when a user selects a document with a specific extension, follow these steps:

1. Open the group policy for editing, as described in "Accessing The Software Installation Settings In A Group Policy" earlier in this Immediate Solutions section.

2. In the console tree pane, right-click on the Software Installation leaf and select Properties from the context-sensitive pop-up menu.

3. On the File Extensions page, select the file extension that you want to manage from the drop-down list box at the top of the page. The applications associated with the extension will be displayed in the Application Precedence window below the list box.

4. Use the Up and Down buttons to rearrange the order of the applications.

5. Click on Apply to confirm your changes, and then click on OK to close the Properties dialog box and return to the Group Policy Editor.

## Creating Categories For Managed Applications

If you are deploying several similar or related applications, you can create categories that can help your users to make the right selection when they access the list of published applications in Add/Remove Programs. You can apply these categories to your managed applications and you can place an application in more than one category.

For example, you could create categories for each department in your organization and include each application that authorized users in the department might want to install. In addition, you could create categories for each major type of application, such as data management, graphics, or Web site development. When an authorized user accesses the Add/Remove Programs utility in Control Panel, the managed applications available to him will be grouped by category.

---

**NOTE:** *The category settings that you make will be universal. All existing categories will be available for all software installations in all group policies throughout your domain. By the same token, any modifications or removals that you do will also affect the category settings in each of these policies.*

---

To add, remove, or modify categories, follow these steps:

1. Open the group policy for editing, as described in "Accessing The Software Installation Settings In A Group Policy" earlier in this Immediate Solutions section.

2. In the console tree pane, right-click on the Software Installation leaf and select Properties from the context-sensitive pop-up menu.

3. In the Properties dialog box, select the Categories page. Existing categories, if any, will be displayed in a window. (See Figure 11.6.)

*Figure 11.6    The Categories page of the Software Installation Properties dialog box.*

4. To add a new category, click on Add to enter the Enter New Category dialog box. Enter the name of the category in the edit box and click on OK to return to the Categories page.

5. To modify an existing category, select it from the list and click on Modify. In the Modify Existing Category dialog box, edit the name of the category and click on OK to return to the Categories page.

6. To remove a category, select it from the list and click on Remove.

7. Click on Apply to confirm your changes, and then click on OK to close the Properties dialog box and return to the Group Policy Editor.

# Working With Applications

If you have implemented all of the Immediate Solutions to this point, you should have a solid foundation for managing software on your network. In this section, we will get down to the basics of installing and managing software packages. Here, you will learn how to deploy new packages, repair a damaged installation, and remove packages that are no longer needed.

## Installing An Application Package

Before you attempt to install an application package, make sure that you have followed the procedures described under "Preparing To Implement Software Management" in this Immediate Solutions section. The steps outlined in "Preparing The Shared Folders And Installation Files" and "Creating A Network Shared Folder" are particularly important.

To install an application package, here is what to do:

1. Open the group policy that will contain the settings for the installed software, as described in "Accessing The Software Installation Settings In A Group Policy" earlier in this Immediate Solutions section.

2. In the console tree pane, right-click on the Software Installation leaf and select New|Package from the context-sensitive pop-up menu.

3. In the Open dialog box, make sure that the Files Of Type drop-down list box is set to Windows Installer Packages (\*.MSI). Click on the down arrow in the Look In drop-down list box at the top of the page. If you have added the root folder for your installation files to the Distributed File System, select this Dfs folder, and then select the child folder that contains the package file for the software that you want to manage. If not, then expand either Computers Near Me or Entire Network to navigate to the folder with the package file.

**WARNING!** *If the package file resides on the local system, do not use the folder tree for the local computer to locate it. If you do, the local addresses of the installation files, rather than their network addresses, will become part of the package. This will cause remote installations to fail. Always use the network addresses, as described in Step 3.*

4. If the folder contains more than one .msi file, place your cursor over the icon to the left of each file name. After a few seconds, you should see a help balloon with a ToolTip showing the name of the program that it installs. (See Figure 11.7.)

5. Click on Open to continue. If you have left the New Packages option at its default setting in the Properties dialog box for the Software Installation leaf, you will see the Deploy Software dialog box. Its three options—Publish, Assign, and Advanced Published Or Assigned—are described under "Setting Software Installation Defaults" in this Immediate Solutions section.

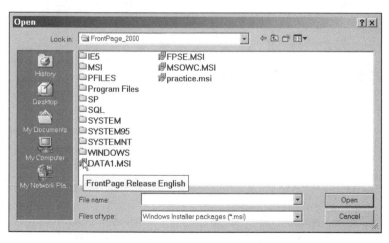

*Figure 11.7   The Open dialog box with a ToolTip help balloon showing.*

*WARNING!   If you intend to install a transform to modify the installation package, you must do it now, before the application is deployed. If so, be sure to select the Advanced Published Or Assigned radio button at this point. In the Properties dialog box for the package, select the Modifications page. (See "Managing Modifications To A Package" elsewhere in this Immediate Solutions section.)*

6. Click on OK to confirm your choice, and then close the Properties dialog box. If you have selected Publish or Assign, you will be returned to the Group Policy Editor. After a few seconds, the new package will appear in the results pane. At that point, the application has been deployed and you can no longer add or manage any transforms that you have created for it. If you have selected Advanced Published Or Assigned, you will eventually see the Properties dialog box for the new package. The settings in this dialog box are covered in the Immediate Solutions section "Working With The Properties Of An Application Package."

## Repairing A Damaged Installation

To repair a damaged installation on a workstation, you must log onto the workstation as an authorized user of the application. On the other hand, the procedure is simple enough that you should be able to walk most users through it over the telephone.

1. Click on Start|Settings|Control Panel|Add/Remove Programs.

2. In the Add/Remove Programs dialog box, select the Change Or Remove Programs icon.

3. Select the program to be repaired, and then click on the Repair button.

4. Follow the prompts to repair the application.

## Removing A Managed Application

When a managed application is no longer needed, you can prevent further deployment or remove it entirely from systems where it has been installed. Here is how to do this:

1. Open the group policy that contains the settings for the installed software, as described in "Accessing The Software Installation Settings In A Group Policy" earlier in this Immediate Solutions section.

2. In the console tree pane, select the Software Installation leaf.

3. In the results pane, right-click on the package to be uninstalled. Select All Tasks|Remove from the context-sensitive pop-up menu.

4. In the Remove Software dialog box select the appropriate option:

   • *Immediately Uninstall Software From Users And Computers*—If you select this option, the software will be uninstalled the next time a workstation that has the program is restarted or an authorized user logs on the workstation. The software will no longer be available for reinstallation.

   • *Allow Users To Continue To Use The Software But Prevent New Installations*—This option, as it suggests, blocks new installations, but it does not interfere with the work of current users.

5. Click on OK to confirm your selection and return to the Group Policy Editor.

If you have selected the option to remove the software completely, and you plan to remove the installation files themselves from the network server, be sure to allow enough time for the installation to be removed from all workstations. You may want to consider archiving the installation files before deleting them from the server. This is particularly important if you have modified the package file or created custom transforms.

# Working With The Properties Of An Application Package

Many options are available in the Properties dialog box of an installed application package. In this section you will learn how to:

• View the properties of a managed application

• Rename a package

• Change a package's deployment settings

• Use a new package to upgrade previously installed packages

• Select the appropriate categories for an application

• Manage transform modifications to a package

• Modify the security options of a package

## Renaming A Managed Software Package

By default, the name of the installed package will be the one specified in the Windows Installer package file. If the default name is not
suitable, you can change it. However, in order to avoid potential problems when the remote installation must be changed, repaired, or removed, you should not change the name once the package has been
installed on any workstation.

Here is how to rename a package:

1. Open the group policy that contains the settings for the installed software, as described in "Accessing The Software
   Installation Settings In A Group Policy" earlier in this Immediate Solutions section.

2. In the console tree pane, select the Software Installation leaf.

3. In the results pane, right-click on the package that you want to
   rename and select Properties from the context-sensitive pop-up
   menu.

4. On the General page of the Properties dialog box, edit the
   name, as appropriate. (See Figure 11.8.)

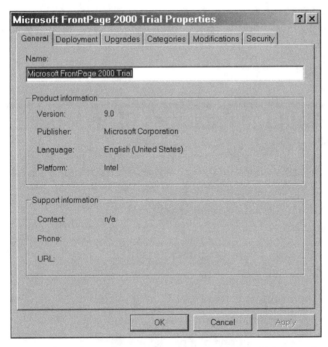

*Figure 11.8   The General page of the Properties dialog box for a managed
application.*

5. Click on Apply to confirm your changes, and then click on OK to close the Properties dialog box and return to the Group Policy Editor.

## Changing An Application's Deployment Settings

After you have installed a managed software package, you may find that you need to change its deployment settings. For example, you may have initially decided to publish an application, leaving it to the user to initiate the actual installation. Many users, however, do not understand how to use Control Panel and may be reluctant to access it. For these users, at least, you may want to assign the application rather than publish it.

Here is how to change an application's deployment settings:

1. Open the group policy that contains the settings for the installed software, as described in "Accessing The Software Installation Settings In A Group Policy" earlier in this Immediate Solutions section.

2. In the console tree pane, select the Software Installation leaf.

3. In the results pane, right-click on the package that you want to modify and select Properties from the context-sensitive pop-up menu.

4. In the Properties dialog box, select the Deployment page. This page often takes some time to appear, so be patient. (See Figure 11.9.)

5. In the Deployment Type area, select either Published or Assigned.

6. In the Deployment Options area, you will find checkboxes for three options. Select them as appropriate to your needs:

   • Automatically install the application whenever the user selects an associated file type.

   • Uninstall the application when the current group policy no longer applies to a specific user or computer. (For example, you may have a user who is authorized to use PowerPoint. She is transferred to another department but continues to use the same workstation. You move her account to the organizational unit for her new department. The software settings for the group policy that has been applied to that unit do not include PowerPoint. The next time that the user logs onto the network at her workstation, PowerPoint will be removed.)

   • Hide the application in Add/Remove Programs.

11. Managing Software

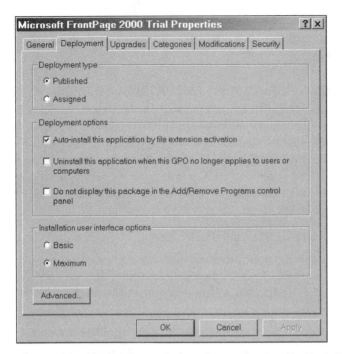

*Figure 11.9   The Deployment page of a managed application's Properties dialog box.*

7. Select either the Basic or the Maximum user interface option. (See "Setting Software Installation Defaults" earlier in this Immediate Solutions section for a description of these options.)

8. Click on Advanced to access options relating to language versions and removal of previous installations that did not use the Windows Installer. The language option will apply only if the application's installation supports multiple languages. Click on OK to return to the main Deployment page.

9. Click on Apply to confirm your changes, and then click on OK to close the Properties dialog box and return to the Group Policy Editor.

## Upgrading A Previously Deployed Application

You can use a managed software package to upgrade a previously deployed application or install service packs for operating systems. Here is how to do this:

1. If you have not already done so, add the upgrade package or service pack to the appropriate group policy, as described in "Installing An Application Package" earlier in this Immediate Solutions section, and then skip to Step 3.

2. If you have already added the upgrade package or service pack, open the group policy that contains the settings for the package, as described in "Accessing The Software Installation Settings In A Group Policy" earlier in this Immediate Solutions section.

3. In the console tree pane, right-click on the Software Installation leaf and select Properties from the context-sensitive pop-up menu.

4. In the Properties dialog box for the package, select the Upgrades page. You will see a list of previously defined upgradable packages, if any.

5. To remove an upgradable package from the list, select the package, click on Remove, and skip to Step 11.

6. To add an upgradable package, click on Add to open the Add Upgrade Package dialog box.

7. In the Choose A Package From area at the top of the page, select the appropriate radio button to indicate the group policy that contains the package to be upgraded. By default, the radio button for the current group policy will be selected and a list of upgradable packages in that policy will be displayed in the Packages To Upgrade window. If the package is contained in another group policy, select the second radio button. Click on Browse to open the Browse For A Group Policy Object dialog box.

8. In the Packages To Upgrade window of the Add Upgrade Package dialog box, select the package to be upgraded.

9. Under the window, select the appropriate radio button to either uninstall the existing software before installing the upgrade or install the upgrade over the existing version.

10. Click on OK to return to the Upgrades page.

11. Click on Apply to confirm your changes, and then click on OK to close the Properties dialog box and return to the Group Policy Editor.

## Specifying Categories For An Application

Grouping your managed applications by category can help your users understand the purpose of the applications available to them and select the appropriate ones for their needs. This is particularly useful for published applications. When a user accesses the Add/Remove Programs utility in Control Panel, the managed applications available to her over the network will be grouped by category.

To manage the categories applied to an application package, follow these steps:

1. Open the group policy that contains the settings for the installed software, as described in "Accessing The Software Installation Settings In A Group Policy" earlier in this Immediate Solutions section.

2. In the console tree pane, select the Software Installation leaf.

3. In the results pane, right-click on the package that you want to modify and select Properties from the context-sensitive pop-up menu.

4. In the Properties dialog box, select the Categories page. The page is divided into two panes, with available categories in the left pane and selected categories in the right pane. (See Figure 11.10.)

5. Highlight the appropriate categories, one at a time, and use the Select and Remove buttons so that the categories that you want to apply appear in the right pane.

---

**NOTE:** *Although you can apply more than one category to a package, for some reason you cannot select multiple categories at the same time in this dialog box.*

---

*Figure 11.10  The Categories page of a managed application's Properties dialog box.*

6. Click on Apply to confirm your changes, and then click on OK to close the Properties dialog box and return to the Group Policy Editor.

## Managing Modifications To A Package

You can customize the installation of a managed application by creating a special type of file called a *transform*. All transforms have an .mst extension. You can apply more than one transform to a package, and you can control the order in which the transforms are applied.

**WARNING!** *In order to apply a transform modification, you must add it to the properties of the managed application's package before the application is deployed. Once the package appears in the results pane of the console tree, it has been deployed. If you access the Modifications page at that point, all of the buttons will be grayed out.*

Here is how to manage transform modifications:

1. Install the package in a group policy, as described in "Installing An Application Package" earlier in this Immediate Solutions section. In Step 5, select Advanced Published Or Assigned.

2. In the Properties dialog box, select the Modifications page. This page includes a window showing the previously installed transforms.

3. To add a transform, click on Add, and then select it in the next dialog box.

4. To remove a transform, select it from the list and click on Remove.

5. To rearrange the order in which the transforms will be applied, select the transform to be moved, and use the Move Up and Move Down buttons.

6. Click on Apply to confirm your changes, and then click on OK to close the Properties dialog box and return to the Group Policy Editor.

## Managing The Security Options For A Package

Managing the security options for a package is much the same as managing the security options for any other Active Directory object. Here is how to do it:

1. Open the group policy that contains the settings for the installed software, as described in "Accessing The Software Installation Settings In A Group Policy" earlier in this Immediate Solutions section.

2. In the console tree pane, select the Software Installation leaf.

3. In the results pane, right-click on the package that you want and select Properties from the context-sensitive pop-up menu.

4. In the Properties dialog box, select the Security page. You will see a list of the users and groups with security permissions for the package, as well as the permissions that they have been granted.

5. To remove a user or group, select the object in the top window and click on Remove. If you do not need to make any other changes, skip to Step 9.

6. To add a user or group, click on Add to open the Select Users, Computers, Or Groups dialog box. Select the desired additions, click on Add, and then click on OK to return to the Security page.

7. To modify the permissions for an object, select the object in the top list, and then select or deselect the checkboxes in the Permissions window, as appropriate.

8. To edit the Access Control List for the managed software package, click on the Advanced button. From here, you can add, remove, view, and edit settings relating to permissions, auditing, and ownership of the object. (An explanation of Access Control List settings is beyond the scope of this book.)

9. On the Security page, click on Apply to confirm your changes, and then click on OK to close the Properties dialog box and return to the Group Policy Editor.

# Using WinINSTALL LE

# In Brief

In Chapter 11, you learned how to use the new features in Windows 2000 to manage software on remote workstations easily and quickly. To do this, however, your software must include installation package files that are compatible with the new features in Windows 2000.

In this chapter, you will learn how to use WinINSTALL LE, a third-party utility that Microsoft has added to the Windows 2000 Server installation CD-ROM, to edit package files. You will also learn how to use the accompanying Discover utility to create package files for legacy applications.

**NOTE:**    *This utility, previously marketed by Seagate Software and now by VERITAS, is known by several different names, which VERITAS seems to have used interchangeably. They include Windows Installer Limited Edition, Windows Installer Package Editor, and WinINSTALL LE. For the sake of brevity, we will use the latter. The VERITAS Software Console serves as a container for the utility, much as the Microsoft Management Console serves as a container for snap-in components.*

## Overview Of WinINSTALL LE

The software management features in Windows 2000, as powerful as they are, require a package file that is compatible with Windows 2000. At this writing, however, very few applications come with this type of file. Even the package definition files included in the Office 97 Resource Kit are not compatible.

To extend the usefulness of these software management features, Microsoft is including a special version of the WinINSTALL Windows Installer Package Editor on the installation CD-ROM for Windows 2000 Server. WinINSTALL LE can be used to edit Windows Installer package files. The accompanying Discover utility can be used to generate package files for legacy applications that do not include them.

The package editor is contained in a tool called the VERITAS Software Console. (See Figure 12.1.) Its interface is similar to that of the Microsoft Management Console, but with some significant differences. The workspace is divided into three main panes. The top left pane, called the Tree View, displays the content of the current package file in a folder tree. The bottom left pane, called the List View, contains a list of the

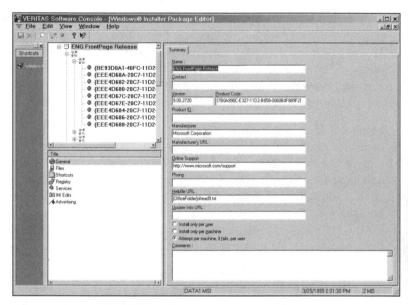

*Figure 12.1    The VERITAS Software Console with the Windows Installer Package Editor module. The package being edited installs the trial version of Microsoft FrontPage 2000.*

types of settings that can be contained in the object selected in the top left pane. The types include General, Files, Shortcuts, Registry, Services, INI Edits, and Advertising.

---

**NOTE:**    *The Advertising settings relate to type libraries and classes and are not covered in this chapter. VERITAS refers users to the documentation for the Windows Installer.*

---

The format of the right pane, called the Data View, depends on the selection in the List View. At times, it is analogous to the results pane of a Microsoft Management Console. Double-clicking on an object opens the appropriate dialog box for modifying the object. In other cases, it resembles a Properties dialog box in which you can edit the settings directly.

The two left panes are used in tandem. The category selected in the bottom pane determines the settings that are displayed in the right pane.

# Overview Of Discover

WinINSTALL's Discover utility will help you to create Windows Installer package files for legacy applications that do not come with them—which, at this time, is likely to include almost every application that your organization already owns. In testing the software management procedures described in this chapter, I used two applications on the Microsoft FrontPage 2000 Trial CD-ROM. FrontPage 2000 came with a package file. Surprisingly, PhotoDraw 2000, which was on the accompanying Bonus Pack disk, did not. I used Discover to create an installation package for PhotoDraw.

Using the Discover feature to generate a package file can be time-consuming but is relatively straightforward. The walkthrough recommends that you set up a "clean" reference workstation that is configured as closely as possible to the workstations on which the application will be installed. This workstation should have only the necessary operating system software and service packs. When creating the reference installation on the workstation, you run Discover from its network location rather than installing it on the workstation.

There are several basic steps in generating a package file with Discover. First, you run Discover to take a snapshot of the current system. Next, you install the legacy application in its normal way. After it has been installed, you modify its default settings if you want to set your own defaults for all users. Finally, you run Discover again.

The second time that you run Discover, it notes the changes that have been made and creates a mirror installation of the legacy application on the network share that you have designated to contain the files. It duplicates the structure of the application's own folders. If the installation routine has added or updated files in the system folders as well, it adds similarly named folders to the network share and copies the appropriate files to those folders. Next, it records all Registry and INI entries, and creates the necessary REG and INI files in the shared folder. Finally, it creates the required package file.

## Drawbacks To Using Discover

Without Discover, it would be extremely difficult to use the software management features in Windows 2000 with legacy applications. However, be aware the packages that it creates have definite limitations.

For example, when an application includes its own Windows 2000-compatible package file, its own installer is used to perform the installation. If a user later needs to install a feature that she did not choose the first time, all she needs to do is open Add/Remove Programs in Control Panel and select the option to change the current installation.

Discover, on the other hand, creates a mirror image of the installation that you perform. When the application is installed on another system through software management, the Windows Installer copies that mirror image, including all of its settings, to the other system. The options that are normally available through the application's installation routine are not available to the end user. The only option presented to the user is the Cancel button. Moreover, she will not be able to modify the installation later in Add/Remove Programs.

Therefore, if the legacy application's installation routine offers you a choice, you may want to do either a custom install, in which you can select all of the features that your users might need, or even a complete install. This might seem wasteful of disk space, both on the server with the installation files and on each workstation where the application is installed. On the other hand, it could save you from having to go to workstations to manually add missing features that your users need. Finally, manually adding components that are not in the package file could cause problems with uninstalling the application later.

**12. Using WinINSTALL LE**

# Immediate Solutions

## Using The WinINSTALL LE Windows Installer Package Editor

The software management features in Windows 2000 require a Windows Installer package file that is compatible with the new operating system. These files are relational databases that cannot be edited with a text editor. Applications written for earlier versions of Windows operating systems, including Windows NT 4, do not include this type of file. To use the new software management features with these applications, you must create your own package files.

---

***TIP:*** *My copy of WinINSTALL LE did not contain any documentation. Look for a technical walkthrough for the program on Microsoft's Web site. Open the \support\walkthru folder on the Windows 2000 Server installation CD-ROM and double-click on walkthru.htm. This file includes a link to the walkthroughs.*

---

Be aware that package files can be very large and complex—much more so than group policies, for example. It is beyond the scope of this book to teach you everything you need to know about editing a package file. To give you an idea of what you can do in a package file, I have included several Immediate Solutions that show you how to perform common tasks. In some cases, however, I have not gone into detail about options and settings that are beyond the scope of this book.

---

***TIP:*** *You may be better off creating a transform file—or even a series of transforms—to customize the installation, rather than modifying the package file itself. The reason is that you can add and remove transform files, and even control the order in which they are applied, when you add the application to a group policy. If the transforms do not work, you can remove the package from the group policy, fix the problem, and redeploy the application. In the meantime, the package file remains unchanged. (Refer to Chapter 11 for information about transform files.)*

---

### Installing WinINSTALL LE

WinINSTALL LE must be installed on a Windows 2000 system. It should not be installed on a workstation, particularly one that will be used as a reference system for creating installation packages for legacy applications. Here is how to install the software:

1. Insert the Windows 2000 Server installation CD-ROM in your CD-ROM drive.

2. Click on Start|Programs|Accessories|Windows Explorer.

3. In Windows Explorer, select the CD-ROM drive and expand the VALUADD, MGMT, and WINSTLE folders.

4. In the WINSTLE folder, view the release notes and readme files, and then double-click on the file swiadmle.msi. This package file includes the actual program files.

5. The installation should proceed very quickly and you may not see a confirmation message. To make sure that the program has been installed, click on Start|Programs. You should see a VERITAS Software folder with the file VERITAS Software Console. This console contains the WinINSTALL LE Windows Installer Package Editor, which appears to be a kind of snap-in for the VERITAS console.

## Opening, Viewing, And Navigating A Package File

You can open a package file in WinINSTALL LE, the Windows Installer Package Editor, to view or edit its contents. The editor is contained in the VERITAS Software Console, which is similar to the Microsoft Management Console.

**WARNING!** *The VERITAS Software Console does not have a File|Save As menu option and does not come with any sample files that are useful for learning purposes. Therefore, I recommend that you set up an application that has a Windows 2000-compatible package file and make a copy of that file to learn how to use the editor. Be sure to remove the read-only attribute of the package file first.*

Here is how to open and navigate a package file:

1. Click on Start|Programs|VERITAS Software|VERITAS Software Console. The console will open with the Windows Installer Package Editor at the root of the Tree View pane at the top left of the console. The first time that you open the console, a default template will appear just below the root. After that, it will be the last-opened package file.

2. To select a different file, click on File|Open. In the Open dialog box, click on the down arrow in the Look In drop-down list box to navigate to the folder that contains the file. Select the file and click on Open. The current package file will be closed and the new one will take its place.

---

**TIP:** *If there are several package files in the same folder, place your cursor over the icon to the left of each one. After a few seconds, you should see a balloon with the name of the program that it installs.*

---

3. In the Tree View pane, expand the tree of the package file to locate the setting that you want to view or edit. When you select an item in the tree, a list of categories (called *titles*, for some reason) will appear in the List View pane at the bottom left of the console. The two panes are used in combination. When you select a category in the bottom pane, the settings relating to that category in the selected Tree View object will appear in the Data View pane at the right of the console. You can edit the settings in the Data View pane.

4. When you are finished, click on File|Save if you have made any changes, and then click on File|Exit to close the VERITAS Software Console.

Table 12.1 includes a list of keyboard shortcuts for navigating the VERITAS Software Console.

**Table 12.1  Keyboard shortcuts for navigating in the VERITAS Software Console.**

| Key or Combination | What It Does |
|---|---|
| F6 | Moves the cursor between the Tree, List, and Data views |
| Alt+Up Arrow | Expands the Tree View |
| Alt+Down Arrow | Expands the List View |
| Alt+Right Arrow | Closes the Data View |
| Alt+Left Arrow | Expands the Data View |
| Alt+Home | Closes both the Tree View and List View |
| Alt+End | Closes the Data View |
| Alt+Page Up | Closes the Tree View |
| Alt+Page Down | Closes the List View |
| Up and Down Arrows | Move the cursor through the Tree View |
| Spacebar or Enter | Selects the highlighted item |
| Page Up and Page Down | Move quickly through the Tree View |
| Home | Moves the cursor to the top of the items in the Tree View |
| End | Moves the cursor to the bottom of the items in the Tree View |

# Adding And Deleting Features And Components In A Package File

The elements of a package file are called features and components. Components are contained within features. For example, the spell checker in Microsoft Word is a *feature*, whereas the DLL files, Registry entries, and other elements needed to implement the feature are *components*. You can add a feature to the root level of the package file or to an existing feature below the root. You can add a component to a feature.

Why would you want to add a feature to a complex commercial application? Why would you want to delete a feature? Perhaps you have developed a custom control or macro that you would like to add to the installation. Perhaps you have found that a certain feature does not work properly and that your users would be better off not having it available. Not being a professional programmer, I cannot say for certain that you can accomplish these tasks through WinINSTALL LE, but my impression is that this is the purpose of the program.

### Adding A Feature To A Package File

To add a feature to a package file, follow these steps:

1. Open the package file in WinINSTALL LE, as described in "Opening, Viewing, And Navigating A Package File" in this Immediate Solutions section.

2. In the Tree View pane, select the package, expand its tree as needed, and highlight the location where you want to add the feature.

3. Right-click on the item in the tree and select Add Feature from the context-sensitive pop-up menu.

4. By default, the new feature will be named "New Feature". Locate and highlight the new item in the Tree View. This will expose a Summary page in the Data View, in which you can change the name, add a description, and select several checkbox options relating to advertising, source, and event. (See Figure 12.2.)

5. Click on File|Save to save your changes.

6. Click on File|Exit to close the console and return to the Windows desktop.

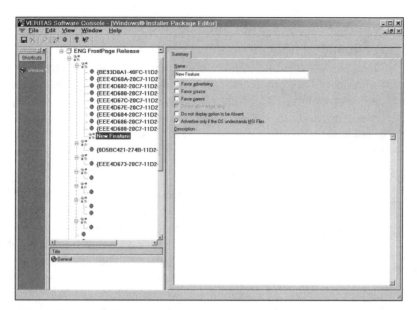

*Figure 12.2   Adding a new feature to a package file.*

### Adding A Component To A Feature In A Package File

Here is how to add a component to a feature:

1. With the package file open, expand the Tree View as needed and highlight the feature to which you want to add the component.

2. Right-click on the feature and select Add Component from the context-sensitive pop-up menu. This will bring up a summary page in the Data View.

3. In their respective fields, enter the source and target directories for the component. In the Component field, enter the unique GUID for the component.

---

**TIP:**   *You will not be able to proceed until you have entered the GUID. If you do not know the GUID and you get stuck in a loop trying to get away from the Summary page, delete the component in the Tree View.*

---

4. Click on File|Save to save your changes.

5. Click on File|Exit to close the console and return to the Windows desktop.

### *Deleting A Feature Or Component In A Package File*

To delete a feature or component, follow these steps:

1. With the package file open, expand the Tree View as needed and highlight the feature or component that you want to delete.

2. Right-click on the feature and select Delete from the context-sensitive pop-up menu.

3. When you see the Remove confirmation message box, click on Yes.

4. Click on File|Save to save your changes.

5. Click on File|Exit to close the console and return to the Windows desktop.

## Working With File Lists In A Package File

A package file includes lists of files to be added or removed during the installation process. Font files are contained in a third, separate list. You can modify the contents of these lists and change some of the properties of files that will be installed, such as their attributes and security permissions.

I can envision some very practical uses for this feature. Here are some examples:

- A program requires the latest version of a Visual Basic runtime module and some of your users may not have it on their systems. Or perhaps you have created a custom template for Word 97 and want to make sure that everyone has it. You could add the required files to the list of those to be installed and specify the destination folders as well.

- You want to protect certain files from viruses, or from being deleted or modified by your users. You could add the read-only attribute to these files.

- Your users have all the fonts that they need, and you want to make sure that the installation program doesn't install more fonts than their systems can handle. You can remove undesired fonts from the list of those that will be installed.

12. Using
WinINSTALL LE

**NOTE:** *The ability to control the fonts that will be installed is very useful. There is a practical limit to the number of fonts that can be installed in Windows 9x, and probably in Windows 2000 as well. Microsoft claims that you can install up to 1,000 fonts in Windows 9x, but experienced desktop publishers, including myself, have found that performance suffers noticeably if you have more than 400 fonts installed. Certain programs, such as CorelDraw, come with many more than 400 fonts. If the person doing the installation is unaware of the problem and exceeds the practical limit, Windows may not even load the next time that it is restarted. In this case, you may need to boot to the command prompt only and delete the font files under MS-DOS. (They will probably be in the system's default fonts folder, such as c:\winnt\fonts.)*

*In addition, many programs install fonts that are virtually identical to others that are already on the system. At best, they add clutter to the fonts list and waste disk space. At worst, there can be a very real difference in quality that may not be obvious immediately.*

*My recommendation is to standardize on high-quality fonts from the same foundry, such as the Bitstream fonts that come with many Corel products. I also suggest using a font manager such as Bitstream Font Navigator. A good font manager will allow you to store the fonts in a folder that you designate rather than in the system's default fonts folder. It will also allow you to create font groups that can be installed and uninstalled as needed. When an installation routine adds new fonts to a system—usually without asking—they will invariably be in the default folder. Switch to a bare-bones font configuration (Arial, Courier, Times New Roman, Symbol, WingDings, Marlett, and Verdana), review the new fonts, delete those that are not needed, and move the others out of the default folder.*

### Working With The Add File List In A Package File

Here are some ways of using the Add file list:

1. Open the package file in WinINSTALL LE as described in "Opening, Viewing, And Navigating A Package File" in this Immediate Solutions section.

2. In the Tree View pane, select the package, expand its tree as needed, and highlight the feature that you want to modify. If you want to see a list of every file to be added or removed, highlight the root of the package file. (See Figure 12.3.)

3. In the List View, select Files. The editor will read the Add, Remove, and Fonts lists and display them in the Data View pane. Depending on the sizes of the lists, this may take some time. Use the tabs at the top of the Data View pane to select the Add page.

4. To remove a file from the list of files to be added, highlight the file and either press Delete or click on the Delete icon at the right of the toolbar above the list. Depending on the importance of the file, you may get a confirmation message before the file is deleted.

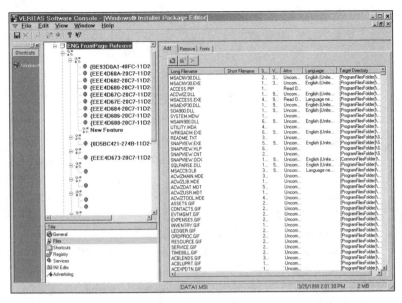

*Figure 12.3   The list of files added in the installation of FrontPage 2000.*

**WARNING!   There is no Undo option in the VERITAS Software Console.**

5. To add a file to the list, click the New icon at the left of the toolbar. This will open the Files To Insert dialog box. Select the file that you want to add, and then click Open to return to the Add page.

6. To modify the properties of a file in the Add list, either double-click on the file in the list or click once on the Properties icon in the middle of the toolbar. This will open the File Properties dialog box. Here, you can assign a short name to the file, modify its attributes, or change the component to which the file relates. If you enable the Auto Register attribute, the file will update the Windows Registry when it is loaded. This makes it easier for applications that depend on the file to find it. When you are ready, click on OK to return to the Add page.

7. To modify the security permissions of a file, open the File Properties dialog box, as described in the previous step, and then click on Permissions. This will open the Lock Permissions dialog box, in which the list of assigned users will be displayed. To remove a user, highlight the name in the list and click on Remove. To add a user, click on Add. This will open the Add Users dialog box. Select the domain that contains the user's account from the drop-down list box, click on Add User to

select the user's name from a list, and select the type of access that you want to grant the user. Click on OK three times to exit the various dialog boxes and return to the Add page.

8.  Click on File|Save to save your changes.

9.  Click on File|Exit to close the console and return to the Windows desktop.

### Working With The Remove File List In A Package File

The package file may also direct the Windows Installer to remove certain files, such as temporary files or features of older versions of the application that are no longer needed. You can prevent this from happening by deleting a file from the Remove list. Here is how to do it:

1.  Open the package file in WinINSTALL LE, as described in "Opening, Viewing, And Navigating A Package File" in this Immediate Solutions section.

2.  In the Tree View pane, select the package, expand its tree as needed, and highlight the feature that you want to modify.

3.  In the List View, select Files. The editor will read the Add, Remove, and Fonts lists and display them in the Data View pane. Depending on the sizes of the lists, this may take some time. Use the tabs at the top of the Data View pane to select the Remove page.

4.  To remove a file from the list of files to be deleted, highlight the name of the file and either press Delete or click on the Delete icon at the right of the toolbar above the list.

5.  To add a file to the list, click on the New button at the left of the toolbar. This will open the File(s) To Remove dialog box. Navigate to the file that you want to add, select the file, and click on Open to return to the Remove page.

6.  To control the point at which a file is removed, highlight the file. Either double-click on the name of the file or click on the Properties button in the middle of the toolbar. This will open the Remove Properties dialog box. Here, you can change the file name, if necessary, as well as the component to which it is attached. You can also select from among three radio buttons to determine whether the file is removed only during installation of the component, only during removal of the component, or at either time.

7.  Click on File|Save to save your changes.

8.  Click on File|Exit to close the console and return to the Windows desktop.

### Working With The Fonts List In A Package File

Here are some ideas for working with the list of fonts that will be installed:

1. Open the package file in WinINSTALL LE, as described in "Opening, Viewing, And Navigating A Package File" in this Immediate Solutions section.

2. In the Tree View pane, select the package, expand its tree as needed, and highlight the feature that you want to modify.

3. In the List View, select Files. The editor will read the Add, Remove, and Fonts lists and display them in the Data View pane. Depending on the sizes of the lists, this may take some time. Use the tabs at the top of the Data View pane to select the Fonts page. (See Figure 12.4.)

4. To remove a font from the list of fonts to be installed, highlight the font in the list and either press Delete or click on the Delete icon at the right of the toolbar above the list.

5. To add a font to the list, click on the New icon at the left of the toolbar. This will open the Font dialog box. Do not enter a font name at this point. Instead, click on the button next to the Font File field to open the Select File dialog box. Navigate to the font that you want to add and click on OK. The font will be copied to the proper installation folder. If the font file has a descriptive

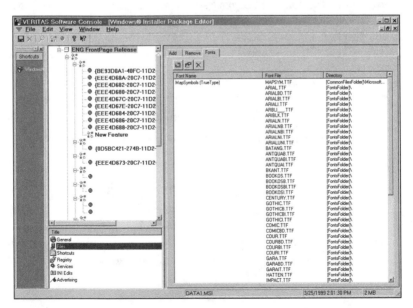

*Figure 12.4   The list of fonts installed with FrontPage 2000.*

**371**

name embedded in it, that name will appear in the Font Name field. You need not fill in or modify the Component field. Click on OK to return to the Fonts page.

**WARNING!** *If the font has an embedded font name, do not change it. There is a definite syntax to font names, and fonts that are part of the same family share the same root name. This makes it possible for you to apply boldfacing and italics to text without having to select a bold or italic font from the font list in your application. In addition, the names of fonts used in a file are embedded in either the file or its accompanying template or style sheet. If you open an existing file and a required font is not available, the file will not display or print properly until you fix the problem.*

6. To modify the properties of a font, either double-click on the font in the list or click once on the Properties icon in the middle of the toolbar. This will open the Font dialog box described in the previous step. Although you normally should not need to modify the properties of a font, you can use this dialog box to substitute a different font for the one selected. To do this, click on the button next to the Font File field, select the new font, click on Open to return to the Font dialog box, and click on OK to return to the Fonts page.

**NOTE:** *You may find that some of the files to be installed do not appear to have proper descriptions. This was the case in the Fonts list for FrontPage 2000. If so, you can add a description in the Font dialog box described previously. You should do this only if you understand the proper syntax for font names. The font name may be embedded in the file, but at a different location from the normal one. Sometimes, you can find the font name by viewing the font in a file viewer such as Vern Buerg's shareware List program, which will show you everything in any file. A better alternative is to install the font in a font manager, and then use that program's features to view and edit the font name.*

7. Click on File|Save to save your changes.
8. Click on File|Exit to close the console and return to the Windows desktop.

## Working With Shortcuts In A Package File

Just about every Windows installation adds shortcuts to the program or programs that it installs. Usually, they wind up every place except where you need them. By editing the package file, you can add, remove, and modify the shortcuts that will be installed.

### Adding A New Shortcut To The Package File

To add a new shortcut to the package file, follow these steps:

1. Open the package file in WinINSTALL LE, as described in "Opening, Viewing, And Navigating A Package File" in this Immediate Solutions section.

2. In the Tree View pane, select the package, expand its tree as needed, and highlight the feature that you want to modify.

3. In the List View, select Shortcuts. The editor will display the current list of shortcuts in the Data View pane.

4. To add a shortcut, click on the New icon at the right of the toolbar above the list. This will open a two-page, untitled dialog box, which probably should have been labeled Properties. (See Figure 12.5.)

5. Select the General page. In the Name edit box, enter the name that you want to appear under the shortcut's icon.

6. In the Shortened Name edit box, enter an alphanumeric name of no more than eight characters.

7. In the Component drop-down list box, select the component to which the shortcut should be attached, if appropriate.

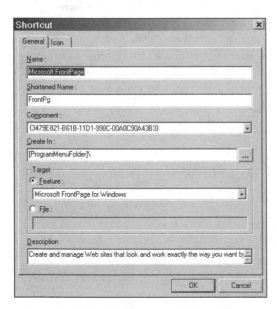

*Figure 12.5    The General page of the untitled properties dialog box for shortcuts.*

8. In the Create In edit box, either enter the name of a new folder or click on the button next to the box. Clicking on the button will open the Directory dialog box, which shows a list of existing folders. Select the folder that you want and click on OK to return to the General page.

9. In the Target area, select the feature or file that the shortcut will point to.

10. In the Description edit box, enter the ToolTip help that will be displayed when a user's cursor hovers over the shortcut.

11. Select the Icon page. In the Shortcut Key edit box, enter the desired shortcut key combination or accept the default setting (None).

12. In the Show Command drop-down list box, select the way that you want the program attached to the shortcut to come up (normal, maximized, or minimized).

13. In the Argument edit box, enter any command-line arguments that may be required.

14. In the Working Directory edit box, enter the folder that you want the program to start in, if any.

15. In the Icon area, click on Select Icon to open the Select Icon dialog box. In the Source Icon File edit box, either enter the name of the file that contains the desired icon or click on the button next to the window to browse for the file. Below this edit box is a window showing the available icons in the selected file. Highlight the icon that you want and press OK to return to the Icon page.

16. Click on OK to close the dialog box and return to the Add page.

17. Click on File|Save to save your changes.

18. Click on File|Exit to close the console and return to the Windows desktop.

### Removing A Shortcut From The Package File

Here is how to remove a shortcut from the package file:

1. Open the package file in WinINSTALL LE, as described in "Opening, Viewing, And Navigating A Package File" in this Immediate Solutions section.

2. In the Tree View pane, select the package, expand its tree as needed, and highlight the feature that you want to modify.

3. In the List View, select Shortcuts. The editor will display the current list of shortcuts in the Data View pane.

4. To remove a shortcut, highlight it in the list. Either press Delete or click on the Delete icon at the right of the toolbar above the list.

5. Click on File|Save to save your changes.

6. Click on File|Exit to close the console and return to the Windows desktop.

### Modifying The Properties Of A Shortcut In A Package File

To modify the properties of a shortcut, follow these steps:

1. Open the package file in WinINSTALL LE, as described in "Opening, Viewing, And Navigating A Package File" in this Immediate Solutions section.

2. In the Tree View pane, select the package, expand its tree as needed, and highlight the feature that you want to modify.

3. In the List View, select Shortcuts. The editor will display the current list of shortcuts in the Data View pane.

4. To modify the properties of a shortcut, highlight the shortcut on the Add page. Either double-click on the item in the list or click once on the Properties icon in the middle of the toolbar above the list. This will open a two-page, untitled dialog box.

5. Follow Steps 5 through 15 in the Immediate Solution "Adding A New Shortcut To The Package File."

6. Click on OK to close the dialog box and return to the Add page.

7. Click on File|Save to save your changes.

8. Click on File|Exit to close the console and return to the Windows desktop.

# Changing The Registry Entries In A Package File

Many installation routines make extensive changes to the Windows Registry. The Registry changes are contained in the package file, which has two lists of Registry modifications—those that will be added and those that will be removed. In both cases, you can add to, remove, and modify the entries on the list.

Here is one example where this might come in handy: Most word processors have their own native file formats, which we use most of the time when we save files. When we install an application, its setup routine modifies the file association settings in the Registry. Later, when we select a file that has been saved in the application's native format, it opens in that application. In most cases, this is exactly what we want to happen.

When it comes to graphics files, however, things are not quite that simple. This is especially true with bitmapped images, such as those normally created in an image editing, or "paint," program. Although many image editors have their own native file formats, many graphics files are saved in an industry-standard format such as TIFF, GIF, or JPEG.

It is not unusual for graphics users to have more than one image editor—a simple one that they use for basic tasks and a full-featured one that they call out only when they need its heavy artillery. In such cases, they may prefer to associate the industry-standard file formats with the simpler—and usually faster-loading—image editor.

The installation routines for most image editors, and for some other applications as well, modify the Registry to associate all of the graphics formats that the application supports with the application itself. In many cases, they will override a previous association. This often happens when a user upgrades one of his image editors. It can be very annoying if you have painstakingly set up the associations that you want, only to have them blown away by a dumb installation routine.

By making changes to both the Add and Remove Registry entries in a package file, you can prevent this from happening. First, review the Remove list and cancel any settings that would delete the current file associations. Second, review the entries to be added and remove any that would replace or override the current settings.

*WARNING!   Be very judicious about modifying the Registry entries in a package file, just as you would be in editing the Windows Registry directly. If you make a mistake in working with the file and shortcut lists, the worst that may happen, at least in most cases, is that the program may not install or run properly. You can always reinstall it. An incorrect Registry entry, on the other hand, can cause serious problems that can be difficult to trace and may even keep Windows from loading.*

### Adding Registry Keys To A Package File

You can add a Registry key to either the Add list or the Remove list of a package file. Here is how to add a Registry key to the Add list:

1. Open the package file in WinINSTALL LE, as described in "Opening, Viewing, And Navigating A Package File" in this Immediate Solutions section.

2. In the Tree View pane, select the package, expand its tree as needed, and highlight the feature or component that you want to modify. (If you want to see all of the Registry modifications that will be made, highlight the root of the package file.)

3. In the List View, select Registry. The Data View pane will be divided into two child panes that look like the Windows Registry Editor. The main folders in the Registry tree, such as HKEY_CLASSES_ROOT, HKEY_CURRENT_USER, and the other predefined Registry keys, will appear in the left pane. The value, type, and data for the selected key will be shown in the right pane, which will have two pages: Add and Remove.

4. In the Data View pane, select the Add page, expand the folders in the Registry tree, and highlight the folder to which you want to add a Registry key. Right-click on the folder and select New Key from the context-sensitive pop-up menu. This will add a folder with the default name of New Key.

5. Change the name of the key, and then right-click on the key and select New Value in the context-sensitive pop-up menu. This will open the Add Value dialog box. (See Figure 12.6.)

6. In the Value Name edit box, enter a name for the new value.

7. In the Data Type drop-down list box, select the data type.

8. Click on OK when you are ready. This will open a second dialog box. The dialog box will depend on the data type that you have selected:

   - If you selected REG_SZ or REG_EXPAND_SZ, you will see the String Editor dialog box. Enter the desired string and click on OK to close the dialog box and return to the Data View pane.

   - If you selected REG_BINARY, you will see the Binary Editor dialog box. Enter the binary information, select either the Binary or the Hex radio button, and click on OK to close the dialog box and return to the Data View pane.

   - If you selected REG_DWORD, you will see the DWORD Editor dialog box. Enter the DWORD data. In the set of radio buttons for Radix, select either Binary, Decimal, or Hex. Click on OK to close the dialog box and return to the Data View pane.

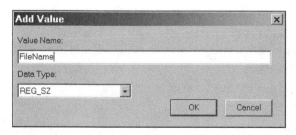

*Figure 12.6   The Add Value dialog box.*

**377**

- If you selected REG_MULTI_SZ, you will see the Multi-String Editor. Enter the required data and click on OK to close the dialog box and return to the Data View pane.

9. Click on File|Save to save your changes.

10. Click on File|Exit to close the console and return to the Windows desktop.

Here is how to add a Registry key to the list of those to be removed:

1. Open the package file in WinINSTALL LE, as described in "Opening, Viewing, And Navigating A Package File" in this Immediate Solutions section.

2. In the Tree View pane, select the package, expand its tree as needed, and highlight the feature or component that you want to modify.

3. In the List View, select Registry. The Data View pane will be divided into two child panes that look like the Windows Registry Editor. The main Registry tree folders will appear in the left pane and the value, type, and data for the selected key will be shown in the right pane. The right pane will have two pages: Add and Remove.

4. In the Data View pane, select the Remove page, expand the folders in the Registry tree, and highlight the folder to which you want to add a Registry key. Right-click on the folder and select New Key from the context-sensitive pop-up menu. This will add a folder with the default name of New Key.

5. Change the name of the key, and then click on a blank area in the Registry tree window. This will open a message box, asking whether the key and its subkeys should be deleted. If this is what you want, click on OK to return to the Remove page and skip to Step 8. The value will then read Delete All Subkeys And Values.

6. If this is not what you want, click on No. The value will then read Delete Key Only If Empty. To change the value, right-click on the key and select New Value in the context-sensitive pop-up menu. This will open the Add Value dialog box.

7. In the Value Name edit box, enter a name for the new value. The Data Type setting will be grayed-out. Click on OK to return to the Remove page.

8. Click on File|Save to save your changes.

9. Click on File|Exit to close the console and return to the Windows desktop.

### Removing A Registry Key In A Package File

You can remove a Registry key from either the Add list or the Remove list. Here is how to do it:

1. Open the package file in WinINSTALL LE, as described in "Opening, Viewing, And Navigating A Package File" in this Immediate Solutions section.

2. In the Tree View pane, select the package, expand its tree as needed, and highlight the feature or component that you want to modify.

3. In the List View, select Registry. The Data View pane will be divided into two child panes that look like the Windows Registry Editor. The main Registry tree folders will appear in the left pane and the value, type, and data for the selected key will be shown in the right pane. The right pane will have two pages: Add and Remove.

4. In the Data View pane, select the appropriate page, expand the folders in the Registry tree, and highlight the key to be removed. Right-click on the key to be removed and select Delete from the context-sensitive pop-up menu. (Pressing the Delete key did not work for me in this context.)

**WARNING!** *You will not see a delete confirmation message, and there is no Undo feature in the VERITAS Software Console.*

5. Click on File|Save to save your changes.

6. Click on File|Exit to close the console and return to the Windows desktop.

### Modifying Registry Key Properties In A Package File

You can modify the values of Registry keys in either the Add list or the Remove list. Here is how to modify the values of a key that will be added:

1. Open the package file in WinINSTALL LE, as described in "Opening, Viewing, And Navigating A Package File" in this Immediate Solutions section.

2. In the Tree View pane, select the package, expand its tree as needed, and highlight the feature or component that you want to modify.

3. In the List View, select Registry. The Data View pane will be divided into two child panes that look like the Windows Registry Editor. The main Registry tree folders will appear in the left

12. Using WinINSTALL LE

pane and the value, type, and data for the selected key will be shown in the right pane. The right pane will have two pages: Add and Remove.

4. In the Data View pane, select the Add page, expand the folders in the Registry tree, and highlight the folder that contains the key that you want to modify. Right-click on the key and select New Value from the context-sensitive pop-up menu. This will open the Add Value dialog box.

5. In the Value Name edit box, you can edit the name of the value. If you do not need to change the data type, click on OK to close the dialog box and return to the Add page.

6. In the Data Type drop-down list box, you can change the data type. Click on OK when you are ready. This will open a second dialog box. The dialog box will depend on the data type that you have selected:

   • If you selected REG_SZ or REG_EXPAND_SZ, you will see the String Editor dialog box. Edit the string and click on OK to close the dialog box and return to the Data View pane.

   • If you selected REG_BINARY, you will see the Binary Editor dialog box. Edit the binary information, select either the Binary or the Hex radio button, and click on OK to close the dialog box and return to the Data View pane.

   • If you selected REG_DWORD, you will see the DWORD Editor dialog box. Edit the DWORD data. In the set of radio buttons for Radix, select either Binary, Decimal, or Hex. Click on OK to close the dialog box and return to the Data View pane.

   • If you selected REG_MULTI_SZ, you will see the Multi-String Editor. Edit the required data, and click on OK to close the dialog box and return to the Data View pane.

7. Click on File|Save to save your changes.

8. Click on File|Exit to close the console and return to the Windows desktop.

Here is how to modify the value of a Registry key that will be removed:

1. Open the package file in WinINSTALL LE, as described in "Opening, Viewing, And Navigating A Package File" in this Immediate Solutions section.

2. In the Tree View pane, select the package, expand its tree as needed, and highlight the feature or component that you want to modify.

3. In the List View, select Registry. The Data View pane will be divided into two child panes that look like the Windows Registry Editor. The main Registry tree folders will appear in the left pane and the value, type, and data for the selected key will be shown in the right pane. The right pane will have two pages: Add and Remove.

4. In the Data View pane, select the Remove page, expand the folders in the Registry tree, and highlight the folder that contains the key that you want to modify. Right-click on the key and select New Value from the context-sensitive pop-up menu. This will open the Add Value dialog box.

5. In the Value Name edit box, edit the name of the value, and then click on OK to close the dialog box and return to the Remove page. (The Data Type settings will be grayed-out.)

6. Click on File|Save to save your changes.

7. Click on File|Exit to close the console and return to the Windows desktop.

### Renaming A Registry Key In A Package File

Sometimes, all you need to do is rename a Registry key. Here is how to do it:

1. Open the package file in WinINSTALL LE, as described in "Opening, Viewing, And Navigating A Package File" in this Immediate Solutions section.

2. In the Tree View pane, select the package, expand its tree as needed, and highlight the feature or component that you want to modify.

3. In the List View, select Registry. The Data View pane will be divided into two child panes that look like the Windows Registry Editor. The main Registry tree folders will appear in the left pane and the value, type, and data for the selected key will be shown in the right pane. The right pane will have two pages: Add and Remove.

4. In the Data View pane, select the page that contains the key to be renamed. Expand the folders in the Registry tree and highlight the folder that contains the key that you want to rename. Right-click on the key and select Rename from the context-sensitive pop-up menu. When you do, the name will be highlighted and your cursor will be at the end of the name. Unless you want to delete the current name entirely, move your cursor before pressing a key.

**12. Using WinINSTALL LE**

---

**NOTE:**   *Pressing F2 did not work for me in this context.*

---

5. Edit the name as needed, and then click on a blank area of the Registry tree.

6. Click on File|Save to save your changes.

7. Click on File|Exit to close the console and return to the Windows desktop.

# Working With Windows 2000 Services In A Package File

You can add a Windows 2000 service to a component in a package file, change the properties of that service, and modify the way in which existing services that the application uses are controlled. The package file contains separate lists of services to be added and services to be controlled.

---

**NOTE:**   *The dialog boxes in WinINSTALL LE for working with Windows 2000 Services are very different from those shown in the walkthrough for the program. Because there is no online help in the WinINSTALL LE dialog boxes, some of the steps outlined below are unavoidably vague.*

---

### Adding A Service To The Add List

Here is how to add a service to the list of those to be added:

1. Open the package file in WinINSTALL LE, as described in "Opening, Viewing, And Navigating A Package File" in this Immediate Solutions section.

2. In the Tree View pane, select the package, expand its tree as needed, and highlight the feature or component that you want to modify.

3. In the List View, select Services. The Data View pane will display two pages, Add and Control, which show the services that have already been added to those lists.

4. In the Data View, select the Add page and click on the New icon at the left of the toolbar above the main window. This will open the Add Service dialog box, with General and Options pages. (See Figure 12.7.)

5. Select the General page. In the Name edit box, enter the actual name of the service as it will be identified in the Windows Registry.

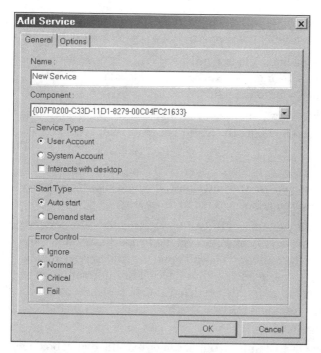

*Figure 12.7    The General page of the Add Service dialog box.*

6. In the Component drop-down list box, select the component to which the service will be attached.

7. In the Service Type, Start Type, and Error Control areas, select the appropriate radio buttons.

8. Select the Options page. In the Display Name edit box, enter the name that users will see in a list of system services.

9. In the Load Order Group, indicate the appropriate group from the Group Order List in the Windows Registry, if appropriate.

10. In the Dependencies areas, indicate any dependencies that may exist.

11. If appropriate, enter the required information in the Domain\Username and Password fields.

12. Click on OK to confirm your settings, exit the dialog box, and return to the Add page.

13. Click on File|Save to save your changes.

14. Click on File|Exit to close the console and return to the Windows desktop.

### Modifiying The Properties Of A Service On The Add List

Here is how to modify the properties of a service that will be added:

1. Open the package file in WinINSTALL LE, as described in "Opening, Viewing, And Navigating A Package File" in this Immediate Solutions section.

2. In the Tree View pane, select the package, expand its tree as needed, and highlight the feature or component that you want to modify.

3. In the List View, select Services. The Data View pane will display two pages, Add and Control, which show the services that have already been added to those lists.

4. In the Data View, select the Add page. Highlight the service that you want to modify and click on the Properties icon in the middle of the toolbar. This will open the Add Service dialog box, with General and Options pages. For information on modifying the properties in this dialog box, see Steps 5 through 11 under "Adding A Service To The Add List" in this Immediate Solutions section.

5. Click on OK to confirm your settings, exit the dialog box, and return to the Add page.

6. Click on File|Save to save your changes.

7. Click on File|Exit to close the console and return to the Windows desktop.

### Adding A Service To The Control List

Adding a service to the Control list is somewhat simpler than adding one to the Add list. Here is how to do it:

1. Open the package file in WinINSTALL LE, as described in "Opening, Viewing, And Navigating A Package File" in this Immediate Solutions section.

2. In the Tree View pane, select the package, expand its tree as needed, and highlight the feature or component that you want to modify.

3. In the List View, select Services. The Data View pane will display two pages, Add and Control, which show the services that have already been added to those lists.

4. In the Data View, select the Control page and click on the New icon at the left of the toolbar above the main window. This will open the Control Options dialog box. (See Figure 12.8.)

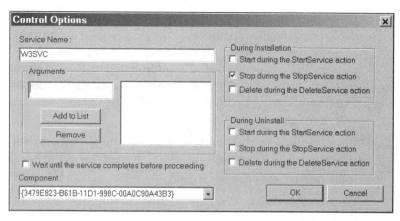

*Figure 12.8    The Control Options dialog box.*

5. In the Service Name edit box, enter the name of the service as it appears in the Windows Registry.

6. In the Arguments edit box, enter any arguments that may be required, one at a time. Click on Add To List to add the argument to the window at the right of the Arguments area. Click on Remove to remove an argument from this window.

7. In the Component ID drop-down list box, select the component to which the service is attached.

8. Select the appropriate checkboxes in the During Installation and During Uninstall areas.

9. Click on OK to confirm your settings, exit the dialog box, and return to the Control page.

10. Click on File|Save to save your changes.

11. Click on File|Exit to close the console and return to the Windows desktop.

### Modifiying The Properties Of A Service On The Control List

Here is how to modify the properties of a service on the Control list:

1. Open the package file in WinINSTALL LE, as described in "Opening, Viewing, And Navigating A Package File" in this Immediate Solutions section.

2. In the Tree View pane, select the package, expand its tree as needed, and highlight the feature or component that you want to modify.

3. In the List View, select Services. The Data View pane will display two pages, Add and Control, which show the services that have already been added to those lists.

4. In the Data View, select the Control page. Select the service that you want to modify and click on the Properties icon at the left of the toolbar above the main window. This will open the Control Options dialog box. For information on how to modify the settings in this dialog box, see Steps 5 through 8 under "Adding A Service To The Control List" in this Immediate Solutions section.

5. Click on OK to confirm your settings, exit the dialog box, and return to the Control page.

6. Click on File|Save to save your changes.

7. Click on File|Exit to close the console and return to the Windows desktop.

### Removing A Service From The Add Or Control List

Here is how to remove a service from the list of those to be added or controlled:

1. Open the package file in WinINSTALL LE, as described in "Opening, Viewing, And Navigating A Package File" in this Immediate Solutions section.

2. In the Tree View pane, select the package, expand its tree as needed, and highlight the feature or component that you want to modify.

3. In the List View, select Services. The Data View pane will display two pages, Add and Control, which show the services that have already been added to those lists.

4. In the Data View, select the appropriate page and highlight the service that you want to remove. Either press the Delete key or click on the Delete icon at the right of the toolbar.

**WARNING!**   *You will not see a delete confirmation message, and there is no Undo feature in the VERITAS Software Console.*

5. Click on File|Save to save your changes.

6. Click on File|Exit to close the console and return to the Windows desktop.

## Working With INI Edits In A Package File

With all of the information that is installed in the Windows Registry, nevertheless some installation routines, including the one for FrontPage 2000, continue to create or modify INI files. This is done for cross-platform compatibility reasons. Package files contain separate lists for additions and removals. You can add and remove your own modifications, or edit the properties of the changes that the installer will make. The procedures for modifying each list are the same.

### Adding An INI Edit To A List

You can add new files to the Add and Remove lists, as well as sections and values to files already on the lists. Here is how to add your own edits to an INI list in a package file:

1. Open the package file in WinINSTALL LE, as described in "Opening, Viewing, And Navigating A Package File" in this Immediate Solutions section.

2. In the Tree View pane, select the package, expand its tree as needed, and highlight the feature or component that you want to modify.

3. In the List View, select INI Edits. The Data View pane will be divided into two child panes. The left pane will display folders for each INI file to be modified. Expanding the folder will display the sections to be modified. The values to be changed or added will be displayed in the right pane. Above the panes will be tabs for Add and Remove pages.

4. Select the appropriate page.

5. If you want to modify an INI file that is not listed, right-click on the INI File Data root and select New File from the context-sensitive pop-up menu. This will open the INI File Name dialog box. You can either enter the full path name of the INI file or click on the button next to the edit box, which will open the Select File dialog box. After you have entered or selected the name of the file, click on OK to return to the Add page. The file that you have selected will be added to the tree, where you can enter your modifications.

6. To edit a section in an INI file, including one that you have added, right-click on the file in the INI File Data tree and select New Section from the context-sensitive pop-up menu. This will open an edit window in which you enter the name of the section to be added or modified.

7. To add a new value to a section, right-click on the section in the INI File Data tree and select New Value from the context-sensitive pop-up menu. This will open the Properties dialog box.

8. Enter the appropriate information in the Value and Data edit boxes, and select the appropriate action (Create Or Update, Create New, or Append) in the set of Action radio buttons.

*12. Using WinINSTALL LE*

9. Click on OK to confirm your settings and return to the Add page.

10. Click on File|Save to save your changes.

11. Click on File|Exit to close the console and return to the Windows desktop.

### Modifying The Values In An INI Edit

Here is how to modify the properties of an INI edit in a package file:

1. Open the package file in WinINSTALL LE, as described in "Opening, Viewing, And Navigating A Package File" in this Immediate Solutions section.

2. In the Tree View pane, select the package, expand its tree as needed, and highlight the feature or component that you want to modify.

3. In the List View, select INI Edits. The Data View pane will be divided into two child panes. The left pane will display folders for each INI file to be modified. Expanding the folder will display the sections to be modified. The values to be changed or added will be displayed in the right pane. Above the panes will be tabs for Add and Remove pages.

4. Select the appropriate page. Expand the INI File Data tree to highlight the section that you want to modify. The values will be displayed in the right pane.

5. Double-click on the value to open the Properties dialog box. (See Figure 12.9.) Edit the information in the Key and Value edit boxes, as needed. Select the appropriate action (Add Line, Create Line, or Add Tag) in the set of Action radio buttons.

6. Click on OK to confirm your settings and return to the Add page.

7. Click on File|Save to save your changes.

8. Click on File|Exit to close the console and return to the Windows desktop.

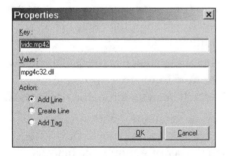

*Figure 12.9    The Properties dialog box for an INI edit.*

### Removing An INI Edit From A List

Here is how to remove an INI edit from a package file:

1. Open the package file in WinINSTALL LE, as described in "Opening, Viewing, And Navigating A Package File" in this Immediate Solutions section.

2. In the Tree View pane, select the package, expand its tree as needed, and highlight the feature or component that you want to modify.

3. In the List View, select INI Edits. The Data View pane will be divided into two child panes. The left pane will display folders for each INI file to be modified. Expanding the folder will display the sections to be modified. The values to be changed or added will be displayed in the right pane. Above the panes will be tabs for Add and Remove pages.

4. Select the appropriate page. Expand the INI File Data tree to highlight the file or section that you want to modify. Values will be displayed in the right pane.

5. Right-click on the item to be deleted and select Delete from the context-sensitive pop-up menu.

6. Click on OK to confirm your settings and return to the Data View pane.

7. Click on File|Save to save your changes.

8. Click on File|Exit to close the console and return to the Windows desktop.

# Using Discover To Create A New Package File

Perhaps the most useful feature of WinINSTALL LE is its Discover utility. Discover can be used to create package files for legacy applications that do not include a Windows 2000-compatible package file. Moreover, the program is easy to use and does not require any specialized knowledge.

The process for creating a package file with Discover involves three basic steps:

• Preparing a reference system.

• Taking a "before" snapshot of the system and installing the legacy application.

- Taking an "after" snapshot and creating the installation package.

Discover compares the two snapshots and determines what the installation program did. In this respect, Discover is similar to a good uninstaller utility. Finally, it uses this information to copy the necessary files to the appropriate shared folder on your network and creates the package file.

---

**NOTE:**   *Because the procedures for preparing a reference workstation and installing a legacy application differ from one situation to another, I have described them in general terms only and have not attempted to break them down into numbered steps.*

---

## Preparing A Reference Workstation

The first step in using Discover is to select and prepare a reference workstation, on which you will temporarily install the legacy application. The workstation must be running Windows 2000 Professional. The hardware and operating system configurations of the workstation should be as similar as possible to those of the workstations where the application will be installed.

---

**TIP:**   *If you cannot dedicate a workstation for this purpose, consider using swappable hard drives. You will need a docking bay that you install in an external 5.25-inch drive bay; two or more standard 3.5-inch by 1-inch form factor hard drives of any capacity; and one caddy for each drive. Good-quality docking bay/caddy sets sell for about $40 and are available for both SCSI and IDE drives.*

*Shut down the system and install the docking bay. Disconnect the ribbon cable from the current primary drive and connect it to the rear of the docking bay. Remove the primary drive and install it in a drive caddy. Label the caddy, insert the caddy into the docking bay, and lock it down with the provided key. When you boot the system, everything should work just as before.*

*Install one of the new drives in a second caddy and label the caddy. Shut down the system and swap the drives. Install Windows 2000 Professional on the new drive with only those features that are necessary. Now, you have a good reference platform.*

*If you are using IDE drives, run your hardware setup's IDE hard drive detection procedure whenever you swap drives. Windows NT 4 insisted on running CHKDSK whenever I used my BIOS' auto-detect feature. I did not try this with Windows 2000, preferring to play it safe.*

---

For best results, the configuration of the workstation should be as clean as possible. VERITAS defines a clean reference workstation as one that has only the necessary operating system software and service packs.

There should be no application software installed on the reference workstation because the presence of other applications can influence the way that the installation of the legacy application is carried out. For example, if you install Excel 97 on a workstation that already has Word 97, certain common files and folders will already be on the system. Therefore, the Excel installer will not copy those files from the installation CD-ROM or attempt to create folders that already exist. Consequently, these files and folders will not be among the ones that Discover later copies to the shared network folder. Any attempt to install Excel 97 on a remote workstation that does not already have Word 97 will fail.

In addition, any operating system applications and processes that write to the hard disk or modify the Windows Registry should be disabled until the task is finished. The walkthrough for WinINSTALL LE describes this as a "quiet" workstation.

On the server that contains the WinINSTALL program files, make the primary folder for the WinINSTALL files shareable. At the reference workstation, you will run this network installation of Discover. Be sure to add the Administrators group to the list of users and groups with specific permissions for the folder, give the group full control, and then change the setting for the Everyone group to allow only read access.

There is one apparent exception to the "no application software" rule. For Discover to work properly, the walkthrough for WinINSTALL LE states that you must copy all of the files in the folder that contains the Discover executable file (disco7.exe) from the network to the workstation. In most cases, they will be in the c:\program files\VERITAS software\winstall folder.

---

**NOTE:** *This instruction is contained in the technical walkthrough "Using WinINSTALL LE to Repackage Applications for the Windows Installer," available on Microsoft's Web site. The reason for it is unclear, particularly because the instructions in the walkthrough also say to run the network copy of Discover. Moreover, they do not indicate that you must add the local folder to your path command, which would seem to be logical, or even that the folder must have a specific name. I am repeating the instruction here because I do not see where it can do any harm.*

---

Finally, I recommend that you back up the files on the workstation, including the Windows Registry, before you start Discover. Later, you can uninstall the legacy application using the Add/Remove Programs utility in Control Panel or the application's own uninstall routine.

Unfortunately, these methods of uninstalling a program are not always as thorough or as accurate as they should be. If you have a reliable backup, you will have a better chance of being able to restore the configuration of the workstation to its prior state.

## Taking A "Before" Snapshot And Installing The Legacy Application

After you have selected and prepared the reference workstation, you are ready to begin the process of creating an installation package for the legacy application. The first stage involves running Discover to take a "before" snapshot. As soon as the snapshot has been created, you will be asked to start the application's setup program, so be sure that you have its installation disks handy.

Here are the steps to follow at this stage:

1. Log onto the reference workstation as an administrator.

2. Click on Start|Run, and then click on Browse. This will open the Browse dialog box.

3. Click on the down arrow in the Look In drop-down list box. Expand either Computers Near Me or Entire Network to locate the VERITAS Software folder.

4. Double-click on the VERITAS Software folder, and then double-click on the Winstall child folder.

5. In the Winstall folder, select disco7.exe and click on Open to return to the Run dialog box.

6. Click on OK to start Discover. After a minute or so, you should see the initial WinINSTALL Discover screen. Click on Next to continue.

7. This will open a dialog box with three edit boxes. In the first edit box, enter a name for the application. This name will appear in the results pane of the Group Policy Editor and in the list of available programs in the Control Panel Add/Remove Programs utility.

---

**NOTE:** *Unlike most of the dialog boxes mentioned in this book, the Discover dialog boxes do not have unique names, except as noted. Therefore, I have described the most important ones in some detail to help you keep your place in these procedures.*

---

8. In the second edit box, enter the network path to the folder that you have created to contain the application's installation files. This is where Discover will copy the application's files and create the package file. When you are ready, skip to Step 10.

**WARNING!** *If the folder is a mapped network drive, do not use the drive mapping. This will cause remote installations to fail. Always enter the network path. For this reason, you may prefer to use the dialog box described in Step 8.*

9. If you do not know the network path to the folder, click on the Browse button next to the edit box. This will open the Target Application MSI Package dialog box. (See Figure 12.10.) Click on the down arrow in the Look In drop-down list box. If you have added the root folder for your installation files to the Distributed File System, select that Dfs folder, and then double-click on it to expose the child folder for the legacy application. Otherwise, expand either Computers Near Me or Entire Network to drill down to the folder. Select the folder, and then click on Open to return to the previous dialog box.

10. In the third edit box, select the language to be used for installer messages. (See Figure 12.11.) When you are ready, click on Next to continue.

11. In the next dialog box, select the drive where Discover should create its temporary work files, and then click on Next to continue.

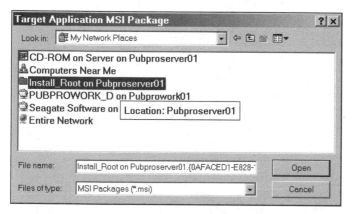

*Figure 12.10    The Target Application MSI Package dialog box with the Dfs root folder selected.*

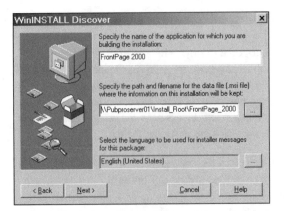

*Figure 12.11    Identifying the application and the folder for the installation files.*

12. This will open a dialog box in which you will be asked to select the drives that Discover should scan. The left window will show the available drives and the right window will show the selected drives. Use the Add and Remove buttons to move the selected drives from one window to the other. If you intend to install the application on drive C—and you should—selecting only that drive should be sufficient. When you are ready, click on Next to continue.

13. This will open a dialog box in which you will be asked to define those files and folders that should be excluded from the scan. (See Figure 12.12.) At the top left is a drop-down list box with

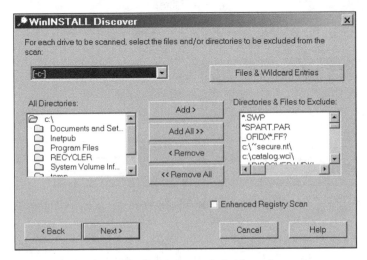

*Figure 12.12    Selecting files to be excluded from the scan.*

the drives that you selected in the previous dialog box. Under this is a folder tree for the selected drive. To the right is a window with a list of files and folders that are excluded by default. To add more folders to the list, select the folder in the tree at the left and click on Add. To remove a folder from the list, highlight it in the right window and click on Remove.

14. To refine the list of excluded files, click on the File & Wildcard Entries button at the top right of the dialog box. This will open the Directories And Files To Exclude dialog box. Make your selection, and then click on Open to return to the previous dialog box.

*WARNING! Be cautious about adding to the list of excluded files and folders. The default list of exclusions is quite good and should be sufficient for most situations. Failing to exclude a folder that the legacy application's installation routine does not modify will add slightly to the time required for Discover to perform its scans. Excluding a folder that the installation does modify will make this entire process useless. Never exclude the root of the Program Files folder tree.*

15. If you want to perform an enhanced Registry scan, which helps to ensure that Discover picks up all changes to Registry keys, click on the checkbox at the bottom right of the dialog box. When you are ready, click on Next to continue.

16. Discover will now perform the "before" scan. You will see a progress screen with only a Cancel button. The scan will take several minutes.

17. At the end of the scan, you will see the Launch Application Setup Program screen. Click on OK to open the Run Application Setup Program dialog box.

18. Navigate to the folder that contains the legacy application's setup program. Double-click on the file to start the installation. At this point, Discover will close.

19. Follow the installation routine's prompts and install the application in the normal way.

*WARNING! Do not install the application on a drive that may not be present in some workstations. Always install the application on drive C, and accept the default folder locations as well. If you install the application on drive D, for example, and then attempt to install it on a system that does not have a D drive, the installation may fail.*

20. Reboot the workstation if you are prompted to do so.

21. Open and test the application, change its default settings as needed, and then close the application.

## Taking An "After" Snapshot And Creating The Installation Package

To complete the process and generate the installation package, you must run Discover again as soon as you have tested the application. This is what you need to do:

1. Log onto the reference workstation as an administrator.

2. Click on Start|Run, and then click on Browse. This will open the Browse dialog box.

3. Click on the down arrow in the Look In drop-down list box. Expand either Computers Near Me or Entire Network to locate the VERITAS Software folder.

4. Double-click on the VERITAS Software folder, and then double-click on the Winstall child folder.

5. In the Winstall folder, select disco7.exe, click on Open to return to the Run dialog box, and then click on OK to start Discover.

6. Next, you will see a dialog box showing the name of the application that you have just installed. (See Figure 12.13.) The dialog box contains two radio buttons. If everything has gone smoothly, choose the first (default) button to perform the "after" snapshot. If not, select the second button to scrap the "before" snapshot and start over. When you are ready, click on Next to continue.

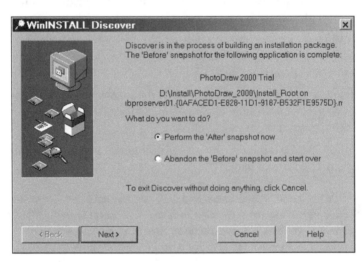

*Figure 12.13    Preparing to begin the "after" scan.*

7. Discover will now perform the "after" scan if you selected the first radio button. You will see a progress screen with only a Cancel button. The scan will take several minutes.

8. After the scan, you should see a Conversion Successful message box. This may include one or more warnings about problems that you may need to address in the package file. A typical problem is a reference to an absolute path, or UNC, that may not be available on the target system when the application is deployed. Click on OK to continue.

9. Next, you should see an After Snapshot Complete! confirmation message box. Click on OK to return to the Windows desktop.

At this point, the package should be ready to install in a group policy. After you have installed the package and tested the remote installation on another workstation, remember to uninstall it from the reference workstation.

**12. Using WinINSTALL LE**

# Managing User Data

# *In Brief*

With the popularity of laptop computers and home computers, many users take work with them to do at home or on trips away from the office. Because of this, they often have one version of a file on the network and another version on their laptop or home system. Over the years, network administrators have tried to deal with the problem by instructing their users to regularly back up their files to and from the network, or by providing them with third-party utilities designed for synchronizing files and folders. In either case, the user must initiate the procedure manually and regularly.

Human nature being what it is, users do not always follow these procedures as often as they should. Even when they do, mistakes happen. If more than one person is using the file, version control can be a nightmare. Newer files are often overwritten by older ones.

User Data Management, which works only on Windows 2000 Professional workstations, addresses these problems in two ways:

- Its folder redirection feature allows you to redirect certain folders from the local workstation to a shared network folder. The redirection is transparent to both the user and the applications that she is using.

- Automatic synchronization of files and folders enables the user to open and save files on the network and still have those files available to her when she is working offline.

## Overview Of User Data Management

Roaming user profiles and software management, discussed in Chapters 7 and 11, enable a user's Windows environment and installed applications to follow her from one workstation to another on the network. User Data Management does the same for her data files. In addition, it enables her to continue to work on the files whenever she is offline.

The user can then make the contents of any shared file or folder on the network available offline. These files are stored in a special cache on the user's local system. This enables her to access them any time that she is not connected to the network, including occasions when the network goes down while she is connected to it.

As with so many of the other subjects covered in this book, User Data Management requires an understanding of both the Active Directory (covered in Chapters 3 through 5) and Group Policy (covered in Chapter 6). In addition, you should know how to use disk quotas (covered in Chapter 8). If you have not already done so, I recommend that you read those chapters before proceeding.

# Folder Redirection

By using folder redirection, you can channel the content of certain Windows 2000 special folders, installed by default on a Windows 2000 Professional workstation, to a network folder instead. You can redirect the following folders:

- Application Data
- Desktop
- My Documents and its child folder, My Pictures
- Start menu and its child folders, Programs and Programs\Startup

The My Pictures folder can be redirected independently of its parent folder, My Documents. (You can also choose to have it follow the parent folder, as it normally does.) When you redirect the Start Menu folder, however, you also redirect its child folders. You cannot redirect them independently.

Implementing folder redirection is a two-stage process. First, you must create the shared network folders where the users' local folders will be redirected, and then you must enable folder redirection in a group policy. The next time that a user who is governed by the policy logs on, any files that she saves to a redirected folder, such as My Documents, will be saved to the network instead of to her local drive.

Folder redirection seems to have value, if only because the user's files will be protected by your network backup procedures. It makes even more sense when the user is running any of the components of Microsoft Office, all of which seem to default to the My Documents or My Pictures folders when saving files.

### *Drawbacks Of Folder Redirection*

Despite its advantages, however, folder redirection is far from fool-proof. There is nothing in folder redirection itself that prevents a user from saving her files to another folder on her local drive. In fact, many experienced computer users have their own methods of organizing the files and folders on their local drives. These systems often make more sense than dumping everything into one folder. Creating a sensible folder structure under My Documents does not solve anything because the only child folder that you can redirect is My Pictures.

The local folders that are available for redirection are also among the folders that are copied to the network when the user has a roaming profile. With a roaming profile, the files in these local folders are synchronized with the copies on the network at logon and logoff. When the network is unavailable, the local copy is used temporarily. If the files that are normally included in a local copy of a roaming profile do not exist on the local drive, however, then the roaming profile will not work as intended.

On the other hand, if the user does not have a roaming profile, then folder redirection begins to make sense because most of her important files and folders would need to be redirected. This would seem to have some of the advantages of roaming profiles while requiring much less work from you.

If you determine that folder redirection may be of value to you, follow the procedures under "Working With Folder Redirection" in the Immediate Solutions section of this chapter to implement the feature. Be sure to test it out afterward, however, by logging onto a Windows 2000 Professional workstation as a user governed by the policy.

---

**TIP:**   *If you decide to implement folder redirection for a large number of users, you should also consider enabling disk quotas on the volumes that will contain the redirected files. When you enable disk quotas for a volume on which your users already have files, Windows 2000 Server arbitrarily assigns quotas to each of these users in a way that might not meet your needs. Therefore, you should enable and configure disk quotas before you implement folder redirection. (Refer to Chapter 8 for more information on disk quotas.)*

---

# Synchronization Of Offline Files

Unlike most of the other features described in this book, the responsibility for enabling and using offline files rests with the user on the workstation, not with you as network administrator. She can choose to make any shared file or folder anywhere on the network available to her offline, as long as she has at least read permission. The rights and permissions that she has for the network files or folders continue to apply.

On a Windows 2000 Professional workstation, offline files are enabled by default. (The feature is enabled or disabled in My Computer|

ToolslFolder OptionslOffline Files.) To make a shared network file or folder available offline, the user opens My Network Places, drills down to the desired file or folder, highlights the desired item, and selects Make Available Offline from the current folder's File menu.

The first time that a user makes an item available offline, the Offline Files Wizard helps her to set up a synchronization schedule. After that, the Synchronization Manager keeps the network and local copies of the files coordinated, using the options that she has selected. She can configure synchronization to occur at logon, logoff, whenever the local computer is idle, or at scheduled intervals. These settings can be modified later by selecting My ComputerlToolsl Synchronize. The user can also initiate synchronization manually at any time that she is connected to the network.

In a typical scenario, offline files are synchronized at logon and logoff. When a user logs onto the network, the Synchronization Manager checks the network versions of the offline files with the ones in the user's local cache. If she has modified a file while offline and the network copy has not been changed by anyone else, her local version will be copied to the network. If she logs onto a different workstation that does not have a copy of her offline folders and files, the network copies will be downloaded to the workstation's local cache.

What if the network copy of the file has been modified by someone else since it was last opened by the user? In that case, the user will be given an opportunity to decide which version to keep, or to save her version to the network under a different name.

It is important to understand that even when a user selects entire folders to be made available offline, only the files are downloaded to the local system, not the folder structure that contains them. All offline files are contained in the local cache, and the size of the cache can be set by the user. The files can be accessed through the Offline Files Folder, which was created the first time she makes an item available offline. The folder window contains a fair amount of information about each file, including the path to the network copy.

The Offline Files Wizard includes an option to create a shortcut to the folder on her Windows desktop. I recommend that you select it whenever you set up offline files for a user. It makes it much easier for her to access the files.

13. Managing User Data

**NOTE:**   The Offline Files Folder appears to be a common folder accessible to every user on the workstation. I discovered this when logging onto the same workstation as several different users, with different levels of rights and permissions. In each case, the folder showed all the offline files for all users. I expected that each user would have their own private folder as a part of their custom Windows environment. I did not test to see whether a user who did not have write permissions for these files on the network could modify the local copies, but the fact that I could see someone else's offline files concerned me.

# *Immediate Solutions*

## Working With Folder Redirection

By using folder redirection, you can reroute files in certain default Windows 2000 folders from the local drive to a shared folder on your network. To do this, you must create the shared folders, place the users whose folders you want to redirect in the appropriate object on your domain, and create or modify the appropriate group policy for the object.

The following folders may be redirected: Application Data, Desktop, My Documents, My Documents\My Pictures, and Start Menu. When you redirect the Start Menu folder, you also redirect two of its child folders, Programs and Programs\Startup.

### Creating A Shared Root Folder For Redirection

The redirected files and folders must be placed in a shared folder on your network. Follow these steps to make the root folder for your redirected files shareable:

1. Click on Start|Programs|Accessories|Windows Explorer. Select the root folder of the drive that will contain the redirected files.

2. Create a new folder and name it "Redirect".

3. Right-click on the folder and select Properties from the context-sensitive pop-up menu.

4. In the Redirect Properties dialog box, select the Sharing page. (See Figure 13.1.)

5. By default, the folder will not be shared. Select the Share This Folder radio button to expose the sharing options.

6. In the appropriate edit boxes, enter a name for the shared folder and a descriptive comment.

7. Click on Caching to open the Caching Settings dialog box. (See Figure 13.2.)

8. Make sure that the Allow Caching Of Files In This Shared Folder checkbox is selected.

9. In the Setting drop-down list box, select Automatic Caching For Documents. Click on OK to close the Caching Settings dialog box and return to the Sharing page.

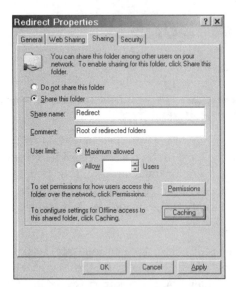

*Figure 13.1    The Sharing page of a folder's Properties dialog box.*

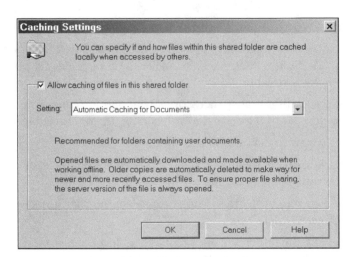

*Figure 13.2    The Caching Settings dialog box.*

10.  Click on Apply to confirm your changes, and then click on OK to close the Properties dialog box and return to Windows Explorer.

11.  Click on File|Close to exit Windows Explorer.

---

**NOTE:**    *In order to make folder redirection work properly, you may also need to create a child folder for each user whose folders are being redirected. Use their logon names when naming the folders and grant each user full control permission for his own folder.*

---

## Creating A Group Policy For Implementing Folder Redirection

The next step in implementing folder redirection is to organize the user accounts for the people whose folders will be directed. You must assign them to an object in the Active Directory that is managed by the appropriate group policy.

Later, when you edit the group policy to enable redirection, you will have two options for locating the redirected folders:

- You can place everyone's folders under the same network share. If you do this, you will need to make sure that there is adequate free space on the network drive.

- You can assign specific folders to individual security groups. In this case, the folders can be on different servers.

Before you apply folder redirection through a group policy, you should make sure that the groups and user accounts on your network are organized in a way that will permit the feature to work properly for you. For example, let's assume that you intend to apply folder redirection to a large number of users whose accounts are assigned to the domain rather than to sites or organizational units within the domain. Placing all of the redirected folders on the same network volume could overload the volume. In this case, you should organize your users into security groups, so that you can distribute their folders among several volumes and servers. On the other hand, if your users are distributed among several organizational units and the appropriate group policies have been applied at that level, placing each user's redirected folders under the same root folder becomes a viable option because you can set a different location for redirection in each policy.

Here is how to create a new group policy for an Active Directory object:

1. Click on Start|Programs|Administrative Tools|Active Directory Users and Computers.

2. Expand the console tree to expose the object to which you want to attach a policy.

3. Right-click on the object. On the context-sensitive menu, select Properties.

4. Select the Group Policy page. (See Figure 13.3.)

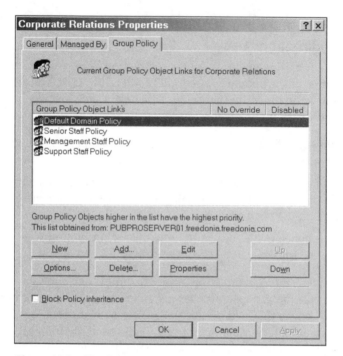

*Figure 13.3    The Group Policy page of an organizational unit.*

5.  Click on the New button to create a new policy and assign it to the object. Its default name will be New Group Policy Object, so change the default name to a more-suitable one.

6.  By default, the new policy will be disabled; that is, it will not be applied to the current object. To enable the policy, click on the Options button, uncheck the Disabled box, and click on OK to return to the Group Policy properties page.

7.  If there are several policies assigned to the current object and you need to change the order in which they are applied, select the policy to be moved and click on the Up or Down buttons, as needed.

8.  Click on Apply to confirm your changes, and then click on OK to exit the Properties dialog box and return to the console.

9.  Click on File|Close to exit the console.

| Related solutions: | Found on page: |
| --- | --- |
| Managing Sites | 79 |
| Administering Organizational Units | 172 |
| Managing Group Policies Assigned To Active Directory Objects | 196 |

## Accessing The Folder Redirection Settings In A Group Policy

To use folder redirection, you must edit the appropriate group policy. Because there are several ways to open a policy in the Group Policy Editor, we will cover them once here rather than repeat the instructions in each of the other Immediate Solutions in this section. Follow these steps:

1. This step assumes that you have created the Microsoft Management Console for group policies suggested in Chapter 6 and added the appropriate group policies to that console. If so, click on Start|Programs, select the program group that contains the shortcut to the console, select the console, select the policy to be edited, and then skip to Step 5.

2. If you have not created the console mentioned in Step 1, click on Start|Programs|Administrative Tools. Depending on where you have applied the group policy, select either Active Directory Users and Computers or Active Directory Sites and Services.

3. Expand the console tree to expose the Active Directory object to which you have applied the policy that you want to edit. Right-click on the object and select Properties from the context-sensitive pop-up menu.

4. In the Properties dialog box, select the Group Policy page, and then select the policy to be edited. Click on Edit to open the policy in the Group Policy Editor.

5. Expand the User Configuration, Windows Settings, and Folder Redirection folders. (See Figure 13.4.)

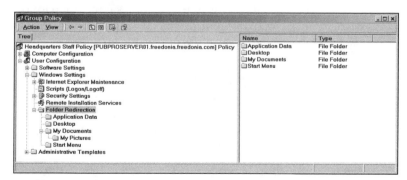

*Figure 13.4    Selecting the Folder Redirection folder in a group policy.*

6. Follow the procedures described throughout this Immediate Solutions section to manage folder redirection. When you are finished, close the Group Policy Editor.

7. If you have accessed the policy from the Properties dialog box of an Active Directory object, click on OK to close the dialog box, and then click on Console|Exit to exit the open console.

| *Related solutions:* | *Found on page:* |
|---|---|
| Managing Group Policies Assigned To Active Directory Objects | 196 |
| Creating Your Own Group Policy Administrative Tool | 211 |

## Enabling Folder Redirection In A Group Policy

Now that you have created the necessary network shared folder and group policy, you are ready to enable folder redirection in that policy. Here is how to do it:

1. Open the policy in the Group Policy Editor, as described in "Accessing The Folder Redirection Settings In A Group Policy" in this Immediate Solutions section.

2. Select and expand the Folder Redirection folder in the console tree pane. The folders available for redirection will be displayed in the results pane.

3. Right-click on the folder that you want to redirect. For the sake of this example, select the My Documents folder because it has a few more options than the other folders. This will open the Properties dialog box for the folder.

4. On the Target page of the dialog box, you will find that the default selection in the Setting drop-down list box is No Administrative Policy Specified. This setting disables redirection for the current folder. To enable redirection, click on the down arrow in the list box and select one of the following two options:

   • *Basic - Redirect Everyone's Folder To The Same Location—* If you select this option, the home folder for each user's redirected folders will be a child of the root folder that you have created. This option is a good choice for policies that have been applied to sites or organizational units with a relatively small and well-defined number of users.

   • *Advanced - Specify Locations For Various User Groups—*If you select this option, you will be able to specify a different folder for each group that you choose. This option is a good choice for policies that have been applied at the domain level, where you may have a very large number of users.

What happens next will depend on the option that you selected in Step 4. If you selected the Basic option, continue with Step 5. If you selected the Advanced option, skip to Step 7.

5.  When you select the Basic option, the Target Folder Location edit box will appear. Enter the network path of the shared folder that you created for redirection. If you prefer, click on Browse to open the Browse For Folder dialog box, expand My Network Places, select the shared folder, and click on OK to return to the Target page.

6.  Append the environmental variable %username% to the end of the network path that you defined in Step 5, and then skip to Step 11. (See Figure 13.5.)

7.  When you select the Advanced option, a Security Group Membership window will appear. Here, you can select the security groups that will be affected by the policy and select a different redirection folder for each one. Click on Add to open the Specify Group And Location dialog box.

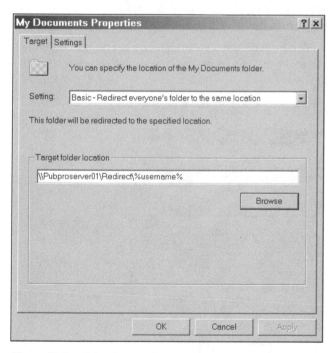

13. Managing User Data

*Figure 13.5*   *Selecting the Basic setting on the Target page, with the variable %username% appended to the path of the main redirection folder on the network.*

8. In the Security Group Membership edit box, enter the name of the group to be added. If you prefer, click on Browse to open the Select Group dialog box, choose the group that you want, and click on OK to return to the Specify Group And Location dialog box.

9. In the Target Folder Location edit box, enter the network path of the shared folder that you have created for this group's redirected folders. If you prefer, click on Browse to open the Browse For Folder dialog box, expand My Network Places, select the shared folder, and click on OK to return to the Specify Group And Location dialog box. (See Figure 13.6.)

10. Click on OK to return to the Target page. The name of the group that you have added and the path to its folder will appear in the Security Group Membership window.

11. Click on Apply to confirm your choices, and then click on the Settings page.

12. Review the options on the Settings page. (See Figure 13.7.) The options are self-explanatory; in most cases, the default choices will be appropriate.

13. Click on Apply to confirm your changes, if any, and then click on OK to exit the Properties dialog box and return to the Group Policy Editor.

14. Click on File|Close to exit the editor.

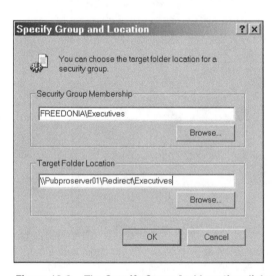

*Figure 13.6   The Specify Group And Location dialog box.*

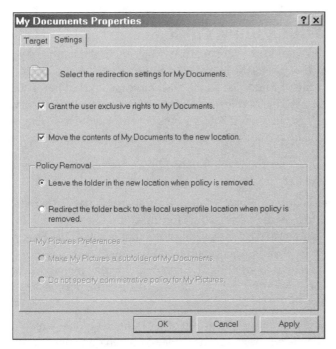

*Figure 13.7    The Settings page of the Properties dialog box, with the default options selected.*

## Modifying Folder Redirection Settings

The process for modifying folder redirection settings is essentially the same as that for enabling them. Follow the steps described in "Enabling Folder Redirection In A Group Policy" elsewhere in this Immediate Solutions section, and change or edit the settings as required.

If you selected the Advanced option and you need to make changes to the security groups list, open the group policy and select the Settings page in the Properties dialog box for the folder. You can make the following changes:

- To add a group to the list, repeat Steps 8, 9, and 10 under "Enabling Folder Redirection In A Group Policy."

- To change the settings for a security group, select the group from the displayed list and click on Modify. This will open the Specify Group And Location dialog box, described in Steps 8, 9, and 10.

- To remove a group from the list, select the group and click on Remove.

# Working With Offline Files

The control of the offline files feature is largely in the hands of your users rather than you as the network administrator. A user can choose to make any file or folder for which she has some level of permission available offline. This applies not only to items on a network server, but also to those in shared folders on other workstations. The permissions that she has for the original file also apply to the local copy.

Even so, you have some level of control over the situation. Here are some of the ways:

- If the user is not a member of any group that you have created and that has specific permissions for the shared network folder, then she is governed by the permissions that apply to the Everyone group. By default, this group has full control over a folder when you make it shareable. You can override this by making her a member of a group that is specifically denied the permissions that you select.

- If the user is a member of a group other than Everyone, which has specific permissions for the folder, you can deny her certain permissions that you have extended to the group as a whole. First, add her to the Permissions list. Next, specifically deny her permissions, as appropriate. Denied permissions take precedence over allowed ones.

*NOTE:*   *You can also create a group for this purpose, but making a person a member of two groups with conflicting permissions can cause you problems down the line. In this case, it is better to add the individual user to the Permissions list.*

- Through settings in a group policy, you can control the offline files options that are available to users who are managed by the policy.

I assume that you already know how to manage sharing permissions, so I have not covered the subject here. In the Immediate Solutions that follow, you will learn how to manage offline files at the workstation level and how to use group policy to control the options available to users.

*NOTE:*   *If you want to configure offline files for a specific user, including yourself, you should log onto a Windows 2000 Professional workstation as that user. You can also use the feature on a system running Windows 2000 Server, applying it to shared files and folders on other systems. You should do this only for testing and learning purposes, however, and only if you do not have a Windows 2000 Professional workstation available to you.*

**13. Managing User Data**

## Enabling, Configuring, And Modifying Settings For Offline Files

To use offline files, the feature must first be enabled. By default, it is enabled in Windows 2000 Professional and disabled in Windows 2000 Server. After you have enabled offline files, you can configure their settings. Later, you can follow the steps to modify your settings.

You can enable and configure the settings for offline files through menu options in either My Computer or Windows Explorer. Here is how to do it:

1. Open either My Computer or Windows Explorer.

2. Click on Tools|Folder Options, and then select the Offline Files page. (See Figure 13.8.) Make sure that the Enable Offline Files box is checked. This will expose the other options on the page. Accept the default settings unless you have a reason to change them.

3. At the bottom of the dialog box, click on Advanced. This will open the Offline Files - Advanced Settings dialog box. (See Figure 13.9.) The settings here control how the feature reacts when the connection to a folder on another system is lost.

13. Managing User Data

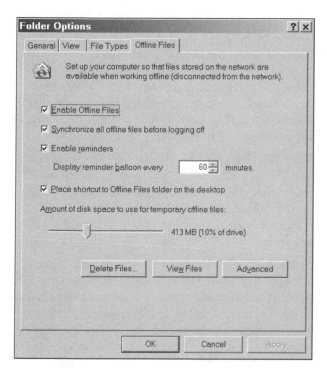

*Figure 13.8   The Offline Files page of the Folder Options dialog box.*

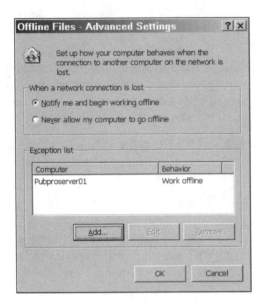

*Figure 13.9    The Offline Files - Advanced Settings dialog box.*

These settings apply, for example, if the network server that contains the source files becomes unavailable for any reason.

In this dialog box, you must choose between one of two radio buttons:

- *Notify Me And Begin Working Offline*—If you select this option, you will be able to continue working on any of the offline files. You will be using the copy in the local cache. When the system that has the source file becomes available again, the two copies will be synchronized automatically. This radio button is selected by default.

- *Never Allow My Computer To Go Offline*—The wording of this option is a little confusing because it will often be the other system that goes offline, not yours. If you select this option and the system that has the source file becomes unavailable, you will not be able to work on the offline files in your local cache.

4. Under the radio button is an area where you can create an Exception List. You can use it for specific computers, overriding the option that you have just selected and applying the alternate option instead. You might want to do this, for example, if you have selected the first radio button as your general preference, but do not want that option to apply to a specific system. If you do not need to add to the Exception List, skip to Step 7.

*Figure 13.10    The Offline Files - Add Custom Action dialog box. Use this to add a computer to the Exception List.*

5.  To add a system to the Exception List, click on Add to open the Offline Files - Add Custom Action dialog box. (See Figure 13.10.) Enter the name of the system to be added to the list. If you prefer, click on Browse to open the Browse For Computer dialog box, expand My Network Places as needed, select the desired system, and click on OK to return to the previous dialog box.

6.  Select the appropriate radio button, click on OK to return to the Advanced Settings dialog box, and click on OK again to return to the Offline Files page.

7.  Click on Apply to confirm your changes, and then click on OK to exit the Folder Options dialog box and return to My Computer or Windows Explorer.

## Making A File Or Folder Available Offline

Now that you have enabled and configured the settings for offline files, you can select a shared file or folder on another system for offline availability. Here is how to do it:

1.  Open My Network Places.

2.  Drill down to the file or folder that you want to make available offline. If you select a folder, all files in that folder for which you have permission will be added to your Offline Files Folder. If you select a file, only that file will be made available to you.

3. Select the file or folder, and then click on File|Make Available Offline. The setting is a toggle. This will place a checkmark next to the menu option.

4. The first time that you select a file or folder for offline availability, the Offline Files Wizard will run. Read the information in the first screen, and then click on Next to continue.

5. In the second screen, make sure that the option to automatically synchronize the files when you log on and off is selected. (See Figure 13.11.) If you do not select this checkbox, you will need to either synchronize the files manually or configure other options in the Synchronization Manager, such as creating a schedule for synchronization. Click on Next to continue.

---

**NOTE:**   *Unlike most other wizards and dialog boxes in Windows 2000, the individual screens in the Offline Files Wizard are not labeled.*

---

6. In the third screen, the Enable Reminders checkbox is selected by default. Accept this setting unless you have a reason to change it. Unfortunately, the option to create a shortcut on the desktop to the Offline Files Folder is not selected by default. This shortcut makes it much easier to access offline files when you are not connected to the source system, and the folder is not added to My Computer or Windows Explorer. Therefore, I recommend that you select this option. (See Figure 13.12.)

*Figure 13.11   The second screen of the Offline Files Wizard.*

**Offline Files Wizard**

While you are offline, a message appears periodically to remind you that you are not connected to the network.

☑ Enable reminders

Whether you are working online or offline, you can access your Offline Files in the same network folders or in the Offline Files folder.

☑ Create a shortcut to the Offline Files folder on my desktop

< Back    Finish    Cancel

*Figure 13.12    The third screen of the Offline Files Wizard, with the option to create a shortcut to the offline files selected.*

7. Click on Finish to continue. If you have selected a folder that contains child folders, this will open the Confirm Offline Subfolders dialog box. You can select whether to make only the selected folder available offline or all of the subfolders available. Click on OK to confirm your selection and continue.

8. After you have exited the wizard, the file or folder that you have selected will be copied to your system and placed in a local cache, where you can access them through the Offline Files Folder. You will see a synchronization progress report, followed by the Synchronization Complete screen. If there are no errors, you will be returned to My Network Places as soon as the process is complete. If there are errors, they will be displayed in a larger version of the synchronization screen. Review the errors and click on OK to return to My Network Places.

The next time that you make a file or folder available offline, the Offline Files Wizard will not start. The only thing that you will see will be the synchronization progress report.

## Discontinuing Offline Availability

To discontinue the offline availability of a file or folder, you need to clear the checkmark that was set when you selected the item. Here is how to do it:

1. Open My Network Places.

2. Drill down to the file or folder that you want.

3.  Select the file or folder, and then click on File|Make Available Offline. The setting is a toggle. This will clear the checkmark next to the menu option.

4.  If you selected a folder that contains subfolders, you will see the Remove Offline Folders dialog box. Here, you can choose whether you want to delete only the parent folder or the subfolders as well. Click on OK to confirm your choice and return to My Network Places.

## Configuring Synchronization Options

When you ran the Offline Files Wizard, it helped you to set some basic default options for synchronization. You can modify those settings and many more as well. Here is how to do it:

1.  Open My Computer, Windows Explorer, the Offline Files Folder, or any other folder, such as My Network Places, that shares the My Computer interface.

2.  Select Tools|Synchronize. This will open the Items To Synchronize dialog box. The root folder for each shared file or folder that you have selected will appear in a window. (See Figure 13.13.)

*Figure 13.13    The Items To Synchronize dialog box, with a list of currently available offline folders.*

---

**NOTE:** *This may not be the folder that you would expect. For example, long before I wrote this chapter, I made the root folder of the D drive on my production workstation shareable so that I could easily access anything on the drive from my server. When I was writing this chapter, I tested the offline files feature on the server as well as on the workstation. The workstation folder that I selected at the server was several levels deep on drive D. This was the folder that I expected to see in the Items To Synchronize dialog box. Instead, what I saw was the root folder of drive D. The files in the Offline Files Folder, however, were from the folder that I had specifically selected for offline availability.*

---

3. To see the list of files in a folder, select the folder and click on Properties. This will open the Offline Files Folder in a second window, which you can keep open if you prefer. Switch back to the Items To Synchronize dialog box when you are ready.

4. To configure your synchronization options, click on Setup. This will open the Synchronization Settings dialog box.

5. Select the Logon/Logoff page. (See Figure 13.14.) Click on the drop-down arrow in the edit window at the top of the page and select the type of network connection for which you are setting options. For example, you might have both a normal LAN connection and a remote access connection. If you have more than one, you will need to set options for each one.

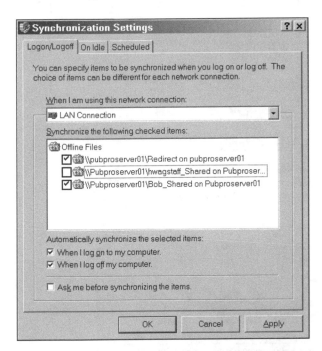

*Figure 13.14    The Logon/Logoff page of the Synchronization Settings dialog box.*

6. In the Synchronize The Following Checked Items window, you will see the same list of folders as in the previous dialog box. Check the ones that you want to synchronize at logon and/or logoff, and leave the others unchecked.

7. Under the list of items to be synchronized is a set of checkboxes with options for synchronizing at logon and logoff, and for prompting you before beginning synchronization. By default, the first two are checked and the prompting option is unchecked. I recommend that you accept the default settings here.

8. Click on Apply to confirm your choices, repeat Steps 5 through 7 as needed for your other types of network connections, and then select the On Idle page. (See Figure 13.15.)

9. By default, the On Idle option is not selected. Here, too, if you choose to enable this option, you may need to do so for each type of network connection that you have. If you want to fine-tune this option, click on Advanced to open the Idle Settings dialog box. If not, skip to Step 11.

10. In the Idle Settings dialog box, select the number of minutes of idle time that the Synchronization Manager should wait before beginning synchronization, as well as the number of minutes that it should wait before repeating the synchronization. You

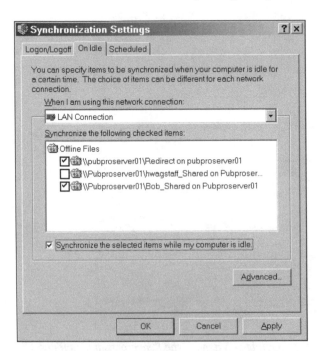

*Figure 13.15    The On Idle page of the Synchronization Settings dialog box.*

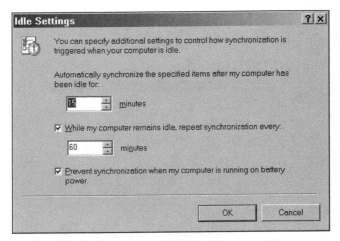

*Figure 13.16    The Idle Settings dialog box.*

can also disable synchronization if your system is running on battery power during idle time. (See Figure 13.16.) Click on OK to return to the On Idle dialog box.

11. Click on Apply to confirm your changes, repeat Steps 9 and 10 as needed for other network connections, and select the Scheduled page.

12. On the Scheduled page, you can create schedules for synchronization. Click on Add to start the Scheduled Synchronization Wizard. Read the information on the first screen, and then click on Next to continue.

13. On the second screen, select the type of network connection that you are using, and then select the items that you want to synchronize. Also, select the checkbox at the bottom of the screen if you want the Synchronization Manager to connect to the network automatically if you are offline at the time. (See Figure 13.17.) Click on Next to continue.

14. On the third screen, select the start time, start date, and frequency of the schedule. (See Figure 13.18.) Click on Next to continue.

15. On the fourth screen, enter a name for your schedule, and then click on Next to continue. This will open a confirmation box, showing the settings that you have entered.

16. Click on Back to modify your previous settings, or click on Finish to exit the wizard and return to the Scheduled page. Your new schedule will appear in the list of current synchronization tasks.

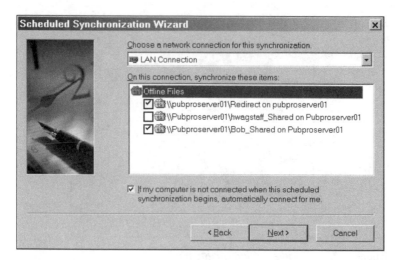

*Figure 13.17    The second screen of the Scheduled Synchronization Wizard.*

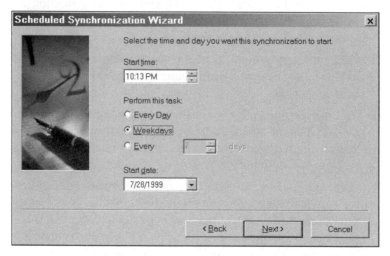

*Figure 13.18    The third screen of the Scheduled Synchronization Wizard.*

17. Repeat Steps 12 through 16 as needed for other network connections.

18. Click on Apply to confirm your actions, and then click on OK to exit the Synchronization Settings dialog box and return to the Items To Synchronize dialog box.

19. If you want to synchronize the selected items now, click on Synchronize. This will launch the synchronization progress meter. If not, click on Close to return to the Windows desktop.

## Removing A Synchronization Schedule

Removing a synchronization schedule is a straightforward process. Here is how to do it:

1. Open My Computer, Windows Explorer, the Offline Files Folder, or any other folder, such as My Network Places, that shares the My Computer interface.

2. Select Tools|Synchronize. This will open the Items To Synchronize dialog box.

3. Click on Setup to open the Synchronization Settings dialog box, and then select the Scheduled page.

4. Highlight the schedule that you want and click on Remove. This will open a Confirm Schedule Delete message box.

5. Click on OK to confirm your deletion and return to the Scheduled page.

6. Click on Apply to confirm your changes, click on OK to exit the Synchronization Settings dialog box, and then click on Close to exit the Items To Synchronize dialog box and return to the Windows desktop.

## Setting Advanced Scheduling Options For Synchronization

After you have added a synchronization schedule, you can modify it with advanced settings that were not available the first time around. Here is how to do it:

1. Open My Computer, Windows Explorer, the Offline Files Folder, or any other folder, such as My Network Places, that shares the My Computer interface.

2. Select Tools|Synchronize. This will open the Items To Synchronize dialog box.

3. Click on Setup to open the Synchronization Settings dialog box, and then select the Scheduled page.

4. Highlight the schedule that you want and click on Edit. This will open the My Scheduled Update dialog box, in which you can refine the settings.

5. To change the name of the schedule, select the General page and edit the name as needed.

6. To modify the list of folders to be synchronized for any network connection, select the Synchronization Items page. This is very similar to the second screen of the Scheduled Synchronization Wizard. (Refer to Figure 13.17.)

**13. Managing User Data**

7. To change the schedule, select the Schedule page. Here, you can refine the schedule by specifying the days on which it is to be run.

8. To fine-tune the schedule even more, click on Advanced. This will open the Advanced Schedule Options dialog box. (See Figure 13.19.)

9. To expose all of the options available to you, select the End Date and Repeat Task checkboxes. If you want the task to be repeated indefinitely, deselect the End Date checkbox before you finish. When you are ready, click on OK to confirm your settings and return to the Schedule page.

10. To control how the synchronization is done, select the Settings page. (See Figure 13.20.) On this page, you can set options for deleting a task that is not scheduled to run again or stopping a task if it runs for more than a specified length of time. You can also set idle time and power management options. The options are self-explanatory.

11. When you are ready, click on Apply to confirm your changes, and then click on OK to close the dialog box for the selected schedule and return to the Scheduled page.

12. Click on Apply again, if necessary, to confirm your changes, click on OK to exit the Synchronization Settings dialog box, and then click on Close to exit the Items To Synchronize dialog box and return to the Windows desktop.

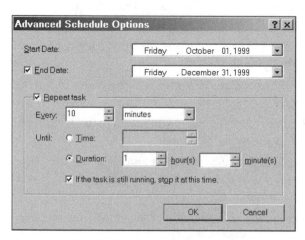

*Figure 13.19    The Advanced Schedule Options dialog box.*

13. Managing User Data

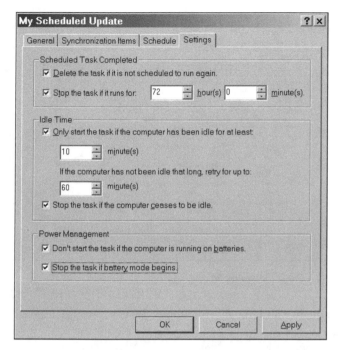

*Figure 13.20    The Settings page for setting advanced schedule options.*

## Managing The Files In The Offline Files Folder

The Offline Files Folder shares the My Computer interface and works much like any other folder under My Computer. The menu options are slightly different because of the special nature of this folder. For example, because the folder is not a part of either My Computer or Windows Explorer, it is difficult to copy or move files to another folder. To compensate for this, there is a Copy To Folder option on the Edit menu. This opens the Browse For Folder edit box.

Also, if you delete a file, you will see a Confirm File Delete message box. The message informs you that you are deleting the offline version of the file but not the network version. Nevertheless, the deleted file will no longer be available offline. To make it available again, you will have to open My Network Places, select the file, and then click on File|Make Available Offline.

Here is how to access the Offline Files Folder:

1. If you selected the option in the Offline Files Wizard to add a shortcut to the folder on your Windows desktop, just double-click on the shortcut to open the folder. (See Figure 13.21.)

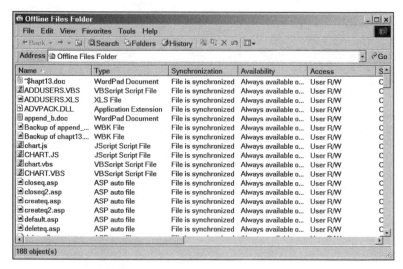

*Figure 13.21    The Offline Files Folder.*

2. If you did not add the shortcut, open My Computer, Windows Explorer, or My Network Places and then click on Tools|Synchronize.

3. On the Items To Synchronize page, highlight the folder that contains the files that you need to access and click on Properties. This will open the Offline Files Folder in a separate window.

4. If you no longer need it open, switch back to the Items To Synchronize page, click on Close, and return to the Offline Files Folder window.

## Configuring Offline Files Settings In A Group Policy

You can control the offline files options available to users—and even block them altogether—through a group policy. Here is how to access the settings that apply to offline files:

1. This step assumes that you have created the Microsoft Management Console for group policies suggested in Chapter 6 and added the appropriate group policies to that console. If so, click on Start|Programs, select the program group that contains the shortcut to the console, select the console, select the policy to be edited, and then skip to Step 5.

2. If you have not created the console mentioned in Step 1, click on Start|Programs|Administrative Tools. Depending on where you have applied the group policy, select either Active Directory Users and Computers or Active Directory Sites and Services.

3. Expand the console tree to expose the Active Directory object to which you have applied the policy that you want to edit. Right-click on the object and select Properties from the context-sensitive pop-up menu.

4. In the Properties dialog box, select the Group Policy page, and then select the policy to be edited. Click on Edit to open the policy in the Group Policy Editor.

5. Expand the User Configuration, Administrative Templates, and Network folders.

6. In the console tree, select Offline Files. The results pane will display the available settings. (See Figure 13.22.)

7. To modify a setting, double-click on it in the results pane to open its Properties dialog box.

8. When you are finished, click on Console|Exit to exit the Group Policy Editor.

| Related solutions: | Found on page: |
|---|---|
| Managing Group Policies Assigned To Active Directory Objects | 196 |
| Creating Your Own Group Policy Administrative Tool | 211 |

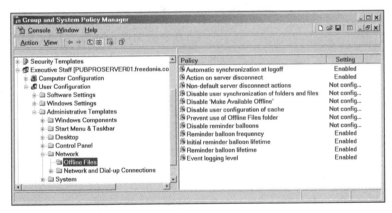

*Figure 13.22   The Offline Files settings in a group policy.*

# Where To Find Group Policy Settings

The structure and content of most group policies, including those that you create, follow those of the Default Domain Policy. When you create a new policy, it is virtually identical in structure and content to the Default Domain Policy, except that none of the settings in the new policy are configured.

This appendix provides a detailed explanation of the structure of a group policy and the settings available in each folder or branch container. Use it to help find the location of policy settings in any group policy.

## Computer Configuration

Each policy has two main sections: Computer Configuration and User Configuration. Child folders under Computer Configuration include Software Settings, Windows Settings, and Administrative Templates. See Figure A.1 for the structure of this section.

## Software Settings

The Software Settings folder has one child folder—Software Installation—in which you will add software installation packages for remote installation on client workstations. There are no preinstalled packages in the Default Domain Policy. See Chapter 11 for information on how to install and manage software installation packages.

## Windows Settings

The Windows Settings folder has one child folder—Security Settings—and one branch with leaves—Scripts (Startup/Shutdown).

### Security Settings

Under Security Settings, you will find child folders and branches named Account Policies, Local Policies, Event Log, Restricted Groups, System Services, Registry, File System, IP Security Policies on Active Directory, and Public Key Policies.

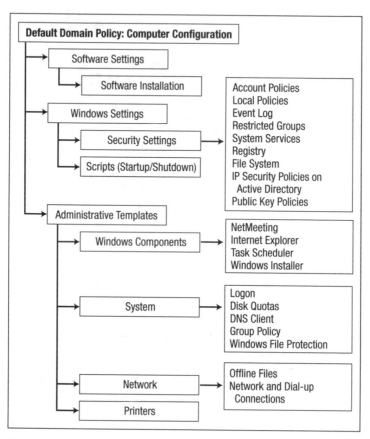

*Figure A.1    The structure of the Computer Configuration section.*

- *Account Policies*—The Account Policies folder has three branches: Password Policy, Account Lockout Policy, and Kerberos Policy. See Table A.1 for a list of the settings within each branch.

- *Local Policies*—The Local Policies container has three branches: Audit Policy, User Rights Assignment, and Security Options. See Table A.2 for a list of the settings within each policy.

- *Event Log*—The Event Log container has one child folder, Settings for Event Logs. See Table A.3 for a list of available settings.

- *Restricted Groups*—There are no restricted groups in the Default Domain Policy. You can add groups to the folder by right-clicking on the folder, selecting Add Group from the context-sensitive menu, and following the prompts. Later, you can modify the security settings for the objects that you have added to the folder.

*Table A.1   Account Policies settings in the Computer Configuration section.*

| Folder | Settings |
|---|---|
| Password | Store password using reversible encryption |
| | Enforce password history |
| | Maximum password age |
| | Minimum password age |
| | Minimum password length |
| | Passwords must meet complexity requirements of installed password filter |
| Account Lockout | Account lockout threshold |
| | Account lockout duration |
| | Reset account lockout counter after x minutes |
| Kerberos Policy | Enforce user logon restriction |
| | Maximum lifetime for service ticket |
| | Maximum lifetime for user ticket |
| | Maximum lifetime for user ticket renewal |
| | Maximum tolerance for computer clock synchronization |

*Table A.2   Local Policies settings in the Computer Configuration section.*

| Folder | Settings |
|---|---|
| Audit | Audit account logon events |
| | Audit account management |
| | Audit directory service access |
| | Audit logon events |
| | Audit object access |
| | Audit policy change |
| | Audit privilege use |
| | Audit process tracking |
| | Audit system events |
| User Rights Assignment | Access this computer from network |
| | Act as part of the operating system |
| | Add workstation to domain |
| | Back up files and directories |
| | Bypass traverse checking |
| | Change the system time |
| | Create a pagefile |

**Appendix A Where To Find Group Policy Settings**

*(continued)*

**433**

**Table A.2** *Local Policies settings in the Computer Configuration section (continued).*

| Folder | Settings |
|---|---|
| User Rights Assignment | Create a token object |
| | Create permanent shared objects |
| | Debug programs |
| | Deny access to this computer from network |
| | Deny logon as a batch job |
| | Deny logon as a service |
| | Deny logon locally |
| | Enable computer and user accounts to be trusted for delegation |
| | Force shutdown from a remote system |
| | Generate security audits |
| | Increase quotas |
| | Increase schedule priority |
| | Load and unload device drivers |
| | Lock pages in memory |
| | Log on as a batch job |
| | Log on as a service |
| | Log on locally |
| | Manage auditing and security log |
| | Modify firmware environment values |
| | Profile single process |
| | Profile system performance |
| | Remove computer from docking station |
| | Replace a process-level token |
| | Restore files and directories |
| | Shut down the system |
| | Synchronize directory service data |
| | Take ownership of files and other objects |
| Security Options | Additional restrictions for anonymous connections |
| | Allow Server Operators to schedule tasks |
| | Allow system to be shut down without having to log on |
| | Allowed to eject removable NTFS media |
| | Amount of idle time required before disconnecting sessions |

*(continued)*

**Table A.2** *Local Policies settings in the Computer Configuration section (continued).*

| Folder | Settings |
|---|---|
| Security Options | Audit access to global system objects |
| | Audit use of Backup and Restore privilege |
| | Automatically log off users when logon time expires |
| | Automatically log off users when logon time expires (local) |
| | AutoDisconnect: Allow sessions to be disconnected when they are idle |
| | Clear virtual memory pagefile when system shuts down |
| | Digitally sign client-side communication (always) |
| | Digitally sign client-side communication (when possible) |
| | Digitally sign server-side communication (always) |
| | Digitally sign server-side communication (when possible) |
| | Disable Ctrl+Alt+Delete requirement for logon |
| | Do not display last username in logon screen |
| | LANManager authentication level |
| | Message text for users attempting to log on |
| | Message title for users attempting to log on |
| | Number of previous logons to cache in case domain controller is not available |
| | Prevent system maintenance of user account password |
| | Prevent users from installing print drivers |
| | Prompt user to change password before expiration |
| | Recovery Console: Allow administrative logon |
| | Recovery Console: Allow floppy and access to all drives and all folders |
| | Rename administrator account |
| | Rename guest account |
| | Restrict CD-ROM access to locally logged-on user only |
| | Restrict floppy access to locally logged-on user only |
| | Restrict management of shared resources |
| | Secure Channel: Digitally encrypt or sign secure channel data (always) |
| | Secure Channel: Digitally encrypt secure channel data (when possible) |
| | Secure Channel: Digitally sign secure channel data (when possible) |

**Appendix A Where To Find Group Policy Settings**

*(continued)*

*Table A.2  Local Policies settings in the Computer Configuration section (continued).*

| Folder | Settings |
|---|---|
| Security Options | Secure Channel: Require strong (Windows 2000 or later) session key |
| | Secure system partition (for RISC platforms only) |
| | Send unencrypted password in order to connect to third-party SMB servers |
| | Shut down system immediately if unable to log security audits |
| | Smart Card removal behavior |
| | Strengthen default permissions of global system objects |
| | Unsigned driver installation behavior |
| | Unsigned non-driver installation behavior |

*Table A.3  Event Log settings in the Computer Configuration section.*

| | |
|---|---|
| Maximum log size for application log | Maximum log size for security log |
| Maximum log size for system log | Restrict Guest access to application log |
| Restrict Guest access to security log | Restrict Guest access to system log |
| Retain application log | Retain security log |
| Retain system log | Retention method for application log |
| Retention method for security log | Retention method for system log |
| Shut down the computer when the security audit log is full | |

*Table A.4  System Services settings in the Computer Configuration section.*

| | |
|---|---|
| Alerter | Application Management |
| ClipBook | COM+ Event System |
| Computer Browser | DHCP Client |
| DHCP Server | Distributed File System |
| Distributed Link Tracking Client | Distributed Link Tracking Server |
| Distributed Transaction Coordinator | DNS Client |
| DNS Server | Event Log |
| Fax Service | File Replication |
| FTP Publishing Service | IIS Administration Service |
| Internet Connetion Sharing | Indexing Service |
| Intersite Messaging | IPSEC Policy Agent |
| Kerberos Key Distribution Center | License Logging Service |

*(continued)*

***Table A.4*** ***System Services settings in the Computer Configuration section (continued).***

| | |
|---|---|
| Logical Disk Manager | Logical Disk Manager Administrative Service |
| Messenger | Microsoft Fax Service |
| Microsoft SMTP Service | Net Logon |
| NetMeeting Remote Desktop Sharing | Network Connections |
| Network DDE | Network DDE DSDM |
| NT LM Security Support Provider | Performance Logs and Alerts |
| Plug and Play | Print Spooler |
| Protected Storage | QoS RSVP |
| Remote Access Auto Connection Manager | Remote Access Connection Manager |
| Remote Procedure Call (RPC) | Remote Procedure Call (RPC) Locator |
| Remote Registry Service | Removable Storage |
| Routing and Remote Access | RunAs Service |
| Security Accounts Manager | Server |
| Simple Mail Transport Protocol (SMTP) | Smart Card |
| Smart Card Helper | SNMP Service |
| System Event Notification | Task Scheduler |
| TCP/IP NetBIOS Helper Service | Telephony |
| Telnet | Terminal Services |
| Uninterruptible Power Supply | Utility Manager |
| Windows Installer | Windows Management Instrumentation |
| Windows Management Instrumentation Driver Extensions | Windows Time |
| Workstation | World Wide Web Publishing Service |

- *System Services*—See Table A.4 for a list of System Services settings that can be configured here.
- *Registry*—The default Registry folder is empty. You can add Registry keys to the folder by right-clicking on the folder, selecting Add Key from the context-sensitive menu, and following the prompts. Later, you can modify the security settings for the objects that you have added to the folder.
- *File System*—The default File System folder is empty. You can add files to the folder by right-clicking on the folder, selecting Add File from the context-sensitive menu, and following the

prompts. Later, you can modify the security settings for the objects that you have added to the folder.

- *IP Security Settings on Active Directory*—Settings for this branch include Server (Request Security), Secure Server (Require Security), and Client (Respond Only).

- *Public Key Policies*—The Public Key Policies folder has four child folders: Encrypted Data Recovery Agents, Automatic Certificate Request Settings, Trusted Root Certification Authorities, and Enterprise Trust. In the Default Domain Policy, each of these child folders is empty. You can add objects to them by right-clicking on the folder and selecting the appropriate option from the context-sensitive menu.

### Scripts

Under the Scripts branch, you will find objects in which you can set Startup and Shutdown scripts. See Appendix C for information on using scripts.

## Administrative Templates

The final large group under Computer Configuration is Administrative Templates. Three administrative templates are installed by default: conf.adm, system.adm, and inetres.adm. You can install other templates that come with Windows 2000 Server or create your own. In the default configuration, the Administrative Templates folder is broken out into four child folders: Windows Components, System, Network, and Printers.

---

**NOTE:**   *Creating and modifying administrative templates require knowledge of both basic programming techniques and the Windows 2000 Registry. Those subjects are beyond the scope of this book.*

---

### Windows Components

The Windows Components folder is broken out into four child folders: NetMeeting, Internet Explorer, Task Scheduler, and Windows Installer. See Table A.5 for a list of available settings.

### System

The System folder breaks out into five child folders: Logon, Disk Quotas, DNS Client, Group Policy, and Windows File Protection. See Table A.6 for a list of available settings.

***Table A.5** Windows Components settings in the Computer Configuration section.*

| Folder | Settings |
|---|---|
| NetMeeting | Disable remote desktop sharing |
| Internet Explorer | Disable automatic installation of Internet Explorer components |
| | Disable periodic check for Internet Explorer software updates |
| | Disable showing the splash screen |
| | Disable software update shell notifications on program launch |
| | Make proxy settings per-machine rather than per-user |
| | Security zones: Do not allow users to add or delete sites |
| | Security zones: Do not allow users to change policies |
| | Security zones: Use only machine settings. |
| Task Scheduler | Disable advanced menu |
| | Disable drag and drop |
| | Disable new task creation |
| | Disable task deletion |
| | Hide property pages |
| | Prevent task run or end |
| | Prohibit browse |
| Windows Installer | Allow admin to install from Terminal Services session |
| | Always install with elevated privileges |
| | Cache transforms in secure location or workstation |
| | Disable IE security prompt for Windows Installer scripts |
| | Disable Windows Installer |
| | Disable browse dialog box for new source |
| | Disable patching |
| | Disable rollback |
| | Enable user control over installs |
| | Enable user to browse for source while elevated |
| | Enable user to patch elevated products |
| | Enable user to use media source while elevated |
| | Logging |

**Appendix A Where To Find Group Policy Settings**

*Table A.6   System settings in the Computer Configuration section.*

| Folder | Settings |
|---|---|
| System | Disable AutoPlay |
| | Disable Boot/Shutdown/Logon/Logoff status messages |
| | Disable legacy run list |
| | Disable the run once list |
| | Do not automatically encrypt files moved to encrypted folders |
| | Do not display welcome screen at logon |
| | Download missing COM components |
| | Remove Disconnect item from Start menu (Terminal Services only) |
| | Remove Security option from Start menu (Terminal Services only) |
| | Run these programs at user logon |
| | Verbose versus normal status messages |
| Logon | Automatically detect slow network connections |
| | Delete cached copies of roaming profiles |
| | Do not detect slow network connections |
| | Log users off when roaming profile fails |
| | Maximum wait time for group policy scripts |
| | Run logon scripts synchronously |
| | Run shutdown scripts visible |
| | Run startup scripts asynchronously |
| | Run startup scripts visible |
| | Slow network connection timeout for user profiles |
| | Timeout for dialog boxes |
| | Wait for remote user profile |
| Disk Quotas | Apply policy to removable media |
| | Default quota limit and warning level |
| | Enable disk quotas |
| | Enforce disk quota limit |
| | Log event when quota limit exceeded |
| | Log event when quota warning level exceeded |
| DNS Client | Primary DNS suffix |

*(continued)*

*Table A.6  System settings in the Computer Configuration section (continued).*

| Folder | Settings |
|---|---|
| Group Policy | Apply group policy for computers asynchronously during startup |
| | Apply group policy for users asynchronously during logon |
| | Disable background refresh of group policy |
| | Disk Quota policy processing |
| | EFS recovery policy processing |
| | Folder redirection policy processing |
| | Group policy refresh interval for computers |
| | Group policy refresh interval for domain controllers |
| | Group policy slow link detection |
| | IP security policy processing |
| | Registry policy processing |
| | Scripts policy processing |
| | Security policy processing |
| | Software installation policy processing |
| | User group policy loopback processing mode |
| Windows File Protection | Hide the file scan progress window |
| | Limit Windows File Protection cache size |
| | Set Windows File Protection scanning |
| | Specify Windows File Protection cache location |

### Network

The Network folder is broken out into two child folders: Offline Files and Network and Dial-up Connections. See Table A.7 for a list of available settings.

### Printers

The options in the Printers folder enable you to control certain aspects of the way Windows 2000 Server manages the printers on your network. See Table A.8 for a list of available settings.

# User Configuration

Child folders under User Configuration include Software Settings, Windows Settings, and Administrative Templates. See Figure A.2 for the structure of this section.

**Table A.7   Network settings in the Computer Configuration section.**

| Folder | Settings |
| --- | --- |
| Offline Files | Action on server disconnect |
| | Administratively assigned offline files |
| | At logoff, delete local copy of user's offline files |
| Offline Files | Default cache size |
| | Disable "Make Available Offline" option |
| | Disable reminder balloons |
| | Disable user configuration of offline files |
| | Enabled |
| | Event logging level |
| | Files not cached |
| | Initial reminder balloon lifetime |
| | Non-default server disconnect actions |
| | Prevent use of Offline Files folder |
| | Reminder balloon frequency |
| | Reminder balloon lifetime |
| | Subfolders always available offline |
| | Synchronize all offline files before logging off |
| Network and Dial-up Connections | Allow configuration of connection sharing |

**Table A.8   Printers settings in the Computer Configuration section.**

| | |
| --- | --- |
| Allow printers to be published | Allow pruning of published printers |
| Automatically publish new printers in the Active Directory | Check published state |
| Computer location | Custom support URL in the Printers Folder's left pane |
| Directory pruning interval | Directory pruning priority |
| Directory pruning retry | Pre-populate printer search location text |
| Printer browsing | Prune printers that are not automatically republished |
| Web-based printing | |

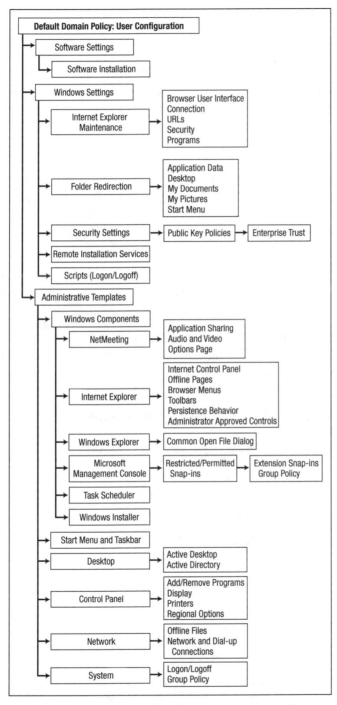

*Figure A.2   The structure of the User Configuration section.*

# Software Settings

The Software Settings folder is identical to that in the Computer Configuration section. Software Settings has one child folder, Software Installation, where you add software installation packages for remote installation on client workstations. There are no preinstalled packages in the Default Domain Policy. See Chapter 11 for information on how to install and manage software installation packages.

# Windows Settings

The Windows Settings folder breaks out into three folders—Internet Explorer Maintenance, Folder Redirection, and Security Settings—and two branches with leaves: Remote Installation Services and Scripts (Logon/Logoff).

### *Internet Explorer Maintenance*

Under Internet Explorer Maintenance are child folders for Browser User Interface, Connection, URLs, Security, and Programs. See Table A.9 for a list of available settings.

### *Folder Redirection*

Under Folder Redirection, you can force redirection of several user-related folders that are installed by default on the local drive of each

*Table A.9     Internet Explorer Maintenance settings available in the User Configuration section.*

| Folder | Settings |
|---|---|
| Browser User Interface | Browser Title |
| | Animated Bitmaps |
| | Custom Logo |
| | Browser Toolbar Buttons |
| Connection | Connection Settings |
| | Automatic Browser Configuration |
| | Proxy Settings |
| | User Agent String |
| URLs | Favorites and Links |
| | Important URLs |
| | Channels |
| Security | Security Zones and Content Ratings |
| | Authenticode Settings |
| Programs | Programs |

computer. The folders include Application Data, Desktop, My Documents, My Pictures, and Start Menu.

The settings apply to groups of users. You can use this to redirect one or more of these folders to a folder on the network that can be shared by each member of the group.

### Security Settings

The Security Settings folder has one child folder, Public Key Policies. This folder, in turn, has its own child folder, Enterprise Trust. In the Default Domain Policy, this last folder is empty. You can add a Certified Trust List to the folder or run the Certificate Manager Import Wizard by right-clicking on the folder, selecting the appropriate option from the context-sensitive menu, and following the prompts. Later, you can modify the security settings for the objects in the folder.

### Remote Installation Services

The Remote Installation Services branch has a single leaf, Choice Options. Here, you can configure the options that are available to users when they run the client-side installation wizard for software installations managed by your network. For example, you can disable the Custom Setup option here.

### Scripts

Under scripts, you will find objects in which you can set logon and logoff scripts. See Appendix C for information on using scripts.

# Administrative Templates

The final large group under User Configuration is Administrative Templates. In the default configuration, it includes child folders for Windows Components, Start Menu and Taskbar, Desktop, Control Panel, Network, and System. You can install additional templates that come with Windows 2000 Server or create your own.

### Windows Components

The Windows Components folder includes six child folders: NetMeeting, Internet Explorer, Windows Explorer, Microsoft Management Console, Task Scheduler, and Windows Installer. Here is where you can set options that control the Windows interface presented to your users.

- *NetMeeting*—The NetMeeting folder contains numerous settings for Microsoft's conferencing software, as well as three child folders: Application Sharing, Audio & Video, and Options Page. See Table A.10 for a list of available settings.

*Table A.10    NetMeeting settings available in the User Configuration section.*

| Folder | Settings |
|---|---|
| NetMeeting | Enable automatic configuration |
| | Disable directory services |
| | Prevent adding directory servers |
| | Prevent viewing Web directory |
| | Set the intranet support page |
| | Set call security options |
| | Prevent changing call placement method |
| | Prevent automatic acceptance of calls |
| | Prevent sending files |
| | Prevent receiving files |
| | Limit the size of sent files |
| | Disable Chat |
| | Disable NetMeeting 2.x whiteboard |
| | Disable whiteboard |
| Application Sharing | Disable application sharing |
| | Prevent sharing |
| | Prevent desktop sharing |
| | Prevent sharing command prompts |
| | Prevent sharing Explorer windows |
| | Prevent control |
| | Prevent application sharing in true color |
| Audio & Video | Limit the bandwidth of audio and video |
| | Disable audio |
| | Disable full duplex audio |
| | Prevent changing DirectSound audio setting |
| | Prevent sending video |
| | Prevent receiving video |
| Options Page | Hide the General page |
| | Disable the Advanced Calling button |
| | Hide the Security page |
| | Hide the Audio page |
| | Hide the Video page |

- *Internet Explorer*—Windows 2000 comes with Internet Explorer 5, so these settings apply to that version. The folder contains a number of settings in the main folder and also breaks out into six child folders: Internet Control Panel, Offline Pages, Browser Menus, Toolbars, Persistence Behavior, and Administrator Approved Controls. See Table A.11 for a list of settings in each of these folders.

*Table A.11    Internet Explorer settings available in the User Configuration section.*

| Folder | Settings |
|---|---|
| Internet Explorer | Disable AutoComplete for forms |
| | Disable Internet Connection Wizard |
| | Disable caching of Auto-Proxy scripts |
| | Disable changing Advanced Page settings |
| | Disable changing Automatic Configuration settings |
| | Disable changing Calendar and Contact settings |
| | Disable changing Messaging settings |
| | Disable changing Profile Assistant settings |
| | Disable changing Temporary Internet Files settings |
| | Disable changing accessibility settings |
| | Disable changing certificate settings |
| | Disable changing color settings |
| | Disable changing connection settings |
| | Disable changing default browser check |
| | Disable changing font settings |
| | Disable changing history settings |
| | Disable changing home page settings |
| | Disable changing language settings |
| | Disable changing link color settings |
| | Disable changing proxy settings |
| | Disable changing ratings settings |
| | Disable external branding of Internet Explorer |
| | Disable importing and exporting of Favorites |
| | Disable the Reset Web Settings feature |
| | Display error message on proxy script download failure |
| | Do not allow AutoComplete to save passwords |
| | Identity Manager: Prevent users from using identities |

*(continued)*

Appendix A Where To
Find Group Policy
Settings

*Table A.11* **Internet Explorer settings available in the User Configuration**
**section (continued).**

| Folder | Settings |
|--------|----------|
| Internet Explorer | Search: Disable Find Files via F3 within the browser |
| | Search: Disable Search customization |
| | Use Automatic Detection for dial-up connections |
| Internet Control Panel | Disable the Advanced page |
| | Disable the Connections page |
| | Disable the Content page |
| | Disable the General page |
| | Disable the Programs page |
| | Disable the Security page |
| Offline Pages | Disable adding channels |
| | Disable removing channels |
| | Disable adding schedules for offline pages |
| | Disable editing schedules for offline pages |
| | Disable removing schedules for offline pages |
| | Disable offline page hit logging |
| | Disable all scheduled offline pages |
| | Disable channel user interface completely |
| | Disable downloading of site subscription content |
| | Disable editing and creating of schedule groups |
| | Subscription limits |
| Browser Menus | Disable Context Menu |
| | Disable Open In New Window menu option |
| | Disable Save This Program To Disk option |
| | File Menu: Disable New menu option |
| | File Menu: Disable Open menu option |
| | File Menu: Disable Save As Web Page Complete menu option |
| | File Menu: Disable Save As menu option |
| | File Menu: Disable closing the browser and Explorer windows |
| | Help Menu: Remove "For Netscape Users" menu option |
| | Help Menu: Remove "Send Feedback" menu option |
| | Help Menu: Remove "Tip Of The Day" menu option |
| | Help Menu: Remove "Tour" menu option |

*(continued)*

*Table A.11* **Internet Explorer settings available in the User Configuration section** (continued).

| Folder | Settings |
| --- | --- |
| Browser Menus | Hide Favorites Menu |
| | Tools Menu: Disable Internet Options menu option |
| | View Menu: Disable Full Screen menu option |
| | View Menu: Disable Source menu option |
| Toolbars | Configure toolbar buttons |
| | Disable customizing browser toolbar buttons |
| | Disable customizing browser toolbars |
| Persistence Behavior | File size limits for Internet zone |
| | File size limits for Intranet zone |
| | File size limits for Local Machine zone |
| | File size limits for Restricted Sites zone |
| | File size limits for Trusted Sites zone |
| Administrator Approved | Carpoint |
| Controls | DHTML Edit Control |
| | Investor |
| | MSNBC |
| | Media Player |
| | Menu controls |
| | Microsoft Agent |
| | Microsoft Chat |
| | Microsoft Scriptlet Component |
| | Microsoft Survey Control |
| | NetShow File Transfer Control |
| | Shockwave Flash |

**Appendix A Where To Find Group Policy Settings**

- *Windows Explorer*—The Windows Explorer folder contains a number of settings, as well as one child folder, Common Open File Dialog. See Table A.12 for a list of settings available in these folders.

- *Microsoft Management Console*—The Microsoft Management Console folder has one child folder: Restricted/Permitted Snap-ins. This folder, in addition to containing settings for all standalone snap-ins, contains two child folders: Extension Snap-ins and Group Policy. See Table A.13 for a list of available settings. If you enable the

"Restrict users to the explicitly permitted list of snap-ins" setting in the main folder, you can use the settings in the child folders to enable the snap-ins that they may use. If you do not enable any of the snap-ins, you effectively prevent users from using any snap-ins.

- *Task Scheduler*—The Task Scheduler folder has seven settings: Disable Advanced menu, Disable drag and drop, Disable new task creation, Disable task deletion, Hide property pages, Prevent task run or end, and Prohibit Browse.

- *Windows Installer*—The Windows Installer folder has four settings: Always install with elevated privileges, Disable rollback, Disable media source for any install, and Search order.

**Table A.12   Windows Explorer settings in the User Configuration section.**

| Folder | Settings |
|---|---|
| Windows Explorer | Disable DFS tab |
| | Disable UI to change keyboard navigation indicator settings |
| | Disable UI to change menu animation settings |
| | Disable Windows Explorer's default context menu |
| | Do not request alternate credentials |
| | Do not track Shell shortcuts during roaming |
| | Enable Classic Shell |
| | Hide Hardware tab |
| | Hide these specified drives in My Computer |
| | Hide the Manage item in the Windows Explorer context menu |
| | Maximum number of recent documents |
| | No "Computers near Me" in My Network Places |
| | No "Entire Network" in My Network Places |
| | Only allow approved Shell extensions |
| | Prevent access to drives from My Computer |
| | Remove "Map Network Drive" and "Disconnect Network Drive" |
| | Remove File Menu from Windows Explorer |
| | Remove Search button from Windows Explorer |
| | Remove the Folder Options menu item from the Tools menu |
| | Request credentials for network installation |
| Common Open File Dialog | Hide the common dialog back button |
| | Hide the common dialog places bar |
| | Hide the dropdown list of recent files |

**Table A.13   Microsoft Management Console settings in the User Configuration section.**

| Folder | Settings |
|---|---|
| Microsoft Management Console | Restrict the user from entering author mode<br>Restrict users to the explicitly permitted list of snap-ins |
| Restricted/Permitted Snap-ins | Active Directory Domains and Trusts |
| | Active Directory Sites and Services |
| | Active Directory Users and Computers |
| | Certificates |
| | Component Services |
| | Computer Management |
| | Device Manager |
| | Disk Defragmenter |
| | Disk Management |
| | Distributed File System |
| | Event Viewer |
| | FAX Service |
| | Indexing Service |
| | Internet Authentication Service (IAS) |
| | Internet Information Services |
| | IP Security |
| | Local Users and Groups |
| | Performance Logs and Alerts |
| | QoS Admission Control |
| | Removable Storage Management |
| | Routing and Remote Access |
| | Security Configuration and Analysis |
| | Security Templates |
| | Services |
| | Shared Folders |
| | System Information |
| | Telephony |
| | Terminal Services Configuration |
| | WMI control |

*(continued)*

**Table A.13    *Microsoft Management Console settings in the User Configuration section* (continued).**

| Folder | Settings |
|---|---|
| Extension Snap-ins | AppleTalk Routing |
| | Certification Authority |
| | Connection Sharing (NAT) |
| | DCOM Configuration Extension |
| | Device Manager |
| | DHCP Relay Management |
| | Event Viewer |
| | IAS Logging |
| | IGMP Routing |
| | IP Routing |
| | IPX RIP Routing |
| | IPX Routing |
| | IPX SAP Routing |
| | Logical and Mapped Drives |
| | OSPF Routing |
| | Public Key Policies |
| | RAS Dial-in–User Node |
| | Remote Access |
| | Removable Storage |
| | RIP Routing |
| | Routing |
| | Send Console Message |
| | Service Dependencies |
| | SMTP Protocol |
| | SNMP |
| | System Properties |
| Group Policy | Administrative Templates (Computers) |
| | Administrative Templates (Users) |
| | Folder Redirection |
| | Group Policy Tab for Active Directory tools |
| | Group Policy snap-in |

*(continued)*

**Table A.13 Microsoft Management Console settings in the User Configuration section (continued).**

| Folder | Settings |
|---|---|
| Group Policy | Internet Explorer Maintenance |
| | Remote Installation Services |
| | Scripts (Logon/Logoff) |
| | Scripts (Startup/Shutdown) |
| | Security Settings |
| | Software Installation (Computers) |
| | Software Installation (Users) |

### Start Menu And Taskbar

The Start Menu and Taskbar folder has numerous settings for controlling options available to users. See Table A.14 for a list of settings.

### Desktop

The Desktop folder has a number of options for controlling the appearance of the user's desktop as well as two child folders: Active Desktop and Active Directory. See Table A.15 for a list of settings.

### Control Panel

The Control Panel folder has four child folders: Add/Remove Programs, Display, Printers, and Regional Options. See Table A.16 for a list of settings in each one.

### Network

The Network folder has two child folders: Offline Files and Network and Dial-up Connections. See Table A.17 for a list of settings.

### System

The System folder contains several settings and two child windows: Logon/Logoff and Group Policy. See Table A.18 for a list of settings.

**Table A.14 Start Menu and Taskbar settings in the User Configuration section.**

| | |
|---|---|
| Add "Run in Separate Memory Space" checkbox to Run dialog box | Add Logoff to the Start menu |
| Clear history of recent opened documents on exit | Disable Logoff on the Start menu |
| Disable and remove links to Windows Update | Disable and remove the Shut Down command command |

*(continued)*

Appendix A Where To Find Group Policy Settings

**Table A.14    Start Menu and Taskbar settings in the User
        Configuration section (continued).**

| | |
|---|---|
| Disable changes to Taskbar and Start Menu settings | Disable context menus for the Taskbar |
| Disable drag-and-drop context menus on the Start Menu | Disable personalized menus |
| Disable programs on Settings menu | Disable user tracking |
| Do not keep history of recently opened documents | Do not use the search-based method when resolving shell shortcuts |
| Do not use the tracking-based method when resolving shell shortcuts | Gray non-available Windows Installer programs Start Menu shortcuts |
| Prohibit users from enabling instrumentation | Remove Documents menu from Start Menu |
| Remove Favorites menu from Start Menu | Remove Help menu from Start Menu |
| Remove Network and Dial-up Connections from Start Menu | Remove Run menu from Start Menu |
| Remove Search menu from Start Menu | Remove common program groups from Start Menu |
| Remove user's folders from Start Menu | |

**Table A.15    Desktop settings in the User Configuration section.**

| Folder | Settings |
|---|---|
| Desktop | Disable adding, dragging, dropping, and closing the Taskbar's toolbars |
| | Disable adjusting desktop toolbars |
| | Do not add shares of recently opened documents to My Network Places |
| | Do not save settings at exit |
| | Hide Internet Explorer icon on desktop |
| | Hide My Network Places icon on desktop |
| | Hide all icons on desktop |
| | Prohibit user from changing My Documents path |
| | Remove My Documents icon from Start menu |
| | Remove My Documents icon from desktop |
| Active Desktop | Active Desktop wallpaper |
| | Add/Delete items |
| | Allow only bitmapped wallpaper |
| | Disable Active Desktop |

*(continued)*

**Table A.15   Desktop settings in the User Configuration section** (continued).

| Folder | Settings |
|---|---|
| Active Desktop | Enable Active Desktop |
| | Prohibit adding items |
| | Prohibit changes |
| | Prohibit deleting items |
| | Prohibit editing items |
| Active Directory | Enable filter in Find dialog box |
| | Hide Active Directory folder |
| | Maximum size of Active Directory searches |

**Table A.16   Control Panel settings in the User Configuration section.**

| Folder | Settings |
|---|---|
| Control Panel | Disable Control Panel |
| | Hide specified Control Panel applets |
| | Show only specified Control Panel applets |
| Add/Remove Programs | Disable Add/Remove Programs |
| | Disable Support Information |
| | Go directly to Components Wizard |
| | Hide Add New Programs page |
| | Hide Add/Remove Windows Components page |
| | Hide Change or Remove Programs page |
| | Hide the "Add a program from CD-ROM or floppy disk" option |
| | Hide the "Add programs from Microsoft" option |
| | Hide the "Add programs from your network" option |
| | Specify default category for Add New Programs |
| Display | Disable display in Control Panel |
| | Disable changing wallpaper |
| | Hide the Appearance tab |
| | Hide the Background tab |
| | Hide the Screen Saver tab |
| | Hide the Settings tab |
| | No screen saver |
| | Password protect the screen saver |
| | Screen saver excecutable name |

*(continued)*

Appendix A   Where To Find Group Policy Settings

**455**

**Table A.16    Control Panel settings in the User Configuration section** (continued).

| Folder | Settings |
|---|---|
| Printers | Browse a common Web site to find printers |
| | Browse the network to find printers |
| | Default Active Directory path when searching for printers |
| | Disable addition of printers |
| | Disable deletion of printers |
| Regional Settings | Restrict selection of Windows 2000 menus and dialogs language |

**Table A.17    Network settings in the User Configuration section.**

| Folder | Settings |
|---|---|
| Offline Files | Action on server disconnect |
| | Administratively assigned offline files |
| | Disable Make Available Offline option |
| | Disable reminder balloons |
| | Disable user configuration of offline files |
| | Event logging level |
| | Initial reminder balloon lifetime |
| | Non-default server disconnect actions |
| | Prevent use of Offline Files folder |
| | Reminder balloon frequency |
| | Reminder balloon lifetime |
| | Synchronize all offline files before logging off |
| Network and Dial-up Connections | Allow TCP/IP advanced configuration |
| | Allow access to current user's RAS connection |
| | Allow configuration of connection sharing |
| | Allow connection components to be enabled or disabled |
| | Display and enable the Network Connections Wizard |
| | Enable access to properties of RAS connections available to all users |
| | Enable access to properties of a LAN connection |
| | Enable access to properties of components of a LAN connection |

*(continued)*

*Table A.17  Network settings in the User Configuration section* (continued).

| Folder | Settings |
|---|---|
| Network and Dial-up Connections | Enable access to properties of components of a RAS connection |
| | Enable adding and removing components for a RAS or LAN connection |
| | Enable connecting and disconnecting a LAN connection |
| | Enable connecting and disconnecting a RAS connection |
| | Enable deletion of RAS connections |
| | Enable deletion of RAS connections available to all users |
| | Enable renaming of RAS connections belonging to the current user |
| | Enable renaming of connections, if supported |
| | Enable status statistics for an active connection |
| | Enable the Advanced Settings item on the Advanced menu |
| | Enable the Dial-up Preferences item on the Advanced menu |

*Table A.18  System settings in the User Configuration section.*

| Folder | Settings |
|---|---|
| System | Century interpretation for Year 2000 |
| | Code signing for device drivers |
| | Custom user interface |
| | Disable Autoplay |
| | Disable Registry-editing tools |
| | Disable the command prompt |
| | Do not display welcome screen at logon |
| | Do not run specified Windows applications |
| | Download missing COM components |
| | Run only allowed Windows applications |
| Logon/Logoff | Connect home directory to root of the share |
| | Disable Change Password |
| | Disable Lock Computer |
| | Disable Logoff |
| | Disable Task Manager |
| | Disable legacy run list |
| | Disable the run once list |

Appendix A Where To
Find Group Policy
Settings

*(continued)*

*Table A.18   System settings in the User Configuration section* (continued).

| Folder | Settings |
|---|---|
| Logon/Logoff | Exclude directories in roaming profile |
| | Limit profile size |
| | Run legacy logon scripts hidden |
| | Run logoff scripts visible |
| | Run logon scripts synchronously |
| | Run logon scripts visible |
| | Run these programs at user logon |
| Group Policy | Create new Group Policy Object links disabled by default |
| | Disable automatic update of ADM files |
| | Enforce Show Policies Only (applies to the View menu option for the Administrative Templates nodes in the Group Policy Editor) |
| | Group Policy domain controller selection |
| | Group Policy refresh interval for users |
| | Group Policy slow link detection |

# Remote Installation Services

The Remote Installation Services (RIS) feature of Windows 2000 is a natural extension of the software management features of IntelliMirror. RIS allows you to install the Windows 2000 Professional operating system on a remote client computer. Under the right circumstances, you don't even have to go to the client computer to turn it on—let alone baby-sit the installation and configuration of the operating system.

As powerful as it may be, this feature will not be for everyone because of its stringent requirements. In addition, the procedure for installing and using RIS is very involved. During beta testing of Windows 2000, Microsoft posted an excellent Beta 3 Technical Walkthrough, "Remote OS Installation," on its Web site. In it, Microsoft presented step-by-step procedures for installing and using RIS. These procedures are not unlike those in this book. The procedures occupied 35 pages. For these reasons, I decided to devote an appendix, rather than a main chapter, to the subject.

In this appendix, I will give you a brief overview of the feature. I recommend that you download the Walkthrough from Microsoft's Web site. Log onto **www.microsoft.com** and search for both "Remote OS Installation" and "Remote Installation Services," in case the title has changed.

## Overview Of Remote Installation Services

RIS works much like the software management features in IntelliMirror. In one scenario, you create a network share, and then copy the files from the Windows 2000 Professional CD-ROM to that share. In another scenario, you can take things a step further by using a supplied utility called RIPrep, as follows:

- Install the operating system on a workstation.
- Configure its Windows environment.
- Install the applications software to be used on it.
- Run RIPrep to create a mirror image of the installation on a network server.

This second scenario could be very useful if you have a large number of workstations that need to be configured the same way.

There are two ways in which a workstation without an operating system can connect to the network and request an installation. If the workstation has a remote-boot-enabled BIOS and a compatible network interface card (NIC), you can boot the workstation from a remote server and install the operating system without ever having to visit the workstation. If it does not have this BIOS feature, but it does have a compatible NIC, you can create a remote boot floppy. The software on the floppy will create a connection to the network, determine which operating systems are available there, present the user with a list of choices, and initiate the remote installation.

---

**NOTE:** *Although the remote boot floppy offers the user a choice of all of the operating systems that are available, RIS supports only Windows 2000 Professional. You cannot use it to install Windows 2000 Server. If you have created mirror images of entire setups, you may have several different types of Windows 2000 Professional installations available. If you are relying on another person to initiate the installation, be sure to tell them which option to select.*

---

# Requirements For Using RIS

The management of software applications, described in Chapter 11, is straightforward. If the software has a compatible Windows Installer package file, all that you need to do is copy the installation files to a network share and add the package to a setting in the appropriate group policy. The features needed to use software management are installed by default. Moreover, they do not place any special demands on your network configuration.

This is not the case with RIS and RIPrep, however. Here are some of the most important considerations to keep in mind:

- RIS is an optional component of Windows 2000 Server. It is not installed by default. You will need to install it by opening the Add/Remove Programs utility in Control Panel, selecting Add/Remove Windows Components, and then selecting Remote Installation Services from the displayed list of available components.

- RIS requires Dynamic Host Configuration Protocol (DHCP), Domain Name Service (DNS), and the Active Directory. It must be installed on either a domain controller or a member server in a domain that has access to the Active Directory. The domain must also be running DHCP and DNS servers. DHCP and DNS are also optional components that are not installed by default.

- The DNS server in your domain must be running the Windows 2000 version of DNS, although RIS is compatible with the Windows NT 4 version of DHCP. DHCP has been included with Windows 2000 primarily for backward-compatibility with Windows NT 4. If all of the servers in your domain are running Windows 2000 and your domain controller is running in native mode, you might not otherwise need DHCP.

---

**TIP:** *If you do not already have DHCP and DNS servers in your domain, and you are planning to install these components on the same server as RIS, make sure that the server has at least a Pentium II-class central processor and 128MB of memory. When I installed these components on a server that met only Microsoft's minimum requirements, I found that they slowed the server to a crawl.*

---

- The volume on which you plan to install the Windows 2000 Professional installation files must be formatted for NTFS and have at least 1GB of free space. The files cannot be on the same volume as the server's system files and cannot be on a Distributed File System volume.

- For a completely automatic remote installation, the workstation must have a remote-boot-enabled BIOS and a compatible network interface card (NIC). A semiautomatic, locally initiated network installation also requires a compatible NIC. At this writing, only a very small number of NICs are compatible with RIS, although the list is certain to grow. Be sure to check your documentation for an up-to-date list.

# Limitations Of RIPrep

The RIPrep utility can be used to create a mirror image of a local workstation's hard drive on a network share. This mirror image can be installed on another system, even if it has different hardware than the one used to generate the image.

Although this can be very useful, there are the following limitations to consider:

- The process works only on a local, single-partition C drive.

- The network share should have plenty of extra capacity because the entire source drive, not just the files on it, is copied to the image file.

- Both the source system and the one to which its image file is being copied should have only Plug-and-Play-aware hardware. The process depends on the Plug-and-Play features in Windows 2000 Professional to identify and configure the hardware on the system.

# The Windows Script Host

One of the drawbacks of all previous versions of Microsoft Windows has been the lack of a native batch file or scripting language. Until recently, the only native option has been the MS-DOS batch file. Many power users who want to automate Windows processes have taken to writing Visual Basic or Java scripts, and then running them within Internet Explorer. Many users who are proficient with batch files have not had the time or inclination to learn these far more complex scripting languages.

Internet Explorer, beginning with version 3, has supported these scripts, as well as the ActiveX controls that provide their user interface. As an environment for executing scripts on a local system, however, it has several significant drawbacks. Scripts must be contained within HTML pages. The browser takes a long time to load and makes heavy demands on memory and system resources.

Microsoft partially addressed the needs of power users in 1997, when it released what was then called the Windows Scripting Host (WSH) as part of its Zero Administration for Windows initiative. The utility is included with Windows 2000 Server and Professional as well as with Windows 98. A Windows 95 version is available on Microsoft's Web site. Point your browser to **www.microsoft.com** and search for "Windows Script Host."

The shipping releases of the Windows 2000 network operating systems include the latest version of the utility. The name has been shortened slightly. This version also works with Windows 98 and is available as a download.

The WSH requires the user to know either the Visual Basic or Java scripting language. Because of this, I did not cover it in the main part of this book. Nevertheless, the WSH can be of value to you if you know one of these languages. This appendix will give you an overview of the utility.

# Overview

The Windows Script Host (WSH) serves as an environment for executing scripts. It uses the Visual Basic and Java scripting engines included with version 3 or greater of Internet Explorer. Microsoft expects that third-party developers will provide engines for other scripting languages, such as Perl, TCL, REXX, and Python.

The WSH makes far fewer demands on the system than Internet Explorer. Scripts can be executed directly from the desktop, as well as from the Run line and the command prompt. The WSH is particularly appropriate for scripts that do not require interaction with the user, such as logon and logoff scripts. The current version adds the capability to include multiple scripts and functions in the same file, as well as a command-line parameter to call the desired script within the file.

The package includes a Windows version (wscript.exe) and a command-line version (cscript.exe), as well as several sample scripts. The installation routine copies the program files to the %windir%\system32 folder, where %windir% is the home folder for your system files. Look for the samples in a child folder called Samples or Wsamples. By default, the .vbs and .js extensions are associated with the Windows version. When a user double-clicks on the file name or shortcut for a script, the script is executed.

---

**TIP:** *You can download sample scripts from Microsoft's Web site. Point your browser to* **www.microsoft.com** *and search for "Windows Script Host."*

---

Table C.1 lists the sample scripts that are included with the downloadable version of the WSH. They are not included on the Windows 2000 CD-ROM. Most of the scripts come in both Visual Basic and Java versions. A few also come with sample Excel files.

**Table C.1   Sample scripts provided with the Windows Script Host.**

| Script Name | What It Does |
| --- | --- |
| Addusers | Reads an Excel file that contains a list of users and adds them to the Active Directory. |
| Chart | Creates an Excel file and adds a chart. |
| Delusers | Reads an Excel file that contains a list of users and deletes them from the Active Directory. |
| Excel | Displays Windows Script Host properties in Excel. |

*(continued)*

*Table C.1    Sample scripts provided with the Windows Script Host (continued).*

| Script Name | What It Does |
|---|---|
| Network | Demonstrates how to use the WSHNetwork object. |
| Registry | Demonstrates how to add and remove Registry keys. |
| Shortcut | Adds a shortcut to Notepad on the Windows desktop. |
| Showvar | Lists the environmental variables on the current system. |

# Modifying Script Properties

You can set default properties for both the Windows version of the WSH (wscript.exe) and any script file. Modifications to the properties of the executable file become the default settings for all scripts. Modifications to the properties of a script apply only to that script.

To change the default settings for wscript.exe, double-click on the file name in Windows Explorer or My Computer, or execute the file from the Run line without any parameters. This will open the Windows Script Host Settings dialog box. (See Figure C.1.) Here, you can specify the number of seconds after which the script should be

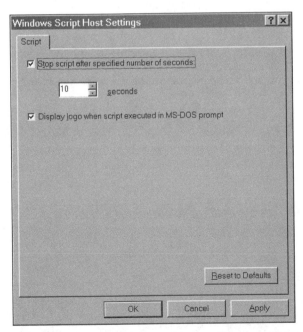

*Figure C.1    The Windows Script Host Settings dialog box.*

stopped. You may want to do this for scripts that have a tendency to get caught in a loop. You can also decide whether Windows Script Host version information should be displayed when the script is executed from an MS-DOS prompt.

To change the settings for a script, right-click on the file name in My Computer or Windows Explorer, and select Properties. The General page displays information about the file and has no user-configurable options. Switch to the Settings page to set a limit on execution time, or to enable or disable the display of version information at runtime. On the Summary page, you can include information about the file itself, such as its author. On the Security page, you can set security permissions for the file. Click Apply to confirm your changes, and then click OK to exit the Properties dialog box.

When you customize the properties for a script, a Windows Script Host control file with the same name as the script file and a .wsh extension is automatically generated in the same folder as the script. This is an ASCII text file with the settings that you have made. (See Figure C.2.) Double-clicking on the control file executes the script, just as if you had double-clicked on the script itself.

In the current version of the WSH, you can also create a file that contains multiple scripts and the routines that they use. This is an ASCII text file with a .ws extension. The command-line version of the WSH has a parameter that allows you to call a script within a .ws file.

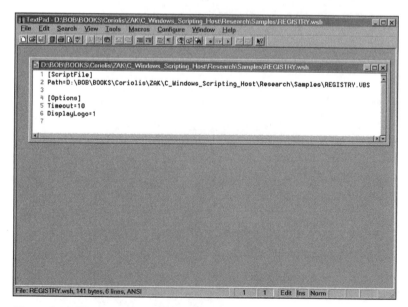

*Figure C.2    The .wsh control file for the Registry sample script.*

# Using The Command-Line Version

The syntax for the command-line version of the WSH (cscript.exe) uses two types of parameters, in addition to the script name:

- *Host parameters*—These parameters enable or disable various WSH options. They come before the script name and are always preceded by two forward slashes (//).

- *Script parameters*—These parameters follow the script name and are passed to the script. They are always preceded by a single forward slash (/). The required parameters, if any, depend on the script being run.

Here is the syntax of the command line for cscript.exe:

```
cscript [host parameters] script name [script parameters]
```

Parameters are optional. Only the script name is mandatory. If you execute the program without a script name, you will get a screen of help information.

Table C.2 lists the available host parameters.

**Table C.2    Host parameters for cscript.exe.**

| Parameter | What It Does |
|-----------|--------------|
| //I | Executes the script in interactive mode (default). Allows the display of user prompts and script errors. |
| //B | Executes the script in batch mode (the opposite of inter-active mode). Suppresses the display of user prompts and script errors. |
| //T:nn | Sets the number of seconds that the script can run before it times out. (The default is no timeout.) |
| //logo | Displays a banner with version information when the script is run (default). |
| //nologo | Suppresses the display of the banner at runtime. |
| //H:CScript or //H:WScript | Sets the default version for running scripts. (The normal default is WScript.) |
| //S | Saves the command-line options for the current user. |
| //? | Shows help information for the command line. |
| //E:engine | Executes the script with the specified scripting engine. |
| //D | Enables the script debugger. |
| //X | Launches the program in the script debugger. |
| //Job:<JobID> | Runs the specified JobID in the named script file (in this case, a .ws file). |

# Index

# S

# Windows 2000 Titles from Coriolis

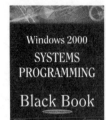
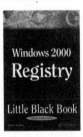